MORAL IMPERIALISM

CRITICAL AMERICA

GENERAL EDITORS: Richard Delgado and Jean Stefancic

EDITED BY BERTA ESPERANZA
HERNÁNDEZ-TRUYOL

MORAL IMPERIALISM

A Critical Anthology

New York University Press • *New York and London*

NEW YORK UNIVERSITY PRESS
New York and London

© 2002 by New York University

Library of Congress Cataloging-in-Publication Data
Moral imperialism : a critical anthology /
edited by Berta Hernandez-Truyol.
p. cm. — (Critical America series)
Includes bibliographical references and index.
ISBN 0-8147-3613-0 (cloth : alk. paper) —
ISBN 0-8147-3614-9 (pbk. : alk. paper)
1. Human rights—History. 2. Human rights—
Cross-cultural studies. 3. Imperialism—History.
I. Hernandez-Truyol. II. Critical America.
JC571 .M783 2002
323—dc21   2002006498

New York University Press books are printed on acid-free paper,
and their binding materials are chosen for strength and durability.

Manufactured in the United States of America

10 9 8 7 6 5 4 3 2 1

Contents

Acknowledgments

Many persons have made the preparation of this book possible through their support, heartening conversations, inspiration, collaboration, and research. The innumerable hallway, conference, classroom, and restaurant discussions with colleagues, friends, and students all provided insights that are part of the fabric of this work. So at the outset I want to thank all the various communities that formed the constellation of systems that provided the support and inspiration necessary to this project.

I owe special gratitude to Tom Franck, a mentor and friend who has inspired and challenged me to pursue my vision of international human rights, and to the unique team of Richard Delgado and Jean Stefancic, editors of the Critical America series—both dear friends and valued colleagues—who encouraged me to pursue that vision in a critical and self-critical way. The essay authors—friends and admired colleagues—have provided the intellectual spirit of the anthology. Claire Moore Dickerson, Jane E. Larson, and Christy Gleason have always been generous friends and have once again given me their time and energy, engaged in countless hours of conversation, and provided advice and inspiration with respect to the work as a whole as well as to my contributions. Shelbi Day, Dana Gryniuk, and Cindy Zimmerman were invaluable in seeing this work to completion.

At NYU Press, Niko Pfund helped me launch the project, kept in close touch throughout the process, and deserves special mention. Jennifer Hammer saw the book to completion.

I have been fortunate to complete this work at my new home, the University of Florida Levin College of Law. Dean Jon Mills has been most generous with his intellectual and research support and personal encouragement. My new friends and colleagues have afforded welcoming and inspirational company. The Faculty Support Office effectively and cheerfully provided word processing assistance while also keeping my spirits up and my coffee cup full. St. John's University School of Law, where I started this book, dedicated needed time and resources; Linda Ryan and Barbara Traub afforded invaluable library resources.

Finally I want to thank my family and friends, especially Meika, for unselfishly providing time, understanding, emotional support, nourishment, and much needed reality checks.

Introduction

Berta Esperanza Hernández-Truyol and Christy Gleason

THE EVENTS OF September 11, 2001, had a transformative impact on U.S. life and society. On 9–11, a date that will live in infamy, nineteen terrorists—men whose presence within these borders ranged from the illegal to the mysterious—armed with box cutters, hijacked four civilian aircraft—two American Airlines and two United Airlines planes—and strategically turned them into human-controlled jet-fueled missiles of mass destruction. The terrorists, some of whom learned how to fly in U.S. flight schools, crashed two of the planes into the towers of the World Trade Center (WTC) in New York City and a third into the Pentagon outside Washington, D.C. Thousands of innocent persons, including the passengers and crew of the four aircraft, workers in the WTC and in the Pentagon, rescue workers and bystanders, were killed or injured. These included citizens of the United States as well as over sixty other nations. Hundreds of millions of dollars worth of property was damaged or destroyed. The United States, sole surviving superpower in this twenty-first century, was transformed from a safe state to a besieged one; from a state where calm prevailed to one permeated by fear and uncertainty.

On the morning of the attacks, President Bush called them "an act of war" and three days later declared a state of emergency. Congress did not, and perhaps cannot, formally declare war, probably because the attack came from persons in a group which was neither a government nor the representative of a state. Because of the actors, these terrorist attacks seem to be creating a new kind of "war." Interestingly, notwithstanding the anomalous state of aggression being experienced, by joint resolution Congress condemned both the attacks and their sponsors and declared "that these premeditated attacks struck not only at the people of

America, but also at the symbols and structures of our economic and military strength and that the United States is entitled to respond under international law."[1]

In addition, also by joint resolution, Congress "authorize[d] the use of United States Armed Forces against those responsible for the [9–11] attacks launched against the United States," calling the acts "treacherous violence" that "render[ed] it both necessary and appropriate that the United States exercise its rights to self-defense and to protect United States citizens both at home and abroad."[2] The acts were deemed to pose "an unusual and extraordinary threat to the national security and foreign policy of the United States." Congress recognized the president's authority to "take action and to deter and prevent acts of international terrorism against the United States."

Therefore, Joint Resolution 23 authorized the president "to use all necessary and appropriate force against those nations, organizations, or persons he determine[d] planned, authorized, committed, or aided the terrorist attacks that occurred on September 11, 2001, or harbored such organizations or persons, in order to prevent any future acts of international terrorism against the United States by such nations, organizations, or persons."[3]

While at first blush the U.S. legislative responses smack of arrogance, imperialism, and unilateralism, the heinous nature of the terrorist attacks in fact resulted in a fast-forming international coalition. The day after the attacks, President Vladimir Putin of Russia expressed support for retaliation. German Chancellor Gerhard Schroder called the attacks "a declaration of war against the entire civilized world," and leaders from France, Russia, and Britain joined him in talks to coordinate a European response, including the possibility of joint military action. Two days after the attacks, NATO members invoked Article 5 of the founding treaty, a mutual defense clause which states that an armed attack against any of the allied nations in Europe or North America is considered an attack against all. This invocation, in turn, triggered Article 51 of the UN Charter which preserves the right of individual or collective self-defense.

Significantly, during the month of September, the Bush Administration's effort to form a coalition seemed immensely successful. Pakistan, Saudi Arabia, North Korea, Egypt, and China all offered some level of support. By the end of September, arrests of those with suspected terrorist links were made in nations across the world, including the Netherlands, Spain, Belgium, Britain, and the United Arab Emirates. In addition, in order to stop the source of funds to terrorists, President Bush ordered that the assets of suspected terrorist entities be frozen, an action that went beyond U.S. borders. Germany, Britain, China, Colombia, Costa Rica, and the Czech Republic cooperated in freezing bin Laden/Al Qaeda/Taliban-linked assets.

However, cooperation came at a price. Many Middle Eastern states wanted the United States to become more involved in eliminating violence in their region. Pakistan demanded the end of eleven-year-old sanctions, the restoration of the flow of U.S. arms, and the reduction of its debt load in exchange for the use of bases or the right to fly in Pakistani airspace. Russia had grievances against NATO expansion, and the United States, in order to obtain public support, turned a blind eye to the massive human rights violations Russia was carrying out in Chechnya, including armed incursions into territory that sought to be independent. By October, Uzbekistan, Turkmenistan, and Tajikistan, three of the world's worst violators of human rights, became allies of the United States against Afghanistan.

On October 7, U.S.-led air strikes began in Kabul, targeting forces associated with Al Qaeda and the Taliban. At this juncture, additional states, such as the Philippines, gave the United States their full support—a support that was reiterated by countries such as China, Britain, France, Germany, and others in the European Union. Similarly, Asian leaders, meeting at the Asia Pacific Economic Cooperation Summit, signed a statement against terrorism. In November, Turkey became the first Muslim nation to join the United States in the air strikes, with Britain, Australia, and Canada committing to sending troops, and France considering doing so. African states, such as Sudan and Nigeria, also joined the coalition, as did Jordan and North Korea. Others, such as Iran and Iraq, condemned the U.S.-led air strikes.

The coalition, however, may prove to be fragile. The U.S.-backed Northern Alliance that is taking territory from the Taliban is exhibiting some level of gross disregard for human rights. To be sure, pictures of men cutting their beards, of women walking the streets, and of music permeating the air have been broadcast across the globe. However, we also receive news of wounded Taliban soldiers being dragged and executed.

Within the United States, under the cover of its claim to be fighting terrorism, the government has begun to act in a fashion that smacks of racism and appears to erode basic civil rights. For example, in October, Rudolph Giuliani, the Mayor of New York, refused to accept a $10 million donation for disaster relief from a Saudi prince after the latter suggested that U.S. policies in the Middle East had contributed to the attacks. In November, the State Department announced that, in an effort to prevent future terrorist attacks, it would slow down the process for granting visas to young men from Arab and Muslim nations, including Afghanistan, Algeria, Bahrain, Djibouti, Egypt, Eritrea, Indonesia, Iran, Iraq, Jordan, Kuwait, Lebanon, Libya, Malaysia, Morocco, Oman, Pakistan, Qatar, Saudi Arabia, Somalia, Sudan, Syria, Tunisia, Turkey, the United Arab Emirates, and Yemen. At the same time that the visa policy was announced, the Bush Administration's Justice Department announced a separate new antiterror policy that allows authorities to monitor all communications between certain persons in federal custody and their lawyers.

And in an action that elicited opprobrium both at home and abroad, on November 13, 2001 the Bush Administration issued a military order directing the Department of Defense to establish military commissions to decide the guilt of noncitizens suspected of involvement in terrorist activities. The order allows persons to be detained inside or outside the United States, be subjected to secret trials, and receive punishment of life imprisonment or death. All this may occur without the mandated application of "the principles of law and the rules of evidence generally recognized in the trial of criminal cases in the United States district courts."[4] The order has raised numerous legal concerns. Some in Congress have objected to the creation of the commissions (adjudicating bodies) based on the principle of "separation of powers." Others question its compliance with constitutional and international due process standards. Yet others note that the order violates binding U.S. treaty obligations, including the International Covenant on Civil and Political Rights, ratified by the United States in 1992, and the third Geneva Convention of 1949, ratified by the United States in 1955. Our international friends have protested the secret nature of the trials, their lack of process, and the possibility of the imposition of the death penalty. Indeed, this possibility has led Great Britain, probably the strongest U.S. ally in the so-called war against terrorism, to not only refuse to extradite captured fighters but also to demand the return of suspected British citizens to Britain for trial.

A further threat to the fragile coalition emerged from the U.S. treatment and classification of the captives. Pictures of Taliban/al-Qaeda fighters in shackles, either hooded or wearing blacked-out goggles, in prisoner jumpsuits, and sometimes brought to their knees, have generated protests from around the world and from within the United States as well. One source of contention is the sight of human beings being transported like animals, and kept in chain-link fence, cagelike structures at the U.S. naval base in Guantánamo Bay, Cuba—a state of exposure that has resulted in the camp's name: Camp X-Ray. The other source of contention is the status of the prisoners who include over one hundred fifty citizens of over twenty states, including three from Great Britain and one from Australia. The United States has designated the captives "unlawful combatants" rather than "prisoners of war"—a classification that not only would require certain treatment under the Geneva Conventions but also could impede trial in the military tribunals set up by order of President Bush. One obstacle to designating these captives "prisoners of war" is that it requires that they were acting on behalf of a state, whereas they, as well as the actors in the 9–11 attacks as discussed earlier, were acting on behalf of al-Qaeda, which is not a state. The huge rub, however, is that under the Geneva Conventions captives have to be considered "prisoners of war" unless a competent tribunal finds differently.

In response to the global demands for the captives to be treated according to accepted international norms, the United States declares simply—and contrary to the real pictures the world is seeing on television —that the prisoners are being treated humanely. Secretary of Defense Rumsfeld claims that allegations to the contrary are mere "hyperbole" and that "these people are committed terrorists," as if that designation should excuse any inhumane treatment that might be meted out. Similarly, Vice President Cheney dismisses criticism of the treatment by suggesting that the prisoners are probably being treated "better than they deserve." It is not surprising that this attitude on the part of the United States, while embraced by many within the country in the aftershock of the attacks, is being condemned by human rights organizations and others who fear erosion of civil liberties inside and outside the country. The U.S. attitude is also being severely denounced by friendly governments who object to the U.S. refusal to follow accepted rules of conduct, including those that, as in the treatment of prisoners, limit its freedom of action. But this is not the first time that such accusations have been leveled against the United States.

These events reveal the propensity of the United States to go it alone, to cut corners when expedient, to make the law, and to push forward with its agenda. While it is laudable that a diverse international community has emerged to fight terrorism, it is important to underscore the human rights sacrifices that are being made in the process. Moreover, while the United States protests human rights violations vocally, it now conveniently turns a blind eye to some egregious infringements and commits some abuses itself—such as the visa denials and the military commissions—in the name of national security.

It should be recalled that during the aftermath of the terrorist bombings of two U.S. embassies, the United States was quick to invoke human rights guidelines and treaties in defense of its attack on alleged terrorist training camps located inside Afghanistan. Ironically, at the same time, it bluntly dismissed Amnesty International and Human Rights Watch when they pointed out human rights violations closer to home in terms of the disproportionately high rate of capital punishment for black men and the inhumane conditions in prisons.

Current critical legal scholarship focuses primarily on the domestic issues of race, gender, sexuality, ethnicity, and citizenship. Little scholarship, however, turns outward to consider the ramifications of current majoritarian-based U.S.[5] jurisprudence on a global scale, or the lessons to be learned from the international legal context. The status of the United States as the only remaining superpower leaves it relatively unchecked in its ability to claim "moral authority" in the international sphere.

To take another example, in the controversy over female genital mutilation, the U.S. Congress was quick to condemn practices throughout Africa and the Middle East, and to take action criminalizing the practice domestically and placing conditions on foreign aid to locations that engage in such practices. Nonetheless, domestic policy ignores the disempowerment of women, particularly poor women under new draconian welfare rules, and the realities of physical, psychological, and economic violence against women. The irony of condemnation of international activities—the same types of activities which are permitted within its own borders—is not lost on third world countries.

More recently, in a global setting not directly involving the United States, the Pinochet saga plainly pit human rights against sovereignty—that universal indicia of state authority. In 1999 a London magistrate ruled that Gen. Augusto Pinochet, a *chileno*, should be extradited to

Spain to stand trial on charges that during his rule he ordered the torture, in Chile, of political adversaries. The accusation came from a Spanish judge, Baltasar Garzón, who issued an arrest warrant and charged Pinochet with orchestrating a campaign of terror against opponents during his seventeen-year dictatorship.[6]

The central question for the English court was whether Pinochet was immune from prosecution for acts committed while he was head of state. There was no likelihood of prosecution in Chile because of a wide-ranging amnesty law that Pinochet arranged before he stepped down.[7] For extra protection and to remain immune from prosecution for life, after relinquishing power in 1990, Pinochet made himself a senator for life. Despite Chile's amnesty law and Pinochet's senatorial status, the House of Lords—Britain's highest appeals court—ruled that Pinochet did not have immunity for any alleged acts of torture, or for any conspiracy to commit torture, which occurred after 1988—the date when an international law making torture a crime prosecutable in any nation became law in Britain.[8]

In light of the facts and the House of Lords's ruling, the London magistrate concluded that the allegations constituted extraditable crimes and that, notwithstanding the absence of Spanish victims, Spain had jurisdiction. Pinochet's response to the magistrate's ruling was that "the events in Chile have nothing whatsoever to do with Spain."[9] He observed that "Spain does not have jurisdiction over me" and that Spain's actions were "in violation of the sovereignty of Chile."[10]

In the end, England deemed Pinochet too sick to stand trial and returned him to Chile where his reception was mixed. After vigorous debate, however, the Chilean court also concluded that Pinochet was unfit to stand trial. But the Pinochet case affirms the Nuremberg precept regarding human rights norms: some conduct is so heinous that no matter where committed and by whom, it is subject to prosecution by anyone, anywhere.[11] This articulation of human rights law shows how one or more states—here England and Spain—can rely on those norms to the erosion of Chile's pre-Nuremberg sacrosanct sovereign prerogative to do as it wishes within its national borders.

Most recently, and also expanding on the Nuremberg legacy, we have evidenced a similar erosion of state sovereignty by international bodies. The people of Serbia turned over their unapologetic former head of state, Milosevic, to an ad hoc international criminal tribunal for Yugoslavia (ICTY) for trial under international norms for crimes against humanity. The spectacle of the alleged mass murderer refusing to recognize the legitimacy of the body before which he appeared on a bone-chilling indictment detailing atrocities too many and too depraved to have been carried out by human hands was paralyzing.

The ominous sense of higher justice prevails. Nonetheless, the United States, a major proponent and supporter of ICTY and the Milosevic indictment, steadfastly refuses to ratify the Statute of a Permanent International Criminal Court that would institutionalize international criminal justice proceedings because it does not want its citizens (meaning soldiers) subject to the jurisdiction of such an international forum. The United States justifies its stance by claiming that tyrannical regimes or terroristic rogue governments will fabricate undeserved falsehoods as pretexts to get even with the United States—a benevolent state.

In the meantime, decorated veterans who have lived as respected public servants are found to have been less than truthful about their participation in the killing of women and children during the Vietnam war—an ugly secret many conspired to hide. At the same time, a Pulitzer Prize-winning historian and college professor is exposed for having repeatedly lied about having served in-country during the Vietnam war (he was teaching at the U.S. Military Academy), playing in a championship football game (he never played on the football team), and major involvement in the antiwar movement (friends don't remember his participation at all).

Because of the increased reach and popularity of a corporate-controlled media serving as an "arbiter of truth," the power of corporations and individuals to act as nongovernmental imperialists grows without effective means of legal protection. As these same recent cases demonstrate, once a news story appears, even a court-ordered retraction and civil settlement cannot remove the stain on a person's reputation. Revelations of the still disputed events of a nighttime attack in 1969 led many in the media to question Bob Kerry's honesty, integrity, and heroism—despite (or because of) his receiving the Congressional Medal of Honor for his service at other times during the war. Similarly, following the uncovering of the scholar's dishonesty, the media and his professional critics questioned not only his personal ethics and honesty, but his scholarly abilities, the accuracy of his award-winning research, and his fitness to teach the "fact-based" subject of history. Throughout the public trials of both men in and by the media, the search for the whole story—the complete picture—fell victim to the rush to judge another person's flaws without revealing or recognizing one's own. This kind of moral imperialism with a supranational megaphone works best when the rules of "objectivity" allow one's own past to remain unseen.

Who is right and who is wrong? Should England be able to send Pinochet to Spain to stand trial for his Chilean crimes? Should the international community hold Milosevic accountable for his dastardly deeds? Who, if anyone, should hold a war hero turned public servant accountable for killing innocent civilians in the course of an undeclared war? Does it matter that a history professor lied about his own past? As important, who gave the media the power to make such judgments with impunity, and is there anything the international legal system can do to challenge the corporate media's supranational power?

The affront to sovereignty, to unfettered state power, and even to the claims to be able to define reality and to establish truth exposes myriad potential fault lines concerning the strong abusing the weak, the big imposing their morality on the small. These concerns are complex and multifaceted; the human rights system is useful in its analysis. Yet the human rights system is not perfect; it is fraught with stresses that emerge from the diversity of cultures, languages, and religions around the world, and it is plagued with contradictions that result from its ideological origins. The challenge, as discussed by the essays in this book, is to be able to make the laudable and desirable human rights rules and principles a reality without depending on power disparities between or among domestic, international, and even supranational actors.

This book attempts to bring international human rights solutions to bear on current international and domestic legal, political, and cultural crises. It also explores U.S. moral domination during a time of clear domestic moral shortcomings. Some essays reveal that insisting on other nations' adherence to norms that derive from U.S. culture and history may do harm in societies—both within and outside the United States—which have radically different cultures and histories.

This book interrogates the age-old question—why should U.S.-Western ideology guide the world?—but addresses it through an international and interdisciplinary lens, including a broad range of scholarly perspectives that incorporate the multiple and diverse voices of "others"—both within and outside U.S. borders. It focuses on the systemic use and abuse of power that perpetuates moral hierarchy in both the local and global contexts, weaving together historical, legal, social, political, and policy analysis with empirical investigation.

This anthology's analyses merge two interrelated approaches that have developed along seemingly parallel paths: human rights regimes and critical theory. This critical human rights approach is applied to contemporary and often controversial themes in domestic and international law—themes as diverse as female genital mutilation and immigration in the United States, citizenship and state responsibility for children, adoption and prostitution, and labor and slavery—all of which are then explored on the common axis of imperialism.

These critical human rights themes are organized around the international human rights framework that evolved after World War II when international actors failed to agree upon a single convention that would incorporate the broad range of civil, political, social, economic, and cultural rights embraced in the Universal Declaration of Human Rights, the first broad international pronouncement about the rights of individuals within the international sphere. "Core" states such as the United States, on the one hand, and "peripheral" and communist countries such as those in Latin America and Africa and the former Soviet Union, on the other, differed greatly with respect to precisely which rights should be protected—a North-South polarization that resulted in the segregation of rights into three broad categories or "generations," each embodied in a different document. The hierarchy attributed to the generations reflects the dominance of the Northern or Western powers. The first generation includes civil and political rights— those most like the ones contained in the U.S. Bill of Rights and, consequently, widely embraced by the Northern or Western states, including the United States. These "rights of Man" were in their apogee in the eighteenth century and can be traced to the "bourgeois" revolutions, particularly the French and American. The American Declaration of Independence and the French *Declaration des Droits de l'Homme* form the foundation for the civil and political rights of the first generation. Ironically, these revolutions—founded on individualism and the desire for freedom from government intrusion as well as the right to private property—coexisted with the institution of slavery and with women's status as chattel.

Civil and political rights, as conceived and articulated, are "negative rights" that do not impose any obligations on the government with respect to its citizenry. Rather, they provide only that individuals are to be free from government interference in their actions in certain realms. This "freedom from" government interference includes the rights to life, liberty, dignity, and bodily integrity; freedom of opinion, conscience, religion, expression, the press, assembly, and movement; freedom from arbitrary detention or arrest and interference with correspondence; and the right to property.

Significantly, although the right to property could well be viewed as an economic right, it is often located in the first generation because of its centrality to the interests for which the French and American Revolutions were fought, thus highlighting the interdependence and indivisibility of these rights. Moreover, the categorization of first-generation rights as negative is challenged when one realizes that some civil and political rights are more aptly recognized as positive—imposing an affirmative obligation on governments to ensure their observance. These include the right to participate in free elections and the right to a fair trial, "rights" that could not be effectuated without some government participation or control.

It is noteworthy that the first-generation narrative—as well as the second's—provides that all persons are entitled to the enumerated rights on an equal basis. Broad nondiscrimination and equality principles, on the basis of race, gender, language, religion, culture, family, ethnicity, and national and social origin, are the backbone of the first and second generations alike. Yet these rights as they exist today are far from being equally enjoyed by either individuals or the protected groups. For example, women around the globe do not enjoy equality with men in either the public or private spheres.

Indeed, first-generation rights have been criticized for neglecting the material realities of the working classes and of all peoples in postcolonial economies. On the other hand, second-generation rights—social, economic, and cultural rights—were driven by the peripheral states' and the second world's concern with social welfare. In fact, third world states together with the-then second world insisted on the centrality of these rights for social well-being and suggested that first-generation rights simply permitted the continued exploitation and subjugation of colonized people.

Second-generation rights were inspired by the socialist revolutions of the first two decades of the twentieth century, and were incorporated in the postsocialist Mexican and Russian Constitutions of 1917 as well as the 1919 constitution of the International Labor Organization. These rights, rather than ensuring freedom from government tyranny, sought state intervention to prevent and stop the exploitation of people. These rights that aspire to the well-being of the collective, as opposed to solely the individual, are called "positive rights."

The second generation's three groupings of rights aim to provide broad general welfare protections. Social rights include the right to an adequate standard of living, as determined by adequate food, nutrition, clothing, housing, education, and healthcare, among other things. Economic rights range from the right to social security to the right to work in a safe and healthy environment. Finally, cultural rights span a broad spectrum of traditions and practices which include the right to take part in cultural life, to enjoy the benefits of scientific progress and its applications, and to preserve the cultural identity of minority groups. Cultural rights are significant because culture forms the foundation of identity, which is central to the well-being and self-respect of persons, rights generally conceived of as first-generation.

In general, Western states originally resisted the notion of second-generation rights, although the International Covenant on Social, Economic, and Cultural Rights (Economic Covenant)—the document embodying "second"-generation rights—has now been widely accepted internationally. Interestingly, U.S. President Franklin Delano Roosevelt wholeheartedly embraced what would be called second-generation rights, recognizing that "true individual freedom cannot exist without economic security and independence; . . . [that] people who are hungry and out of a job are the stuff of which dictatorships are made." Nonetheless, the United States has categorically rejected social and economic rights as obligations both domestically (by refusing to recognize rights to work, housing, shelter, food, and welfare) and internationally (by refusing to ratify the Economic Covenant).

As with first-generation rights, it is noteworthy that the enjoyment of second-generation rights has not been evenly spread. Women, for example, have been and still are deprived of equal opportunities to work and education. Ironically, such denial of equality is sometimes explained as grounded upon tradition and culture—thus denying rights on the very grounds that are supposed to protect them.

"Third"-generation rights, like the first two, were also born of a revolution—the anticolonialist revolutions that followed World War II and ostensibly resulted in the independence of many nations. These revolutions influenced the text of human rights, contextualizing the rights of self-determination and nondiscrimination contained in both the International Covenant on Civil and Political Rights (ICCPR)—the docu-

ment embodying "first"-generation rights—and the Economic Covenant. The conceptual framework of this generation rejects foreign domination and occupation, and promotes freedom from aggression and
from threats against national sovereignty. Like second-generation
rights, third-generation rights also rely on the state to guarantee their
implementation.

Third-generation rights, although still works in progress, comprise
"solidarity" or group rights, such as the right to development—a right
the existence of which the United States rejects—the right to enjoy a safe
environment, to democracy, to peace, and to a common heritage and
humanitarian assistance, as well as the emerging right to democratic
governance.

Notwithstanding the generational paradigm, the reality is that
rights are interdependent and indivisible. The ICCPR recognizes the
natural rights basis of contemporary human rights norms—they derive
from the inherent dignity of the human person—as well as the generations' interdependence and indivisibility. "The ideal of free human beings enjoying civil and political freedom and freedom from fear and
want can only be achieved if conditions are created whereby everyone
may enjoy his[/her] civil and political rights as well as his[/her] economic, social and cultural rights." The Economic Covenant has a similar provision. Other human rights documents, such as the Convention
on the Elimination of All Forms of Discrimination against Women, the
international Convention on the Elimination of All Forms of Racial Discrimination, and even the Convention on the Rights of the Child support the indivisibility model by integrating both first- and second-generation protections.

Using the generational construct, this book is structured in three
parts. Because this work assumes the indivisibility, interdependence,
and interrelatedness of human rights, the three-generational structure
is simply an organizational tool. We believe that normative issues
raised by poverty, hunger, violence, power disparities, and other patterns of inequality are better examined in a context which assumes the
interrelatedness of rights rather than one that segregates them. For example, the right to work in a safe, healthy, and nondiscriminatory environment is as much a first-generation right to equality as a second-generation right to work; the right to use one's mother tongue in the courts,
in school, or in the street pertains as much to the right to individual fairness in treatment as to the right of culture.

Seeking to locate a right in a generation in order to ascertain whether it is protected, or pitting an individual against a group to resolve conflicts based on race, sex, religion, ethnicity, or power, misses the mark. The important point is whether the conflict or tension abridges, interferes with, or creates an impediment to an individual's or group's enjoyment of full personhood and, if so, what guidance the human rights system can offer. Viewing issues through this lens renders the human rights structure instrumental to human flourishing. This critical human rights approach engages in analysis without hegemonic presuppositions regarding any one correct model to facilitate personhood in a complex and diverse world.

The twenty essays in this volume, all original works, address moral concerns in various ways. They discuss the phenomenon of globalization and the resulting hybridization of norms, cultures, and understandings (Hernández-Truyol, Santos, Sassen); the extent to which race plays a role in hierarchies (Fernández-Kelly, Rush, Scantlebury/McKinley/Jesson); skepticism about the human rights system stemming from its imperialistic origins and applications (Gott, Johnson, Yamamoto/Shirota/Kim); the role cultural norms play in subordinating minorities—within larger society as well as minorities within a minority group (Akram, Greene, Santos); the potential of political or cultural hierarchies to strip peoples of their own identities and self-determination (Perry and Obiora, Román, Scantlebury/McKinley/Jesson); the inefficacy of legal rules crafted from a singular perspective to offer protections to those differently situated (Fakazis, Maguigan, Niemi-Kiesiläinen); the imposition of imperialistic epistemologies constructed by narratives which marginalize the nontraditional, the disempowered, or the outsider (Fakazis, Gott, Lyndon); the incompleteness that results from an analysis of economics without regard to individual rights (Connor, Hernández-Truyol and Larson, Moore Dickerson). Some authors expose hierarchies and some propose solutions, but all unveil the perils of the claim of moral authority left unchecked, suggesting novel strategies and coalitions as well as charting paths where further inquiry is necessary.

This work covers a tremendous amount of ground in seeking to expose the imposition of moralistic imperial stances that hurt both individuals and communities. Throughout this book, threads of history and religion, sex and race, nationality and citizenship reveal the omnipresence of claims to moral superiority by the strong against the weak, the rich against the poor, the normative against the "other" both within and across national borderlands. This imposition also confirms that the rights of generations are interrelated and indivisible. The right to vote is meaningless to a hungry person; the right to democracy means little without the right to development; the claims of truth are contextual and cannot be absolute, universal, or imperial if they are to be utilitarian. Cultures and religions can be as oppressive to their members as they may be to outsiders. The only means to achieving a real global community is by facing global inequalities, respecting differences, and fostering the full personhood of all people.

NOTES

1. S.J. Resolution 22, One Hundred Seventh Congress, First Session.

2. S.J. Resolution 23, One Hundred Seventh Congress, First Session.

3. *Id.* at sec. 2.

4. Military Order, "Detention, Treatment, and Trial of Certain Non-Citizens in the War against Terrorism," The White House, November 13, 2001.

5. Throughout this introduction and in the chapters that I authored or coauthored, I use the designation United States for the United States of America. Many, if not most or all of the other authors use the terms United States and America interchangeably. I decided not to alter the authors' choice of language in that regard. I do find it necessary to comment thereon, however, because I find it ironic that in a book on imperialism the imperialistic practice of denominating the United States as "America" remains normative. Indeed, America is much larger than the United States alone; there is also Canada in North America, and all of Latin America and the Caribbean (some locations commonly referred to as Central America, some as South America).

6. *See* Richard J. Wilson, *Prosecuting Pinochet in Spain*, 6 Hum. Rts. Br. 3 (1999). Chilean documents confirm 3,197 deaths or disappearances while Pinochet was in power.

7. Indeed, in 1999 the Supreme Court of Chile held that the missing were kidnap victims, not murder victims, and therefore the original crimes were "continuing events" that went beyond the amnesty law's 1978 deadline. *See* Clifford Krauss, *Chilean Military Faces Reckoning for Its Dark Past*, N.Y. Times, Oct. 3, 1999, at 1.

8. In a 3–2 majority, the first law Lords' decision, on November 25, 1998, held that Pinochet was not entitled to immunity for the acts alleged in the second arrest warrant, because such acts did not constitute official functions, and therefore were not protected under head-of-state immunity. First Law Lords'

Decision, 3 W.L.R. 1499–1502 (Lord Nicholls), 1506 (Lord Steyn), 1508 (Lord Hoffman) [1998].

While the House of Lords's reliance on the 1988 torture law provided the court with positivitic grounding for its decision, customary international law provides support for the conclusion that Pinochet's actions violated international law.

9. *See Judge in Britain Orders Extradition for Pinochet; Ex-Chile Dictator to Appeal Order to Face Trial in Spain,* Chicago Tribune, Oct. 9, 1999, at N3.

10. *See* Warren Hoge, *British Court Rules Pinochet Extraditable for Trial in Spain,* N.Y. Times, Oct. 9, 1999, at A4.

11. *See The Nuremberg Trial,* 6 F.R.D. 69, 110 (1946). Under the doctrine of *jus cogens,* certain peremptory norms are considered so fundamental that states cannot agree to contravene them.

PART I

CIVIL AND POLITICAL RIGHTS

I

Imperial Humanitarianism

History of an Arrested Dialectic

Gil Gott

THE HISTORICAL ANTECEDENTS of present-day human rights discourse and practice are usually sought in the tenets of liberal political philosophy and Enlightenment-era ideas about universal human dignity. A critical historicization of modern human rights, however, must include looking beyond inherited intellectual frameworks to a consideration of the social and political contexts of precursor movements. By studying such movements we can see how humanitarian norms have interacted with broader sociohistorical frameworks. A historicized understanding of these dynamics is indispensable as we strive to reconstruct human rights discourse and practice in light of shifting (globalizing) social and political contexts that "contaminate" human rights-based normativities and projects.

This chapter contributes to a critical historicization of the modern human rights project by examining the development of transnational humanitarianism during the "long nineteenth century," from the 1780s through the first decade of the twentieth century. By analyzing the relationships between the early humanitarian movements, the Victorian era's imperial system in Africa, and the initial international legal codification of the humanitarian impulse as part of the imperial dual mandate to "civilize" and control subaltern peoples, this chapter will provide a historical dimension to the current project of constructing a critical human rights theory and practice.

The record of nineteenth-century European imperialism in Africa is remarkable for its blending of humanitarian thought and action with a callous, sometimes bloodthirsty aggressiveness. Despite this record few scholars make a point of problematizing the integral connections between humanitarianism and imperialism as mutually constituting sides of a single dialectic: "imperial humanitarianism" or "humanitarian imperialism." Histories of nineteenth-century imperialism typically include "add-on" descriptions of contemporaneous missionary and humanitarian activities, while specific histories of the era's humanitarianism treat the imperial context as background, or offer economic determinist explanations that view humanitarianism as a function of class interest. To the extent that a more complex relationship between imperialism and humanitarianism is problematized, scholars usually conclude that sincere humanitarians sometimes unwittingly, tragically, and perhaps even carelessly served the European states' and capitalist interests in colonizing the periphery.[1]

In the period under review the most prominent form of humanitarianism was the movement to end slavery. The antislavery movement, rooted in Great Britain, with French and American branches, initially targeted primarily European and American slave traders and owners, but later focused on the slave trade in Africa. Along the way slavery became a key impetus for intensified missionary activity in Africa, the "civilizing mission" pursued there by both religious and secular humanitarians, and a rhetorical centerpiece in the creation of an international legal regime for the "orderly" conquest of Africa. In a reversal of sorts, the final campaign of the nineteenth-century antislavery movement was the humanitarian effort to end the colonial forced labor system of King Leopold II of Belgium in the Congo. The argument presented here is that nineteenth-century humanitarian and imperial projects were indeed intertwined and mutually constitutive. As narrative, the history provides a cautionary tale for twenty-first-century human rights advocates who might wish to transcend or ignore discomfiting social and political contexts and conjunctural determinants of human rights in the new global era.

European intellectuals of the seventeenth and eighteenth centuries, from Swift to Montesquieu, Diderot, and Rousseau, questioned the morality of slavery from both religious and secular humanist perspectives. While slavery had been officially denounced within the territorial domain of England prior to any significant organized humanitarian action (through the 1772 *Somerset* case championed by Granville Sharp) and in France (by law in 1794 as a result of successful slave revolts in the French colonies of Martinique and St. Domingue, only to be "relegalized" under Napoleon from 1802 to 1815), the international *trade* in slaves was outlawed as a result of formidable metropolitan activism starting in the late 1780s. At that time an "embryonic internationale"[2] comprising British, French, and American abolitionists emerged to translate the moral objections of Enlightenment thinkers into social and political actions. These campaigns, led by members of noncomformist religious sects such as the Quakers (Anthony Benezet), Methodists (John Wesley), Evangelicals of the Clapham sect of the Anglican church (Henry Thornton, William Wilberforce, and Thomas Clarkson), and Catholic outriders (Abbé Grégoire), won legal abolition of the slave trade between 1802 and 1815 in Denmark, England, the United States, and France.

After this initial phase, the antislavery movement was able to solidify its gains through a series of treaties, created between 1815 and 1840, facilitating international cooperation to enforce legal abolition of the slave trade. By the latter part of the nineteenth century the antislavery crusade had become the most widely supported and successful of the early modern humanitarian causes, and humanitarianism generally had achieved a notable presence in both the international and domestic affairs of Western states. Activists in Britain, the United States, Brazil, and France continued the work of the earlier abolitionist internationale, developing a modern transnational humanitarian movement which finally achieved global abolition of the slave trade by the 1880s through a series of formal treaties.[3] Slavery itself was declared universally illegal by the end of the century. Major organizations of the period, such as the British and Foreign Anti-Slavery Society (founded in 1839), a few of which survive today as the oldest functioning nongovernmental human rights organizations, are cited along with the international antislavery campaign by historians as key precursors of the modern human rights movement.

IMPERIAL COMPLICATIONS

Despite the creation of the post-1815[4] treaties of cooperation and the ascendance of Great Britain as de facto antislave trade enforcer, the early international regime was fairly ineffectual, as widespread illicit trafficking of African slaves continued throughout the first two-thirds of the nineteenth century. Thus, the second generation of antislavery activists in the 1830s looked for other means by which to undermine the international slave system. These activists, such as Thomas Buxton, set their humanitarian sights on the internal conditions of African society and, as signaled by the 1840 founding of the African Civilization Society, plotted to "redeem" Africa itself.

Informed by Victorian worldviews, the second generation of activists believed Europeans could end slavery by bringing Christianity, commerce, and civilization to "unregenerate" African peoples.[5] This belief was consistent with the early Victorian faith in human progress (historicism) and the (Eurocentric) midcentury understanding of slavery as indigenous African and Arab institutions. Whereas earlier abolitionists had condemned Europeans and white North Americans for instituting modern slavery, the Victorian era activists imagined that the root of the problem was somehow internal to African societies. The new thinking led to such ill-conceived ventures as the so-called Niger Expedition of 1841–42, which failed famously in its plan to establish a model plantation as a commercial and civilizational beachhead in western Africa.

Victorian-era humanitarianism thus departed conceptually from the altruism of the earlier "Romantic era" (1770–1830). Especially noticeable was a shift in the representation of African, Asian, and native peoples and their societies. During the Romantic period, abolitionists generally adopted what we might recognize today as a form of cultural relativism. The ubiquitous image of the "noble savage" was characteristic of the kind of "Enlightenment objectivity" which humanitarians of the era strove to bring to intercultural discourse. Although patronizing and distorting, the noble savage imagery differed from outright supremacist depictions of non-Europeans as irredeemable subhumans or civilizationally inferior. Romantic antislavery literature often represented Africa itself as a kind of "despoiled sylvan idyl,"[6] within which African peoples could exist admirably without the need for European intervention or civilization.[7]

By midcentury, Victorian abolitionists had dropped these relatively positive images of Africans and Africa from their repertoire. The noble savage and sylvan idyl gave way to the cannibal and the Dark Continent. Even David Livingstone, the popular missionary explorer typically viewed as one of the genuinely humanitarian figures of the mid-Victorian period, railed against the ongoing slave trade in East Africa in terms that relegated Africa and African peoples to a kind of ontological barbarism. Livingstone likened African peoples to children and savages, declared them benighted, and surmised that the only hope for Africa was to have contact with "superior races" through commerce and Christianization.[8]

For Thomas F. Buxton as well, organizer of the 1840s Niger Expedition and a leader of the second-generation antislavery movement, Africa was a dark and diabolical place. Indeed, Buxton and other antislavery activists of the period helped popularize various negative stereotypes, for example, the myth that African societies routinely practiced ritual human sacrifice.[9] Later, the related myth of African cannibalism became standard fare in Darwinian-inspired anthropological literature. An unintended though perhaps inevitable consequence of Buxton's ill-conceived Niger Expedition was that it became a symbol for the mid- to late-Victorian view of Africans as unredeemable.

Victorian antislavery activists tactically deployed such negative imagery in order to shock the conscience of European and North American publics and thus motivate them to act against the enslavement of Africans. From the early 1840s onward these negative images became an indispensable part of the call for direct intervention by Europeans in African affairs. Buxton's speech at the founding of the African Civilization Society in 1840 was an early example of such an incitement to penetrate into the heart of Africa, and civilize with missionaries and schools, as well as agricultural and commercial undertakings.[10]

The usefulness of the melodrama that Victorian abolitionists created—modern enlightened European civilization on one side, African barbarism-cum-savagery on the other—was not lost on imperialist statesmen of the late Victorian period. Belgium's notorious King Leopold II, for example, formally began his drive for empire during the opening speech of the Brussels Geographic Conference of 1876, in which he ably deployed the rhetoric of Victorian humanitarianism: "To open to civilization the only part of our globe where it has yet to penetrate, to pierce the darkness which envelops whole populations, it is, I dare say, a crusade worthy of this century of progress."[11] Leopold could simultaneously establish his humanitarian credentials while promoting his International Association for Africa, the precursor of the Congo Free State which would become his personal colonial possession. Only after thirty years and the suffering and death of millions of Africans in the Congo region would the international community grasp and be repulsed by the imperial dimension of Leopold's humanitarianism.

Leopold's Africa expert and Livingstone's alter ego, Henry Morton

Stanley, also trafficked fluidly in the Victorian humanitarian idiom, while ruthlessly serving his own and Leopold's interests in Africa. Stanley's late-Victorian-era book *Slavery and the Slave Trade in Africa* is a virtual lexicon of double-edged humanitarian rhetoric. Stanley addressed his antislavery exposé to those interested in "the progress of the negro races, and their advancement toward civilization."[12] He decried a three-hundred-year absence of African "intellectual or moral progress," attributing it to the implicitly Iberian-driven slave trade.[13] He then suggested that proper colonial governments (implicitly British and Belgian) should provide "care, knowledge, prudence, and security" to "the ignorant native," who would be saved from slavery, and recruited for colonial or coolie labor.[14] The heart of the book is a detailed description of the *Arab* slave trade ("[a]ll that was bestial and savage in the human heart was given fullest scope"),[15] and a celebration of Leopold's humanitarian undertaking to combat it. Finally, Stanley credited the European partition of Africa with being "the first effective blow dealt to the slave trade in inner Africa."[16]

Although many European imperialists such as Leopold and Stanley clearly did not act out of some sincere though misguided belief in the West's duty to civilize Africa, the record shows that less cynical forms of humanitarianism often did circulate beyond the Victorian salon to shape the imperial encounter. In particular, European missionaries who spread Christianity among indigenous African peoples formed a tenacious presence in Africa throughout the imperial era. These missionaries were not simply pawns in their governments' imperial gambits, nor did they typically seek to enrich themselves at the Africans' expense. They often conflicted with colonial administrators who did not share the same primary concern of converting Africans to Christianity. In the end the missionaries' prospects rose or fell with the success of the European states' imperial projects, but their prominence in the imperial undertaking suggests a complex relationship between various instrumental and more straightforward, not to say unproblematic, humanitarian motivations.[17]

The relationship of Victorian-era humanitarianism to the imperial project can thus be specified culturally through a shared discourse of historicist or religious self-aggrandizement, condescension, and Eurocentrism, and institutionally through the central role played by missionaries and antislavery societies in mounting expeditions into African territory. Beyond these, a third aspect of the relationship between humanitarianism and imperialism lies in the formation of an international law of empire. In the late nineteenth century, international law and politics accommodated and absorbed the humanitarian impulse at a time of intensifying attention to formal empire construction. As opposed to informal imperialism, the formal phase, known as the Scramble for Africa (1880–1905), involved moving beyond coastal trading relationships with the periphery to physical conquest, occupation, and the establishment of colonies. During the short twenty-five years of the Scramble for Africa, European imperial powers took possession of almost the entire land mass of the African continent.[18] The story of how Victorian humanitarianism cotravels with the modern international law of imperialism provides an important sight line for the critical historicization of humanitarianism.

EMPIRES RATIONAL AND HUMANE

In just over a generation, an estimated 100 million African people became colonial subjects. The Scramble for Africa was accompanied by widespread atrocity, in some cases of Holocaust-like scale and depravity. In the Congo region alone, as many as 10 million Africans are estimated to have died "unnatural deaths" due to the inhumane policies of the Belgian colonizers, ranging from outright mass murder to lethal forced-labor policies. In the end, many African women in the region chose to stop bearing children, so utterly hopeless was their situation.

Why did the European colonial powers choose to inaugurate a modern round of direct imperial expansion so many centuries after the earlier era of "discovery" and conquest had passed? The causes are myriad, and theories of empire abound. Some scholars explain the prominence of imperial dynamics in the mid- to late-nineteenth century as a function of the structure of monopoly capitalism and systemic surpluses in both production and investment capital. Emphasizing (European) geopolitics, others have argued that each country involved acted on the belief that it could not afford to lose international prestige by falling behind in acquiring territories, or failing to protect strategic interests in Africa and, by extension, Asia. When a European power asserted itself in Africa, it started a chain reaction of claims by others, a process Bismarck referred to as the "colonial scrimmage." A third explanation is that imperial expansion ameliorated European states' internal social problems either by distributing the economic benefits of imperialism to the working classes or, ideologically, through the glorification of a unified imperial national identity. Yet another theoretical focus looks to conditions in the periphery itself, including the self-interested dynamics of colonialist administrators and settlers and putative "power vacuums" or other political shortfalls among indigenous peoples.

Most theorists of modern European imperialism relegate humanitarian justifications to a secondary level of significance. However, at the time of the Scramble humanitarian motivations appear to have been integrally linked to the economic and political worldviews of imperialists. Infamously captured by imperialist poet Rudyard Kipling in his celebration of "the White Man's Burden," humanitarian justifications of imperialism reflected the Victorian era's belief in the providence of Anglo-Saxon dominion among the "less civilized" peoples of Africa, Asia, the Caribbean, and Latin America.[19] In this moral mythology, whites possessed the duty to civilize the "backward races." But the idea of the White Man's Burden was more than a simple bad faith rationalization of European imperialist activity in Africa. Colonialists such as Sir Frederick Lugard would monumentalize as colonial doctrine the European "dual mandate," which simultaneously denied colonized peoples' right of self-determination and sovereign control over natural resources including land, while upholding the basic human dignity of all people including the colonized on whose behalf Europeans were to govern.[20] More broadly, efforts to mold international law to the new imperialism occurred on the force of an imagined civilizational (humanitarian) interest and obligation in the African continent.

Whatever theory best explains imperialism, the Scramble for Africa prominently featured unique elements of so-called multilateral cooperation, a hallmark of "pragmatic" twentieth-century approaches to international relations and law. The efforts to establish a rational approach to the conquest of Africa began formally at the Berlin West African Conference in 1884–85. The Conference brought together thirteen European nations, the United States, and Turkey to resolve problems related to the Scramble. Contrary to popular perception, the participating countries at the Berlin Conference did not use the formal occasion of the Conference and resulting treaty to partition Africa. Instead, the powers divided Africa among themselves in separate back-room agreements, and through action "on the ground" over the next two decades.

Nevertheless, the Berlin Conference addressed a range of important technical and legal questions regarding African colonization, while infusing a humanitarian disposition into the legal imperial project. Indeed, humanitarianism was the discursive glue that made this imperial multilateralism possible. The Berlin Conference protocols and concluding treaty (the General Act) thus provide a rich record for understanding the ways in which humanitarianism interfaced with the legal and political processes of empire.

By the time of the Berlin Conference, the hypercompetitive phase of imperial expansion in Africa had begun. Britain, France, Germany, and Portugal began openly vying with one another to expand their imperial reach. The Berlin Conference resulted from an elaborate confluence of diplomatic strategies, not least influential of which was Leopold's scheme to take control of the Congo region. Indeed, one of the most important outcomes of the Berlin Conference was its official recognition of Leopold's privately organized International Association of the Congo as a sovereign entity.[21] The three main areas addressed at the Conference involved the establishment of freedom of commerce in central Africa, freedom of navigation on the Congo and Niger river systems, and a general framework of rules for "effective occupation" of African lands by European states. However, in addition to these areas, humanitarianism was omnipresent in the conference deliberations, as reflected in both the official text of the General Act treaty and throughout the record of the four-month-long Conference.

Bismarck's opening speech, which welcomed the delegates and announced the Conference agenda, squarely placed Victorian humanitarianism at the discursive center:

> In extending invitations to this Conference, the [German] Imperial Government was guided by the conviction that all the Governments invited shared the desire to promote the civilization of the natives of Africa by opening the interior of that continent to commerce, by furnishing the means of instruction to its inhabitants, by encouraging missions and enterprises calculated to diffuse useful knowledge, and by preparing the way to the abolition of slavery, and especially of the slave trade.[22]

Bismarck adopted the Victorian humanitarian mantra in tying abolition to commerce, Christianity, and civilization, but he did so in order
to posit a sense of common mission among the European states competing for territory and influence in Africa. His speech built on this
theme by recommending that the Conference devise an imperial system that would be "founded upon the equality of rights [among the
imperial states] and upon the solidarity of interests of all the commercial nations."[23]

In his opening statement, Great Britain's representative at the
Berlin Conference, Sir Edward Malet, continued in the same vein as Bismarck, emphasizing the need for regulated commerce in central Africa
in order to "secure the benefits of civilization to the Africans."[24] Malet
took Bismarck's humanitarianism a step further by also raising a point
that anticipated a modern democratic sensibility usually not found
among late-Victorian humanitarians: "that the natives are not represented at this Conference, and that, nevertheless, the decisions of this
body will be of the gravest importance to them."[25] Malet included in the
proposed legal framework for "legitimate commerce" in the imperial
territories the principle of religious freedom,[26] which, remarkably, is in-
scribed in the General Act treaty as a right ("liberty of conscience and
religious toleration") not only of Europeans, but also of "natives," "al-
legiants," and "strangers."[27] Like Bismarck, Malet invoked humanitarian principles in order to achieve the commonality of purpose (and
identity) requisite for the successful (geopolitically nondisrupting) pursuit of empire in Africa.

Although U.S. delegate John Kasson echoed the consensus humanitarian concerns of conference attendees regarding "civilization of the
native races" and "abolition of the slave trade,"[28] the particular package
of humanitarian values he championed failed to properly interpellate a
collective humanitarian and imperial identity. After supporting
Leopold's Congo initiative, characterizing his International Association
as a purveyor of humanitarian values "formed under high and philan-
thropic European patronage,"[29] Kasson misstepped by valorizing native peoples' agency. He foregrounded consent as a criterion in establishing legal authority over African territories, thereby implicitly as-
cribing to native peoples international legal status, at least insofar as
necessary to legitimate native conveyances of sovereignty and property
to European adventurers.

Kasson later invoked the experience of the colonial settlers in the United States to argue for the establishment of military neutrality in central Africa. Here Kasson argued that, in the interests of those "whom our action shall induce to undertake the work of reducing Africa to civilization, it is our duty to save them from the repetition of the fatal experiences which characterized the like conditions in America."[30] The proposed declaration of colonial neutrality was thus forwarded as a means of protecting members of the "white race" pursuing the civilizing mission in Africa. Neither of these proposals by Kasson was adopted by the Conference, and it appears that he missed the general tenor of invocations of the humanitarian and imperial collective sounding repeatedly around him. International legal status for Africans violated the Eurocentric nature of the collective identity (undermining the ability of the identity to control its object-Other), while the neutrality proposal aspired too liberally to an international (regional) order the neoimperial conditions for which would not arrive for another hundred years.

At the conclusion of the Conference the delegates approved clauses in the formal General Act treaty that committed the imperial powers to "watch over the conservation of indigenous populations and the amelioration of their moral and material conditions of existence and to strive for the suppression of slavery and especially the negro slave trade."[31] Moreover, the powers agreed to "protect and favor without distinction of nationality or of worship, all the institutions and enterprises religious, scientific or charitable, created and organized . . . to instruct the natives and to make them understand and appreciate the advantages of civilization."[32] As well, chapter II, article 9 of the General Act creates an obligation to prevent the slave trade in the imperial territories and a commitment on the part of the states parties, using all means within their power, to punish those engaged in the slave trade.[33] While it is clear that these humanitarian commitments did not reflect the primary motivations for state actions in Africa, the use of international law to further the ends of multilateral colonial diplomacy hinged upon the repeated appeals to a humanitarian European collective.

The Berlin Conference declarations in turn facilitated calls by European humanitarians such as the French Cardinal Archbishop of Algeria Charles Lavigerie to renew civil society's efforts toward "a great crusade of faith and humanity" to end the slave trade.[34] This new wave of activism originally paralleled the legal regime in its internationalist orientation. Soon, however, it lapsed into a nationalist particularism better befitting the political sentiments of the time, as Lavigerie's calls for international cooperation led instead to the formation of *national* antislavery organizations. Lavigerie's efforts to create a kind of international volunteer militia to combat the slave trade never bore fruit, but instead may have inadvertently provided cover for a joint German and British naval blockade against insurgents in East Africa.[35]

The new round of antislavery activism led to a second major international conference in Brussels in 1889–90 which focused specifically on the slavery issue. Once referred to as Africa's Magna Carta,[36] the Brussels Conference Final Act treaty reiterated the antislave trade commitments of the Berlin Conference, but again tied these commitments to further imperial domination of Africa. Indeed, even more directly than Berlin, the Brussels Conference was premised on the carving up of Africa into colonial territories to be monopolized by their respective European metropoles.[37] Leopold manipulated the Conference to his ends, winning support for an import duty scheme in the Congo (in spite of his earlier commitment to free trade there) by convincing the delegates that the revenue was needed to sustain his antislavery campaign there.

Both the Berlin and Brussels Conference treaties were concerted attempts to create an international law of empire through which to facilitate the "peaceful" takeover and exploitation of Africa. Both leaned heavily on the force of a transnational humanitarian identity. The subsequent "end of slavery" in Africa changed little in terms of the social and political domination of Africans by Europeans. Forced labor and grossly inadequate wage labor conditions characterized the European-administered economies in Africa well into the period of anticolonial struggle. The relationship described here between the multilateral diplomacy of the imperial powers (channeled through formal international law creation) and the internationalist aspirations of the humanitarians, however, is not strictly ideological. The humanitarian discourse did more than provide cover for the raw power ambitions of the imperial states. Rather, the imperial and the humanitarian formed a kind of partially arrested dialectic, whereby the transnational humanitarian identity became an important articulation point of imperialism, although, as shown in the next section, it was never fully contained or exhausted in the imperial project.[38]

POST-VICTORIAN HUMANITARIANISM

We must still consider briefly a final chapter in the story of nineteenth-century humanitarianism. This may be accomplished by examining three figures who in different ways embody the humanitarian legacy of the nineteenth century: an African American, George Washington Williams, and two British activists, E. D. Morel and Sir Roger Casement. While these individuals do not entirely escape the arrested dialectic described above, they do reflect a politics that looked beyond Victorian humanitarianism and, thus, provide useful models from which to draw positive lessons about moving from conjuncturally conditioned normativities to a transformative normativity, a move elaborated on in the conclusion.

W. E. B. Du Bois called George Washington Williams "the greatest historian of the [black] race" because of his two-volume history of blacks in America published in the early 1880s.[39] In the short span of years before his early death at age forty-one, the great historian also served as a soldier in the Civil War, an elected member of the Ohio legislature, a Baptist minister, a lawyer, journalist, and public lecturer. He was nominated by President Chester A. Arthur to serve as U.S. consul in Haiti, though Arthur was out of office before Williams could be approved for the post. During a trip to the White House Williams became interested in the possibility of using the "opening up" of the Congo as a way of furthering the interests of American blacks through what he believed could be a mutually beneficial commercial and political relationship with Africans. Williams traveled to Europe and interviewed Leopold for a newspaper article, leaving with a favorable impression of the Belgian king for his apparently selfless commitment to humanitarian action in Africa.

Williams resolved to visit the Congo region to pursue his political and entrepreneurial vision of establishing an African American presence there. During the trip Williams quickly dropped his plans for a transatlantic African partnership based on commercial development and turned instead to the painful task of recording the many examples of slavery, torture, murder, exploitation, and treachery that he was forced to observe or learn about from indigenous sources. His "Open Letter" to King Leopold and a report to President Harrison documented the atrocities, to which he assigned the then rare phrase "crimes against humanity,"[40] using the Berlin General Act treaty provisions as a legal basis from which to denounce the king's administration of the colony.

The "Open Letter" was published in 1890 and predictably met with great rancor from the Belgian king and disfavor from Williams's U.S. patron, a white railroad magnate named Colis Huntington. Williams's character was impugned in the Belgian press, which referred to him as an "unbalanced negro."[41] Within a year of publishing his exposé, most of which was fully verified over the next two decades, Williams was dead of tuberculosis. He had courageously rebuked a powerful king and called for an international investigation of the criminal abuses of the imperial system, alienated his vital source of funding, and abandoned his dream of pioneering transatlantic African enterprise. Among the many Europeans and Americans who had been to the Congo, it was Williams, himself contending with the racist mores of his day, who first observed and confronted the hypocrisies of humanitarian imperialism.

A few years after Williams had died, E. D. Morel and Roger Casement took the lead in mounting a crusade to expose and depose Leopold's reign in Africa. Morel, a clerk in the British shipping industry, and Casement, who served as the first British consul to the Congo Free State, became coconspirators in one of the first and most remarkable human rights victories of the twentieth century. From his knowledge of the shipping records generated in the "trade" between Belgium and the Congo Free State, Morel was able to deduce that King Leopold's colony was using forced or slave labor to extract ivory and rubber products worth five times the value of goods sent from Belgium in exchange. Casement, like Williams before him, witnessed the atrocities in the Congo region firsthand. In 1904 Morel and Casement together formed the Congo Reform Association, the protest vehicle that would force King Leopold to relinquish control of the Congo within just four years.[42]

Though close personal friends and loyal allies, Morel and Casement are interesting studies in contrast. Morel was able to mount a popular campaign against the forced labor system in the Congo precisely because he did not seriously doubt the overall moral appropriateness of imperialism. He had a Victorian's faith in free trade and the civilizing mission. This bias led him to write approvingly of Britain's own inhumane colonialism in west Africa. Moreover, he shared the earlier humanitarians' top-down approach to reform with all its attendant condescensions and Eurocentrism. He was nevertheless dogged in his opposition to the inhumane treatment of Africans in the Congo colony, and later he would virulently protest Britain's involvement in World War I.

Casement was a gay man facing a stifling Victorian sexual morality. He was also a militant Irish nationalist who would eventually be hanged by the British for treason. In contrast to Morel, Casement thus had a lived affinity with what we might today call subaltern politics. Indeed, at his trial on charges of treason for conspiring to form an Irish anticolonial force (with plans to assist an Egyptian revolt against British rule), Casement gave a powerful speech about the rights of colonized people to self-government. The speech later struck a resonant chord with Jawaharlal Nehru, one of the twentieth century's great anticolonial leaders, perhaps suggesting a certain positional affinity between Casement and other subaltern activists.

The campaign to end King Leopold's reign pressured the British and U.S. governments to withdraw their support for the Congo colony. Morel managed the flow of public information through his adept production of several publications which he used to enlist the support of celebrities and members of "high society."[43] In addition to providing financial and moral support and strategic advice to Morel and the Congo Reform Association, Casement had written an early official report, commissioned by the British Foreign Office, on the atrocities in the Congo. Anticipating the genre of human rights reporting of the later twentieth century, Casement spent over three months in the interior of the Congo colony documenting conditions there. His sober official report verified what Williams had alleged years earlier, but it did not please his superiors in the British Foreign Office. Remarkably, the Congo campaign ended King Leopold's reign, though the system of forced labor continued in the Congo region well into the middle of the twentieth century.[44]

The Congo campaign stands out as an early example of post-Victorian humanitarianism, a blend of old and new. Morel and Casement represent different moments in this hybrid sensibility. Morel, though critical of the colonial system and an avowed pacifist, held a Victorian and nationalist faith in the imperial destiny of the British. He understood the need for land reform in the colonies, but did not champion the political independence of colonized peoples. His was a passionate though top-down humanitarianism, which adopted a rather patronizing posture while remaining physically and psychically distant from the people he wanted to help. Casement, who died fighting for the cause of anticolonial self-government, and who suffered the lifelong indignity of having to conceal his gay sexuality, operated as a kind of early human rights field-worker. Like Williams, he understood in a way Morel did not, that the ultimate goal of humanitarian work could be the political empowerment of subaltern groups (their "self-government") and the need, if necessary, to engage in direct forms of political, even armed, struggle to achieve that end.

CONCLUSION

Contemporary human rights discontents share a healthy skepticism toward a postwar legal cosmopolitanism that codifies, and aspires to extend geographically, a Western conception of rights. Critics of the existing orthodoxy offer instead a variety of approaches that would privilege subaltern values in a regenerated human rights agenda. Increasingly, these outsider critiques deny the privileged normativity of universalist human rights discourse and practice both on a philosophical and political basis. Beyond offering a cultural relativist critique of international human rights (as particularist in origin and substance), scholars increasingly question the emancipatory potential of a human rights basis for social and political struggle. In this perspective, human rights discourse and practice face intense scrutiny as potentially hegemonic legitimators of neoimperial relations.[45]

This chapter somewhat self-consciously projects the contemporary critique onto a complex historical record and, not surprisingly, derives a cautionary tale. Like the Victorian adventurer in Africa tracing the easy cohabitation of early humanitarian internationalism with Victorian-era imperialism, we confront a somewhat fractured though discernible likeness of ourselves, of the way today's mainstream human rights culture may channel power.[46] The (hi)story shows how transnational humanitarianism is integrally linked to a deeper cultural process of representation, whereby a Victorian cosmopolitan identity arises from a process of mutual constitution between the metropolitan/national self and its international/subaltern other. Humanitarianism and imperialism come together as part of a representational structure that is a distinctive and central feature of modern international engagement. The cosmopolitan self, the subject of modern international engagement, is fixed through a process of projection in which humanitarianism has played a leading role. This projection process occurs in various cultural, social, and legal sites, each of which is touched on above.

From here, the moral of the (hi)story is that a critical human rights project must break with received forms of humanitarianism and concomitant representational structures. It is not just that legal structures, doctrines, and rights are culturally inflected, as legal anthropologists have told us. Rather, cultural (representational) structures provide the very conditions of possibility for modern cosmopolitan legal projects such as human rights. Legal rights channel power in a way that constitutes "a political principle which orders and selects from a surplus of signifiers" in the cultural realm.[47] But, in addition, international human rights discourse and practice themselves derive from a powerful historical system of signification, which has always drawn on humanitarian-imperial constructions of others.

On another level, Marxian-inspired critiques of human rights identify as problematic a fundamental conceptual bifurcation of, on the one hand, a sacred realm of political community "in the state" in which the abstract rights of citizens comprise the moral dimension, and, on the other, a profane realm of civil society in which (egoistic) individuals materially exist.[48] From this perspective human emancipation cannot be achieved through campaigns for the realization of liberal (bourgeois) rights. Further, the normative force of such claims cannot escape the original bifurcation that structurally locates universalist ideals outside the realm of the real. This separation of the sacred, the moral, and the universal from the material world of civil society renders oxymoronic a "politics of human rights," insofar as "politics" implies an aspiration to a set of emancipatory universalist ideals.

Such a structural critique of rights-based normativity is helpful in historicizing humanitarianism, even though few nineteenth-century humanitarians seriously contemplated extending full citizenship status to subalterns. From studying the record of imperial humanitarianism it is tempting to conclude, along with Marx, that a liberal humanitarianism, beholden to the fundamental bifurcation at the heart of liberal political theory, could never possess transformative potential. A transformative dialectic, whereby a rationality-based normativity could challenge and alter a given social order, will not obtain given the original reduction of the moral to a moment in the nonredeemable state-civil society bifurcation.

However, implicit in the notion of an arrested dialectic, inductively derived from the relationship between nineteenth-century humanitarianism and imperialism outlined in broad terms here, is the possibility of a humanitarian, or human rights-based, politics. The universalist rights-based normativity which we inherit from the Enlightenment is no doubt contaminated by capitalism and its international aspect, imperialism. However, such a contamination does not render forms of struggle galvanized by human rights normativity *structurally* bereft of transformative potential. This is an opening to be exploited, perhaps through the vehicle of affinity-based discourse and practice, namely, various instances of globalized identity politics.

Tracing the relationship of mutual reinforcement between nineteenth-century humanitarianism and imperialism is difficult for many of the same reasons that few of today's human rights critics dismiss the entire human rights project as an unmitigated neoimperial ruse. Relationships between the normative and social dimensions of a given conjuncture evince great indeterminacy. It is an imperfect science at best that allows us to identify mechanisms of social control and resistance, and the overlapping ideational and material aspects of each. Indeed, one important lesson to be gained by critically historicizing humanitarianism involves a methodological reminder to collapse the comfortable normative-descriptive dichotomy that is a cornerstone of legal and social scientific scholarship. Human rights simply cannot be allowed the privileged status of a "trumping" normativity that is divorced from social and political contexts; but likewise, purposive action guided by norms (of diverse origin) constitutes a vital aspect of social and political power dynamics.

NOTES

1. For an excellent overview and critique of the economic determinist explanations of humanitarianism, *see* the two-part article by Thomas L. Haskell, *Capitalism and the Origins of Humanitarian Sensibility*, 90 Am. Hist. Rev. 339, 547 (1985).

2. Yves Benot and Jennifer Curtiss Gage, *The European Conscience and the Black Slave Trade: An Ambiguous Protest*, 97 Diogenes 93, 102 (1997).

3. *See* Paul Gordon Lauren, *The Evolution of International Human Rights: Visions Seen* 43 (1998).

4. The Vienna Congress of 1815 was a turning point in antislavery history,

since the European powers for the first time acknowledged slavery's repugnance, stopping just short of declaring its illegality.

5. Howard Temperley, *White Dreams, Black Africa: The Antislavery Expedition to the River Niger 1841–1842* 4, 14 (1991).

6. *See* Winthrop D. Jordan, *White over Black: American Attitudes toward the Negro, 1550–1812* 370 (1968; reprint, 1977). Compare the negative depictions of Africa contained in proslavery literature. *Id.* at 304–8.

7. Peter Brantlinger, "Victorians and Africans: The Genealogy of the Myth of the Dark Continent," in *"Race," Writing, and Difference* 185, 197 (Henry Louis Gates, Jr. ed. 1985).

8. *Id.*

9. *See id.* at 12.

10. *Id.* at 3–4.

11. Thomas Pakenham, *The Scramble for Africa: 1876–1912* 21 (1991).

12. Henry M. Stanley, *Slavery and the Slave Trade in Africa* 2 (1893).

13. *Id.* at 5.

14. *Id.* at 15.

15. *Id.* at 24.

16. *Id.* at 69.

17. Eric J. Hobsbawm, *The Age of Empire, 1875–1914* 71–72 (1987). For a discussion of the subtle ways in which the missionary presence destroyed African social structures, *see* Michael W. Doyle, *Empires* 170–72 (1986).

18. In addition to sharing the stage with the late phases of antislavery internationalism, the Scramble is contemporaneous with two other transnational social movements that are also viewed as forerunners of modern human rights. International movements for women's equality and a humanitarian law of war grew and consolidated gains during the period. *See* Lauren, *supra* note 3, at ch. 2.

19. *See* Ronald Robinson and John Gallagher, with Alice Denny, *Africa and the Victorians: The Climax of Imperialism in the Dark Continent* ch. 1 (1961).

20. Sir Frederick Lugard, *The Dual Mandate in British Tropical Africa* (1919).

21. The transformation was completed at the Conference's final session when Bismarck announced without objection that the Association had acceded to the General Act treaty, an action only open to state sovereigns. *See* S. E. Crowe, *The Berlin West African Conference, 1884–1885* 142–51 (1970).

22. *State Department Report to the United States Senate Relating to the Independent State of the Congo*, Senate Executive Doc. No. 196, 49th Cong., 1st sess., 1886, at 25 [hereinafter *Congo Report*].

23. *Id.*

24. *Id.* at 27.

25. *Id.*

26. *Id.* at 28.

27. *General Act of the Conference of Berlin concerning the Congo*, Feb. 26, 1885, ch. I, art. 6, Official Documents, 3 Am. J. Int'l L. (Supp. 7) (1909) [hereinafter *General Act*].

28. *Congo Report, supra* note 22, at 34.

29. *Id.*

30. *Id.* at 63–64.

31. *General Act, supra* note 27, at ch. I, art. 6.

32. *Id.*

33. *Id.* at ch. II, art. 9.

34. *See* John D. Hargreaves, *The Elephants and the Grass* 4 (1985).

35. *Id.* at 6.

36. The Magna Carta reference is Reginald Coupland's. *See* Moses Nwulia, *Britain and Slavery in East Africa* 163 (1985).

37. Hargreaves, *supra* note 34, at 7–8.

38. *See* Annelise Riles, *Aspiration and Control: International Legal Rhetoric and the Essentialization of Culture*, 106 Harv. L. Rev. 723–40 (1993). I borrow the term "arrested dialectic" from Pierre Schlag, *Normative and Nowhere to Go*, 43 Stan. L. Rev. 167, 180 n.38 (1990).

39. *See* Adam Hochschild, *King Leopold's Ghost: A Story of Greed, Terror, and Heroism in Colonial Africa* 104 (1998).

40. *Id.* at 111–12.

41. *See* John Hope Franklin, *George Washington Williams: A Biography* 212 (1985).

42. *See* Hochschild, *supra* note 39, at 206–7.

43. *Id.* at 212–17.

44. *Id.* at 278–79.

45. *See, e.g.,* Noam Chomsky's recent treatment of the new norm of humanitarian intervention. Noam Chomsky, *The New Military Humanism* (1999).

46. There are two famous instances of the Victorian confronting himself in Africa: Stanley meeting Livingstone and Conrad's Kurtz finding his primal self in *Heart of Darkness*.

47. *See Human Rights, Culture and Context: Anthropological Perspectives* 6 (Richard Wilson ed. 1997).

48. *See* Karl Marx, "On the Jewish Question," in *Karl Marx: Early Writings* 211–41 (Rodney Livingstone and Gregor Benton, trans. 1975).

2

Toward a Multicultural Conception of Human Rights

Boaventura de Sousa Santos

FOR THE PAST few years I have been puzzled by the extent to which human rights have become the language of progressive politics. For many years after World War II human rights were part and parcel of Cold War politics, and were so regarded by the Left. Double standards, complacency toward friendly dictators, defense of trade-offs between human rights and development—all made human rights suspect as an emancipatory script. Whether in core countries or throughout the developing world, progressive forces preferred the language of revolution and socialism to formulate an emancipatory politics. However, now that those approaches are decidedly out of favor, those same progressive forces find themselves resorting to human rights to reconstitute the language of emancipation. It is as if human rights has been called upon to fill the void left by socialist politics. Can the concept of human rights fill such a void? My answer is a qualified yes.

The specification of the conditions under which human rights can serve a progressive politics illuminates some of the dialectical tensions that lie at the core of Western modernity.[1] I identify three such tensions. The first is that between social regulation and social emancipation—a creative tension which forms the basis of the paradigm of modernity. Yet at the end of the twentieth century emancipation had ceased to be the "other" of regulation and had become its double. Until the late sixties social regulation was met by the strengthening of emancipatory politics. Today we witness a double social crisis: the crisis of social regulation, symbolized by the failures of the regulatory and welfare states, and the crisis of social emancipation, symbolized by the crisis of the social revolution and socialism as paradigms of radical social transformation. Human rights politics, which has been both a regulatory and an emancipatory politics, is trapped in this double crisis, while attempting at the same time to overcome it.

The second dialectical tension occurs between the state and civil society. The modern state, though a minimalist regulatory state, is potentially a maximalist state, to the extent that civil society reproduces itself through laws and regulations which emanate from the state and for which there seems to be no limit as long as the democratic rules of law-making are respected. Human rights are at the core of this tension: while the first generation of human rights was designed as a struggle of civil society against the state, considered to be the sole violator of human rights, the second and third generations of human rights resort to the state as the guarantor of human rights.

Finally, the third tension occurs between the nation-state and what we call globalization. The political model of Western modernity is one of sovereign nation-states coexisting in an international system of equally sovereign states, the interstate system. The privileged unit and scale of both social regulation and social emancipation are the nation-state. The interstate system has always been conceived of as a more or less anarchic society, run by a very soft legality. On the other hand, internationalist emancipatory struggles, namely, working-class internationalism, have always been an aspiration rather than a reality. Today, the selective erosion of the nation-state due to the intensification of globalization raises the question whether social regulation and social emancipation are both to be displaced to the global level. We have started to speak of a global civil society, global governance, global equity, and transnational public spheres. Worldwide recognition of human rights politics is at the forefront of this process. The tension, however, lies in the fact that in very crucial respects human rights politics is a cultural politics. We can even think of human rights as symbolizing the return of the cultural and even of the religious at the beginning of the twenty-first century. But to speak of culture and religion is to speak of difference, boundaries, particularity. How can human rights be both a cultural and a global politics?

My purpose here, therefore, is to develop an analytical framework to highlight and support the emancipatory potential of human rights politics in the double context of globalization on the one hand, and cultural fragmentation and identity politics on the other.

ON GLOBALIZATION

Globalization is a very difficult term to define. Most definitions focus on the new world economy that has emerged since the 1970s as a consequence of the globalization of the production of goods and services and financial markets. As a result, transnational corporations (TNCs) and multilateral financial institutions have risen to new and unprecedented preeminence as international actors.

I prefer a definition of globalization that is more sensitive to social, political, and cultural factors. What we usually call globalization consists of sets of social relations; as these sets of social relations change, so does globalization. There is strictly speaking no single process called globalization; there are, rather, globalizations: bundles of social relations that involve conflicts, and hence both winners and losers. More often than not, the discourse on globalization is the story of the winners as told by the winners. The victory appears so absolute that the defeated end up vanishing from the picture altogether. Thus, I define globalization as the process by which a given local condition or entity succeeds in extending its reach over the globe and, by doing so, develops the capacity to designate a rival social condition or entity as local.

The most important implications of this definition are the following. First, in the Western capitalist world system there is no genuine globalization. What we call globalization is always the successful globalization of a given localism; there is no global condition for which we cannot find a local root, a specific cultural embeddedness. The second implication is that globalization entails localization. We live in a world of localization as much as we live in a world of globalization. The reason why we prefer the term globalization is that hegemonic scientific discourse tends to prefer the story of the world as told by the winners. There are many examples of how globalization entails localization. The English language, as lingua franca, is one such example. Its expansion as global language has entailed the localization of other potentially global languages such as French.

Once a given process of globalization is identified, its full meaning and explanation may not be obtained without considering related processes of relocalization occurring in tandem and intertwined with it. The globalization of the Hollywood star system represented the French or Italian actors of the 1960s—from Brigitte Bardot to Alain Delon, from

Marcello Mastroiani to Sophia Loren—who then symbolized the universal way of acting, as rather ethnic or parochially European.

One of the transformations most commonly associated with globalization is time-space compression. This process cannot be analyzed independent of the power relations that account for the different forms of time and space mobility. On the one hand, there is the transnational capitalist class, in charge of the time-space compression and capable of turning it to its advantage. On the other hand, there are subordinate classes and groups, such as migrant workers and refugees, that are also doing a great deal of physical moving but are not at all in control of the time-space compression. There are those, for example, who heavily contribute to globalization but who, nonetheless, remain prisoners of their local time-space. The peasants of Bolivia, Peru, and Colombia, by growing coca, contribute decisively to a world drug culture, but they themselves remain as "localized" as ever. Tourists represent a third mode of production of time-space compression. Global competence sometimes requires the accentuation of local specificity. Most tourist sites today must be highly exotic, vernacular, and traditional in order to enter the market of global tourism. Different modes of production of globalization account for these asymmetries. I distinguish four such modes which give rise to four forms of globalization.

I call the first one *globalized localism*. It consists of the process by which a given local phenomenon is successfully globalized, be it the worldwide operation of TNCs, the transformation of the English language as lingua franca, the globalization of American fast food or popular music, or the worldwide adoption of American intellectual property law and new *lex mercatoria*.

The second form of globalization is *localized globalism*. It consists of the specific impact of transnational practices and imperatives on local conditions that are thereby destructured and restructured in order to respond to transnational imperatives. Such localized globalisms include free-trade enclaves; deforestation and the massive depletion of natural resources to pay for foreign debt; the touristic use of historical treasures, religious sites, ceremonies, arts and crafts, and wildlife; ecological dumping; the conversion of sustainability-oriented agriculture into export-oriented agriculture as part of "structural adjustment"; and the ethnicization of the workplace.

The international division of globalism assumes a distinct pattern. The core countries specialize in globalized localisms, while the choice of localized globalisms is imposed upon the peripheral countries.[2] The world system is a web of localized globalisms and globalized localisms.

The intensification of global interactions entails two other processes that are not adequately characterized either as globalized localisms or localized globalisms. The first one I call *cosmopolitanism*. Cosmopolitanism is the cross-border solidarity among groups that are exploited, oppressed, or excluded by hegemonic globalization. The prevalent forms of domination do not exclude the opportunity for subordinate nation-states, regions, classes, or social groups and their allies to organize transnationally in defense of perceived common interests and to use to their benefit the capabilities for transnational interaction created by the world system. Cosmopolitan activities involve, for example, South-South dialogues and organizations; new forms of labor internationalism; transnational networks of women's groups, indigenous peoples, and human rights organizations; cross-border alternative legal services; North-South anticapitalist solidarity; transformative advocacy non-governmental organizations (NGOs); networks of alternative development and sustainable environment groups; and so on. In spite of the heterogeneity of the organizations that took part, the contestation of the World Trade Organization meeting in Seattle on November 30, 1999 was a good example of what I call cosmopolitanism.[3]

The other process that cannot be adequately described either as globalized localism or as localized globalism is the emergence of issues which, by their nature, are as global as the globe itself and which I would call, drawing loosely from international law, the *common heritage of humankind*. These are issues that only make sense when referred to the globe in its entirety, such as the sustainability of human life on earth, or such environmental issues as the protection of the ozone layer, the Amazon, Antarctica, biodiversity, or the deep-sea bed. I would also include in this category the exploration of outer space. All these issues refer to resources that, by their very nature, must be administered by trustees of the international community on behalf of present and future generations.

Concern with cosmopolitanism and the common heritage of humankind has undergone great development in the last decades. But it has also elicited powerful resistance, showing that what we call globalization is in fact a set of arenas of cross-border struggles.

It is useful to distinguish between hegemonic globalization from above and counterhegemonic globalization from below. What I called *globalized localism* and *localized globalisms* are globalizations from above; *cosmopolitanism* and the *common heritage of humankind* are globalizations from below.

HUMAN RIGHTS AS AN EMANCIPATORY SCRIPT

The complexity of human rights is that they may be conceived either as a form of globalized localism or as a form of cosmopolitanism; in other words, as a globalization from above or as a globalization from below. My purpose is to specify the cultural conditions under which human rights may be conceived of as globalizations of the latter kind.

As long as human rights are conceived of as universal, they will operate as a globalized localism, a form of globalization from above. Human rights will always be an instrument of Samuel Huntington's "clash of civilizations," that is to say, of the struggle of the West against the rest. Their global competence will be obtained at the cost of their local legitimacy. To operate as a cosmopolitan, counterhegemonic form of globalization, human rights must be reconceptualized as multicultural. Progressive multiculturalism is a precondition for a balanced and mutually reinforcing relationship between global competence and local legitimacy. Progressive multiculturalism, as I understand it, is a precondition for a balanced and mutually reinforcing relationship between global competence and local legitimacy. In order to operate as a cosmopolitan, counterhegemonic form of globalization, human rights must be reconceptualized as multicultural and universal, the two attributes of a counterhegemonic human rights politics in our time.

Human rights are not universal in their application. Four international regimes of human rights are consensually distinguished in the world in our time: the European, the Inter-American, the African, and the Asian.[4] Human rights are not universal as a cultural artifact, a kind of cultural invariant, a global culture. Even though all cultures tend to define ultimate values as the most widespread, the question of universality is a particularly Western cultural question.

The concept of human rights rests on a well-known set of presuppositions, all of which are distinctly Western: a universal human nature that can be known by rational means that is essentially different from and higher than the rest of reality; and a concept of the individual as possessing an absolute and irreducible dignity that must be protected from society, the state, or other forms of hierarchies.[5] Because all these presuppositions are clearly Western and liberal, and easily distinguishable from other conceptions of human dignity in other cultures, one might ask why the question of the universality of human rights has become so hotly debated.

A review of the history of human rights in the postwar period shows that human rights policies, by and large, have been at the service of the economic and geopolitical interests of the hegemonic capitalist states. The generous and seductive discourse on human rights has allowed for unspeakable atrocities that have been evaluated and dealt with according to revolting double standards. Writing in 1981 about the manipulation of the human rights agenda in the United States in conjunction with the mass media, Richard Falk spoke of a "politics of invisibility" and of a "politics of supervisibility."[6] As examples of the politics of invisibility he spoke of the total blackout by the media on news about the tragic decimation of the Maubere people in East Timor (taking more than 300,000 lives) and the plight of the hundred million or so "untouchables" in India. As examples of the politics of supervisibility Falk mentioned the relish with which the postrevolutionary abuses of human rights in Iran and Vietnam were reported in the United States. The same could largely be said of the European Union countries, the most poignant example being the silence that kept the genocide of the Maubere people hidden from the Europeans for a decade, thereby facilitating ongoing smooth and thriving international trade with Indonesia.

The Western, and indeed the Western liberal, mark on the dominant human rights discourse can be found in many other instances: in the Universal Declaration of 1948, which was drafted without the participation of the majority of the peoples of the world; in the exclusive recognition of individual rights, with the only exception of the collective right to self-determination which, however, was restricted to the peoples subjected to European colonialism; in the priority given to civil and political rights over economic, social, and cultural rights; and in the recognition of the right to property as the first and, for many years, the sole economic right.

But this is not the whole story. Throughout the world, millions of people and thousands of NGOs have been struggling for human rights, often at great risk, in defense of oppressed social classes and groups that in many instances have been victimized by authoritarian capitalistic states. The political agendas behind such struggles are usually either explicitly or implicitly anticapitalist. A counterhegemonic human rights discourse and practice have been developing, non-Western conceptions of human rights have been proposed, cross-cultural dialogues on human rights have been organized. The central task of an emancipatory politics of our time, in this domain, consists of transforming the conceptualization and practice of human rights from a globalized localism into a cosmopolitan project.

There are five premises for such a transformation. The first is that it is imperative to transcend the debate on universalism and cultural relativism. This is an inherently false debate whose polar concepts are equally detrimental to an emancipatory conception of human rights. All cultures are relative, but cultural relativism, as a philosophical posture, is wrong. All cultures aspire to ultimate concerns and values, but cultural universalism, as a philosophical posture, is wrong. Against universalism, we must propose cross-cultural dialogues on isomorphic concerns. Against relativism, we must develop cross-cultural procedural criteria to distinguish a progressive politics from a regressive politics, empowerment from disempowerment, emancipation from regulation. To the extent that the debate sparked by human rights might evolve into a competitive dialogue among different cultures on principles of human dignity, it is imperative that such competition induce transnational coalitions to race to the top rather than to the bottom. (What are the absolute minimum standards? The most basic human rights? The lowest common denominators?) The often voiced cautionary comment against overloading human rights politics with new, more advanced rights, or with different and broader conceptions of human rights,[7] is a latter-day manifestation of the reduction of the emancipatory claims of Western modernity to the low degree of emancipation made possible or tolerated by world capitalism. Low-intensity human rights act as the other side of low-intensity democracy.

The second premise is that all cultures have conceptions of human dignity, but not all of them conceive of it as a human right. It is therefore important to look for isomorphic concerns among different cultures. Different names, concepts, and *Weltanschauungen* may convey similar or mutually intelligible concerns or aspirations.

The third premise is that all cultures are incomplete and problematic in their conceptions of human dignity. The incompleteness derives from the very fact that there is a plurality of cultures and thus is best visible from the outside, from the perspective of another culture. If each culture were as complete as it claims to be, there would be just one single culture. To raise the consciousness of cultural incompleteness to its possible maximum is one of the most crucial tasks in the construction of a multicultural conception of human rights.

The fourth premise is that all cultures have different versions of human dignity, some broader than others, some with a wider circle of reciprocity than others, some more open to other cultures than others. For instance, Western modernity has unfolded into two highly divergent conceptions and practices of human rights—the liberal and the social-democratic or Marxist—one prioritizing civil and political rights, the other prioritizing social and economic rights.[8]

Finally, the fifth premise is that all cultures tend to distribute people and social groups between two competing principles of hierarchical belongingness. One operates through hierarchies among homogeneous units; the other operates through separation among unique identities and differences. The two principles do not necessarily overlap and for that reason not all equalities are identical and not all differences are unequal.

These are the premises of a cross-cultural dialogue on human dignity which may eventually lead to a *mestiza* conception of human rights, a conception that instead of resorting to false universalisms, organizes itself as a constellation of local and mutually intelligible local meanings, and networks of empowering normative references.

TOWARD A DIATOPICAL HERMENEUTICS

In the case of a cross-cultural dialogue the exchange is not only between different knowledges but also between different cultures. These universes of meaning consist of constellations of strong *topoi*—the overarching rhetorical commonplaces of a given culture, which function as premises of argumentation and make possible the production and exchange of arguments. Strong *topoi* become highly vulnerable and problematic whenever "used" in a different culture.[9] The best that can happen to them is to be moved "down" from premises of argumentation into arguments. To understand a given culture from another culture's *topoi* may thus prove to be very difficult, if not impossible. I therefore propose a *diatopical hermeneutics as the basis for cross-cultural conversation.*

A diatopical hermeneutics is based on the idea that the *topoi* of an individual culture, no matter how strong they may be, are as incomplete as the culture itself. Such incompleteness is not visible from inside the culture itself, since aspiration to the totality induces taking *pars pro toto*. The objective of a diatopical hermeneutics is, therefore, not to achieve completeness—that being an unachievable goal—but, on the contrary, to raise the consciousness of reciprocal incompleteness to its possible maximum by engaging in the dialogue, as it were, with one foot in one culture and the other in another, accounting for its *diatopical* character.[10] A diatopical hermeneutics requires not only a different kind of knowledge, but also a different process of knowledge creation. It requires the production of a collective and participatory knowledge based on equal cognitive and emotional exchanges, a knowledge-as-emancipation rather than a knowledge-as-regulation.[11]

A diatopical hermeneutics can be conducted between the *topos* of human rights in Western culture and the *topos* of *dharma* in Hindu culture, and the *topos* of *umma* in Islamic culture. It may be argued that to compare or contrast a secular conception of human dignity (the Western one) with religious ones (the Islamic and the Hindu) is incorrect or illegitimate.[12] Against this argument, I have two responses. First, the secular-religious distinction is a distinctly Western one and thus what it distinguishes when applied to Western culture is not equivalent to what it distinguishes when applied to a non-Western culture. For instance, what counts as secular in a society in which one or several non-Western cultures predominate is often considered, when viewed from inside these cultures, as a variety of the religious. The second response is that in the West secularization has never been fully accomplished. What counts as secular is the product of a consensus, at best democratically obtained through a compromise involving some religious claim. For this reason, conceptions of secularism vary widely among European countries. In any case, the Judeo-Christian roots of human rights—starting with the early modern natural law schools—are all too visible.[13] Under such conditions, I argue, the secular-religious distinction must be itself subjected to a diatopical hermeneutics.

According to Panikkar, *dharma*

> is that which maintains, gives cohesion and thus strength to any given thing, to reality, and ultimately to the three worlds (*triloka*). Justice keeps human relations together; morality keeps oneself in harmony;

law is the binding principle for human relations; religion is what maintains the universe in existence; destiny is that which links us with the future; truth is the internal cohesion of a thing. . . . Now a world in which the notion of Dharma is central and nearly all-pervasive is not concerned with finding the "right" of one individual against another or of the individual vis-à-vis society but rather with assaying the dharmic (right, true, consistent) or adharmic character of a thing or an action within the entire anthropocosmic complex of reality.[14]

Seen from the *topos* of *dharma*, human rights are incomplete in that they fail to establish the link between the part (the individual) and the whole (reality), or even more strongly in that they focus on what is merely derivative, on rights rather than on the primordial imperative, the duty of individuals to find their place in the order of the entire society and of the entire cosmos. Seen from the perspective of *dharma* and, indeed from that of the *umma* as well, the Western conception of human rights is plagued by a very simplistic and mechanistic symmetry between rights and duties. It grants rights only to those from whom it can demand duties. This explains why, according to Western human rights, nature has no rights: because no duties can be imposed on it. For the same reason, it is impossible to grant rights to future generations: they have no rights because they have no duties.

On the other hand, seen from the perspective of the *topos* of human rights, *dharma* is also incomplete due to its strong undialectical bias in favor of the harmony of the social and religious status quo, thereby occulting injustices and totally neglecting the value of conflict as a way toward a richer harmony. Moreover, *dharma* is unconcerned with the principles of democratic order, with individual freedom and autonomy, and it neglects the fact that, without primordial rights, the individual is too fragile an entity to avoid being run over by whatever transcends him or her. Moreover, *dharma* tends to forget that human suffering has an irreducible individual dimension: societies don't suffer, individuals do.

At another conceptual level, the same diatopical hermeneutics can be attempted between the *topos* of human rights and the *topos* of *umma* in Islamic culture. The passages in the Qur'an in which the word *umma* occurs are so varied that its meaning cannot be rigidly defined. This much, however, seems to be certain: it always refers to ethnic, linguistic, or religious bodies of people who are the objects of the divine plan of salvation. As the prophetic activity of Muhammad progressed, the religious foundations of the *umma* became increasingly apparent and consequently the *umma* of the Arabs was transformed into the *umma* of the Muslims. Seen from the perspective of the *topos* of the *umma*, the incompleteness of individual human rights lies in the fact that on its basis alone it is impossible to ground the collective linkages and solidarities without which no society can survive, much less flourish. Herein lies the problem with the Western conception of human rights: its failure to accept the collective rights of social groups or peoples, be they ethnic minorities, women, or indigenous peoples. This is a specific instance of the much broader difficulty of defining the community as an arena of concrete solidarity and as a horizontal political obligation.

Conversely, from the perspective of the *topos* of individual human rights, the concept of the *umma* overemphasizes duties to the detriment of rights and is bound to condone otherwise abhorrent inequalities, such as the inequality between men and women and between Muslims and non-Muslims. As unveiled by diatopical hermeneutics, the fundamental weakness of Western culture consists of its overly rigid dichotomy between the individual and society, which makes it vulnerable to possessive individualism, narcissism, alienation, and anomie. On the other hand, the fundamental weakness of Hindu and Islamic culture consists of the fact that they both fail to recognize that human suffering has an irreducible individual dimension, which can only be adequately addressed in a nonhierarchically organized society.

The recognition of reciprocal incompletenesses and weaknesses is a condition sine qua non of a cross-cultural dialogue. A diatopical hermeneutics builds on both the local identification of incompleteness and weakness and on its translocal intelligibility. The mobilization of social support for its emancipatory claims is only achievable if such claims have been appropriated in the local cultural context. Appropriation, in this sense, cannot be obtained through cultural cannibalization. It requires cross-cultural dialogue and a diatopical hermeneutics. Abdullahi Ahmed An-na'im[15] provides a good example of a diatopical hermeneutics between Islamic and Western culture.

There is a long-standing debate on the relationships between Islamism and human rights and the possibility of an Islamic conception of human rights.[16] This debate covers a wide range of positions, and its impact reaches far beyond the Islamic world. Two extreme positions can be identified in this debate. One, absolutist or fundamentalist, is held by those for whom the religious legal system of Islam, the Shari'a, must be fully applied as the law of the Islamic state. The Shari'a must prevail in instances of irreconcilable inconsistencies between the Shari'a and the Western conception of human rights. For example, regarding the status of non-Muslims, the Shari'a dictates the creation of a state for Muslims as the sole citizens, non-Muslims having no political rights; based on the premise that peace between Muslims and non-Muslims is always problematic and confrontations may be unavoidable. Concerning women, there is no question of equality; the Shari'a commands the segregation of women and, according to some more strict interpretations, even excludes them from public life altogether.

At the other extreme, there are the secularists or the modernists who believe that Muslims should organize themselves in secular states. Islam is a religious and spiritual movement, not a political one, and, as such, modern Muslim societies are free to organize their government in whatever manner they deem fit and appropriate to the circumstances. The acceptance of international human rights is a matter of political decision unencumbered by religious considerations. Just one example, among many: a Tunisian law of 1956 prohibited polygamy altogether on the grounds that it was no longer acceptable and that the Qur'anic requirement of justice among cowives was impossible for any man, except the Prophet, to achieve in practice.

An-na'im criticizes both extreme positions. The *via per mezzo* he proposes aims at establishing a cross-cultural foundation for human rights, identifying the areas of conflict between Shari'a and "the standards of human rights," and seeking a reconciliation and positive relationship between the two systems. For example, the problem with the historical Shari'a is that it excludes women and non-Muslims from the application of this principle. Thus, a reform or reconstruction of Shari'a is needed. The method An-na'im proposes for such "Islamic reformation" is based on an evolutionary approach to Islamic sources that looks into the specific historical context within which Shari'a was created out of the original sources of Islam by the founding jurists of the eighth and ninth centuries. In the light of such a context, a restricted construction of the other was probably justified. But this is no longer so.

Following the teachings of Ustadh Mahmoud, An-na'im shows that a close examination of the contents of the Qur'an and Sunna reveals two levels or stages of the message of Islam, one of the earlier Mecca period and the other of the subsequent Medina stage. The earlier message of

Mecca is the eternal and fundamental message of Islam and it emphasizes the inherent dignity of all human beings, regardless of gender, religious belief, or race. Under the historical conditions of the seventh
century (the Medina stage) this message was considered too advanced,
was suspended, and its implementation postponed until the appropriate circumstances emerged in the future. The time and context, says An-
na'im, are now ripe for it.

What is significant about An-na'im's approach and what distinguishes a diatopical hermeneutics from Orientalism is the attempt to
transform the Western conception of human rights into a cross-cultural
one that vindicates Islamic legitimacy rather than relinquishing it. In
the abstract and from the outside, it is difficult to judge whether a religious or a secularist approach is more likely to succeed in an Islam-
based cross-cultural dialogue on human rights. However, one would be
inclined to suggest that, in the Muslim context, the mobilizing energy
needed for a cosmopolitan project of human rights will be more easily
generated within an enlightened religious framework. If so, An-na'im's
approach is very promising.

In India a similar *via per mezzo* is being pursued by some human
rights groups, particularly by untouchable social reformers who seek to
ground the struggle of the untouchables for justice and equality in the
Hindu notions of *karma* and *dharma*. The reformers revise and reinterpret these concepts or even subvert them selectively in such a way as to
turn them into sources of legitimacy and strength for contestation and
protest. An illustration of such revisions is the increasing emphasis
given to *"common dharma"* (*sadharana dharma*) in contrast with the *"specialized dharma"* (*visesa dharma*) of caste rules, rituals, and duties. According to Khare, the *common dharma*,

> based on the spiritual sameness of all creatures, traditionally promotes
> a shared sense of mutual care, avoidance of violence and injury, and a
> pursuit of fairness. It traditionally promotes activities for public wel-
> fare and attracts progressive reformers. Human rights advocates
> might locate here a convergent indigenous Indian impulse. The *com-
> mon dharma* ethic also eminently suits untouchable social reformers.[17]

The "Indian impulse" of the *common dharma* provides human rights
with cultural embeddedness and local legitimacy whereby they cease to

be a globalized localism. The revision of the Hindu tradition to create an opening for human rights claims is thus another good example of a diatopical hermeneutics. The outcome is a culturally hybrid claim for human dignity, a *mestiza* conception of human rights.

A diatopical hermeneutics is not a task for a single person writing within a single culture. For example, An-na'im's approach, though a true *examplar* of diatopical hermeneutics, is conducted with uneven consistency. In my view, An-na'im accepts the idea of universal human rights too readily and acritically, becoming surprisingly ahistorical and naively universalist as far as the Universal Declaration goes.

The diatopical hermeneutics conducted by An-na'im from the perspective of Islamic culture, and the human rights struggles organized by Islamic feminist grassroots movements following the ideas of "Islamic reformation" proposed by him, must be matched by a diatopical hermeneutics conducted from the perspective of other cultures and particularly from the perspective of Western culture. This is probably the only way to embed in Western culture the idea of collective rights, the rights of nature and of future generations, and of duties and responsibilities vis-à-vis collective entities, be they the community, the world, or even the cosmos.

DIFFICULTIES OF A PROGRESSIVE MULTICULTURALISM

A diatopical hermeneutics offers a wide range of possibilities for debates going on in the different cultural regions of the world system on the general issues of universalism, relativism, the cultural frames of social transformation, traditionalism, and cultural revival.[18] However, such a dialogue is only made possible by the temporary simultaneity of two or more different contemporaneities. The partners in the dialogue are only superficially contemporaneous; indeed each of them feels himself or herself only contemporaneous with the historical tradition of his or her respective culture. This is most likely the case when the different cultures involved in the dialogue share a past of interlocked unequal exchanges. What are the possibilities for a cross-cultural dialogue when one of the cultures *in the present* has been itself molded by massive and long-lasting violations of human rights perpetrated in the name of the other culture?

Cultural imperialism and epistemicide are part of the historical trajectory of Western modernity. After centuries of unequal cultural exchanges, is the equal treatment of cultures fair? Is it necessary to render some aspirations of Western culture unpronounceable in order to make room for the pronounceability of other aspirations of other cultures? It is precisely in the field of human rights that Western culture must learn from the South[19] if the false universality that is attributed to human rights in the imperial context is to be converted into the new universality of cosmopolitanism in a cross-cultural dialogue. The emancipatory character of a diatopical hermeneutics is not guaranteed a priori and indeed multiculturalism may be the new mark of a reactionary politics.

One of the most problematic presuppositions of a diatopical hermeneutics is the conception of cultures as incomplete entities. The dilemma of cultural completeness is as follows. If a given culture considers itself complete, it has no interest in entertaining an intercultural dialogue. If, on the contrary, it enters such a dialogue out of a sense of its own incompleteness, it makes itself vulnerable and, ultimately, offers itself up to cultural conquest.

It may be argued that only a powerful and historically victorious culture, such as Western culture, can grant itself the privilege of proclaiming its own incompleteness without risking dissolution. This line of argument is particularly convincing when applied to those non-Western cultures that in the past have endured the most destructive "encounters" with Western culture that led in many cases to their utter cultural extinction. This is the case of indigenous peoples' cultures in the Americas, Australia, New Zealand, India, and elsewhere. These cultures have been so aggressively *incompleted* by Western culture that the demand for incompleteness as a precondition for a diatopical hermeneutics is a ludicrous exercise.[20]

The problem with this line of argument is that it leads logically to two alternative outcomes, both of them quite disturbing: cultural closure or conquest as the sole realistic alternative to intercultural dialogue. In a time of intensified transnational social and cultural practices, cultural closure occults and implicitly condones chaotic and uncontrollable destructuring, contamination, and hybridization. Such processes reside in unequal power relations and in unequal cultural exchanges, so much so that cultural closure becomes the other side of cultural conquest. The question, then, is whether cultural conquest can be replaced by intercultural dialogue based on mutually agreed upon conditions and, if so, what conditions.

CONDITIONS FOR A PROGRESSIVE MULTICULTURALISM

The conditions for a progressive multiculturalism vary widely across time and space, mainly according to the specific cultures involved and the power relations among them. However, I venture to say that the following contextual procedural orientations and transcultural imperatives must be accepted by all social groups interested in intercultural dialogue.

I. From Completeness to Incompleteness

Cultural completeness, the starting point, is the condition prevailing before intercultural dialogue starts. The true beginning of this dialogue is a moment of discontent with one's own culture, a sense that it does not provide satisfactory answers to some of one's queries, perplexities, or expectations. This sensibility is linked to a vague knowledge of and an inarticulate curiosity about other cultures and their answers. The moment of discontent involves a preunderstanding of the existence and possible relevance of other cultures and translates itself into an unreflective consciousness of cultural incompleteness. The individual or collective impulse for intercultural dialogue and thus for a diatopical hermeneutics starts from here.

Diatopical hermeneutics deepens as it progresses in the cultural incompleteness; the objective of a diatopical hermeneutics is to create a self-reflective consciousness of cultural incompleteness.

2. From Narrow to Wide Versions of Cultures

Far from being monolithic entities, cultures have rich internal variety. The consciousness of such variety increases as the diatopical hermeneutics progresses. Of the different versions of a given culture, one must be chosen which represents the widest circle of reciprocity within that culture, the version that goes furthest in the recognition of the other. As we have seen, of two different interpretations of the Qur'an, An-na'im chooses the one with the wider circle of reciprocity, the one that involves Muslims and non-Muslims, men and women alike. In the same way and for the same reason, the untouchable social reformers emphasize "*common dharma*" to the detriment of "*specialized dharma.*" The same must be done within Western culture. Of the two versions of human rights existing in our culture—the liberal and the social-democratic or Marxist—the social-democratic or Marxist one must be adopted for it extends to the economic and social realms the equality that the liberal version only considers legitimate in the political realm.

3. From Unilateral to Shared Times

The time for intercultural dialogue cannot be established unilaterally. Each culture, and therefore the community or communities that sustain it, must decide if and when they are ready for intercultural dialogue. Because of the fallacy of completeness, when one given culture starts feeling the need for intercultural dialogue it tends to believe that the others feel an equal need and are equally eager to engage in dialogue. This is probably most characteristically the case with Western culture, which for centuries felt no need for mutually accepted intercultural dialogue. Now, as the unreflective consciousness of incompleteness sets in in the West, Western culture tends to believe that all other cultures should or indeed must recognize their own incompleteness and be ready and eager to enter into intercultural dialogue with the West.

If the cultures and social groups involved must agree upon the time to enter into an intercultural dialogue, the time to end it provisionally or permanently must be left to the unilateral decision of each culture and social group involved. There should be nothing irreversible about a diatopical hermeneutics. A given culture may need to pause before entering into a new stage of the dialogue; or it may feel that the dialogue has caused more harm than benefit and, accordingly, wish to end it indefinitely. The reversibility of the dialogue makes it an open and explicit political process. The political meaning of a unilateral decision to terminate the intercultural dialogue is different when the decision is taken by a dominant culture or by a dominated culture. While in the latter case it may be an act of self-defense, in the former it will probably be an act of aggressive chauvinism. It is up to the politically progressive forces within a given culture and across cultures—what I have called cosmopolitanism from above—to defend the emancipatory politics of diatopical hermeneutics from reactionary deviations.

4. From Unilaterally Imposed to Mutually Chosen Partners and Issues

Intercultural dialogue is always selective both in terms of partners and of issues. The insistence that neither partners nor issues be unilaterally imposed and that they be mutually agreed upon is probably the most demanding condition of a diatopical hermeneutics. The specific historical, cultural, and political process by which the otherness of a given culture becomes significant for another culture at a given point in time varies widely. But in general, colonialism, liberation struggles, and postcolonialism have been the most decisive processes behind the emergence of significant otherness. Issues of discussion are problematic because in a given culture some issues are not easily translatable into another culture. In addition, in every culture there are always non-negotiable or even unspoken issues. A diatopical hermeneutics has to focus not on the "same" issues, but on isomorphic concerns, on common perplexities and the uneasiness from which the sense of incompleteness emerges.

5. From Equality or Difference to Equality and Difference

Cultures tend to distribute people and groups according to two competing principles of hierarchical belongingness—unequal exchanges among equals, such as exploitation, and unequal recognition of difference, such as racism or sexism—and thus according to competing conceptions of equality and difference. Neither the recognition of equality nor that of difference suffices to found an emancipatory multicultural politics. The following transcultural imperative must thus be accepted by all partners in the dialogue if a diatopical hermeneutics is to succeed: people have the right to be equal whenever difference makes them inferior, but they also have the right to be different whenever equality jeopardizes their identity.

CONCLUSION

As they are now predominantly understood, human rights are a kind of esperanto which can hardly become the everyday language of human dignity across the globe. It is up to the diatopical hermeneutics sketched above to transform human rights into a cosmopolitan politics connecting mutually intelligible and translatable native languages of emancipation. This project may sound rather utopian. But, as Sartre once said, before it is realized an idea has a strange resemblance to utopia.

NOTES

Earlier versions of this essay prompted intense debates on different occasions and it would be fastidious to mention all the people from whose comments this version has so greatly benefited. Nevertheless, I would like to mention two crucial moments in the framing of my ideas as they stand now: the "First National Seminar on Indigenous Special Jurisdiction and Territorial Autonomy," held in the first week of March 1997 in Popayan (Colombia), organized by the Consejo Regional Indigena del Cauca (CRIC) and by the Colombian Government and attended by more than five hundred indigenous leaders and activists; and an unforgettable seminar at the Center for the Study of Developing Societies in New Delhi, on April 25, 2000, whose participants included, among others, D. L. Sheth, Ashis Nandy, Shiv Visvanathan, Shalini Randeria, Achyut Yagnik, Gabrielle Dietrich, and Nalini Nayak. Many thanks to all of them, and also to Rajeev Bhargava and Elizabeth Garcia. My special thank you to Maria Irene Ramalho.

1. Elsewhere, I deal at length with the dialectical tensions in Western modernity. *See* Boaventura de Sousa Santos, *Toward a New Common Sense: Law, Science and Politics in the Paradigmatic Transition* (1995).

2. It has been claimed that the new global economy, based on informational capital, has eliminated the distinction between core, peripheral, and semiperipheral countries. *See* Manuel Castells, *The Rise of the Network Society* 92, 112 (1996). In my view, the distinction holds as well as the hierarchy it contains. More than ever it resides in the specific mix of core and peripheral activities, productions, sectors, employment systems, and the like, in each country. The predominance of core traits in the mix implies that the country specializes in globalized localisms; the predominance of peripheral traits, on the contrary, brings with it the predominance of localized globalisms. The semiperipheral countries are those with an unstable balance between localized globalisms and globalized localisms.

3. Such groups either as hyperlocalized populations (for example, the indigenous peoples of the Andean cordillera) or as hyper-transnationalized populations (such as the indigenous peoples in Brazil, Colombia, or India displaced by "development projects," and illegal immigrants in Europe and North America) experience a space-time compression over which they have no control.

Thus, I don't use cosmopolitanism in the conventional, modern sense. In Western modernity cosmopolitanism is associated with rootless universalism and individualism, world citizenship, and negation of territorial or cultural borders or boundaries. This idea is expressed in Pitagoras's "cosmic law," in Democritus's *philallelia*, in the medieval ideal of the *res publica christiana*, in the Renaissance conception of "humanitas," in Voltaire's saying that "to be a good patriot one needs to become the enemy of the rest of the world," and, finally, in early twentieth-century labor internationalism.

4. For an extended analysis of the four regimes, *see* Santos, *supra* note 1, at 330–37.

5. Raimundo Pannikar, *Is the Notion of Human Rights a Western Concept?* 81 Cahier 28, 30 (1984).

6. Richard Falk, *Human Rights and State Sovereignty* (1981).

7. Jack Donnelly, *Universal Human Rights in Theory and Practice* 109–24 (1989).

8. *See, e.g., Human Rights in Cross-Cultural Perspective: A Quest for Consensus* (Abdullahi A. An-na'im ed. 1992) [hereinafter An-na'im, *Human Rights*]; *Human Rights: Cultural and Ideological Perspectives* (Adamantia Pollis and P. Schwab eds. 1979) [hereinafter Pollis and Schwab].

9. In intercultural exchanges one very often experiences the need to explain and justify ideas and courses of action which in one's own culture are so self-evident and commonsensical that to provide an explanation or justification for them would be strange or awkward, if not utterly foolish.

10. Etymologically, *diatopical* evokes *place* (Gr. *topos*), *two* (Gr. *di-*), and *through* or *cross* (Gr. *dia-*).

11. *See* Santos, *supra* note 1, at 25, for the distinction between these two forms of knowledge, one that progresses from chaos to order (knowledge-as-regulation) and the other that progresses from colonialism to solidarity (knowledge-as-emancipation).

12. It has often been stated that Hinduism is not a well-defined, clearly identifiable religion in the sense of Christianity or Islam "but rather a loosely coordinated and somewhat amorphous conglomeration of 'sets' or similar formations." Wilhelm Halbfass, *Tradition and Reflection: Explorations of Indian Thought* (1991).

13. Ashis Nandy has been one of the most influential and consistent critics of Western secularism as applied to the Indian context. *See* Ashis Nandy, *The Twilight of Certitudes: Secularism, Hindu Nationalism and Other Masks of Deculturation*, 1 Postcolonial Studies 283 (1998). Bhargava provides a detailed and insightful analysis of the concept of secularism. He highlights the complex issues raised by the concept in the Indian context and offers a new and innovative perspective on secularism in Western societies. *Secularism and Its Critics* (Rajeev Bhargava ed. 1998).

14. *See* Panikkar, *supra* note 5, at 28, 39; *see also* Kenneth K. Inada, "A Buddhist Response to the Nature of Human Rights," in *Asian Perspectives on Human Rights* (Claude Welsh, Jr. and Virginia Leary eds. 1990). According to David Knipe, *dharma* is "the spiritual duty in accord with cosmic law and order; perhaps the closest Sanskrit word for 'religion.'" David Knipe, *Hinduism: Experiments in the Sacred* 156 (1991).

15. An-na'im, *supra* note 8; Abdullah An-na'im, *Toward an Islamic Reformation* (1990) [hereinafter An-na'im, *Islamic Reformation*].

16. Besides An-na'im, *Human Rights, supra* note 8, and An-na'im, *Islamic Reformation, supra* note 15, *see* Kevin Dwyer, *Arab Voices: The Human Rights Debate in the Middle East* (1991); *Faith and Freedom: Women's Human Rights in the Muslim World* (Mahnaz Afkhami ed. 1995). On the broader issue of the relationship between modernity and Islamic revival, *see, e.g.,* Hisham Sharabi, *Modernity and Islamic Revival: The Critical Tasks of Arab Intellectuals*, 2 Contention 127 (1992); Ali Shariaty, *What Is To Be Done: The Enlightened Thinkers and an Islamic Renaissance* (1986).

17. R. S. Khare, "Elusive Social Justice, Distant Human Rights: Untouchable Women's Struggles and Dilemmas in Changing India," in *Changing Concepts of Rights and Justice in South Asia* 198, 204 (Michael Anderson and Sumit Guha eds. 1998).

18. For the African debate, *see* Henk Prodcee, *Beyond Universalism and Relativism*, 6 Quest 45 (1992); Mogobe B. Ramose, *African Democratic Traditions: Oneness, Consensus and Openness*, 6 Quest 63 (1992); Ernest Wamba dia Wamba, *Some Remarks on Culture Development and Revolution in Africa*, 4 J. of Historical Sociology 219 (1991).

A sample of the rich debate in India can be found in *Multiculturalism, Liberalism and Democracy* (Rajeev Bhargava, Amiya Bagchi, and R. Sudarshan eds. 1999) and in Thomas Pantham, *On Modernity, Rationality and Morality: Habermas and Gandhi*, 1 Indian J. of Social Science 187 (1988).

A bird's-eye view of cultural differences can be found in Johan Galtung, *Western Civilization: Anatomy and Pathology*, 7 Alternatives 145 (1981).

19. Elsewhere, I deal in detail with the idea of "learning from the South." Santos, *supra* note 1, at 475–519.

20. In this essay I concentrate on the diatopical hermeneutics between Western culture and the "great Oriental cultures" (Hinduism and Islam). I am aware that a diatopical hermeneutics involving indigenous peoples' cultures raises other analytical issues and demands specific preconditions. Focusing on the indigenous peoples of Latin America, I deal with this topic in Boaventura de Sousa Santos and Mauricio Garcia Villegas, *El Caleidoscópio de Justiças en Colombia* (2000).

3

Orientalism Revisited in Asylum and Refugee Claims

Susan Musarrat Akram

THIS ESSAY LOOKS at a particular aspect of the stereotyping of Islam both by advocates and academics, in the context of "neo-Orientalism." In the asylum and refugee context neo-Orientalism particularly affects women, and damages refugee rights both in and outside the Arab and Muslim world.

THE NEW ORIENTALISM

Edward Said describes the Western perception that "Orientals," persons of Middle Eastern or Islamic descent, are somehow fundamentally different from Westerners, in the following passage:

> [T]here are still such things as *an* Islamic society, *an* Arab mind, *an* Oriental psyche. . . . Cliches about how Muslims (or mohammedans, as they are still sometimes called) behave are bandied about with a nonchalance no one would risk in talking about blacks or Jews. At best, the Muslim is a "native informant" for the Orientalist.[1]

One aspect of Orientalism is the Western belief that there is a profound difference between the very mind-set of people from Middle Eastern or Islamic cultures and those from the West. Some Orientalists portray this difference in a romanticized, simplified version of the Eastern mind. Some portray it as much more sinister, describing Muslims as warmongers and Arabs as "terrorists." Another aspect of Orientalism is the acute tendency of Westerners to explain every facet of Eastern and

Muslim societies in light of the Muslim religion—as if there were no complexity, diversity, or other influences in the philosophies or practices of Muslim societies. Observers describe this as characteristic of Western neocolonialism, or embedded in the philosophy of cultural relativity—calling it a form of cultural imperialism.

Orientalism is also reflected in the tendency to simplistically explain the experiences of well over a billion people by reference to a supposedly monolithic and rigid way of thinking called "Islam." The absurdity of such a proposition should be obvious to anyone who realizes that Islam is practiced in such diverse cultures and places as China, Indonesia, Pakistan, Tunisia, Somalia, and the United States. "Neo-Orientalism" here refers to the phenomenon so scathingly attacked by Said and others, but promoted by more recent movements such as modern feminism and human rights, including universalism and cultural relativism. The concern here is both with universalists who misunderstand and misconstrue Islamic concepts in their effort to ensure a single standard of human rights, and with cultural relativists who similarly stereotype Islam as a set of "cultural values" that cannot or should not be changed in any positive "Western-oriented" way. The motivations of the proponents of these philosophies are not identical, but the result is essentially the same.

Such stereotyping leads to several very destructive outcomes— aside from dehumanizing and trivializing the beliefs of a large segment of humankind. First, neo-Orientalist stereotyping supports and promotes the most repressive and extreme versions of Islamic interpretation currently being manipulated by fundamentalist regressive regimes. Thus, it further strengthens and entrenches these regimes' efforts to distance "Islam" from universal human rights. Second, such stereotyping divides Western human rights promoters from their counterparts in the Muslim world. Human rights promoters within the Islamic world are repelled by Western stereotyping, and are criticized in their own societies for apparently identifying with outsiders who promote such stereotypes. Moreover, Muslim human rights promoters are discouraged by these Western attitudes from advocating alternative interpretations of Islam which are compatible with universal human rights. Third, within human rights advocacy in asylum and refugee law, many are denied human rights protections because neo-Orientalist stereotyping privileges Western interpretations over a more accurate interpretation of persecution occurring in the Muslim milieu.

This essay focuses on the manner in which neo-Orientalism affects the presentation and outcome of asylum and refugee claims made in the West by individuals from the Muslim world. Neo-Orientalist portrayals of Islam doom asylum and refugee applicants' cases from the very start in two major ways. First, the distorted view of "Islam" put forward by refugee advocates can be proven wrong by government research and expert testimony, thus undermining the credibility of the refugee's account. Second, the portrayals silence the voice of the refugee herself, with a number of destructive consequences.

FALLACIES ABOUT ISLAM AND THEIR NEGATIVE IMPACT ON ASYLUM CLAIMS

Certain stereotypes about Islam appear repeatedly in the presentation and defense of asylum-refugee claims. Westerners' perception that Islam somehow lacks ethical and humanitarian roots and that "Allah" is a warmongering God different from the Jewish-Christian God reflects a fundamental Western ignorance about Islam. Critical to understanding Islam is a recognition of its cardinal principle of belief in one God— the same God as the Judaic and Christian God—and that the great prophets reiterated the word of God, with Muhammad being the last of God's messengers. For Muslims, the word of God is contained in the Qur'an, which was revealed to Prophet Muhammad and written down exactly as revealed to him. The ethical principles of the Old and New Testaments are embodied in the Qur'an. Muslims believe in all the early Jewish and Christian prophets, from Abraham to Jesus, but their view of the purpose and mission of the prophets differs from that of Jews and Christians. When Westerners insist on coupling the Jewish and Christian religions because of their shared roots and basic principles, but omit Islam, Muslims are rightly puzzled.

The basic requirements of Islam are extraordinarily simple to understand. It has five "pillars" or precepts for every Muslim to follow: belief in one God and in his prophet Muhammad's message; daily prayer; giving *zakat* (charity) to the needy; performing the pilgrimage to Mecca, if possible, once in an individual's lifetime; and fasting during Ramadan.

Contrary to Western myth, every Muslim is free to select the religious precepts that make the most sense to him or her. There are three corollaries to this principle that are the reverse of Western myth. First, every Muslim should read and understand the Qur'an for him- or herself because each individual Muslim makes his or her own individual reckoning with God. Second, Islam has no church or priesthood, and thus there are no "clerics" or "clergy" with power, for example, to excommunicate or absolve Muslims of their sins. Third, Muslim jurisprudence legitimizes a huge range of interpretations of religious precepts, as long as these are based on good faith and pious intent.

Another Western myth is that there is a single "Islamic tradition." The "Islamic tradition" is actually comprised of the Qur'an, the *sunnah* and *hadith*, the *fiqh*, the *madahib*, and the *shari'a*. There are enormous inconsistencies and disagreements in the interpretations of the content of these sources, and between and among the sources themselves. It is thus inaccurate to talk about "Islam" or the "Islamic tradition" as a monolith. The primary source of Islamic religion and Islamic law is the Qur'an. The Qur'an, as the revealed word of God, is the source of all Muslim religious truth; other sources that comprise the "traditions" of Islam are secondary and inferior to the Qur'an. Any interpretation of religion or religious law that conflicts with the Qur'an must accede to the Qur'anic principle. The secondary sources of religious law are the *sunnah*, the ways or traditions of the Prophet, and the *hadith*, the sayings of the Prophet as recorded by the Prophet's followers or others who obtained their information on more or less sound authority. The interpretation of the Qur'an by collectors of *hadith* and jurists has become the core of the Islamic tradition. *Fiqh* is Islamic jurisprudence, which developed historically through many different legal schools, or *madahib*, and is based on all the recognized sources. The final source of "Islamic tradition" is the *shari'a*, or body of legal rules. The Qur'an itself is not a code of law as relatively few verses deal with purely legal principles. Moreover, those verses themselves are subject to many interpretations, beginning with whether they are mandatory or permitted, and whether they address public or purely private sanctions. Thus it is more accurate to define Islamic law as Qur'anic principles interpreted by different jurists, incorporating the customary law of the Arabs, and applied to a particular legal situation.

The Western myth of a monolithic "Islamic law" is also contrary to the historical and current reality of "Islamic laws and traditions." Muslim scholars resorted to the Qur'anic requirement that a Muslim should apply *ijtihad* (individual logical interpretation) to clarify or explain the meaning of Qura'nic verses. Four Sunni schools of interpretation survive: the Hanafi (in Turkey, Central Asia, China, Iraq, and the Indo-Pakistan subcontinent); Maliki (in Egypt, North Africa, and parts of West Africa); Shafi'i (in Jordan, Palestine, Syria, Lebanon, Yemen, Egypt, Malaysia, Thailand, Singapore, and Sri Lanka); and Hanbali (in Saudi Arabia). The Hanbali school teaches the most rigid adherence to the *sunnah* of all the schools of jurisprudence. The main Shi'a sect, the *Twelvers*, follow a fifth school. Needless to say, the interpretations of each of these schools on any particular Qur'anic principle may differ widely from the others. In general, these five schools of thought agree on some basic interpretive principles: (1) Islamic laws change with time, place, and circumstance; (2) Islamic laws are meant to avoid doing harm; (3) laws may be set aside if they are based on a reason which has ceased to apply; and (4) laws must be interpreted in the public interest. Most countries which base their family law on Muslim law have adopted the *ijtihad* of one or other of these schools, resulting in widely differing legal provisions. At the same time, few states have adopted Muslim *shari'a* principles in criminal law—with some exceptions such as Iran, Saudi Arabia, and Pakistan—because there is so little agreement on what *shari'a* criminal law requires.

The roots of Islamic sectarianism are also misunderstood in the West. In addition to the many schools of interpretation of religious law, there is great variety of Islamic practice among different sects. The *Shi'a* and *Sunni* are only two of these sects, although they represent the majority of the Muslim world. Although the initial source of the conflict was their competing claims to political and religious succession to the Prophet—not much different from the Catholic-Protestant rift over who was entitled to lead the Christian Church—their division has since led to major interpretative differences over Islamic principles. In that sense, Iran's *Twelver Shi'ism* is as far removed from Saudi Arabia's *Sunni Wahhabism* as Roman Catholicism is from Protestantism. In both religious schisms, each sect accuses the other of heresy. Yet many Westerners consider both the Saudi and Iranian regimes to be representative of "Islamic ideology." In so lightly dismissing the huge differences in these countries' interpretations and applications of "Islam," Westerners ignore the serious human rights ramifications of many regimes' political manipulation of Islam for their own repressive ends.

Finally, contrary to Western stereotypes, Islam does not sanction inequality between man and woman, or suppress women's rights or freedoms. The ideas supporting the current unequal and oppressive treatment of women in much of the Muslim world is not based on the Qur'an, but on questionable interpretations of the Qur'an by a succession of male patriarchal interpreters working in male-dominated systems for whom such religious interpretations serve political ends.

Because it is not just the threat to male dominance but also to the dominance of the particular regime in power that is at issue, claims related to Islam are not confined to women refugees alone. However, asylum and refugee claims relating to Islam or Islamic law have arisen most frequently in connection with claims made by women. Under the definition of the term refugee by the 1951 Refugee Convention,[2] an applicant for refugee status must establish persecution or a well-founded fear of persecution based on a particular ground: race, religion, nationality, political opinion, or social group. Countries adopting the Refugee Convention interpret each of these terms in varying ways, but essentially apply the same definition.

Refugee lawyers and academics make a distinction between gender-related claims, referring to persecution that particularly affects women, and gender-based claims, referring to persecution of women precisely because they are women. The United Nations High Commissioner for Refugees (UNHCR), entrusted with the protection of refugees worldwide, has defined a number of categories of gender-related claims that are useful in assessing the claims of women fleeing the repressive applications of Islamic "law." These categories have been incorporated in some countries' official guidelines to refugee-asylum adjudicators in assessing gender-related claims. However, few of these guidelines recognize the relationship between the oppressive use of religion and political motives.

The UNHCR's role is to assess the type of persecution claimed against the relevant international law instruments which provide the framework for human rights protections, including the Convention against Torture, the International Convention on the Elimination of Discrimination against Women, and the International Convention on the Rights of the Child. The universal application of the standards established in these instruments is undisputed. But the relevant issue from the perspective of a neo-Orientalist critique is *what is the source of persecution?* In most such cases, the sources of persecution are portrayed as "Islamic law" and "Muslim mores." This is an inaccurate characterization; rather, the sources of persecution in these cases are the singular interpretations of Islam enforced by patriarchal, male-dominated societies in a way that reinforces male power structures and the political hegemony of the dominant political and religious elite.

The monolithic portrayals of Islam in refugee and asylum claims are not simply incorrect and open to empirical rebuttal, but they also silence the voice of the refugee. Forcing the refugee to reject her religion entirely—which is the apparent strategy in many cases—comes at an enormous personal cost. On the other hand, turning the claim into an attack on mores alone makes it impossible for the woman to make a claim based on religion or political opinion. Therefore, she is left with only a social group claim—most commonly expressed as the social group of women. Courts and immigration authorities hesitate to grant asylum on such an ambiguous ground. Moreover, the social group in such cases is so broadly defined—Muslim women—that it raises floodgate concerns.

The movement to present women's asylum claims as gender-based persecution is implicitly Orientalist. This position effectively claims that all women seeking asylum from the Muslim world are refugees, in that Islam persecutes women because they are women. This position falsifies, stereotypes, and diminishes the real claims of persecution by Muslim women. Moreover, it does real harm to the Muslim feminist movement in all its complexity and diversity—both within Muslim cultures and without.

A. Asylum Claims from the Islamic World That Are Factually Incorrect: Apostasy from Islam Is a Capital Offense under Islamic Law

In the 1992 case *Bastanipour v. INS*,[3] the applicant argued to the court that he feared he would be summarily executed in Iran for having converted from Islam to Christianity, a capital offense under Islamic religious law. Although the court variously referred to the claim of apostasy as a claim "under Iranian law" and "Muslim religious law," making no distinction between the two, asylum was granted. The court found that the asylum claim was based on a well-founded fear of persecution for the crime of apostasy under Islamic law.

Although the court was correct in interpreting Iranian law as requiring death for apostasy, its error, which was made in reliance on counsel, lay in claiming that such punishment was mandated under

Islamic law. Only two sources were cited for the proposition: Thomas Patrick Hughes's *A Dictionary of Islam* (1895), and a law review article, "Criminal Law and the Legal System in Revolutionary Iran," *8 Bost. Coll. Third World L.J.* 91, 97 (1988). For the Court to rely on a single 1895 text—written by a Westerner—makes one wonder whether the judges knew that Islam was a religion at all. Nowhere in the case is there a citation to original authority. The hundreds of Muslim jurists, writers, and activists knowledgeable about the subject who fundamentally disagree with such a conclusion were thus summarily dismissed without mention, and *Bastanipour* further entrenched Orientalists' belief about the barbarism of Islam. Although the distortion of Islam appeared to actually help Bastanipour to prevail in his case, the risks of such an approach based on false or exaggerated claims of "Islamic law" are highlighted in the similar case of *Elnager v. INS*.[4]

"Conversion to another religion is an act condemned by the Koran and is punishable by death"[5]

In *Elnager v. INS*, an Egyptian man sought political asylum on the basis that he would be persecuted by radical Muslims for having converted to Christianity. The statement that the "Koran" requires death as punishment for apostasy was presumably made by Mr. Elnager's counsel, and quoted without question by the court. The court looked at whether Egypt itself adopts the death penalty for conversion. The court relied on an opinion by the Bureau of Human Rights and Humanitarian Affairs (BHRHA) in finding no evidence that there was such a provision in Egyptian law or practice. The entire thrust of Mr. Elnager's application for relief was based on this premise, but the fallacy lost him his case.

The first aspect of the fallacy is the absolute notion that Islamic law requires the death penalty for apostasy. There is no unequivocal injunction in the Qur'an that mandates death as punishment for apostasy. Many Islamic scholars seriously question whether there is even any Islamic requirement of death for apostasy.[6] They point to a plethora of contrary evidence: the substantial body of Qur'anic verses as well as sources in the *hadith* that require honoring religious freedom, ban compulsion in religion, and make clear that punishment for such acts as religious conversion is left to the hereafter—again, a matter between the individual and his Maker.[7]

There is not even any agreement about what constitutes "apostasy." A careful examination of the application of the principle of punishment for apostasy reflects political rather than religious interpretations. In Saudi Arabia, for example, members of the large *Shi'a* minority are condemned as apostates by the orthodox *Sunni Wahhabis* who hold power.[8] In Iran, the ruling *Twelver Shi'a* theocrats persecute the *Sunni* minority in southeastern Iran as apostates.[9] Their persecution of Bah'ais as people who have strayed from Islam is well-documented. In Pakistan, members of the Ahmediyya, or Qadiyani, sect, have in recent years been subjected to severe discrimination for alleged apostasy, and have left the country in large numbers because of mistreatment.[10] In all these countries the ruling elites have appeared quite ready to label as apostates opponents of the state, including Muslims who criticize their peculiar brand of the religion or challenge their fundamentalist doctrine.[11]

In *Elnager*, a more accurate presentation of the evidence could have shown that there are strong fundamentalist forces in Egypt seeking political power on the basis of their brand of Islam, and that they advocate death to those who express ideas and opinions they find offensive, including those who convert from Islam.[12] The Egyptian government does not agree with these interpretations, and does not have or enforce such laws; however, it is unable to control the fundamentalist groups within Egypt. Elnager would have had to show that the risk was that his conversion would readily become known to the fundamentalists and that they were quite capable of punishing him with death. Presenting the case in this way, rather than the simplistic and erroneous ground that "Islam requires the death penalty for apostasy," is both accurate, and legally and empirically provable. A more analytical interpretation of the effect of "Islamic law" on his claim of persecution may have won the case.

B. Silencing Women Refugees from Expressing Religious or Political Beliefs

In Muslim women's refugee cases, Western advocates frequently assist in silencing the women's voices in a number of ways. One way this occurs is by forcing women refugees to express their opposition to the policies of their countries in a way that conforms to their Western advocates' view of "Islam," rather than their own true characterization of the form of persecution they have suffered.

Islam requires women to wear the veil, and any woman who refuses to do so is not a Muslim woman.

In a 1991 asylum case in Canada, Nada,[13] a young Saudi woman, claimed she had been persecuted in her country for refusing to wear the veil and for protesting the regime's enforcement of sexist laws. She listed the repressive laws applying to her and her fear of the *mutawwa'in*—the semiofficial Saudi agency known as the Committee for the Promotion of Virtue and Prevention of Vice.

Nada's lawyer argued her case by claiming that her political beliefs of feminism and her membership in a particular social group, that of women, subjected her to persecution from the Saudi authorities. Nada's claim was rejected on the ground that it was not credible that an Arab Muslim woman would disagree with the authorities of a Muslim state. The Refugee Board found that her feminism was not a "political opinion" for purposes of refugee status, and that she should "comply with the laws of general application she criticizes."[14] The Canadian Minister of Employment and Immigration said he did not think Canada should "try to impose its values on the rest of the world."[15]

After much publicity, Nada was granted the right to remain in Canada on humanitarian grounds. In fashioning the claim in a way that made it ludicrous for Nada to maintain her feminism and still profess herself a Muslim, her advocates also fell into the trap of Orientalizing her. Nada publicly stated her own view of the Orientalist attitudes she confronted in Canada:

> The discrimination and repression I lived with in Saudi Arabia had political and not cultural roots. . . . The claim that such practices are cultural is dangerous, if not racist. When a woman walks down the street in Saudi Arabia without a veil and the Mutaww'ain [religious police] flog her, this is not cultural, it's political. Islam is being manipulated. In the Middle East, as everywhere else, men would do anything to preserve their power and authority. In Saudi Arabia the veil is just a form of oppression, a way for men to say they have power over women.[16]

Another way in which neo-Orientalism silences refugee women is by falsely characterizing Muslim women's claims as gender-based persecution instead of religious or political. Women refugees are silenced first by being given a choice of either denouncing "Islam" altogether or foregoing their claim; and second, when the government's actions are portrayed as being legitimately required by the religion itself, the applicant's opposition to such actions can never be seen as political.

In *Fatin v. INS*,[17] the applicant claimed asylum based on her membership in a particular social group and on her political opinion. She defined the social group as "the social group of upper class Iranian women who supported the Shah of Iran, a group of educated Westernized free-thinking individuals." Alternatively, Fatin suggested that she would be persecuted solely because she was a woman. This contention was rejected because there was insufficient evidence that Fatin would be persecuted based simply on her gender. However, the court found that Fatin's claim based on the social group of Iranian women who find the laws toward women "so abhorrent that they 'refuse to conform'. . . may well satisfy the definition of [social group]." However, Fatin did not establish that her beliefs were so "fundamental to [her] identity or conscience that [they] ought not to be required to be changed." Her claim failed because she did not show that the consequences to her would amount to persecution. The court made a distinction between women who had such an abhorrence to wearing the veil that it might be persecution to require them to do so, and women for whom wearing the veil was merely inconvenient, but not persecutory.[18]

On the political opinion claim, the court found that it failed for the same reasons as the social group argument, in that the record simply did not establish that she had a well-founded fear of persecution on that ground. Had Fatin's lawyers attempted to present the claim in a more sophisticated and non-Muslim-stereotyping manner, the court's reasons for denial may well have been overcome. Instead of claiming that she would be unable to play the role of a religious *Shi'a* woman, her advocates could have focused on developing the testimony concerning Fatin's own belief in religious freedom based on her and her family's interpretation of Islam.

Fatin could have been allowed to explore how she felt that Islam was being fundamentally misinterpreted and misused by the Iranian regime. In support of her case she could have presented expert testimony and evidence of the use of such precepts to solidify political power by the Iranian theocracy. Fatin could then have convincingly defined the social group to which she belonged, and shown that this group faced a well-founded fear of persecution in Iran, as "Muslim women who fundamentally disagree with the interpretation of Islam imposed by the *Twelver Shi'a* theocracy through gender-specific laws."

There is tremendous confusion about how to define "social group." Thus, it is not surprising that membership in a broadly defined social group has not been a ground found persuasive by asylum adjudicators. Defining the social group as suggested here makes the link between the social group and its political opinion or imputed political opinion clear as grounds for legal action.

On Fatin's political opinion and social group claims, the court may have been justified in finding the evidence weak and unconvincing. Fatin's claim that she was a "Westernized free-thinking individual," that she had a "deep-rooted" belief in freedom and equality for women, and that she "would avoid practicing a religion" did not convince the court that the basis for her beliefs was fundamental to her conscience. Fatin nowhere claimed she did not believe in Islam. This is at the heart of the dilemma Western feminist advocates find themselves in when representing Muslim refugee women: few of the latter articulate their objections to the particular "Islamic" regime in question as a fundamental rejection of the faith itself.

In *Safaie v. INS*,[19] the court found that an Iranian woman who refused to conform to gender-specific laws did not have a well-founded fear of persecution. In describing Safaie's claim and evidence, the court asserted that Safaie began wearing "Islamic dress"[20] when it became mandatory in 1982, but she did not have the "mentality of a Moslem." Safaie had specifically claimed asylum on the basis of her gender. The court took the view that "[N]o factfinder could reasonably conclude that all Iranian women had a well-founded fear of persecution based solely on their gender."

Safaie's second social group claim was based on the group of "Iranian women who advocate women's rights or who oppose Iranian customs relating to dress and behavior." The court did not believe there was sufficient evidence to indicate that her opposition was of the depth and intensity required. As in *Fatin*, Safaie's claim could have been refashioned to reflect her dissidence as a Muslim woman, with expert testimony to support the fundamental disagreements raging in the Muslim world regarding the requirements of the faith and the political implications of such disagreements.

In other cases, women's claims have also been brought as religiously or politically based claims. However, these have been no more successful than the "gender-as-social-group" claims, nor have they been more reflective of Islamic complexity from a non-Orientalist point of view. This is because refugee advocates have failed to distinguish between the "Islam" that is practiced by the government and the Islamic beliefs the applicant herself holds and practices. It also silences the woman refugee's voice, preventing her from articulating as political opinion her opposition to the actions of the government she fears.

In *Fisher v. INS*,[21] Saideh Hassib-Tehrani ("Fisher") based her claim on the assertion that the government of Iran would persecute her because of her religious or political beliefs. The court said, "Fisher's assertion that the government will prosecute her for violating the dress and conduct rules does not alone amount to persecution on account of religious or political beliefs. She 'merely has established that [she] faces a possibility of prosecution for an act deemed criminal in Iranian society."[22] The court found: "The mere existence of a law permitting the detention, arrest, or even imprisonment of a woman who does not wear the chador in Iran does not constitute persecution any more than it would if the same law existed in the United States."[23] The court's assumption was clearly that the failure to wear the chador was not in itself necessarily an expression of religious belief: it may be nothing more than nonconformity.

Fisher was denied asylum. She might have prevailed in her claim had it been more accurately portrayed. For example, she could have shown her complete disagreement with the *Twelver Shi'a* interpretation of the aspects of Islam which those in power in Iran use to repress women, including the requirement to wear a chador, and explained that, based on Muslim principles, she had a right to a fundamentally different interpretation. Her argument would have been that in forcing her to conform to interpretations of Islamic practices with which she intrinsically disagreed, the government was violating her fundamental human right of freedom of conscience and religious belief. Moreover, her fundamentally different religious interpretation was perceived by the ruling religious establishment as a threat to its power; hence, anyone who appeared to disagree with its peculiar Muslim theocratic principles was both a religious and a political opponent.

She could also have explained that she would be persecuted for belonging to the social group of women whose actions indicated that they fundamentally disagreed with the religious interpretation imposed on them. Not all Iranian women are part of this social group. Contrary to the Western view promoted by neo-Orientalists, many women in the Muslim world do not object to wearing a veil, many adopt it voluntarily on the basis of custom, and many who wear it do not perceive a law requiring it to be persecutory. Women in these categories would be unable to make the essential showing that they would in some way be singled out because of, or on account of, a political, religious, or social group ground.

Nada's case also exemplifies how refugee voices are silenced by the neo-Orientalists' approach, by refusing to recognize women's opposition to their government's use of Islam as religious opposition or political opinion. A more sophisticated approach to the relevance of Islam in Nada's claim might have refashioned the claims of religious and political persecution based on expert and documentary evidence. Specifically, on her claim of religious persecution, Nada could have provided expert testimony concerning the Saudi interpretation of Islamic precepts concerning women, shown the differing views about these precepts within Islam, and shown that *as a Muslim*, Nada legitimately disagreed with the interpretation of the Saudi rulers. This presentation would have allowed Nada to retain her identity as a *Muslim feminist*, while also allowing her to disagree with the Saudi government's use of Islam to oppress her.

Such an approach has been taken in cases assessing the impact of Islam on refugee claims in some other countries. New Zealand, for example, has developed a relatively sophisticated jurisprudence on the issue, with predictably accurate and generous results for refugees. In *Refugee Appeal No. 2039/93 Re MN* (12 February 1996), the Refugee Appeals Authority (RSAA) decided the case of an Iranian woman of Arab ethnicity. She claimed asylum on two grounds: first, that she opposed the male-dominated society of her Arab family; and second, that she opposed the male domination of Iranian society. The RSAA found that she had established a well-founded fear of persecution based on her political opinion on both grounds.

The RSAA was persuaded by evidence that families in Iranian and Arab societies applied tribal social values as well as Islamic ideology as a way of controlling women. The RSAA further found that the rules that oppress women in Iran are disguised by a façade of religion, but are put in place to acquire and maintain the power structure exclusively for men. Nowhere in the case is there evidence that either the reviewing tribunal or counsel relied on arguments that Islamic law requires the oppressive rules against which the applicant complained; nor did the applicant herself state that she did not consider herself a Muslim.

Most important is the recognition that if the woman's belief is not seen purely as opposition to "Islam," then her repudiation of the type of government repression she faces can be articulated as political opinion. This permits her to give voice to the full expression of her own experience of persecution, and, in doing so, does not require her to denounce her religion.

CONCLUSION

Orientalist perspectives have grave consequences in the human rights context. The new Orientalism emerging from feminist perspectives on human rights advocacy threatens accurate presentations of human rights violations and victimization.

Neo-Orientalism not only denies refugees protection because the stereotypes are fundamentally not provable, but it also diminishes the voices and dignity of the refugees themselves. Simplifying the experience of persecution by Muslims as being due to "Islamic law" dooms the refugee's claim and continues the oppression by forcing her to falsify the bases of her fear. These fallacies reflect a failure to understand the complexity of the Muslim world and Muslim reality—a failure of sophistication that would not be tolerated if the stereotype were of a religion other than Islam.

NOTES

1. Edward Said, *Orientalism* 336 (1978).

2. Convention Relating to the Status of Refugees (1951 Refugee Convention), art. 1D, 189 U.N.T.S. 137, July 28, 1951.

3. 980 F.2d 1129 (7th Cir. 1992).

4. *Elnager v. INS*, 930 F.2d 784 (9th Cir. 1990).

5. *Id.* at 785.

6. Several *ayahs* from Surat *Al-Nisaa* are often cited as implying such a requirement. They state: "why are ye two parties on the subject of the hypocrites. . . . If they turn back, then seize them, and slay them wherever ye find them . . . (4:88–91). This has been interpreted both as requiring death for apostasy and death for those who oppose Islam [through force, as in a state of war], not reversion from the Islamic religion. *See* Majid Khadduri, *The Islamic Law of Nations, Shaybani's Siyar* 196, n.4 (1966).

Khadduri's translation of Shaybani contains the editorial comment that the Prophet Muhammad's practice was to permit any of his followers who wished to do so to return to Makka and rejoin the polytheists without prohibition, citing Ibn Hisham, *Kitab Sirat Rasul Allah*, Vol. II, at 747–48. However, he also cites contrary authority to this *hadith*, Ali b. Abi Talib, Abd-Allah v. Masud, and Mu'adh b. Jabal, in Abu Yusuf, *Kitab-ul-kharaj* 179 (Abid Ali trans. 1962). The most painstaking assessment of authority for the proposition that Islam mandates death for conversion is S. A. Rahman's *Punishment of Apostasy in Islam* (1972). Among his conclusions are:

> Our study of the relevant Qur'anic verses establishes that the punishment for apostasy is postponed to the Hereafter, in the same way as that for original disbelief. There is absolutely no mention in the Qur'an of mundane punishment for defection from the faith by a believer, except in the shape of deprivation of the spiritual benefits of Islam or of the civil status and advantages that accrue to an individual. . . . Not only is there no specific provision in the Qur'an, prescribing punishment for an apostate in the phenomenal world, but several verses of the Holy Book envisage the natural death of the apostate in his condition of disbelief and even contemplate repeated apostasies and reversions to the true faith. (*Id*. at 131)
>
> The Fuqha' [jurists] acknowledge generally that no punishment for apostasy is prescribed in the Qur'an. Their principal reliance for the view that apostasy must be punished with death is on certain quali [verbal] hadith, but as has been brought out in the discussion of those sayings, the relevant occasion or the circumstances to which they might have reference are not fully explained . . . [and] . . . the orthodox dictum [has] questionable logic and reasoning. (*Id*. at 135)

The author draws the distinction between private obligations, which are a matter between the individual and God (Huquq Allah), and public obligations, which are governed by the state (Huquq al-Ibad). The Qur'an clearly places matters of conscience in the first category (*Id*. at 135). Rahman notes the Qur'anic requirement and variations that require "civil death" to the person converting from Islam (i.e., termination of marriage and inheritance rights), and the historical reasons for these consequences. Current legislation in most Muslim countries does away with such consequences. *See* Ann E. Mayer, *Islam and Human Rights, Tradition and Politics* (1995).

7. The clearest verses on freedom of religion are found in Surah *al-Baqarah*: "Let there be no compulsion in religion: Truth stands out clear from error." Qur'an, 2:256; "If it had been thy Lord's will, they would all have believed, all who are on earth. Will you then compel mankind against their will to believe?" Qur'an, 10:99.

8. Amnesty International, *Saudi Arabia: Religious Intolerance: The Arrest, Detention and Torture of Christian Worshippers and Shi'a Muslims* (1993).

9. Amnesty International, *Iran: Violations of Human Rights: Documents Sent by Amnesty International to the Government of the Islamic Republic of Iran* 45–46, 63–65 (1987). The rubric of "religious offense" or apostasy is frequently used to repress political opponents in some Islamic countries. *Id.* at 162.

10. Ordinance XX of the *Pakistan Penal Code* proclaims that members of the Ahmediyya, or Qadiayani, sect are non-Muslims, and prohibits them from engaging in many of the religious practices of Islam. For cases of members of the Ahmediyya sect seeking asylum in Canada based on Pakistan's Ordinance, *see, e.g.,* CRDD No. T90-04196, Sultan, Dualeh, May 1, 1991.

11. *See* Ann E. Mayer, "Fundamentalist Impact in Iran, Pakistan, and the Sudan," in *Fundamentalisms and the State: Remaking Politics, Economies, and Militance* 110, 117, 125, 137 (Martin Marty and Scott Appleby eds. 1993).

12. For example, the secular Egyptian intellectual Farag Fuda was assassinated by fundamentalist terrorists in 1992; Nasr Hamid Abu Zayd, a University of Cairo professor, was declared an atheist in 1993 based on his linguistic research and had to go into hiding due to fundamentalist death threats. Youssef Ibrahim, *Egypt Fights Militant Islam with More of the Same*, N.Y. Times, Aug. 18, 1993, at A3.

13. Nada is the fictitious name used by her counsel to protect her identity. *See* Julie Wheelwright, *One Giant Step for Women in Search of Asylum*, Guardian, Mar. 22, 1993, at 11.

14. *Id.* at 11.

15. Judy Steed, *Refugee Board Chief Knows Racism First Hand*, Toronto Star, Feb. 28, 1993, at B5.

16. Nada, *A Serious Step toward Accepting Female Refugees*, Ottawa Citizen, Mar. 11, 1993, at A13.

17. 12 F.3d 1233 (3d Cir. 1993).

18. *Id.* at 1242.

19. 25 F.3d 636 (8th Cir. 1994).

20. There is no such thing as "Islamic dress." The clothing worn in the countries where Islam is practiced reflects the same cultural diversity as in the rest of the world. The same is true of the "veil," which refers neither to a specific garment nor to a universally accepted concept in Islam.

21. 37 F.3d 1371 (9th Cir. 1994).

22. *Fisher v. INS*, 79 F.3d 955, 962 (1996). *Fisher* was a trilogy of cases, first decided in 1994, amended a year later, and then reheard and decided *en banc* in 1996 at the Ninth Court.

23. *Id.*

4

Homophobia/Heterosexism in African Americans

Internalized Racism and African American Lesbians and Bisexual Women

Beverly A. Greene

Somewhere on the edge of consciousness there is what I call a mythical norm, which each one of us within our hearts knows "that is not me." In America, this norm is usually defined as white, thin, male, young, heterosexual, Christian, and financially secure. . . . Those of us who stand outside that [mythical norm's] power often identify one way in which we are different, and we assume that to be the primary cause of all oppression, forgetting other distortions around difference, some of which we ourselves may be practicing.[1]

INTRODUCTION: THE MULTIDIMENSIONAL LIVES OF AFRICAN AMERICAN LESBIANS AND BISEXUAL WOMEN

African American lesbians and bisexual women are a large and diverse group whose members represent every category of age, class, education, physical ability, and geographical region, as well as others. Thus they have multiple identities and nobody should make arbitrary assumptions about which of these are most salient to a given individual, particularly as the saliency of these identities may shift depending on the context of a woman's life and the different stages in her life.

The heterogeneity of African women notwithstanding, black lesbians in the diaspora have been integral members of black communities. Throughout history, they have experienced varying levels of tolerance for their sexual orientation, and have shared the same devalued position born of racism and sexism as their heterosexual counterparts.[2] The intolerance of African American lesbians expressed in homophobia and heterosexism within the African American community has a range of determinants, including internalized oppression and racism by African Americans.

Based on conservative population estimates there are some 1.8 million African American women who could be defined as lesbian and bisexual in the United States. Yet few published empirical studies include all or significant numbers of African American lesbian and bisexual respondents, raising questions about the accuracy of the assumptions made about their psychologies.[3] Thus it is not appropriate to limit one's understanding of African Americans to dominant cultural analyses which may reinforce preexisting racist, sexist, and heterosexist biases. It is also imperative when analyzing the history of discrimination of any ethnic group to incorporate group members' own understandings of their history, oppression, and coping strategies. Thus, this work addresses internalized racism in the African American community.

While African Americans within the United States share an inherited legacy of racial discrimination and oppression by the dominant culture, African American lesbians and bisexual women have multiple stigmatized identities and are affected by the conflation of institutional racism and sexism both within the African American and the dominant cultural communities. To understand the meaning and reality of being an African American woman who is lesbian or bisexual, this essay explores the impact of a range of factors that include ethnicity, gender, sexual orientation, socioeconomic class, and their dynamic interactions in the individual. In addition, the work reviews the nature of the traditional gender-role stereotypes among African Americans; the role and importance of family and community; and the role of religion and spirituality in the lives of African Americans. The essay shows that powerful factors affecting lesbians' and bisexual women's lives include the role of racial stereotypes about African Americans, the degree of sexism, internalized racism, and homophobia by African Americans as a group, and racist and sexist barriers and challenges from the dominant culture. These factors have contributed to the development of ethnosexual myths imposed on all people of color and to the sexual identity and sexual behavior of African Americans and hence of African American lesbian and bisexual women.

FAMILY OF ORIGIN: TOLERANCE AND SILENCING

The African American family has functioned as an important refuge which has protected group members from the racism of the dominant culture and has been an important socializing tool for African Americans as an oppressed group in a hostile environment. The importance of African American family and community as survival tools makes the coming out process for African American lesbians fraught with greater difficulty and perhaps with greater risk than their white counterparts. On the other hand, because of the strength of family ties, there may be a reluctance to formally "expel" a lesbian from the family despite an undisputed rejection of a lesbian sexual orientation; typically lesbians are not "disowned." The apparent "tolerance" of some families does not however constitute approval and is usually contingent on a lesbian's silence about her sexual orientation. This "closeted sexuality" which exists in African American communities "should be seriously interrogated," as it contributes significantly to internalized homophobia by lesbians and gay persons.[4]

African American culture accepts close and emotionally intense ties between adult women, embracing a role within the community for the nonrelated adult girlfriend who has an often very intense but nonsexual, spiritual, and emotionally connected relationship with an African American woman and her family.[5] The role of the close female friend makes it easy for African American families to avoid acknowledging the lesbian nature of a relationship between two adult women.[6] In interracial relationships, a non–African American partner's race may become scapegoated as a more comfortable focus for the family's anger about the disclosure.[7] It is not unusual, however, for *any* partner to be scapegoated as a bad influence who seduced or influenced their family member into the lifestyle. For some family members this approach can represent their way of rejecting a lesbian sexual orientation while relieving their loved one of any responsibility for her sexuality and maintaining the family tie.

Moreover, in some African American families, lesbian, even interracial, relationships may be openly accepted by family members. Reactions by families are as diverse as are African American families themselves. However, the African American community is perceived as extremely homophobic; thus many women remain closeted.

THE ROLE OF ETHNOSEXUAL STEREOTYPES IN HETEROSEXISM

In ethnosexual stereotypes the sexuality or sexual behavior of a disadvantaged ethnic group is devalued, degraded, or exaggerated. Negative stereotypes have been used to objectify African American men and women, degrade African American women in comparison to their idealized white counterparts, and to rationalize and promote their sexual exploitation and control. Such myths affect lesbians' and bisexual women's understanding of their sexuality.

Since they came to America as slaves, African American women were deemed chattel—mere pieces of property—with no human or civil rights. Forced sexual relationships with African males and white slave masters were the norm. Slave masters used African American women's bodies for the satisfaction of sexual desire without their consent—what is now called rape—as well as for breeding purposes, to increase their stock of slaves and profits.

Ethnosexual stereotypes about African American women have their roots in images created by a white society that struggled to reconcile the contradictions between its ideals and espoused values of freedom, liberty, and democracy and its inhumane and debased treatment of African Americans generally and their use of African American women's bodies specifically.[8] Making up distortions about the sexual behavior and proclivities of African Americans, depicting them as bestial, animal-like, and therefore less than human, was a means of rationalizing their unfair and deplorable treatment.

African American women clearly did not fit the traditional stereotypes of women as fragile, weak, and dependent, as they were never allowed to be "dependent" on anyone. The "Mammy" figure is the historical antecedent to the stereotype of African American women as assertive, domineering, and strong. Assertiveness was considered the equivalent of being antimale and even castrating. Popular images of African American women, and any other strong assertive woman, as castrating were created in the interest of maintaining the status quo. In this arrangement of social power, African American men and women were subordinate to whites and women were subordinate to men.

These images, though, have historical antecedents. Slavery defined African women as workers and from the very moment they arrived on these shores required that they work to a greater degree outside the home than their white counterparts. While this arrangement may have facilitated a greater level of cultural gender role flexibility among African American families, it deprived slave women of the customary perks of "femininity" accorded other American women.[9] Such flexibility among African American women notwithstanding, sexism is still a visible and prevalent phenomenon in African American communities.

The sexual objectification of African Americans during slavery was rationalized by the creation of distorted images of excessive sexual desire, promiscuity, and moral looseness. Such conceptions are relevant to the current self-images of African American lesbians and bisexual women, and to the way a lesbian's family and the African American community views its lesbian and bisexual members, as well as their own sexuality. Psychological theories that portrayed assertive women as castrating were also used to scientifically stigmatize any woman who wanted to work outside the home or who violated the strict gender-role stereotypes of a patriarchal culture.[10] Today's stereotypes are a product of those myths and depict African American women as not sufficiently subordinate to African American men, inherently promiscuous, morally loose, assertive, matriarchal, defective, and "other" when compared to white women.

African American males are encouraged to view strong women, rather than the practices of racist institutions, as responsible for their oppression. Racism, sexism, and heterosexism converge to blame African American women for the failure of their men to live up to the Western ideal of the male role, and consequently for the "failure" of African American families. In this analysis, the prescribed remedy for liberating people of African descent is male dominance and female subordination.[11] Many African American women, including lesbians, have internalized these myths.

Stereotypes of lesbians as masculinized females are conflated with images of African American women as "too strong" and "domineering." Both are depicted as defective females who want to be or act like men and are sexually promiscuous. African American men and women who have internalized the racism, sexism, and heterosexism inherent in the patriarchal values of Western culture may scapegoat any "strong" woman who defies traditional gender role norms. As women whose primary romantic and emotional attractions are to other women, lesbians and bisexual women are easy targets. Normative traditional analyses are replete with racist, sexist, classist, and heterosexist biases and assumptions[12] that reinforce rather than mitigate the multiple levels of discrimination that African American lesbians and bisexual women routinely encounter.

Mental health institutions have played a distinct role in supporting hegemonic heterosexist beliefs and values. Among them is the belief that lesbians either want to be or naturally look like men, are unattractive or less attractive than heterosexual women, are less extroverted, are unable to get men or have had traumatic experiences with men that presumably "turned" them against men, or are simply defective females. The assumption that sexual attraction to men is intrinsic to being a normal woman is as acceptable among African American communities as it is in the dominant culture.

A significant assumption deriving from ethnosexual myths is the belief that reproductive sexuality is the only form of sexual expression that is both psychologically normal and morally correct;[13] and that there is a direct relationship between sexual orientation and conformity to traditional gender roles.[14] These assumptions are used to threaten women with the stigma of being labeled lesbian if they do not adhere to the traditional gender role stereotypes of the African American community in which males are dominant and females are submissive.

Such an atmosphere can perpetuate the invisibility of African American lesbians and bisexual women. It creates a society in which for women attraction to only men, male dominance, and female subordination have been viewed as normative. There is often a connection between homophobia and the internalized racism that resides in the psyches of many African Americans—both of which are psychologically destructive to individuals as well as to the African American community.

HOMOPHOBIA/HETEROSEXISM AMONG AFRICAN AMERICANS: INTERNALIZED RACISM

"[T]o talk about the history of heterosexism and the history of homophobia is to talk about ways in which various institutions and persons have promoted unjustified suffering and unmerited pain."[15] An analysis of homophobia and heterosexism among African Americans should not be used to support the notion that this phenomenon is any worse among African Americans than it is in any other group. In fact, an April 1993 Gallup poll showed that greater numbers of African American respondents favored equal rights for lesbians and gay men in job opportunities and lifting military bans against them than did their white counterparts. Also, the Congressional Black Caucus has been most supportive of lesbian and gay rights. Nonetheless, black communities often engage in vitriolic homophobic rhetoric and action that are harmful to African American lesbians and bisexual women.

Some writers believe that lesbians and gay men were tolerably treated in poor African American communities, such as Harlem, New York, in the 1940s through the 1950s.[16] One reason for this was the relative invisibility of lesbians and gay men within the African American community and the dominant culture. Another explanation has been seen as "seizing the opportunity to spite the white man," and to express the empathy African Americans may have experienced, as oppressed people, toward members of another oppressed group.[17]

The dissolution of that tolerance may be the result in part of the heightened visibility of lesbians in contemporary majority and ethnic minority communities. In the past the survival of the black community was a higher priority than its homophobia. But as black communities undergo crisis and disintegration, their most vulnerable members—black women; lesbian, gay, bisexual and transgendered (LGBT) people; and children—become scapegoats and vicious acts of violence against them increases. In some quarters such violence is viewed as not only acceptable but necessary to protect the community.

Historically oppressed groups, specifically African Americans and Native Americans, have accorded reproductive sexuality great importance. Many group members view it as the only way to guarantee their continued presence in a society that wants to be rid of them and that uses racist and genocidal practices to accomplish its goal. Many African Americans therefore see nonreproductive sexual practices as another threat to the group's survival;[18] these practices cause "fears of extinction."[19] A lesbian and gay sexual orientation is sometimes viewed as part of a larger scheme on the part of white America to accomplish its goal. In this context, women's primary role is to reproduce; those who reject this role are viewed as traitors to the race.[20] Although fears of genocidal practices against African Americans as a group are warranted, this view unfairly scapegoats lesbian and gay members of the community.

Furthermore, having a lesbian or bisexual sexual orientation does not preclude having children, particularly among African American and other lesbians of color. Despite this reality, the internalization of these myths may be used as a barrier between heterosexual and lesbian or bisexual members of the African American community.[21]

LESBIAN SEXUALITY: CHOICE, OUTING, PASSING

"Passing is an obscene form of salvation. . . . Just as a Black woman passing for white is 'required to deny everything about her past,' a Black lesbian who passes for heterosexual is required to deny everything about her present."[22] An important dimension of any analysis of African American homophobia is the relation between sexuality and gender, and culture.

One form of homophobia is represented in the belief that lesbian sexual orientation represents consciously chosen behavior. Many African Americans, like members of the dominant culture, hold the homophobic belief that lesbian or gay sexual orientation is not an identity component but rather a poorly chosen "lifestyle." As such, they see the discrimination that results from it as an "inconvenience" rather than the protracted, involuntary hardship of being black.[23] This attitude reveals heteropatriarchal hegemony: the origins of heterosexuality need not even be questioned, are not chosen, and are presumed to be natural. The belief that lesbian sexual orientation is chosen and that race is not is a key factor in the oppression of lesbians causes many heterosexual African Americans to resent the comparison between racism and homophobia.

The relative visibility of race and ethnicity among African Americans and the invisibility of lesbian sexual orientation play significant roles in the belief that lesbian sexual orientation is chosen. Many in the community believe that if lesbians would simply shut up, remain invisible, and hide, they would not suffer discrimination, nor would they require legal or other protection. The implication is that lesbians who are "out" are not only inviting negative treatment but that perhaps they even deserve it. As one lesbian puts it, the demand by the black community that lesbians be invisible is "a demand for a lie I was able to tell by not telling."[24]

In African American communities and families, the simple act of "telling" someone that you are a lesbian, or engaging in any other behavior that is routine among heterosexuals, is often viewed as "flaunting" something distasteful. As noted, the implication is that lesbian sexual orientation, unlike racial identity, can and should be concealed, and that any hardship that results from identifying oneself presumably could be avoided. This makes homophobia appear to be more controllable than racism. It is assumed that the problem rests in being known and that there is no cost to remaining silent. This assumption requires serious interrogation[25] as a stark representation of heterosexual privilege.

Both the lesbian and gay literature and the cultural and psychological literature on people of color document the deleterious, dehumanizing effects of passing.

> [W]hen you are *not* dismissed from work because you stayed in the closet; when there is *no* anti-lesbian explosion from your parents because you have de-dyked your apartment before their visit. . . . heterosexism is functioning in its most effective and deadly way. . . . it is not necessary to murder or torture us to ensure our silence and invisibility. [26]

Creating a climate of terror insures that most group members will choose to remain silent.

The community mandate that the principle applied to racial pride not be applied to sexual orientation constitutes an exercise in heterosexual privilege. Heterosexual African Americans exercise heterosexual dominance by defining being "out" racially and ethnically as healthy and imperative, while defining being "out" as a lesbian as unhealthy, undesirable, and an invitation to abuse.

Similarly, African Americans see discrimination against the descendants of Africans as racism and the structural bias, not the person who is harmed, as the evil force. However, when a lesbian is harmed by discrimination, the heterosexism responsible for the discrimination is not seen as structural bias; rather it is the victim who is defined as the problem. This behavior exemplifies heterosexual privilege and oppression: the very behavior that is defined as psychologically healthy and culturally loyal in a dominant or privileged group—heterosexuals—is deemed a defect in lesbians, the disadvantaged group within the larger African American community. Because of sexism in both the dominant and African American cultures, and racism in the dominant culture, African American women are left with nothing but heterosexual privilege (aside from class for middle- and upper-middle-class African American women) as a means of obtaining privileged status.[27]

Another pernicious source of homophobia among African Americans, and of internalized homophobia among African American lesbians, is religious and theological in origin. Indeed, family members often object to lesbianism on "religious grounds," claiming that if they accept the lesbian family member they will be betraying their faith because a lesbian relationship violates the teachings of biblical scripture, God's law, or God's intent. Strict adherents to Western Christian theology have historically used selective interpretations of biblical scripture to reinforce homophobic attitudes and actions. As African Americans have a strong Christian orientation, it is no surprise that for sexual minorities, their families, and communities religion has been and is the conflict.

The black church has served as a haven for many African Americans in their struggles with racism, and has often been a potent force in liberation theology. But it has either ignored or condemned its sexual minorities: "the African American church sweeps eroticism under the rug, but most congregations don't even give homosexuality a foot in the door."[28] One African American lesbian growing up in a black fundamentalist church has observed that a "don't ask, don't tell" policy of denial was part of an atmosphere in which compulsory heterosexuality was strictly enforced.[29]

There is great variety among mainstream African American denominations in their official policies on homosexuality. The Roman Catholic, Southern Baptist, and Pentecostal denominations maintain the most conservative positions on the subject, while the United Church of Christ appears most welcoming to lesbian and gay members. Others lie between these extremes. Certain non-Christian religious sects view homosexuality as a decadent Western practice as well.

It is noteworthy, however, that interpretation of biblical scripture concerning homosexuality is highly selective. More important, Christian theologians and biblical scholars interpret these issues in a variety of ways. One expert argues that the subject of homosexuality is not even mentioned in the early texts of the Bible and that the word "homosexual" itself, an invention of the late nineteenth century, was never mentioned until the 1946 Revised Standard version.[30] The use of religion to condemn homosexuality, Gomes argues, is simply pretext.

> [T]he legitimization of violence against homosexuals, Jews, women and Blacks, as we have seen, comes from the view that the Bible stigmatizes these people and therefore they are fair game. . . . If the Bible expresses such a prejudice, then it can't be wrong to act on that prejudice. . . . every anti-Semite and racist has used this argument with demonstrably devastating consequences, as our social history all too vividly shows.[31]

The African American church espouses a "profoundly" conservative theological position on sexuality that creates a repressive climate. This conservative theology regarding sexual matters is a derivative of a legacy of slavery, misogyny, and racism. "Theological homophobia," manifested often by the rejection of lesbians (and gay men) by both the black church and the African American community, has some of its roots in internalized racism and sexism among African Americans.

The ministry of misogyny and homophobia in the black church is one in which social action is predicated on the devaluation of women and lesbian, gay, bisexual, and transgendered people—a practice that rests on the belief that black men are the most endangered members of the black community; that they must be protected by and at the expense of African American women, as well as other members of the community. Belief in male superiority and dominance is an active ingredient in homophobia as it supports the preservation of traditional gender roles and the accompanying hierarchies.[32] Roles and hierarchies that maintain female subordination are not viewed as a construction of society but are explained as "God's will." In this analysis, African American lesbians are blamed for not upholding what are perceived to be the roles assigned all women by God rather than being the dictates of a patriarchal society. Secular oppression thereby acquires religious sanction: reinforcing the belief that sexual pleasure is a male domain, which in turn both maintains the status quo of dominance and submission between black men and women, and eroticizes women's submission to men.[33] In this paradigm, lesbians are defiant outlaws.

The leadership of some organized black churches, together with many in the African American community and select black nationalists, also ascribe lesbian and gay sexual orientations among African Americans to the assimilation of decadent Western practices or the "white man's disease." The individual's degree of acculturation or assimilation into a dominant cultural community is thus an important issue in questions of internalized racism. African American families, communities, and places of worship charge that lesbianism is an "acquired" "decadent white sickness" that comes from being too close to white people or trying to be like them. Homophobic beliefs among African Americans are also a function of black nationalists' efforts to claim an African heritage.[34] The basis of these beliefs, however, is the false assertion that there was no homosexuality in Africa. Overall, the view that lesbian and gay sexual orientations are inauthentic in African-descended people, based on the assertion that there is no evidence of them in Africa, lacks support in African reality.

It is noteworthy, however, that the way a culture defines sexuality will determine whether or not the African and Western constructs of sexual orientation are conceptually equivalent. The Western meanings of lesbian, gay, and bisexual are different from the conceptualization and construction of such identities in other cultures, which may render them less visible to the Western observer. A range of methodological obstacles and blinders has interfered with the identification of "lesbians" in Africa and their appropriate study,[35] including the influence of Western taboos, erroneous beliefs about homosexual behavior, and the imposition of Western heteronormativity.

Despite such methodological obstacles, anthropological evidence reveals that there have always been forms of female homosexuality in Africa and in all other human cultures. Black women in the diaspora express what we would consider lesbian relationships. In Kenya Nandi women marry; in Lesotho there are Mummy-Baby relationships in which older women whose husbands are migrant mine workers take younger women as their spouses;[36] in Lovedu in the Northern Province of South Africa, Modjadji, the "Rain Queen," a female hereditary leader keeps as many as forty wives.[37]

In a number of West African regions from which slaves were brought to the "new world," Dahomey and Ashanti women who had sex with other women were not the target of negative sanctions and prohibitions.[38] In Dahomey, a woman could formally marry another woman and the children of one were considered the children of the other. In Suriname, lesbian relationships were tolerated as long as they were not named. A comparison of "lesbian relationships" among black women in the United States with those among black women in Suriname suggests that "Mati"(the Suriname Tongo name for women who have sex with women) display lesbian *behavior* while black lesbians in the United States view themselves as having a lesbian *identity*.[39]

In some parts of southern Africa lesbians are often considered traditional healers (as they were in many Native American tribes). In some cultures their "difference" is believed to give them a special connection with the supernatural. Their healer status also means that they are not required to marry, which allows them to live independent lives as unattached women.[40] It is important to understand the economic structure of a society and its role in defining marriage. Women who must marry men in order to be economically viable may construct their relationships with other women differently than do lesbians in the West.[41]

It is also important to consider the effects of colonization on indigenous cultural practices. In Africa, the advent of Christianity and the influx of Christian missionaries who facilitated Africa's colonization stigmatized the kinds of people and relationships that Westerners regard as lesbian. If and when they were stigmatized, punishment by torture and death was often the price they paid. For this reason, many became hidden members of society. As more African nations turn to democracy, lesbian and gay Africans are becoming more visible and assertive, and are coming into conflict with conservative African leaders. Indeed, South Africa under the leadership of Nelson Mandela is the only nation whose constitution includes protection from discrimination on the basis of sexual orientation.

In any cross-cultural examination of sexual behavior it is crucial to understand that such behavior is mediated and interpreted through the lens of culture. Many contentions about the absence of lesbian or other forms of nontraditional sexuality in precolonial and contemporary Africa are based on myth rather than reality. Despite this, many African Americans believe these contentions, forgetting that they are social creations. These beliefs are significant ingredients in both the internalized racism and homophobia in the African American community, as well as the internalized homophobia among African American lesbians.

A society that objects to and stigmatizes significant elements of African Americans' sexual and other identities transgresses the rights of sexual minorities within its cultural framework. Ethnosexual mythologies are used to justify stigmatized images of African American women and simultaneously support and sustain their exploitation in the social hierarchy.

Many African Americans equate respectability and acceptance by the dominant group with distancing themselves from any image or behavior found in racist stereotypes of African Americans.[42] This of course means distancing themselves from those members of the African American community who cannot or who refuse to attempt to live up to the dominant culture's definition of respectable behavior.[43] Some may reject the stereotypes but may nonetheless feel required to imitate the dominant culture's values. Others, however, believe the degrading stereotypes to be true.

The belief in racial stereotypes of one's own inferiority represents a form of internalized oppression referred to as internalized racism. The shame and distress that many African Americans experience on account of the mythical but negative depictions of black sexuality and the need to negate those depictions can lead them to disparage African American lesbians and gay men. Convincing white people that African Americans were just like them was a strategy used by African Americans in an evolving political arena, but it facilitated the development of a personal mythology among African Americans that is as narrow and misleading as many of the mythologies that whites created about African Americans. A narrow, limited view of black culture, of what "authentic" black behavior is, and anger about anything that differs too much from the mythical ideal of the middle class of the majority culture exemplifies internalized racism.[44]

Because acceptance of lesbian sexual orientation is inconsistent with the dominant culture's ideal, African American lesbians may be an embarrassment to African Americans who strongly identify with the dominant culture.[45] Indeed, the only common names for lesbians in the African American community, "funny women" or "bulldagger women" are derogatory. Homophobia—rooted in religion, false historical beliefs about Africa, and the internalization of the dominant culture's sexual tropes—allows African Americans who have internalized sexual and racial stereotypes to distance themselves personally, and as a community, from the sexual stigma that the dominant culture has associated with black identity, particularly black sexuality. This distancing behavior allows some segments of the African American community to hope for legitimacy and full incorporation into the dominant culture's power structure.

CONCLUSION

The notion of a monolithic racial identity that excludes lesbian sexual orientation represents an attempt to exercise a form of social control designed to establish unilateral conformity among oppressed group members.[46] This mythical uniformity is maintained by ensuring that elements of the community and group are silenced, invisible, and denied. However, the model of the African American community that silences or denies the existence of certain members is neither authentic nor representative. Rejection of African American lesbians by other African Americans represents a kind of pathology in the group that will neither tolerate nor accept the realistic diversity of its members.

One method for silencing nonconforming group members is to lodge accusations of racial disloyalty, lack of authenticity, or of the incompatibility of lesbian sexual orientation with "blackness." The concept of racial loyalty presumes that a lesbian sexual orientation is incompatible with a black identity, or at least an authentic one. This charge shows the hegemonic control of the heteronormative members of one community over sexual minorities within that very community.

African American lesbians are members of a visible oppressed ethnic group, as well as a less visible but nonetheless oppressed sexual minority, in a racially hostile society. African American lesbians may be silent about their sexuality simply to retain the protection and support offered by the African American community and their families. When a minority is relegated to the margins or pushed outside her racial, ethnic, family group—one necessary to her survival—and worse yet, when she is also accused of belonging to the enemy camp or being a confused traitor to her race, she is denied not only her individualism but also her right to participate in her culture.

African Americans share a complex history; it is not ideal. One way of "idealizing" African legacies is to deny the existence of group members or behaviors of which the majority culture disapproves, and which the majority disparages or uses to rationalize the validity of their exploitation. The danger is that the community's denial of many of its members can lead those members in turn to deny or experience shame about legitimate and important parts of themselves.

The denial and subsequent rejection of lesbian and gay members of and by the African American community does not represent an affirmation of African cultural derivatives or of Africans themselves. It simply reflects the acceptance of the Western, hegemonic majority cultural norm of heterosexism that is a function of the gender-based hierarchies of a patriarchal culture. In the long run, it does not serve the interests of the diverse African American community: "there is nothing in me that is not in everybody else, and nothing in everybody else that is not in me."[47] Distortions of what it means to be authentically "black," that silence members (lesbians) of our contemporary communities and purge pieces of our history, must be deconstructed and eradicated. Just as there is no ideal family, there is no ideal nation-family and none is warranted. Nor is the denial of certain aspects of the self or nation, that is, African American lesbians and gays, warranted.

NOTES

This essay contains abridged and revised components of my chapter, "African American Lesbian and Bisexual Women in Feminist Psychodynamic Psychotherapy: Surviving and Thriving between a Rock and a Hard Place," in *Psychotherapy with African American Women: Innovations in Psychodynamic Perspectives and Practice* (L. Jackson and B. Greene eds. 2000).

1. Audre Lorde, "Age, Race and Class," in *Sister Outsider: Essays and Speeches* 116 (A. Lorde ed. 1984).

2. E. Blackwood and S. E. Wieringa, "Sapphic Shadows: Challenging the Silence in the Study of Sexuality," in *Same Sex Relations and Female Desires: Transgender Practices across Cultures* 39 (E. Blackwood and S. E. Wieringa eds. 1999).

3. G. L. Croom, "Lesbian, Gay and Bisexual People of Color: A Challenge to Representative Sampling in Empirical Research," in *Education, Research and Practice in Lesbian, Gay and Bisexual and Transgendered Psychology: A Resource*

Manual 263 (B. Greene and G. L. Croom eds. 2000). Scholarly research suggests that African American lesbians are more likely than their white counterparts to have children; to maintain close relationships with their biological and extended families; to depend on family members or other African American lesbians for support; and to have contact with men and heterosexual peers—a commonality with African women who have sex with women.

4. C. West, "Cornel West on Heterosexism and Transformation," in *Dangerous Liaisons: Blacks, Gays and the Struggle for Equality* 290, 293 (E. Brandt ed. 1999).

5. B. Greene and N. Boyd-Franklin, "African American Lesbians: Issues in Couples Therapy," in *Lesbians and Gay Men in Couples and Families: A Handbook for Therapists* 251 (J. Laird and R. J. Green eds. 1996).

6. Blackwood and Wieringa, *supra* note 2.

7. Greene and Boyd-Franklin, *supra* note 5.

8. B. Greene, "Lesbians and Gay Men of Color: Ethnosexual Mythologies in Heterosexism," in *Preventing Heterosexism and Homophobia* (E. Rothblum and L. Bond eds. 1996).

9. N. Boyd-Franklin, *Black Families: A Multisystems Approach to Family Therapy* (1989).

10. b. hooks, *Ain't I a Woman: Black Women and Feminism* (1981).

11. *Id.*; B. Greene, "Family, Ethnic Identity and Sexual Orientation among African American Lesbians and Gay Men," in *Lesbian, Gay and Bisexual Identity: Psychological Research and Social Policy* 40 (C. Patterson and A. D'Augelli eds. 1998).

12. J. Glassgold and S. Iasenza, *Lesbians and Psychoanalysis: Revolutions in Theory and Practice* (1995).

13. L. Garnets and D. Kimmel, "Lesbian and Gay Male Dimensions in the Psychological Diversity," in *Psychological Perspectives on Human Diversity in America* 137 (J. Goodchilds ed. 1991); Greene, *supra* note 11.

14. B. S. Newman, *The Relative Importance of Gender Role Attitudes toward Lesbians*, 21 Sex Roles 451 (1989).

15. West, *supra* note 4, at 290.

16. I. Jeffries, *Strange Fruits at the Purple Manor: Looking Back on "the Life" in Harlem*, QW Magazine (formerly NYQ), Feb. 23, 1992, at 40.

17. C. Clarke, "The Failure to Transform: Homophobia in the Black Community," in *Home Girls: A Black Feminist Anthology* 197 (B. Smith ed. 1983); Jeffries, *supra* note 16, at 40.

18. V. Kanuha, *Compounding the Triple Jeopardy: Battering in Lesbian of Color Relationships*, 9 Women and Therapy 169 (1990).

19. *Id.* at 176.

20. C. Cohen, *The Boundaries of Blackness: AIDS and the Breakdown of Black Politics* (1999).

21. *Id.*; Greene, *supra* note 11.

22. Jewelle Gomez, *Black Lesbians: Passing, Stereotypes and Transformation* 164 (1999).

23. H. L. Gates, *Blacklash*, New Yorker, May 17, 1993, at 13.

24. Gomez, *supra* note 22, at 163.

25. C. West, *Race Matters* (1993).

26. C. Kitzinger, "Speaking of Oppression: Psychology, Politics and the Language of Power," in *Preventing Heterosexism and Homophobia* 3, 11 (E. Rothblum and L. Bond eds. 1996).

27. Clarke, *supra* note 17; B. Smith, "Toward a Black Feminist Criticism," in *All the Women Are White, All the Blacks Are Men, But Some of Us Are Brave* 157 (G. Hull et al. eds. 1982).

28. R. J. Weatherford and C. B. Weatherford, *Somebody's Knocking at Your Door: AIDS and the African American Church* 21 (1999).

29. N. Shaka-Zulu, *Sex, Race and the Stained Glass Window*, 19(4) Women and Therapy 27 (1996).

30. P. J. Gomes, *The Good Book: Reading the Bible with Mind and Heart* 144 (1996).

31. *Id.* at 146.

32. Cohen, *supra* note 20; M. E. Dyson, "When You Divide Body and Soul, Problems Multiply: The Black Church and Sex," in M. E. Dyson, *Race Rules* 77 (1996).

33. Cohen, *supra* note 20; I. Monroe, "Louis Farrakhan's Ministry of Misogyny and Homophobia," in *The Farrakhan Factor: African-American Writers on Leadership, Nationhood, and Minister Louis Farrakhan* 275 (A. Alexander ed. 1998).

34. Videotape: *Interview with bell hooks and Barbara Smith. Black Is . . . Black Ain't* (M. Riggs 1996) (on file with author).

35. Blackwood and Wieringa, *supra* note 2.

36. C. Potgieter, "From Apartheid to Mandela's Constitution: Black South African Lesbians in the Nineties," in 3 *Psychological Perspectives on Lesbian and Gay Issues* (B. Greene ed. 1997).

37. M. Gevisser, "Homosexuality in Africa: An Interpretation," in *Microsoft Encarta Africana: Comprehensive Encyclopedia of Black History and Culture* (K. A. Appiah and H. L. Gates eds. 1998).

38. G. Wekker, *Mati-ism and Black Lesbianism: Two Idealtypical Expressions of Female Homosexuality in Black Communities of the Diaspora*, 24 J. Homosexuality 11–24 (1993).

39. *Id.* (finding that Mati retained more African cultural derivatives and working-class elements than black lesbians in the United States, who were observed to have more Eurocentric and middle-class features).

40. Gevisser, *supra* note 37; Kathryn Kendall, "Women in Lesotho and

the Western Construction of Homophobia," in *Same Sex Relations, supra* note 2, at 157.

41. Kendall, *supra* note 40.

42. E. Higginbotham, *Righteous Discontent: The Women's Movement in the Black Baptist Church 1880–1920* (1993); West, *supra* note 25.

43. West, *supra* note 25, at 86.

44. S. Lipsky, *Internalized Racism* (1987).

45. Cohen, *supra* note 20; A. Poussaint, *An Honest Look at Black Gays and Lesbians*, Ebony, Sept. 1990, at 124.

46. Cohen, *supra* note 20; K. Walters, "Negotiating Conflicts in Allegiances among Lesbians and Gays of Color: Reconciling Divided Selves and Communities," in *Foundations of Social Work Practice with Lesbian and Gay Persons* 47 (G. Mallon ed. 1996); H. L. Gates, Jr., *The Charmer*, New Yorker, Apr. 29, 1992, at 116.

47. R. Goldstein, "Go the Way Your Blood Beats: An Interview with James Baldwin," in *James Baldwin: The Legacy* 173, 182 (R. Troupe ed. 1994).

5

Children and Right to a Fair Trial

*Exploring the Relationship between First- and
Second-Generation Human Rights*

Johanna Niemi-Kiesiläinen

INTRODUCTION: ABOUT A CHILD

After a number of years in the profession, a lawyer or legal scholar is
seldom emotionally upset by a decision by a state's highest judicial authority, such as the United States Supreme Court. Occasionally, one may
be struck by a decision by, or the facts presented to, a lower court. However, the cases in the highest courts are usually so refined that while
they may arouse political concerns they rarely elicit an emotional reaction. Uncharacteristically, two recent cases made me forget my de-
tached professional role as a lawyer and scholar. They have one feature
in common: they are both about the fate of a child. In other respects,
they are quite different. One is a constitutional case from a common law
country that deals with child abuse; the other is a civil case from a continental jurisdiction concerning custody. Yet both are salient examples
of the special difficulties that arise when a legal regime designed for rational adults is applied to a child.

Troubled as I was by these cases, I felt compelled to analyze them in
search of some logic. I resorted to what one might call the *Lois Forer*
method. Lois Forer, a retired trial court judge from Philadelphia, looked
back at cases she had decided on the bench and isolated those she considered "wrong." By "wrong" she meant cases which, legally speaking,
had been handled according to due process requirements and decided
according to the law, but the results of which nevertheless might appear
to be unjustified, even outrageous, to the average nonlawyer.[1] Because

legal analysis did not provide her with a common denominator among the "wrong" cases, she sought coherence through a different lens. Looking at the cases as a writer, she found an obvious similarity: the "wrong" cases concerned women, children, or the elderly—"others," as she decided to call them.

The analysis in this essay starts where Forer's ended, as both cases that will be scrutinized concern small children, already labeled as "other" by Forer. Using these cases as my starting point, I will analyze how society perceives the relationship between the law and social problems, and what role we envision the law having in solving these problems. Because the cases come from different jurisdictions, they present an opportunity to highlight the different role of the law in a truly liberal, if not libertarian, state (the United States) and in a Nordic welfare state (Finland). For different, almost opposing reasons, neither paradigm is able to account for the special status of children in the trial. The methodology applied in this critique may also be described as a naive Rawlsian one because the work focuses on Rawls's second principle of justice, according to which social and economic inequalities are justified only if they result in compensating benefits for the least advantaged members of society.[2] In this case my starting point is the most disadvantaged member which can be found, an abused child. I examine the deeper structures of justice in a society and discuss their justification from the child's point of view. Surprisingly, there is a direct link between these "wrong" cases and the deeper understanding of justice.

Given this book's theme on moral imperialism, this essay will warn against the unwarranted advocacy of a wholesale adoption of liberal policies or ideology when legal systems are reformed in different parts of the world. This essay will show the failings of such a wholesale adoption of principles in the context of children: what makes sense as an articulation of rights for adults, results in tensions and ambiguities when applied to children. Changes in contextualization require reformations of the law, not literal translation.

A child is in a precarious legal position. While today, in principle a child is a holder of individual rights, that child is still dependent on others—most likely the family or the state—in the realization of those rights. Legal systems in which children's rights are evaluated, however, are designed by and for adults. Therefore, the realization of the rights of a child presents a special challenge to contemporary legal systems.

In contemporary Western societies, we can distinguish two main paradigms of legal regulation, the liberal legal system and welfare regulation. With the two cases presented here as a starting point, this essay will reveal that both paradigms take a one-sided view of the rights of children, and of anyone else dependent on others. While the liberal paradigm is dependent on patriarchal individualism in realization of these rights, the welfare state depends on government authorities. The liberal paradigm expects the child either to be an autonomous subject or a protegée of the family. The welfare paradigm, on the other hand, treats the child as an object of social policies. When either system fails, the child is left without protection.

Because of the polar locations of the liberal and welfare paradigms, I also look at the importance of building a bridge between two different generations of rights, liberal or civil rights and social rights. In the human rights field, two recent conventions on women's[3] and children's[4] rights have recognized the interdependence of the two generations of rights by incorporating them into one document, much as they had been in the Universal Declaration. The Children's Convention made a remarkable attempt to mold the liberal and welfare approaches by incorporating protections for both civil and social, economic, and cultural rights. But not even the Convention was able to address adequately the most precarious problems related to situations in which a parent has violated the child's rights. This essay suggests that the relatively narrow view of the representation of a child should be broadened in order to ensure that all concerned about the child and the child's well-being can and will be heard and that the child's rights will be protected.

THE TWO CASES

I. The Liberal State and Rights of Children: The *DeShaney* Case

The first case, *DeShaney v. Winnebago County*[5] of the U.S. Supreme Court, represents the liberal paradigm's application of children's rights. It is well known in the United States and has been the subject of wide commentary. The relatively clear-cut but poignant facts of the case are as follows:

Joshua DeShaney, born in 1979, was just a baby when his parents were divorced in Wyoming in 1980. The Court granted custody of Joshua to his father, who subsequently moved to Winnebago County in Wisconsin. Winnebago Social Services was first alerted to possible child abuse in January 1982 when, during a divorce, Joshua's father's second wife complained to the police. Throughout the following year (1983), neighbors, police, and the emergency room reported child abuse to Social Services. Subsequent to Joshua's hospitalization, Social Services released him back to the father's home and after a second hospitalization, the social worker made monthly visits to the home. During this time, the caseworker diligently recorded all her observations with respect to the little boy. These included noting that the father had failed to follow recommendations made by a child protection team (and to which the father had voluntarily agreed) and that she had observed a number of suspicious injuries. But beyond recording these observations, the caseworker did nothing—even after the emergency room notified Social Services in November 1983 that Joshua had again been treated for injuries believed to be a result of child abuse and the social worker was told on her last two visits that Joshua was too ill to see her. Finally, in March 1984, Joshua was beaten so badly by his father that he was rendered severely retarded and will have to be institutionalized for the rest of his life.

The *DeShaney* case was brought by Joshua's appointed legal guardian and his mother against the Department of Social Services in Winnebago County, including those social workers and local officials who had received complaints that the child was being abused by his father but had not removed him from his father's custody. The plaintiffs sued under 42 U.S.C. §1983, alleging that Social Services had deprived Joshua of his liberty interest in bodily integrity in violation of the Due Process Clause of the Fourteenth Amendment of the U.S. Constitution. Specifically the claim was that Social Services had failed to protect Joshua against the risk of violence at his father's hands, a risk of which they were well aware.

The plaintiffs were unsuccessful in their claim. According to the Supreme Court the Due Process Clause prohibits the state from depriving an individual of life, liberty, or property without due process, but it imposes no constitutional duty, no affirmative obligation, on the state to provide members of the general public with adequate protective services. Thus, failure to protect an individual against private violence—even if a government department in charge of protecting children was repeatedly alerted to his danger—does not generally constitute a violation of the clause. In certain circumstances, a special relationship between the state and a person may exist, entitling this person to protection.[6] However, in *DeShaney* the state had not actively imposed limitations on the child's freedom but custody remained with his father. The mere knowledge of risk and harm was not sufficient to create a special relationship. Consequently, the state could not be held liable for the damage Joshua suffered from a third party, in this instance his own father. Interestingly, the Court suggested that the outcome might have been different if the claim had been filed in the state court as a tort case.

The *DeShaney* case highlights difficulties concerning children's rights. For example, in his dissenting opinion, Justice Brennan (joined by Justices Marshall and Blackmun) analyzed the distinction between government's action and inaction. In his dissenting opinion—which, unlike the majority opinion, looks at what the state did rather than what it failed to do—he concluded that Social Services had taken so many steps that the case could not be dismissed simply on the basis of inaction.[7] Noting the involvement of the state in creating an agency designed to receive information or complaints about and to investigate child abuse, the multiple reports to that agency about Joshua, and the assigning of a caseworker who visited Joshua's home and recorded information and observations on the case, the dissenters plainly stated, "[i]t simply belies reality . . . to contend that the state 'stood by and did nothing' with respect to Joshua."[8]

Both the majority and Justice Blackmun in his separate dissenting opinion expressed unease with the outcome of the case. The majority, acknowledging that they as "Judges and lawyers, like other humans, are moved by natural sympathy in a case like this,"[9] nevertheless proceeded to engage in a formalistic reading of the case. Justice Blackmun, in contrast, felt that the case law in point could and should have been interpreted in a way that "comports with dictates of fundamental justice and recognizes that compassion need not be exiled from the province of judging."[10] This "hands-off" approach taken by the majority, maintaining the separation of the public and the private, adopting a formalistic approach to law, and ignoring national reality that results in a patent injustice, is the liberal paradigm's legacy.

II. The Welfare State and Rights of Children: The Grandmother Case

The second case, not as well known, was decided by Finland's Supreme Court KKO:1998:66. The facts of this case are quite different from those of *DeShaney*.

A baby girl was born to A and B in January 1993. In November 1994 B killed his wife A. That same night the girl was brought to her maternal grandmother. In February 1995, Social Services made the decision to take the child into its care. In June, the social agency took the child from the grandmother and placed her with foster parents. In 1996, she was placed in an institutional children's home. In a legal sense, the father remained the custodian, although the decision to transfer the child to the jurisdiction of Social Services terminated his right to make decisions about the child.

The grandmother, together with her other daughter and son-in-law, filed a suit for custody in the local court. According to Finnish law, the relatives or other persons who are close to a child have a right to file for custody if the child is without a custodian due to the death of a parent. The Supreme Court held that in this case, because the child still had a custodian (albeit in prison), the grandmother and other relatives did not have a right to file for custody. According to the Supreme Court, the issue of who was a suitable custodian could not be opened to litigation on the basis of the alleged unsuitability of the parent. Were relatives granted such a right, an improper possibility of interfering with custody could arise.

Finnish law distinguishes between legal custody and the power of Social Services to place an abused child under its care. A parent almost always is a child's custodian, and if not, the parent has priority in being nominated as one. However, when the custodian is unable to take care of the child, the community social service board has the power to assume the care of the child. While the decision of the social service board does not alter the child's legal custodianship, the custodian is effectively prevented from exercising his or her practical rights of custodianship as long as the child is in the care of Social Services.

Whether the grandmother would have been a better custodian than the father and Social Services was never litigated. Custody disputes are litigated in the civil courts, but the decision of the social service board can be appealed to the administrative court. In this case, the grandmother was denied the right to file on the issue of custody but she could have appealed the decision of Social Services. We do not know whether she did so, because it was irrelevant to the outcome of the custody proceedings.

The Supreme Court decision in the Grandmother case was unanimous and, like *DeShaney*, decided solely on formalistic grounds. The Court of Appeals, however, came to a different conclusion, arguing that a formal interpretation of the law would lead to a result that would contravene the main purpose of the law, that is, the best interest of the child. They also pointed out that de facto the child was without a custodian. Both courts touched upon the human rights aspects of the case, and the Supreme Court held that the provisions of the Finnish law were in accordance with the right to a fair trial.[11]

None of the judges expressed any concern about the fairness of the outcome, unless their ambiguous instructions to Social Services are regarded as such. Focusing on this aspect of the case—the silence of the court with respect to the fairness of the outcome—Urpo Kangas, Finnish Professor of Family Law, in a scholarly comment wondered whether the public could accept the outcome in the Supreme Court. Professor Kangas defended the decision of the Court of Appeals and argued that the case should have been decided on material grounds and especially that the principle of the best interest of the child should have been taken into account.

TWO WORLDS: THE LIBERAL AND WELFARE STATES

As the above discussion reveals, both the *DeShaney* and Grandmother cases are examples of the tension between formalistic and material justice goals. In the following analysis, however, I will try to distance myself from the specific legal issues involved and, instead, treat the cases as prime examples of how the law functions in two different legal paradigms, the liberal state and the welfare state.

Several sociological theorists of the twentieth century have utilized the distinction between liberal and welfare state forms. In his book on legal theory, German sociologist Jürgen Habermas presented the concept of legal paradigms as implied knowledge about society, social actors, and legal institutions.[12] Habermas distinguished between the legal paradigms of the contemporary liberal and welfare states as ideal types of modes of regulation. They do not and are not meant to correspond to any given or existing jurisdiction as such. In fact, how much one jurisdiction corresponds to one paradigm is often a matter of degree rather than quality. More specifically, I am not saying that the United States is not, in some senses, a welfare state, nor that the Finnish legal system is not liberal. But in terms of the way the law is conceived, the Habermasian paradigms of law bring to light differences that I find paramount when trying to understand different legal systems.

The two cases examined here provide prime examples of the practical implications of legal decision making in the two different legal paradigms. In addition, the difference between these legal paradigms manifests itself exceptionally well in these cases precisely because the cases concern children. Children's specific legal status exposes deeper structures of the legal system because of the child's incompatibility with the presumptions behind the law.

The Liberal State

The concept of equality in the liberal state is formal and legal. In the liberal paradigm, private law regulates the organization of nonpolitical economic actors who operate in a sphere disconnected from the state. As an economic actor, the individual's positive legal status is protected by law. Because liberty is the most cherished sociolegal value, all state interventions into the private sphere are looked upon with suspicion.[13]

This bias toward nonintervention was patent in the *DeShaney* case's holding that the state had no responsibility to protect little Joshua against violations of his rights from a third person, even if that person was his father. Actually, the Supreme Court's reasoning in *DeShaney* brings to mind the essence of a libertarian policy: "nothing in the language of the Due Process Clause itself requires the State to protect the life, liberty, and property of its citizens against invasion by private actors."[14] Further, referring to precedent, the Court stated that it had "recognized that Due Process Clauses generally confer no affirmative right to governmental aid, even where such aid may be necessary to secure life, liberty, or property interests of which the government itself may not deprive the individual."[15]

This position, however, appears to be at odds with the basic idea of the liberal state itself which, as conceived by Hobbes, was to protect its citizens from violations they would suffer if society was left in a state of nature. According to Hobbes, the state of nature is a violent state, a war of everyone against everyone. To escape that, citizens were ready to accept the rule of the sovereign. Thus, the protection of the members of society from disorder and violence has been understood even by the most libertarian thinkers as being at the core of a state's functions.[16]

The Hobbesian state also presupposed a certain place for women and children. While not citizens, they were under the patriarchal rule and protection of a male citizen. This presupposition of the place of women was implicit in the nineteenth-century political philosophy of political participation and democracy. After the turn of the century, women gained suffrage but, as feminist social theorists have shown, the structures of society still reproduce the male citizen-female dependent structures that lie at the foundation of the liberal state.[17]

The modern liberal-republican theory is ambivalent about gender roles in society. Nowadays, women are entitled to equality on the condition that they perform as men. Yet at the same time, in considering adults' relationship to children, caretaking roles are deeply gendered. Notwithstanding its ambiguity about gender roles, liberal theory is clearer about how the care and protection of children, the weak, and the elderly should be organized: the responsibility lies with the family, kin, church, and community.

The liberal approach to caretaking is explicit in Justice Brennan's dissenting opinion in *DeShaney*. Wisconsin had "established a child-welfare system specifically designed to help children like Joshua." This system channeled all abuse reports to the local departments of social services and thus "law invites—indeed, directs—citizens and other governmental entities to depend on local departments of social services such as respondent to protect children from abuse."[18] Because Justice Brennan evaluated state structures and practices as a whole, he viewed the distinction between action and inaction from a different perspective from the majority. He posited that because, by these structures the "State cuts off private sources of aid"[19] and "displaces private sources of protection,"[20] it could not refuse to shoulder any responsibility on the basis of inaction if things went wrong.

Justice Brennan's reasoning assumed that, even absent a state obligation, there would have been somebody protecting the child. What Justice Brennan failed to address was the assumption of the liberal-republican doctrine of state that a father has a duty to protect a child and absent such protection by "family," the responsibility lies with "kin, church and community." Sadly, the *DeShaney* case is about what can happen when an individual's family, here the father, does not live up to the caretaking expectations of the liberal doctrine. Just how unrealistic Justice Brennan's statement was becomes obvious when we review the facts of *DeShaney*. Joshua's mother lived in another part of the country and thus was unable to provide the caretaking anticipated by the doctrine. Moreover, the community—the neighbors—had done what they could. They called the police and Social Services. It is hard to imagine what additional "community"—or in what additional ways any community—could have intervened on behalf of Joshua to save his young life. Even if there was someone else, it is difficult to envision what that person could have done against a very violent father. It is sheer foolhardiness to encourage somebody to interfere with a dangerously violent person. The modern liberal state is constructed in such a way that only those with public authority can intrude on the privacy of the family and use coercion if necessary.

In light of *DeShaney*, it is evident that there has to be a state or some other public body with responsibility for the protection of children. To deny this is not only to close our eyes to reality but also to embrace a mistakenly constructed liberal ideology. In contrast to both majority and dissenting opinions in *DeShaney*, liberal ideology is based on the responsibility of the state to ensure the safety of its citizens. This liberal ideology failed in the case of an abused child because of its relationship to patriarchy: the ideology fails to take into account a situation where the one entrusted with the protection is the one guilty of abuse.

A liberal state prefers civil remedies. In the United States, civil rights claims have been a crucial tool for changing important public and private policies. *DeShaney*, for example, was preceded by a series of lawsuits by feminist lawyers on behalf of battered women in which the women sought appropriate and nondiscriminatory treatment by police departments.[21] The cases were successful in their political impact; since then most states and police departments have fundamentally changed their policies on domestic violence. It has become harder for battered women to bring an action against state agencies after *DeShaney*, but women can still claim that the practices of the police department or other agencies are discriminatory toward female victims.[22] The law seems to favor strong(er) victims, when the available remedy is a private lawsuit. Thus the law seems to unfairly offer greater protection to an adult woman than to a helpless child.

The Welfare Paradigm

In contrast to the noninterventionist goal of the liberal state, the role of the welfare state is to pursue certain politically chosen goals. According to Habermas, theories of the social or welfare state have an implied image of a society that gives precedence to citizens, to the legislature, and to the practical implementation of laws.[23] If the liberal state is characterized as seeking formal justice, the welfare state seeks material justice. Among the most important acknowledged goals of the welfare state is the protection of citizens against physical and economic risks. Unlike in the liberal states, in Western European welfare states it is difficult to distinguish a dominant section of the law, as the goals of the welfare state are promoted in every branch of the law—in not only civil law (insurance, consumer protection, and the like), but often in social and administrative law as well.

In Finland, where the second case discussed in this essay arose, the welfare of children has been a central goal of state policies. Free healthcare during pregnancy and delivery, the right to paid maternity leave, free healthcare for all children, generous state support for both institutional childcare and care in the home, and free education are examples of Finland's child-friendly policies. The abuse of children has not been a central criminal policy issue, although prosecution does occasionally take place. Instead, Finland has decided to tackle the problem of child abuse as a healthcare and social issue. It is believed that Social Services becomes aware of most cases of child abuse through the healthcare system. If a child's health or development is in danger, Social Services is obliged to remove the child into its care. In practice, the child is then either placed in an institution or in a foster home.

It is sometimes alleged that Scandinavian countries are too eager to intervene in the privacy of the family in the name of child protection. Nonetheless, child protection measures are necessary in the majority of cases, and due to cuts in welfare spending during the 1990s the need for protection exceeds that provided by social services. We too have our Joshuas—children for whom intervention has come too late. The European Court of Human Rights has received cases from Sweden and Finland in which parents have claimed that a child was taken into the care of Social Services in breach of the privacy guarantees of Article 8 of the European Human Rights Convention. In most such cases, however, the

Court has not found that the decisions made by the state courts violated the protection of privacy (art 8.2).[24] Rather, the Court has accepted the principle that the national authorities have jurisdiction in these matters and that "perceptions as to the appropriateness of intervention by public authorities in the care of children vary from one Contracting State to another."[25] On the other hand, the Court has been more inclined to find a breach of the convention where the challenge is to the procedures through which the decision was made or to the excessive limitations of a parent's visitation rights.[26]

In this context it is important to note that in Finland child protection policy and practice promote the child-parent relationship. As the Grandmother case illustrates, the parents usually remain formal legal custodians even while the child is in the care of Social Services. The visitation rights of the parents are encouraged if there is no danger to the child; otherwise, parental custodianship is stripped of its practical content.

Indeed, in the Grandmother case, the Finnish Supreme Court made the following policy statement: "The issue of who was a suitable custodian could not be opened for litigation on the basis of [the] alleged unsuitability of the parent." Were relatives granted such a right, an improper possibility of interference with custody would emerge. Here, the Court agreed with state and community officials that disputes between the relatives should not be transformed into disputes over the custody or placement of the child. Thus, the articulated policy necessarily leads to a situation wherein Social Services was deemed better able to judge the situation of the child than her relatives.

The Grandmother case can be read as an expression of the division of power between general and administrative courts, given that the Supreme Court referred to the grandmother's right to appeal the decisions of the social service board to the administrative court.[27] Notwithstanding the procedural correctness of the Court's decision, it still appears substantively unfair. One cannot help thinking that the grandmother's understandable claim should at least have been litigated.

I suspect that Justice Brennan would see the Grandmother case as a prime example of how the welfare state prevented relatives from taking responsibility for a child. Because the case was not decided on its merits, we do not know whether the grandmother was in fact a good custodian. But the case does show that one-sided reliance on the activity of the authorities can be a problem. Basically this case is about the standard—best interests of the child—and who should represent those interests on behalf of the child.

Together, the *DeShaney* and the Grandmother cases illustrate that neither the state nor some other party should be granted a monopoly to represent the child. Both state and private intervention are needed for the effective protection of children. On their own welfare state structures and legal institutions are as incapable of protecting the children's interests as is the purely liberal legal paradigm. Therefore it is valuable to look for new legal forms combining the two approaches. In the field of human rights, two recent conventions, the Women's Convention and the Children's Convention, recognizing the indivisibility and interdependence of rights or, one might say, both the liberal and welfare state conceptualization of rights, have incorporated civil and social rights into a single document.

THE CHILDREN'S CONVENTION

The 1948 Universal Declaration of Human Rights holds human rights to be indivisible;[28] thus, both so-called first- (civil and political) and second- (social, cultural, and economic) generation human rights are included in the same document. Two decades later, in 1966, when the two main human rights conventions were accepted, the division of human rights into generations was institutionalized. The indivisibility of different human rights was only mentioned in the conventions' preambles.

Later, when the Women's Convention was drafted in the 1970s, the importance of both political and civil rights and social rights for the improvement of women's lot was so evident that both generations of human rights were included in the same convention. With the Children's Convention too, the classical division seems to be missing a purpose. The political rights found in the Children's Convention add little to the rights for young persons in their late teens ensured by the UN International Covenant on Civil and Political Rights and regional human rights conventions, and serve to make adolescents look like precocious young adults.[29] Social rights seem more central to the well-being of children, but realization of social rights for children is perhaps even more complicated than for adults because of the special relation of children to their parents and the state.

The Children's Convention is strained by other, more important, tensions. The general articles (art. 2 and 3) of the Convention reflect the tension between a child's aspiration and right to an autonomous personality and self-determination on the one hand, and her need for and right to special protection on the other.[30] In the realization of these rights, the child is dependent not only on the state but also on her parents. Thus, the child's rights cannot be discussed in terms of a simple bipolar state-citizen relationship but rather as a triangular one, with the child, parent, and state all having salient roles.

However, ignoring the particular location of children, the Children's Convention, like general human rights conventions, basically defines the rights of an individual against the state. Special children's rights, which have the objective of ensuring the child's right to sound development or protection, are written as the rights of an individual child and allocate responsibilities to state parties. To be sure, the Convention also defines a parent's responsibility. According to Articles 3.2 and 18, the primary responsibility for realization of the child's rights lies with her parents, legal custodians, or other persons responsible for her. Indeed some articles even seem to emphasize the rights of the parents over those of the child. Nonetheless, the Convention's text fails to recognize the three-part child-parent-state structure.

The triangular child-parent-state relationship is full of tensions and unresolved issues in the Convention's text. For example, the political rights protect the child against interference by the state, but do not address situations in which she is in conflict with the family. Indeed, the only article which takes into account possible conflict between the parent and the child is the right to religion, which does not endorse the child's rights but rather the right of the family to provide her with religious direction.

Nor does the protection of the rights of children unambiguously address those situations in which the child's rights are violated by the family. The articles that craft specific rights aimed at the protection of children are directed mainly at societal dangers such as economic exploitation (art. 32), drug use and trafficking in drugs (art. 33), sexual exploitation and abuse (art. 34), the sale and trafficking in children (art. 35), the illicit transfer of children abroad (art. 11), other exploitation (art. 36), and starvation and the right to social security (art. 26).

The child's right to protection against violence, abuse, and neglect by a parent is acknowledged in Article 19, which approaches the abuse primarily as a social matter, giving priority to support for the child and the caretaker. The article provides for preventive measures, identification, reporting, referral, investigation, and treatment of child abuse, but does not give a child the right to be separated from an abusive parent. As a last resort, it just mentions the possibility of judicial involvement in family contexts. If the child cannot remain in the family, the state is obliged to give her protection (art. 20).

If the abuse warrants separation from the parent, procedural Article 9 ensures *the parents'* right to judicial review before the child is separated from them. The child also has a procedural right of her own to be heard in matters affecting her. However, this right is contingent on her ability to form and express her views, which are given weight according to her maturity and age (art. 12).

Notwithstanding the ambiguities of these articles, the protections of Articles 19 (against abuse by a parent) and 34 (against emotional exploitation and abuse) would have supported the claims of the plaintiffs in *DeShaney*, if the United States had been party to the Convention.[31] Furthermore, the *DeShaney* plaintiffs might also have found support in the general principles of the Convention.

The Convention does not directly address the issues raised by the Finnish Grandmother case because while it gives all parties a right to be heard when a child is separated from her parents (art. 9.2), it does not specifically give the grandparents status as a party. However, the Convention does not expressly deny grandparents status. It refers to the extended family in Article 20, which mentions the Islamic *kafala* as one possible placement for a child who cannot remain with her family. Article 20 gives *kafala* no priority nor obliges the state to place the child there, but the reference itself suggests that a placement within the extended family is an acceptable option. Thus, though grandparents are neither expressly excluded nor included, they certainly are within the Convention's parameters of an extended family and suitable placement for a child in need of protection.

Thus, in combining both civil and social rights in the same document, the Children's Convention provides children the protections afforded by both liberal and welfare states. Nonetheless, at some level its protection of children is inadequate. While it promotes state intervention, it does not grant the child a specific right to be removed from an abusive situation. Thus, although the Convention does not solve the problems posed by our cases, it nevertheless provides valuable support to efforts to improve child protection measures.

CONCLUSION

The modern human rights approach poses a challenge to all legal regimes, not only "known violators" of human rights. The European Court of Human Rights has oversight over the legal practices of several European countries that have become accustomed to an international monitoring of their legal practices. The United States, on the other hand, rejects the idea of international oversight. But the European experience shows that such monitoring can be a constructive lens that allows us to spot practices that are on the wrong track. In the European context, human rights can also be seen as a constructive discourse in which different rights and legal practices are constantly being tested.

Universal human rights are for everyone. However, the articulation of rights to fit the status of children has proved to be a critical test for both the liberal and welfare law regimes. If the requirement of universality is taken seriously, the barriers between generations of human rights appear artificial and are sometimes counterproductive. The ideological underpinnings of human rights, however, are deep and difficult to overcome. Analysts tend to overemphasize the contradictions between liberal and welfare regulation. By pointing out that a unilateral reliance on either a liberal legal paradigm or on welfare state law actually precludes the realization of cherished values, this essay has shown that these legal regimes should not be seen as opposites but rather as complementary.

To overcome the shortcomings of legal regulation in both the liberal and the welfare states, the political and legal theorists of our time have proposed new models of regulation or legal paradigms which reflect on law as a procedure for creating just outcomes, such as discursive justice (Habermas) and procedural justice (Bayles).[32] Tentative though they may be, these models pay attention to the rules of discourse, to the autonomous subjectivity of the participants, and to the access of all concerned to that discourse. While some theorists have developed these ideas at the global level,[33] here the focus has been on the micro level. In this essay we have seen how difficult access to justice may be for children and others who are dependent on the representation of others. The ideas of discursive justice support the claim that all concerned should be given the opportunity to be heard when the child's rights are determined. Also, the child should have access to justice, and it is paramount to acknowledge that she needs the support of other people—of the state and of the community—to realize that right.

NOTES

1. Lois G. Forer, *Unequal Protection: Women, Children, and the Elderly in Court* 24 (1991).

2. John Rawls, *A Theory of Justice* 14–15, 60 (1971).

3. Convention on the Elimination of All Forms of Discrimination against Women, adopted by the General Assembly of the United Nations on Dec. 18, 1979 [hereinafter Women's Convention].

4. Convention on the Rights of the Child, adopted by the General Assembly of the United Nations on Nov. 20, 1989 [hereinafter Children's Convention].

5. *DeShaney v. Winnebago County Dept. of Social Services*, 489 U.S. 189 (1989).

6. *Id.* at 198–99.

7. *Id.* at 207–10; *see also* Laurence H. Tribe, *The Curvature of Constitutional Space: What Lawyers Can Learn from Modern Physics*, 103 Harv. L. Rev. 1, 10–11 (1989) (relating the issue to the wider perspective of state structures and functions).

8. *DeShaney*, 489 U.S. at 210. The issue of a special relationship had been discussed previously in *Youngberger v. Romeo*, 457 U.S. 307 (1982), and *Estelle v. Gamble*, 429 U.S. 97 (1976), two cases which the *DeShaney* majority and dissent (Brennan joined by Marshall and Blackmun) interpreted quite differently. The existence in *DeShaney* of "a special relationship" between the state and Joshua, sufficient to entitle him to protection from state agencies, is discussed and emphasized in the subsequent *DeShaney* commentary.

9. *DeShaney*, 489 U.S. at 202.

10. *Id.* at 213.

11. Reference was made to Article 6 of the European Human Rights Convention to which Finland is a party. *See* Convention for the Protection of Human Rights and Fundamental Freedoms, Council of Europe, European Treaties ETS No. 5, Nov. 4, 1950.

12. Jürgen Habermas, *Faktizität und Geltung. Beiträge zur Diskurstheorie des Rechts und des demokratischen Rechtsstaats* 473–75 (1992).

13. The current, increasing reliance on criminal sanctions as a disciplinary tool is an indirect consequence of the reluctance to resort to social and adminis-

trative law to solve social problems. I have argued elsewhere that criminal justice intervention has led to increasing regulation of people's lives.

14. *DeShaney*, 489 U.S. at 195. The political inclination of the majority is
confirmed by Justice Brennan's minority opinion. Brennan writes: "The Court's
baseline is the absence of positive rights in the Constitution and a concomitant
suspicion of any claim that seems to depend on such rights." *Id.* at 204.

15. *Id.* at 196.

16. F. A. Hayek, *The Constitution of Liberty* 134 (1969).

17. Carole Pateman, *The Sexual Contract* (1988).

18. *DeShaney*, 489 U.S. at 208.

19. *Id.* at 207.

20. *Id.* at 212.

21. The class action lawsuits against the police officers and departments in
Oakland, California, and New York in the mid-1970s ended in settlements. *See,
e.g., Bruno v. Codd*, 396 N.Y.S.2d 974 (1977) (the New York case). The decisions
finding these claims admissible were highly critical of the police practices described in the testimonies of battered wives.

The most influential case was *Thurman v. City of Torrington*, 595 F. Supp.
1521 (D. Conn. 1984), in which the jury rewarded the plaintiff over 2 million dollars in damages for flagrant negligence in police actions that failed to protect
Mrs. Thurman from her violent former husband.

22. *See* James T. Jones, *Battered Spouses' Section 1983 Damage Actions against
the Unresponsive Police after DeShaney*, 93 W. Va. L. Rev. 251, 296 (1991).

23. Habermas, *supra* note 12, at 472.

24. The decision to take a child into the care of Social Services did not
violate the protection of privacy in the following cases of the European Court
of Human Rights: *L. v. Finland*, judgment 27.4.2000 (Application 25651/94),
Johansen v. Norway, judgment 7.8.1996; *Olsson v. Sweden*, judgment 24.3.1988
A 130.

A violation of the Convention was found in *K. and T. v. Finland*, judgment
12.7.2001 (Application 25702/94). In this case, the child had been taken into
care immediately after her birth from a mother who had a history of mental
problems. Even though the father had started to learn to take care of the baby,
the care order was upheld by the authorities and the courts. While the Court
found that it was not a breach per se of the Convention that Social Services
took the child under its care, a breach was found with respect to the emergency
care order and removal of the child from her mother in the hospital. *Id.* at 163
and 179.

25. *K. and T. v. Finland*, judgment 12.7.2001 (Application 25702/94) ¶ 154.

26. A violation of privacy has been found when parents' visitation rights
have been unneccesarily restricted, even though the placement of the child had
fulfilled the requirements of the Convention. *See Olsson v. Sweden*, judgment

27.11.1992 A 250; *Eriksson v. Sweden*, judgment 22.6.1989 A 156; *Margareta and Roger Andersson v. Sweden*, judgment 25.2.1992 A 226-A.

The procedures followed when the decision was made have been found wanting in a couple of cases against the United Kingdom. *See, e.g., W. v. United Kingdom*, judgement 8.7.1987 A 121. Most recently a violation of the due process clause of art. 6 of the Convention was found in *L. v. Finland*, judgment 27.4.2000 (Application 25652/94).

27. In practice, private control over the welfare state seems to be common. According to Finnish law, any member of the community may appeal the decisions of the communal board. The one whom an administrative decision concerns, of course, may appeal the decision to the administrative court.

28. Universal Declaration of Human Rights, adopted Dec. 10, 1948, preamble; International Covenant on Civil and Political Rights, adopted Dec. 16, 1966, ¶¶ 1–2; International Covenant on Economic, Social and Cultural Rights, adopted Dec. 16, 1966, preamble.

29. The drafting process of the Children's Convention was to some extent dominated by ideological controversy between first-generation civil rights and second-generation economic, social, and cultural rights. For more on the drafting process, *see* Lawrence J. LeBlanc, *The Convention on the Rights of the Child: United Nations Lawmaking on Human Rights* 160 (1995).

30. In 1990, Thomas Hammarberg presented perhaps the first classification of the three "p"s: provide, protect, and participate. *See* Eugeen Verhellen, *Convention on the Rights of the Child: Background, Motivation, Strategies, Main Themes* 79–81 (1997). Glenn Mower's classification highlights the right to life, survival and development rights, and the right to protection. *See* Glenn A. Mower, *The Convention on the Rights of the Child: International Law Support for Children* 15 (1997).

31. In 1999, the United States and Somalia were the only two countries that were not parties to the Children's Convention.

32. *See* Michael Bayles, *Procedural Justice: Allocating to Individuals* (1990).

33. *See, e.g.*, Boaventura de Sousa Santos, *Toward a New Common Sense: Law, Science and Politics in the Paradigmatic Transition* (1995).

6

Domestic and International Adoptions: Heroes? Villains? Or Loving Parents?

The Race and Nationality Precepts as Explanations for International Adoptions

Sharon Elizabeth Rush

IN 1987, WHEN an exceptionally bright exchange student from China in my Constitutional Law class learned that I was in the process of adopting a child, she offered to take me to China to adopt a little Chinese girl. She said we could drive out to the countryside and I could select the child I wanted.

I was dumbstruck and I remember thinking that her plan sounded like kidnapping, but I knew that could not be what she meant. She explained that the Chinese government limited families to one child. Chinese culture values boys more than it does girls, and consequently many families abandon their daughters, leaving them in fields or orphanages in the hope that their next child will be a boy. My student's plan served a double purpose: a Chinese baby could be given a loving home and I could become a mother. Because of the sincerity and generosity of her offer, and also out of compassion for the abandoned girls, I did not summarily dismiss it. After careful thought, I decided not to go and instead proceeded with my plans to adopt a baby in the United States. My decision meant that I did not open my home to even one little Chinese girl who was dehumanized by her government simply because she was female. Instead, I left her and her sisters-in-spirit to lives of destitution, starvation, loneliness, and lovelessness, imagining they were most likely to suffer untimely, youthful deaths.

White Americans, however, have responded in great numbers to the call to adopt Chinese babies. In 1985, around the time of my student's offer, the State Department processed 16 such adoptions.[1] In 1997, the number had increased to 3,500[2] and China became "the leading international source of children for American adoption."[3] White America's generosity in adoption is not limited to China. It has extended to children from other countries as well, particularly following wartime. "Between 1948 and 1962 American families adopted 1,845 German children, 2,987 Japanese children and 840 Chinese children."[4] Following the Korean War and during the period 1953 to 1981, American families adopted 38,129 Korean children.[5] This trend of white Americans adopting international babies continues into the new millennium and the "adoption of Chinese orphans is one of the most preferred forms of intercountry adoption."[6] On a basic humane level, the efforts of parents who adopt across international lines is laudable. As a simple tenet of humanity, every child deserves a loving home.

This is what I have given my adopted African American daughter: a loving home. I did not go to Africa to adopt her. She was born here in the United States. Unlike her Chinese sisters-in-spirit, her government was not communist, but rather a democracy. Moreover, while women in the United States suffer sex discrimination, their devaluation by their government is less draconian than that of Chinese women—at least these abandoned girl-children—by China. In these ways, my adoption of an African American girl is thought by many Americans to be less urgent or morally compelling than if I had adopted a Chinese baby girl or some other international child. Interestingly, however, many Americans think the adoption of my daughter was morally suspect in ways that the adoption of an international baby is not.

The preference of white adoptive parents for international babies over African American ones deserves closer examination. It is different from other types of parental preferences such as a preference for a newborn, a healthy baby, a baby with only moderate physical or mental limitations, or even a preference for a boy or a girl. Perhaps without even realizing it, for some, if not most adoptive white parents, the preference for an international baby stems from their indoctrination in the "Race Precept" and the "Nationality Precept." Specifically, the Race Precept is a belief in and support of the precept of white superiority and black inferiority. Domestic adoptions of African Americans by white Americans may be morally suspect to white Americans because they unconsciously (or consciously) evoke the Race Precept in their minds.

Simultaneously, those adoptions also may be suspect to African Americans because the Race Precept functions in white America as a form of racial and cultural genocide.

Similarly, the Nationality Precept is a belief in and support of the precept of American superiority and every-other-country inferiority. International adoptions not only are not morally suspect to most Americans, but to many Americans they are seen as morally compelling because they offer, consistent with the Nationality Precept, the "best" place of refuge to needy children.

This essay explores how the Race and Nationality Precepts work together in the context of both international and domestic adoptions to promote America's white racism and moral imperialism. Before embarking on this journey, however, an important caveat needs to be mentioned. It is hard to fault anyone for the private preferences they have in the creation of their families. Thus, my analysis of the Race and Nationality Precepts through the lens of domestic and international adoptions is offered to unveil the often unconscious depths of racism and ethnicism in this country.

Given the basic human tenet that every child deserves a loving home, the final part of this essay offers an alternative way of viewing domestic and international adoptions which focuses on what I call "transformative love," an emotion that is most likely to develop in relationships where the parties' love for each other crosses nontraditional lines. Domestic interracial adoptions and international adoptions present an opportunity to understand this concept. Moreover, they serve as a template for the enactment of transformative love which may be helpful or even essential in the struggle to dismantle America's racism and moral imperialism.

I. CHILDREN IN NEED OF FAMILIES

International law recognizes that the family is the basic organizational structure in society. Because of its importance it is protected in human rights instruments. Because of its significance to child development, children's locations within the structure are specifically protected in the Convention on the Rights of the Child.

In the United States far more black children are available for adoption than there are black families available to adopt them.[7] Simultaneously, there is a surplus of white adoptive parents relative to the number of available (healthy) white babies.[8] Simple supply and demand principles could solve this problem: white adoptive parents and black adoptable babies could become families.[9] A recent study reveals, however, that only 8 percent of the adoptions in the United States involve a parent and child of different races,[10] and only 1.2 percent involved a white parent adopting a black child.[11]

Many bureaucratic reasons exist for the overabundance of black children in foster care awaiting adoption.[12] A major impediment to an interracial domestic adoption is a strong preference by agencies and parents for same-race placements. In one study, only one-sixth of the white adoptive parents expressed a willingness to adopt a black child.[13] White parents who are committed to adopting a black baby willingly wind their way through the bureaucratic hoops, which also exist in the adoption of international babies. As an inducement to adopting black babies in the United States, fees are often minimal and certainly substantially lower than they are for international adoptions,[14] which can run to $25,000.[15]

Black children spend at least twice, perhaps three times, as long in foster care than white children.[16] Significantly, even if white Americans did not have the option of international adoption, it may be that black babies would still remain in foster care much longer than white American babies. Given the preference many white Americans have for international babies over black babies, notwithstanding the increased costs and bureaucratic difficulties, and given the strong opposition by the black community to black-white adoptions,[17] it is important to examine closely the way in which the Race and Nationality Precepts function in the adoption context.

A. The Race Precept

Significantly, just as international human rights norms protect families, family life, and children within those social structures, they also proscribe discrimination. In particular, the Convention on the Elimination of All Forms of Racial Discrimination (CERD) forbids discrimination "based on race, colour, descent, or national or ethnic origin." Notwithstanding such international mandates as well as domestic ones, and even with the abolishment of slavery, in the United States, white society initially refused to accept the equal worth of blacks. For over a hundred years, Jim Crow laws mandated the separation of the races throughout society, including in their personal lives. Government attempts to regulate the emotions between persons of different races through antimiscegenation statutes, which prohibited the mixing of black and white blood through marriage and marital procreation, revealed the depth of this taboo. The statutes affirmed whites' emotional disdain for blacks, while they simultaneously attempted to prevent loving, affectionate emotional feelings between blacks and whites from being pursued or rendered a reality. As a "penalty" for being the product of an interracial sexual liaison, either as a violation of the antimiscegenation statutes or as an out-of-wedlock birth, the child and also all the child's descendants and their descendants were legally classified as "black." The use of the "drop of black blood" rule to define race was white society's way of labeling the offspring of interracial sexual relationships as inferior human beings who, regardless of their multiracial ancestry, were no different in whites' eyes from their "pure" black brothers and sisters who were unworthy to mix with whites.

Antimiscegenation statutes were held unconstitutional only in the late 1960s,[18] but, more remarkably, today many whites and some blacks continue to disapprove of white-black marriages.[19] For many white Americans, the notion that a black person and a white person could love each other and want to marry is unimaginable. In fact, many whites see black-white marriages and other personal relationships as deviations from the "natural" order. In this view, it is "unnatural" for a white person to diminish his or her status in society by falling in love with a black person.

When a black-white loving relationship occupies public space, both whites and blacks are reminded of America's historical and current racism. Strangers who see me with my daughter may assume that I had a sexual relationship with my daughter's African American father. For a significant number of white Americans, then, I violated the taboo against such relationships and, from their perspective, the mere existence of my loving family stirs up feelings that many white Americans may not even be aware that they support—sentiments that evidence the persistence of the Race Precept.

Significantly, many blacks who see me with my daughter are also suspicious of our relationship.[20] The need to define and hold fast to their identity also reveals black society's reinterpretation of the "drop of black blood rule." While the rule was "fashioned out of racism, malice, greed, lust, and ignorance, . . . [it] also accomplished good. . . . [The] rule created the African-American race as we know it today."[21] To be African American is to have a dramatically different identity and a dramatically different experience as an American from that of the white American.

Most blacks are less concerned with *how* I became the mother of a black child and more concerned with how I *will mother* the child. Looking upon me as a white person of goodwill, they justifiably wonder what will keep me from acting out the Race Precept by stripping my daughter of her racial identity.[22] Specifically, they might wonder whether I support color blindness, a doctrine that promotes the Race Precept because color blindness teaches my daughter to devalue her blackness by instilling in her the belief that race is irrelevant in America. Implicit in color blindness teachings is that people should pretend that everyone is white because it is better to be white than to be black. Color blindness is synonymous with the Race Precept and, accordingly, blacks are justifiably skeptical that a white person can transcend her racism enough to understand how damaging color blindness is to the self-esteem of her daughter and all children of color.

Ironically, white Americans' willingness to adopt international children, most of whom are children of color,[23] also evidences white society's unwillingness to move beyond racism within its own borders. The desire by prospective white adoptive parents for international babies relative to African American babies supports the persistence of the Race Precept because Chinese, Japanese, Korean, and Mexican babies, to list a few nationalities, are brown in color, but they are not black, either in color or in culture.

Interestingly, many whites curious about my daughter's ancestry remark that she looks Asian, Oriental, Hawaiian, even white with a "really deep tan." When I relate that she is African American, they often respond by assuring me, "You'd never know it." The desire by some white Americans to mask my daughter's African American ancestry and have her pass for a brown Asian[24] or a tanned white American is evidence of their belief in and support of the Race Precept. The racism inherent in such comments is obvious to blacks and antiracist whites. For many whites their unconscious or semiconscious belief in the Race Precept is obscured by their support for the Nationality Precept, especially in the adoption context. The Nationality Precept, unlike the Race Precept, is a public banner that shows white Americans' pride in being American. On closer examination, however, white Americans of goodwill would learn that the Nationality Precept promotes the Race Precept.

B. The Nationality Precept

As provided in CERD, racial discrimination is defined as discrimination on the basis of, among other things, national or ethnic origin. This view, while conflating race and nationality or ethnicity, nevertheless underscores the interdependence of racial and national or ethnic–cultural identities. The fundamental understanding that race and culture are inseparable identity traits becomes confusing for many whites when the issue is adoption. On the domestic front, many whites who adopt blacks teach their children to assimilate into white society, which is precisely the objection blacks have to such adoptions: the alienation of the children from their African American identity.

Similarly, international adoptions, even if the children are white, are becoming morally suspect in the eyes of nationals from other countries who may not only be embarrassed that their country cannot care for all its children,[25] but also distressed that American parents will teach their internationally adopted children to assimilate into American culture and thereby deny the importance of their children's cultural identity. The concern may be more serious with regard to international adoptions of children of color whose racial and cultural identities are inextricably linked.

For example, white American parents who adopt white international babies can choose to hide their family members' cultural differences behind their racial similarity. Because the parents and the baby are white, their racial similarity essentially "domesticizes" the adoption, particularly from the viewpoint of someone who does not know that the parents and child are not biologically related. For example, a Romanian baby's whiteness becomes indistinguishable to strangers within domestic borders from an American baby's whiteness. In fact, the inability to distinguish a biologically related baby from an internationally adopted one may have strongly motivated the parents as they considered their adoption alternatives. Consciously or unconsciously, intentionally or unintentionally, however, the preference by white

Americans for white international babies over African American babies promotes the precept of white superiority and black inferiority.

Promotion of the Race Precept, however, is masked behind promotion of the Nationality Precept. Specifically, white adoptive parents understandably and justifiably are proud to have adopted an international baby and probably tell people the story of how they came to be a family. Thus, the adoption of an international white baby is proudly acknowledged because it is consistent with the Nationality Precept; an international baby who is "saved" from a communist country or a country that otherwise caused the baby to become an orphan can now enjoy living in the "best" country in the world. For most Americans this "truth" is hard to resist, because it is unimaginable that any other country could be "as good" a place to live.

Similarly, white society invokes the Nationality Precept to mask its belief in the Race Precept in the context of the adoption of international children of color, most of whom are of Asian descent. This analysis also requires the unnatural separation of race from culture. For example, unlike a white international baby who is adopted by white parents, the racial differences between a Chinese baby, for example, and her adoptive white parents are obvious. Morever, unlike the white baby, the Chinese baby and all international children of color suffer from race discrimination in America. Such reality notwithstanding, African American babies are more devalued in America than are children of Asian ancestry. The Race Precept does not attach in the same way to Asian Americans; in fact, the stereotype most white Americans have of Asian Americans is that they are intellectually bright.[26] Although this perception masks white society's racism against Asian Americans, it nevertheless significantly differentiates Asian Americans from African Americans in white society's eyes.

Because white society grapples with all racial differences, the international child's foreign culture may become the focus of the differences between the parents and the adopted child. This shift away from racial differences enables white society to discount the baby's Chinese race in the creation of the family unit. Equally important, unlike race which rarely, if ever, can be completely dismissed, culture can be. In this way, white adoptive parents can manipulate the visibility of the baby's culture, valuing it on a theoretical level as the most obvious difference between family members, but also devaluing it as a practical matter, consistent with the Nationality Precept, as they "Americanize" their child.

Most white Americans fail to understand or accept that African Americans have a culture, let alone a culture that is different from white society's "American" culture. Without cultural differences to value and to deflect the issue of racial differences, the Race Precept often becomes inescapable for white Americans of goodwill. Simultaneously, without any urgent need to save the African American baby from destitution or communism, the Nationality Precept is irrelevant and cannot provide a justification for potential white adoptive parents to adopt the African American baby. Because of the way in which the Race and Nationality Precepts function, often unconsciously, many white Americans of goodwill prefer to adopt international babies. An Asian baby who brings a foreign cultural ancestry back with her to the United States provides a way for white America not to talk about the baby's race by focusing on her cultural ancestry in an abstract way. Moreover, white America also rationalizes a decision to adopt internationally because that seems morally compelling, particularly as America becomes increasingly global in its perspective (and as global perspectives become more Americanized). In these ways, the Race and Nationality Precepts work together to help white Americans to consciously or unconsciously create loving families that nevertheless fortify the black-white color line in America.

Although the number of whites adopting African Americans accounts for a minute fraction of all the adoptions in the United States, the indoctrination of even one child in the Precepts is a huge loss to the African American community. Together, the doctrines of color blindness and assimilation threaten African American identity by masking the way in which the Race and Nationality Precepts are founded on white society's moral imperialism both on the domestic and international fronts. The adoptive white parent who denies any child's racial and cultural identity participates in white society's attempt to impose a white American identity on the child.

Thus far I have used the idea of international and domestic adoptions to show how the U.S. concepts of white supremacy and national superiority enable the persistence of racism. I would now like to suggest ways in which international adoptions and domestic adoptions across the color line can help eliminate the Race and Nationality Precepts by suggesting that when such adoptions occur, as they will, the dynamics of family relationships can result in feelings of "transformative love," which can help to dismantle the imperialistic Precepts.

II. TRANSFORMATIVE LOVE

This part of the essay offers a definition of transformative love and distinguishes it from empathy and from other types of love. It also explores how one can move beyond empathy and develop transformative love that ultimately meets the international goals of nondiscrimination and of children flourishing within caring family units. This transformation is important because it may be essential to the attainment of equality for all persons. Even if transformative love is not essential to the attainment of equality for all humans, its existence will move people and societies in that direction.

A. Empathy

People become adoptive parents for many reasons. Fortunately, many adults' empathy moves them to extend their families to include the homeless child. The role empathy plays in adoptions by whites across racial and cultural lines, however, can be problematic because generally the adoptive parents are prone to believe in the Race and Nationality Precepts, perpetuating hierarchies of race and national origin as well as of political philosophy. In fact, if parents' empathy is situated in a "feeling sorry" for the child because he or she is of a particular race or nationality, then their empathy impedes the development of the child's self-esteem and denies the child the basic dignity to be himself or herself and the ability to attain full personhood.

Concern about the limited nature of empathy stems from the suggestion that feeling empathy while maintaining one's identity may be impossible:

> If the self is inseparable from its social circumstances . . . it follows that when I employ projective empathy to understand someone else's circumstances, I inevitably bring the foundational part of my "self"—my own intelligence, self-esteem, and courage, as well as my gender, race, and socioeconomic background—to the experience in a way that prevents any deep understanding of the other. Only if the other person is

substantially the same as I am—that is, shares my social circumstances—is there no distortion of understanding.[27]

This suggestion explains why adoptive parents who espouse, even unconsciously, the Race and Nationality Precepts are inclined to teach their children to assimilate into the family in ways that reflect the parents' identity and lead to the erasure of the child's own racial or cultural heritage and nationality. The adoptive family's projective empathy toward the otherwise homeless child may cause the parents to make the child over into themselves—racially and culturally—so that the child feels like he or she belongs in the family. Many adoptive parents may believe that collapsing the child's identity into their own is the best way to show that they love the child as one of their own.

A different phenomenon known as "imaginative empathy" leads to different results.

> Here empathy becomes not the placement of one's "self" in another's shoes, or even the analogizing of the other's experiences to one's own; rather, it becomes the conscious setting aside of the self in order to construct the unique self of the patient.[28]

Imaginative empathy focuses on knowing someone in ways that require putting aside basic parts of oneself in order to appreciate and understand the other person without collapsing the other person's identity into one's own. Adoptive parents who feel imaginative empathy would be less inclined to teach their children to assimilate into white society in ways that promote the Race and Nationality Precepts.

Still, the concept of imaginative empathy implies a continuing artificial emotional distance between the people in the relationship. Understandably, maintaining a degree of emotional and professional distance in a doctor-patient relationship is natural and probably necessary. In a parent-child relationship, however, it seems unnatural and unnecessary and, in this way, I think even imaginative empathy falls short of disabusing white parents of goodwill of the truth in the Race and Nationality Precepts.

Accordingly, I offer an exploration of an emotion that moves beyond empathy to break down the barriers of racism and nationalism. It is an emotion more powerful than empathy, an emotion that is transformative: "transformative love."

B. "Transformative Love," Authentic Relationships, and Full Personhood

"Love" has more meanings than perhaps any other word in any language. I introduce the concept of transformative love not to deny the beauty or the power of any other type of love. Rather, transformative love is an extension of all types of love and serves to break down any conception of moral, racial, cultural, or national superiority.

Transformative love is ripe for development when a dominant group member develops an authentic relationship with a nondominant group member. By "dominant" group member I mean a person whose fundamental identity traits are those preferred by the society and its culture. In contrast, the nondominant person's fundamental identity traits are devalued by the society and its culture. A society's preference for some traits and its disdain for others is reflected throughout the society, most notably in its legal, political, social, racial, and economic structures. Stated alternatively, transformative love develops in authentic relationships between people on different sides of superiority-inferiority precepts that define the political power structure. In America, authentic relationships can develop across the lines of race, culture, gender, religion, and economics, as well as others.

The authenticity of a dominant-nondominant relationship is critical for the development of transformative love. That is, the dominant person's love for the nondominant person must be premised on an authentic appreciation of the subordinated or subaltern's identity traits. The authenticity of cross-line relationships can be measured by how well two emotions come together. First, the normative's love for the subordinated must be premised on embracing the subordinated's self. To embrace blackness, for example, may sound ridiculously simple. After all, how could the normative love the subordinated *at all* unless there was love for his or her blackness? However, the majority's ability to embrace the minority becomes difficult, if not impossible, if the majority believes in the Race and Nationality Precepts. For the dominant to declare, "I love blackness," is dramatically different from a declaration of love notwithstanding race. The first declaration is premised on embracing the person, whereas the second one is premised on tolerating the person's blackness as if it were a flaw.

Significantly, if the latter were the basis for love, it would be premised on belief in and acceptance of the Race (or Nationality) Precept.

Consequently, the normative person's role in the relationship would be largely about "rescuing" the "other" from her "sorry plight." Trapped in the role of the "imaginative empathizer," the normative would be inclined to support color blindness and assimilation, sincerely believing that this would alleviate some of the other's victimization. The inauthenticity of their relationship in this scenario is readily apparent.

Assuming that the normative authentically embraces the other, then a second emotion must also exist between them if transformative love is to develop. Specifically, the normative must reject that part of himself or herself that participates, often unconsciously, in the subordination of the other. The importance of this second step cannot be overstated because it requires moving beyond imaginative empathy—a limited emotion because empathy, by definition, is premised on power and exists because the "powerless" person lacks agency. Specifically, imaginative empathy depends on the powerful person understanding the powerless person's injury, hurt, or more general victimization in order for the powerful person to fulfill a "rescuing" role.

In contrast, authentic loving relationships—relationships of friendship, commerce, and family that could (and would) break down Race and Nationality Precepts both domestically and internationally, by definition promote the equal dignity of the loved ones. In this way, imaginative empathy is appropriate when a loved one is temporarily in need of that kind of sustenance, as we all are on occasion. Moreover, reciprocity is an essential aspect of caring emotions in loving relationships.

In the context of race and nationality, then, if the normative authentically loves the other, empathy is not situated in feeling sorry for the other because of his or her race or nationality. Rather, empathy is situated in feeling the wrongness of white America's privileging one race over another by its persistent support of the Race and Nationality Precepts through such doctrines as color blindness and assimilation. Moving beyond trying to imagine how the other withstands society's constant devaluation of her because of her race or nationality, once the normative *feels* the unjust way his or her own race and nationality are privileged *at the expense of the other's dignity*, then he or she is open to feeling transformative love.

Thus, unlike imaginative empathy which is focused on rescuing victims, the struggle for someone who feels transformative love is internally focused on rejecting privilege. Specifically, transformative love is about consciously rejecting historically ingrained lessons of the precept of the superior self and the inferior other. Transformative love is based on understanding that one is complicit, however involuntarily, in partaking of the privileges associated with dominant identity traits. It is worth emphasizing that transformative love involves this awakening; one is privileged even if one does not consciously believe in or support any superiority-inferiority precepts.

Unable to escape one's privileged identity, which operates to the direct harm of one's loved one, people who feel transformative love must find ways to repudiate their privileges. For example, white applicants to a state university that has an affirmative action policy can refrain from legally challenging their denial of admission even though they may have higher admission scores compared to some admitted minorities.[29] Their decision to forgo lawsuits can reflect their understanding of the need to repudiate their white privilege for the sake of racial equality. Thus, their love is transformative because it alters not just their perception of the injustice inflicted on their loved ones, but also their self-perception and their role in perpetuating the injustice on all others. The normatives move beyond being empathizers and, to the extent that they are successful at repudiating their privileged status, they make the world more just, even though the system generally remains unjust.

C. Transformative Love and the Parent-Child Relationship

The parent-child relationship is unique to this discussion. In many ways it resembles the doctor-patient one because of the power imbalance between the parent and child, especially during the child's development. As the parent and the dominant person in the relationship, naturally he or she plays a major role in shaping and controlling the child's life. Moreover, the child depends on this power imbalance, particularly during his or her maturation process. In most parent-child relationships there is no doubt about who makes important decisions on behalf of the child. Just as a doctor who has highly developed imaginative empathy makes better treatment decision for her patients, so too, the more developed the parent's imaginative empathy, the better his or her decisions will be for the child.

Unlike the doctor-patient relationship, however, the parent-child relationship is a loving one. The parent not only expects respect from the child, but also has a responsibility as a loving parent to respect the child. Both parent and child owe each other a duty to promote each other's equal dignity, which is not to be confused with the parent's duty to be the decision maker for the child in appropriate circumstances. The child will become an adult, capable of making her own decisions, but the love, respect, and dignity between the parent and child will endure.

Loving cross-line parent-child relationships bring yet another set of special considerations to the discussion. For example, in the context of interracial domestic and international adoptions, the parents not only are empowered as parents with respect to their children, but also by virtue of their whiteness and their American nationality. As the discussion above suggests, transformative love can play an enormous role in such relationships. Once embraced within the most intimate of circles, the concept of transformative love provides an invaluable lens through which to break down morally imperialist enterprises. Whether between states, between commercial actors, between management and labor, or between majority and minority cultures, this concept promotes respect and dignity for all persons alike—North and South, East and West, rich and poor, powerful and disempowered; from dominant and subordinated races, cultures, nations, sexes, sexualities, religions, and ethnicities.

SUMMARY

The challenge is not for persons to forgo domestic and international adoptions that cross racial or nationality lines, but rather to enable persons to develop authentic relationships across racial and nationality lines that serve to dismantle the Race and Nationality Precepts by focusing on personhood.

Each "family," be it the local family unit, a community, a corporate entity, or a nation-state, is unique and all "parents" have unique ways of "parenting" their "children" depending on their "children's" needs. This chapter has used cross-line adoptions to show the perniciousness of the Race and Nationality Precepts. This lens has revealed that adoptive parents who opt for cross-line adoptions must be more aware than they might otherwise have been of racial and cultural differences and authentically embrace those differences in their children. The authenticity of all majority-minority relationships can result in transformative love, which in turn can help eliminate the Race and Nationality Precepts. The lessons adoptive parents learn from their children and from their experiences in cross-line relationships are ones that every white American (and every dominant actor in a heterogenous society) would benefit from learning as well. These lessons are essential to eliminating the Precepts. Only by so doing will doctrines like color blindness and assimilation be rejected and the equal dignity of all persons be enjoyed in America.

NOTES

I am grateful to Berta Hernández-Truyol for inviting me to participate in this project and for her insights and suggestions. I also am thankful to Darby F. Hertz for her research assistance.

1. Michelle Van Leeuwen, *Comment: The Politics of Adoptions across Borders: Whose Interests Are Served?* 8 Pac. Rim L. and Pol'y 189, 190 (1999) (a look at the emerging market of infants from China).

2. *Id.*

3. *Id.* (footnote omitted).

4. *Id.* at 191 n.5 (citing Mary Kathleen Benet, *The Politics of Adoption* 120 (1976)).

5. *Id.*

6. Rita J. Simon and Howard Alstein, *Adoption across Borders: Serving the Children in Transracial and Intercountry Adoptions* 9 (2000).

7. *No Place to Call Home: Discarded Children in America*, H.R. Rep. No. 395, 101st Cong., 2d Sess. 25 (1990) (noting that while the national median length of stay in foster care is seventeen months, the median length of stay for the majority of black children exceeds two years).

8. Simon and Alstein, *supra* note 6, at 5 (quoting the Adoption and Safe Families Act, 1997, Pub. L. 105–89).

9. This is the position advocated by Elizabeth Bartholet in *Nobody's Children: Abuse and Neglect, Foster Drift, and the Adoption Alternative* 181 (1999).

10. Simon and Alstein, *supra* note 6, at 5.

11. *Id.*

12. The primary reason children are removed is because of low family income, which has a disparate impact on black families. *See* Martin Guggenheim, *Somebody's Children: Sustaining the Family's Place in Child Welfare Policy*, 113 Harv. L. Rev. 1716, 1724 (2000) (quoting Duncan Lindsey, *The Welfare of Children* 155 (1994)).

13. Bartholet, *supra* note 9, at 182.

14. For example, the fee for adopting my daughter was reduced by half because she is biracial.

15. *See* Rosanne L. Romano, *Comment: Intercountry Adoption: An Overview for the Practitioner*, 7 Transnat'l L. 545, 546 (1994) (describing adoptions costing between $5,000 and $20,000).

16. *See* 142 Cong. Rec. H4433-03 (daily ed. May 7, 1996) (testimony of Rep. Canady); 141 Cong. Rec. S-13, 770-02 (daily ed. Sept. 19, 1995; H.R. Rep. No. 104-81(I); 140 Cong. Rec. H10, 391–404 (daily ed. Sept. 30, 1994).

17. Simon and Altstein, *supra* note 6, at 2.

18. *See, e.g., Loving v. Virginia*, 388 U.S. 1, 6 n.5 (1967) (identifying thirty states that had antimiscegenation laws at that or some previous time).

19. *See, e.g.,* Isabel Wilkerson, *Black-White Marriages Rise, but Couples Still Face Scorn*, N.Y. Times, Dec. 2, 1991, at A1.

20. *See* David K. Shipley, *A Country of Strangers: Blacks and Whites in America* 115–16 (1997).

21. Christine B. Hickman, *The Devil and the One Drop Rule: Racial Categories, African Americans, and the U.S. Census,* 95 Mich. L. Rev. 1161, 1163 (1997). ("Not all objection to interracial dating comes from whites. In the spirit of black pride, black solidarity, black cultural cohesion, some blacks also resist and resent.")

22. *See* Sharon E. Rush, *Loving across the Color Line: A White Adoptive Mother Learns about Race* 136–39 (2000).

23. Simon and Alstein, *supra* note 6, at 19.

24. Particularly with Asian babies, if any precept attaches at all, it may be just the opposite of the black inferiority precept: Asians are perceived by white society to be extremely bright and intelligent. Yet, when the stereotype fits the reality, as it does in admissions at the University of California when Asians outperformed whites on standardized entrance exams, white America became threatened by Asians' success.

25. For example, South Korea is "working toward the elimination of all intercountry adoption from its country." Simon and Alstein, *supra* note 6, at 19.

26. Robert S. Chang, "Toward an Asian American Legal Scholarship: Critical Race Theory, Post-Structuralism, and Narrative Space," in *Critical Race Theory* 322, 326 (R. Delgado ed. 1995).

27. Cynthia V. Ward, *A Kinder, Gentler Liberalism? Visions of Empathy in Feminist and Communitarian Literature,* 61 U. Chi. L. Rev. 929, 944 (1994).

28. *Id.* at 948.

29. Sharon Elizabeth Rush, *Sharing Space: Why Racial Goodwill Isn't Enough,* 32 Conn. L. Rev. 1, 52–69 (1999).

PART II

SOCIAL, CULTURAL, AND ECONOMIC RIGHTS

PART III

SOCIAL, CULTURAL, AND
ECONOMIC RIGHTS

7

Economic Globalization and the Redrawing of Citizenship

Saskia Sassen

TOGETHER WITH SOVEREIGNTY and exclusive territoriality, citizenship marks the specificity of the modern state. Economic globalization has transformed the sovereignty and territoriality of the nation-state. Just as a strengthening global economy affects the continuity and formation of rights we associate with citizenship, globalization may also have an impact on some of the features of citizenship, particularly people's rights to hold their governments accountable. Historical, underlying conditions have shaped modern citizenship. New conditions created by the global economy constitute another phase in the evolution of the institution of citizenship.[1]

EXPANDING THE ANALYTIC TERRAIN FOR EXAMINING RIGHTS

In a world where globalization challenges the sovereignty of the nation-state and civil solidarity, the proper analytic terrain for examining the question of rights requires the introduction of new elements in the discourse on rights. This is a broad agenda and one to which I cannot do justice in this short essay,[2] so instead I focus on the impact of economic globalization on citizenship. By taking the history of the institution of citizenship seriously by underlining the particular combination of conditions that had to crystallize for citizenship as we know it to emerge, I use the notion of economic citizenship as a construct to destabilize the linearity of that history. The question explored is whether the specific conditions brought on by economic globalization, especially in highly developed countries, have contributed to yet another major transformation or evolution in the institution of citizenship. My answer is yes, but with a twist.[3]

Historicizing the institution means going beyond the latest bundle of rights that came with the welfare state and recognizing the possible erosion of some of the conditions presupposed by citizenship. Today's welfare state crises, growing unemployment in many of the European economies, growing numbers of the employed poor in the United States, and growing earnings inequality in all highly developed countries, can be read as signaling a change in the conditions of citizens.[4] If we take the history of the institution of citizenship seriously, these changing conditions have to be read as having, at least potentially, an impact on the institution.[5]

To what extent the changing conditions of citizens are connected to economic globalization will vary from country to country. But overall, there is now a growing consensus that the race to the bottom in highly developed countries, and in the world at large, is a function of global competition. Further, disinvestment or insufficient investment in industries that contribute middle-income jobs is also partly a function of hypermobile capital in search of the most profitable short-term opportunities around the globe. Finally, the increased liquidity of capital through securitization and the ascendance of finance generally has further stimulated the global circulation of capital and the search for investment opportunities worldwide rather than promoting long-term local economic and social development. These investment decisions typically do not favor the growth of a large middle class, as reflected in one of the most disturbing trends today: the vast expansion in the numbers of unemployed and never-employed people in all the highly developed countries. In developing countries we see the growing masses of poor who lack access to the most basic means for survival.

This growing body of evidence signals that economic globalization has hit at some of the major conditions, even in highly developed countries, that have supported the evolution of citizenship, and particularly the formation of social rights. Thus it could be argued that if there is one type of citizenship that is badly needed it is economic citizenship—the right to a job, the right to work for a living, the right to economic survival. This would be a new bundle of rights representing economic citizenship alongside the social rights corresponding to the welfare state.

There is an emerging body of scholarship and political analysis that posits the need for rights to economic well-being and to economic survival. Some studies place this claim at the heart of democratic theory, arguing that employment and economic well-being are essential conditions for a democratic politics. While I agree with this claim and consider it extremely important, my question here is not about the *claim* to economic citizenship and its legitimacy. Rather I ask whether there exists a *reality* today that represents an aggregation of economic rights that one could describe as a form of economic citizenship in that it empowers and can demand that governments be held accountable in economic matters.

My reading of the evidence is that yes, there is such a reality. But this economic citizenship is located not in individuals, not in citizens, but in global economic "actors." It belongs to firms and markets, specifically to the global financial markets. The very fact that they are global gives these "actors" power over individual governments, a reality closely linked with some of the fundamental changes brought about by economic globalization. Multinationals and the global financial markets are the most powerful of these actors.

This particular instantiation of the notion of economic citizenship has the status of a theoretical provocation; it is not a use that fits in the lineage of the traditional concept of citizenship. I consider the practices in which firms and markets can engage that amount to a bundle of rights, some of them formally specified and others de facto permissions which are a consequence of those practices and formal rights.

When I think of new locations for the aggregation of power and legitimacy that we have historically associated with the nation-state, global financial markets and the covenants on human rights are the two new contestants, alongside the authority of the nation-state, for the redistribution of power and legitimacy. It is the case of the global financial markets I address here. These markets represent one of the most astounding aggregations of new "rights" and legitimacy we have seen in the 1990s.

THE GLOBAL CAPITAL MARKET: POWER AND NORM-MAKING

The formation of a global capital market represents a concentration of power that is capable of influencing national government economic policy and, by extension, other policies. This market now exercises the accountability functions associated with citizenship: it can vote governments' economic policies in or out; it can force governments to take certain measures and not others. As deregulation and new types of reregulation are instituted in a growing number of financial markets in countries around the world, investors worldwide can bring in massive amounts of capital at short notice and they can take it out equally fast. While the power of these markets is quite different from that of the political electorate, they have emerged as a sort of global, cross-border economic electorate, where the right to vote is predicated on the possibility of registering capital.

The deregulation of domestic financial markets, the liberalization of international capital flows, computers, and advances in telecommunications have all contributed to an explosive growth in financial markets.[6] Since 1980, the total stock of financial assets has increased three times faster than the aggregate GDP of all the rich industrial economies. And the volume of trading in currencies, bonds, and equities has increased about five times faster and now surpasses it by far. For instance, aggegate GDP stood at U.S.$30 trillion at the end of the 1990s while the value of interglobal trade of derivatives was U.S.$68 trillion for 1999. This is a figure that dwarfs the value of cross-border trade (U.S.$8 trillion in 2000), foreign direct investment stock (U.S.$6 trillion in 2000), and the aggregate foreign currency reserves of the twenty-three so-called rich countries of the world.

As a consequence of this enormous capital that is highly liquid, the global capital market now has the power to discipline national governments. This became evident with the 1994–95 Mexico financial crisis and the 1997–98 Southeast Asian financial crisis. In all the countries involved, investors were capable of leaving en masse: in the Southeast Asian case they took out well over U.S.$100 billion over a short period of time. The foreign currency markets were large enough to alter exchange rates radically for some of these currencies, to overwhelm each and all the central banks involved, and to override the banks' futile attempts to defend their currencies against the onslaught.

The foreign exchange market was the first one to globalize, in the mid-1970s. Today it is the biggest and in many ways the only truly global market. It has gone from a daily turnover rate of about U.S.$15 billion in the 1970s, to U.S.$60 billion in the early 1980s, and to an estimated $1.3 trillion by the end of the 1990s. In contrast, the total foreign currency reserves of the rich industrial countries amounted to under $1 trillion. Just to make it more concrete, foreign exchange transactions were ten times as large as world trade in 1983; only ten years later, in 1992, they were sixty times larger, and by 2000 seventy times larger. And world trade has itself grown sharply over this period.

According to some estimates, we have reached only the mid-point of a fifty-year process in terms of the full integration of these markets. The financial markets are expected to expand even further in relation to the size of the real economy. Today the total stock of financial assets traded in the global capital market is equivalent to almost three times the GDP of the Organization for Economic Cooperation and Development (OECD) countries. Much more integration and power may lie ahead for capital markets.[7] What really counts is how much capital can be moved across borders and in how short a period of time. It is clearly an immense amount.

In addition to the direct impact on the economy via the market, this massive growth of financial flows and assets and the fact of an integrated global capital market affect states in their economic policy making. Conceivably a global capital market could just be a vast pool of money for investors to shop in without conferring power over governments. The fact that it can discipline governments' economic policy making is a distinct power, one that is not ipso facto inherent in the existence of a large global capital market.

The differences between today's global capital market and the period of the gold standard before World War I are illuminating in this regard. The first set of differences concerns today's growing concentration of market power in institutions such as pension funds and insurance companies. A second major difference is the explosion of financial innovations. Innovations have raised the supply of financial instruments that are tradable, sold on the open market, although there are significant differences by country. Securitization is well advanced in the United States, but just beginning in most of Europe and Japan.[8] The proliferation of derivatives has furthered the linking of national markets by making it easier to exploit price differences between different financial instruments, that is, to arbitrage.[9]

A third set of differences is the impact of digital networks on the functioning and growth possibilities of financial markets. Here the crucial differences are the combination of the speed of circulation made possible by digital networks *and* the innovations that raise the level of liquidity and liquefy what was hitherto considered nonliquid. The properties that the new information technologies bring to the financial markets are instantaneous transmission, interconnectivity, and speed. The speed of transactions has brought its own consequences. Trading in currencies and securities is instant, thanks to vast computer networks. The high degree of interconnectivity in combination with instantaneous transmission signals the potential for exponential growth.

In certain matters, the increase in volumes per se may be secondary. But when these volumes can be deployed to overwhelm national central banks, they become a significant variable explaining the influence the global capital market can exercise over government policy making.[10]

These key features of the current global capital market affect the power of governments over their economies in market-centered systems. This power has been based on the ability to tax, to print money, and to borrow. Before deregulation, governments could (to some extent) directly control the amount of bank lending through credit controls and ceiling imposed on interest rates, which helped make monetary policy more effective than it is today. For instance, to cite a well-known case in the United States, Regulation Q imposed interest rate ceilings and thereby protected the holdings of savings and loan associations by preventing investors' flight to higher interest-bearing alternatives. This in turn kept mortgages and home construction going. In 1985 Regulation Q was lifted. The absence of interest rate ceilings meant that money left the savings and loan association in hordes for higher interest yields, creating a massive slump in mortgages and housing construction.[11]

There are now a series of mechanisms through which the global capital market actually exercises its disciplining function on national governments and pressures them to become accountable to the logic of this market. The financial crises of recent years bring some of this process to the fore in a brutal fashion. But there are others, often difficult to trace. Key policies being instituted today in countries that become integrated into the global capital market reflect the operational logic of this market.[12] One set of policies flows from the anti-inflationary monetary policies of the central banks of these countries. This anti-inflationary emphasis often entails a reversal of prior policies that prioritized employment growth and allowed far higher levels of inflation than are feasible for the functioning of a global capital market. A second set of policies is aimed at making the state "competitive" by cutting down on a variety of social costs.

The global capital market is a mechanism for pricing capital and allocating it to its most profitable opportunity.[13] One of the problems today is that the most profitable opportunity is increasingly being seen as also the most productive. This signals the weight of the financial markets on economic policy. The search for the most profitable opportunities and the increased speed of all transactions, including profit taking, contribute potentially to massive distortions in the flow of capital. The global capital market has a logic in its operation, but it is not one that will lead inevitably to the desirable larger social and economic investments. The issue here is not so much that this market has emerged as a powerful mechanism where those with capital can influence government policy—in many ways an old story.[14] It is rather that the overall operation of this market has an embedded logic that calls for certain types of economic policy objectives. Given the properties of the systems through which this market operates—simultaneity, interconnectivity, and speed—and the magnitude of orders it can produce, it can exercise undue pressure to get the right types of policies instituted, which is precisely what is happening. And this weight can be exercised on any country integrated into the financial markets, and the number of such countries is rapidly growing.[15]

A NEW ZONE OF LEGITIMACY?

These realities beg the question: Is the power of the global capital market a threat to democracy and to the notion that the electoral system is one way in which citizens make governments accountable and exercise some control over them? Where does that leave the electoral system, an essential mechanism for citizens to exercise influence? One way of thinking about the global economic reality is as a partial privatization of key components of monetary and fiscal policies.

Ropke, trying to understand the relation between international law and the international economy before World War I under the Pax Britanica, refers to that particular international realm as a *res publica non christiana*, seeing in it a secular version of the *res publica christiana* of the Middle Ages. Is the transnational web of rights and protections that multinational firms and global markets enjoy today the next step in this evolution—a privatizing of an international zone that was once a *res publica*? Debates around the matter of international public law appear to confirm a move toward such privatization, as legal scholars are positing that we are headed to a situation where international law will predominantly be international private law, largely international economic law.[16] While in principle that includes the individual citizen, in practice such private economic law addresses largely the needs and claims of firms and markets.

There is much to be said about this new zone of legitimacy. Let me begin with two observations. One is that nation-states have participated in its formation and implementation and thereby have reconstituted some of their own features. The other concerns the implicit ground rules of our legal system: a matter that has not been formalized into rules of prohibition or permission constitutes a de facto set of rules of permission.[17] This analysis helps to conceptualize the bundle of rights that has accrued to firms and markets in the 1990s through economic globalization. The ground rules on which economic globalization is proceeding contain far more permissions than have been formalized in explicit rules of prohibition and permission.

A. Denationalized State Agendas

At the level of theory, these observations signal that we need to capture and conceptualize a specific set of operations that take place within national institutional settings but are geared to non-national or transnational agendas (whereas once they were geared to national agendas).[18] I conceptualize this occurrence as denationalization—denationalization of specific, typically highly specialized, state institutional orders and of state agendas. Denationalization thus entails the need to decode what is "national" (as historically constructed) about the particular set of activities and authorities of central banks or ministries of finance.[19]

There is a set of strategic dynamics and institutional transformations at work that may incorporate a small number of state agencies and units within departments, a small number of legislative initiatives and executive orders, and yet have the power to institute a new normativity at the heart of the state. Such changes occur because these strategic sectors operate in complex interaction with powerful private, transnational actors.

The particular types of actors of interest to the argument in this essay are global markets and firms. It is their agendas that get partly institutionalized in key aspects of government policy while much of the institutional apparatus of the state remains basically unchanged. The inertia of bureaucratic organizations, which creates its own version of path dependence, makes an enormous contribution to continuity.

Further, the new types of cross-border collaborations among specialized government agencies, concerned with a growing range of issues emerging from the globalization of capital markets and the new trade order, are yet another aspect of this participation by states in the implementation of a global economic system. A good example is the heightened interaction since the late 1990s among antitrust regulators from a large number of countries. Economic globalization puts pressure on governments to work toward convergence in antitrust regulations even though the competition laws or enforcement practices of different countries are often very diverse.[20] This convergence around specific antitrust issues frequently occurs in the midst of enormous differences among these countries in all kinds of laws and regulations about components of the economy which do not intersect with globalization. It is thus a very partial and specialized type of convergence among different national regulators who often begin to share more with each other than they do with colleagues back home in the larger bureaucracies within which they work.

There are multiple other instances of this highly specialized type of convergence: regulatory issues concerning telecommunications, finance, the Internet, and so on. In some of these sectors there has long been an often elementary convergence, or at least a coordination of standards. What we see today is a sharp increase in the work of establishing convergence, well illustrated by the intensified transactions among central banks in the context of the global capital market. While central banks have long interacted with each other across borders, we can clearly identify a new phase starting in the 1990s. The world of cross-border trade has also brought with it a sharpened need for convergence in standards, as evidenced by the vast proliferation of International Organization for Standardization (ISO) items.

One outcome of these various trends is the emergence of a strategic field of operations that represents a partial disembedding of specific state operations from the broader institutional world of the state once geared exclusively to national agendas.[21] It is a fairly rarified field of cross-border transactions among government agencies and business sectors aimed at addressing the new conditions produced and demanded by economic globalization. It is in many ways a new and increasingly institutionalized framework designed to legitimize various objectives that lie largely in the domain of global markets and firms. This framework allows firms and markets to exercise enormous influence in shaping what the "proper" government policy ought to be. The power of these firms and markets allows them to pressure governments into designing and adopting such policies.[22]

B. Making the Global Economy Work

Private firms in international finance, accounting, and law, the new private standards for international accounting and financial reporting, and supranational organizations such as the WTO, all play strategic nongovernment-centered governance functions. The events following the Mexico crisis of 1994–95 provide us with some interesting insights into these firms' role in changing the conditions for financial operation, the ways in which national states participated, and the formation of the new institutionalized space described above.

J. P. Morgan worked with Goldman Sachs and Chemical Bank to develop several innovative deals that brought investors back to Mexico's markets.[23] Further, in July 1996, an enormous U.S.$6 billion five-year deal that offered investors a Mexican floating rate note or syndicated loan—backed by oil receivables from the state oil monopoly PEMEX—was twice oversubscribed. It became something of a model for asset-backed deals from Latin America, especially oil-rich Venezuela and Ecuador. Key to the high demand was that the structure had been designed to capture investment grade ratings from S&P and Moody's (it got BBB- and Baa3). This was the first Mexican deal with an investment grade. The financial intermediaries worked with the Mexican government, but on their own terms—this was not a government-to-government deal securing acceptability in the new institutionalized privatized space for cross-border transactions—evidenced by the high level of oversubscription and the high ratings. And it allowed the financial markets to grow on what had been a crisis.

After the Mexico crisis and before the first signs of the Asian crisis, a large number of very innovative deals contributed to further expand the volumes in the financial markets and to incorporate new sources of profit, that is, debts for sale. Typically these deals involved novel concepts of how to sell debt and what could be a salable debt. Often the financial services firms structuring these deals also implemented minor changes in depository systems to bring them more in line with international standards. The aggressive innovating and selling on the world market of what had hitherto been thought to be too illiquid and too risky for such a sale further expanded and strengthened the institutionalization of a private intermediary space for cross-border transactions operating partly outside the interstate system. The new intermediaries did the strategic work, exhibiting a kind of "activism" toward ensuring growth in their industry and overcoming the potentially devastating effects of financial crises on the industry and on the goal of integrated global financial markets.

These developments raise a question about the condition of international public law. Do the new private systems for governance and accountability and the acceptance by many states, even if under great pressure, of policies that further the agendas of powerful global economic actors indicate a decline of international public law and the capacity for democratic governance to which individual nation-states aspire?

CONCLUSION

The theoretical-political question running through this essay focuses on which actors gain the legitimacy to govern the global economy and emerge as legitimate claimants to take over the rules and authorities hitherto residing in the nation-state and hence subject, in principle, to citizens' approval. More specifically, the concern was to understand in what ways global economic actors, such as markets and firms, have not only amassed the raw power of their orders of magnitude that can overwhelm the richest states in the world, but have also established policy channels that have made it possible to institute measures within nation-states that further their interests. In the spirit of theoretical provocation aimed at destabilizing somewhat rigid conceptions about the institution of citizenship, I posit that global economic actors have now gained "rights" that allow them to make governments accountable to the operational logic of the global capital market. This outcome signals the emergence of a type of "economic citizenship" that becomes an entitlement of global firms and markets rather than that of citizens. This is an ironic twist on the notion of economic citizenship which concerned individuals' right to a job, to work for a living, and to economic survival. And it is a deeply troubling turn in the longer history of the institution of citizenship. It has the effect of blurring the edges of the institution of citizenship as we have come to construct and represent it, and signals the possibility of a relocation of particular authorities we have associated with individual citizens to strategic institutional domains of the increasingly globalized economy.

The specific development focused on in this essay is part of a larger dynamic that contains countervailing tendencies which also emerge from the conditions produced by economic globalization. The territorial and institutional transformation of state power and authority associated with economic globalization has produced an operational, conceptual, and rhetorical opening for actors other than nation-states to emerge as legitimate in international and global arenas. These actors include not only the global firms and markets focused on here, but also institutional actors such as NGOs, the international human rights regime, first-nation people's initiatives to get direct representation in international fora, particular types of feminist struggles, the global environmental agenda, and the struggle for global labor justice.

NOTES

This essay is based on my research on "Governance and Accountability in the Global Economy." Portions have been published in my book *Losing Control? Sovereignty in an Age of Globalization* (1996). I thank Columbia University Press and the Schoff Fund for its support.

1. *See, e.g.*, the new scholarship on the erosion of citizenship as an institution embedded in nation-states, notably the work by David Jacobson, *Rights across Borders: Immigration and the Decline of Citizenship* (1996); Yasmin Soysal, *Limits of Citizenship* (1994); Rodolfo D. Torres, Jonathan Xavier Inda, and Louis F. Miron, *Race, Identity, and Citizenship* (1999).

2. Elsewhere I have noted that social changes in the role of the nation-state, the globalization of political issues, and the relationship between dominant and subordinate groups have major implications for questions of membership and personal identity. Saskia Sassen, *Guests and Aliens* (1999). Others have called for a critical examination of the limits of nation-based citizenship as a concept for exploring the problems of belonging in the modern world. *See, e.g.*, Soysal, *supra* note 1; Jacobson, *supra* note 1.

3. There is a whole other bundle of issues that is part of the larger inquiry on the issue of citizenship and rights that I cannot focus on here. It has to do with my thesis that we are seeing processes of incipient denationalization within state institutions. *See* Saskia Sassen, *Losing Control? Sovereignty in an Age of Globalization* ch. 1 (1996). This would mean that the institution of citizenship, even if situated in institutional settings that are "national," may have changed if the meaning of the national itself has changed. One empirical question, then, is whether the bundle of transformations we associate with globalization that has changed certain features of the territorial and institutional organization of the political power and authority of the state, may entail changes in the institution of citizenship—its formal rights, its practices, its psychological dimension. I juxtapose this notion with those of postnational citizenship which is centered on locations outside the nation-state and cosmopolitan citizenship. For the transformation of citizenship as it intersects with transformations in the authority of the state, *see* Thomas M. Franck, *The Emerging Right to Democratic Governance*, 86 Am. J. Int'l L. 46 (1992).

4. For a discussion and summary presentation of the evidence on the growing earnings inequality in all the major developed economies, *see* Saskia Sassen, *The Global City: New York, London, Tokyo* chs. 8-9 (2000).

5. Elsewhere I have examined other instantiations of this dynamic, especially as it involves immigrants and human rights. The impact of globalization on sovereignty has also been significant in creating operational and conceptual openings for actors other than the global firms and markets that are the focus of this chapter. NGOs, first-nation people, and agendas centered in the human rights regime are all increasingly emerging as subjects of international law which can make claims on nation-states. For various treatments of this bundle of issues, *see e.g.*, Rodney Bruce Hall, *National Collective Identity* (1999); *Free Markets, Open Societies, Closed Borders?: Trends in International Migration and Immigration Policy in the Americas* (Max Castro ed. 2000).

6. For extensive evidence on the issues discussed in this section, refer to Sassen, *supra* note 4, at chs. 3–4, 7. For a different perspective on some of the issues concerning global finance, *see also* Barry Eichengreen and Albert Fishlow, *Contending with Capital Flows* (1996); Geoffrey Garrett, *Global Markets and National Politics: Collision Course or Virtuous Circle*, 52 Int'l Org. 787–824 (1998).

7. For instance, figures show that countries with high savings have high domestic investment. Most savings are still invested in the domestic economy. Only 10 percent of the assets of the world's five hundred largest institutional portfolios are invested in foreign assets. Some argue that a more integrated capital market would raise this level significantly and hence raise a country's vulnerability to and dependence on that capital market. It should be noted that extrapolating the potential for growth from the current level of 10 percent is somewhat dubious; it may not reflect the potential for capital mobility across borders

of a variety of other factors which may be keeping managers from using the option of cross-border investments. This may well be an underused option and it may remain that way no matter what the actual cross-border capacities of the system.

8. It is estimated that the value of securitization could reach well over U.S.$10 trillion in the Eurozone. In Japan, deregulation is expected to free up about U.S.$13 trillion in fairly immobile and highly regulated assets such as postal savings accounts.

9. It is well known that while currency and interest-rate derivatives did not exist until the early 1980s and represent two of the major innovations of the current period, derivatives on commodities, so-called futures, existed in some version in earlier periods. Amsterdam's stock exchange in the seventeenth century—when it was the financial capital of the world—was based almost entirely on trading in commodity futures.

10. I have explored how the basic features of digital networks—instantaneous transmission, interconnectivity, and speed—produce distributed power in the case of the Internet, or "public-access" digital space, and produce concentrated power in the case of private digital networks such as those in wholesale finance. See Digital Networks and State Authority, paper prepared for the Bi-National Expert Group Jointly Sponsored by the National Academy of Sciences (USA) and the Max Planck Institute for International Law (Germany). A revised copy of this paper was published in Special Issue on Sovereignty, Theory, Culture, Society (Summer 2000).

11. We now also know that the particular organizational structure of savings and loans associations made possible unusually high levels of fraud and that this—rather than the interest rate ceilings, as is often suggested—was a major factor contributing to their financial crisis. We also know from historians on the subject that the possibilities for fraud have long been high in these types of organizations.

12. Sassen, supra note 4.

13. The argument can be and is often made that financial markets are the result of multiple decisions by multiple investors, and therefore have a certain democratic quality. Yet a key condition for participation is ownership of capital, which in itself is likely to produce a particular set of interests and to exclude a vast majority of a country's citizens. Further, small investors, including many households in the case of the United States, typically operate through institutional investors whose interests may not always coincide with those of the small investors. The overall effect is to leave the vast majority of a country's people without any say.

14. See, e.g., Giovanni Arrighi, The Long Twentieth Century: Money, Power, and the Origins of Our Times (1994).

15. The global capital market consists of a variety of specialized financial

markets. These markets discipline governments in a somewhat erratic way even under the premises of market operation: they fail to react to an obvious imbalance for a long time and then suddenly punish the government in question with a vengeance, as was the case with the Mexico crisis, for example. The speculative character of so many markets means that they will stretch the profit-making opportunities for as long as possible, no matter what the underlying damage to the national economy might be. Investors threw money into Mexico even though its current account deficit was growing fast and reached an enormous 8 percent of GDP in 1994. Notwithstanding recognition by critical sectors in both the United States and Mexico that the peso needed gradual devaluation, nothing was done. The rest is history. A sudden sharp devaluation, with the subsequent sharp departure of investors, threw the economy in disarray. The nationality of the investors is quite secondary; an International Monetary Fund (IMF) report says it was Mexican investors who first dumped the peso. Gradual action could probably have avoided some of the costs and reversals. Even in late 1994 many Wall Street analysts and traders were still urging investment in Mexico. It was not until February 1995 that foreign investors began getting out in hordes, that is, selling their Mexican equities. It all started with an excessive inflow, and concluded with an excessive outflow.

16. *See* the work by David Kennedy, including "Some Reflections on 'The Role of Sovereignty in the New International Order,'" in *State Sovereignty: The Challenge of a Changing World: New Approaches and Thinking on International Law* 237 (1992).

17. I am here using work developed for another type of context to the case of the global capital market and multinational firms. In its original formulation, Duncan Kennedy argued that the ground rules in the case of the United States contain rules of permission that strengthen the power of employers over workers, or that allow for a level of concentration of wealth under the aegis of the protection of property rights that is not necessary in order to ensure that protection. *See* Duncan Kennedy, "The Stakes of Law, or Hale and Foucault," in *Sexy Dressing Etc.: Essays on the Power and Politics of Cultural Identity* 83 (1993).

18. For questions on the national state, the global system, and the opportunities for the former to be more active and effective participants in the latter, *see* Alfred C. Aman, Jr., *The Globalizing State: A Future-Oriented Perspective on the Public/Private Distinction, Federalism, and Democracy*, 31 Vanderbilt J. Trans'l L. 769 (1998).

19. The question for research becomes, What is actually "national" in some of the institutional components of states linked to the implementation and regulation of economic globalization? The hypothesis here would be that some components of national institutions, even though formally national, are not national in the sense in which we have constructed the meaning of that term over the last hundred years. Sassen, *supra* note 4. For an in-depth discussion of some

of these issues, *see* R. B. J. Walker, *Inside/Outside: International Relations as Political Theory* (1993).

20. Brian Portnoy, *Constructing Competition: The Political Foundations of Alliance Capitalism*, Ph.D. dissertation, Department of Political Science, University of Chicago (1999).

21. In positing this I am rejecting the prevalent notion in much of the literature on globalization that the realms of the national and the global are two mutually exclusive zones. My argument is rather that globalization is partly endogenous to the national and is in this regard produced through a dynamic of denationalizing what had been constructed as the national. And it is partly embedded in the national, for example, global cities, and in this regard requires that the state reregulate specific aspects of its role in the national.

22. There is a whole other dynamic at work as well that results from certain features of globalization. The ascendance of a large variety of nonstate actors in the international arena signals the expansion of an international civil society. It represents a space where other actors can gain visibility as individuals and as collective actors, and come out of the invisibility of aggregate membership in a nation-state exclusively represented by the sovereign. *See, e.g.*, Franck, *supra* note 3.

23. The U.S.$40 billion emergency loan package from the IMF and the U.S. government and the hiring of Wall Street's top firms to refurbish its image and find ways to bring it back into the market helped Mexico "solve" its financial crisis. With J. P. Morgan as its financial adviser, the Mexican government worked with Goldman Sachs and Chemical Bank to come up with several innovative deals. Goldman organized a U.S.$1.75 billion Mexican sovereign deal in which the firm was able to persuade investors in May 1996 to swap Mexican Brady bonds (Mexican Bradys were a component of almost any emerging market portfolio until the 1994 crisis) collateralized with U.S. Treasury bonds for a thirty-year naked Mexican risk. This is in my reading quite a testimonial to the aggressive innovations that characterize the financial markets and to the importance of a whole new subculture in international finance that facilitates the circulation, that is, sale, of these instruments.

8

The Recognition of the Individual

A Human Rights Perspective for International Commerce

Claire Moore Dickerson

COMMERCE IS A form of dialogue. In international commerce, this dialogue constructs a loose community with its own common language. Intuitively, this has to be correct: how else has cross-cultural commerce flourished since before the Phoenicians put to sea? The result is a legal and practical forum within which recognized participants in international commercial transactions develop applicable norms that govern their interactions.[1]

As with all dialogues, however, not all the relevant parties are necessarily invited to participate, and not all the participants are equally persuasive. Powerful participants in the international commercial dialogue such as supranational organizations and multinational enterprises (MNEs) steeped in the norms of the developed world shape a dialogue that champions their own Northern norms. For example, when the International Monetary Fund (IMF) seeks to help South Korea strengthen its economy, it calls for mass layoffs to achieve its goal, without considering the impact of unemployment in that particular location.[2] Similarly, a major MNE responds to consumer complaints about its foreign suppliers' use of child labor and triggers mass dismissals of child workers. These actions are taken without considering the impact on the individual child workers, whose families need the income and will have to resort to even more dangerous and abusive employment.[3] At best, these behaviors evidence indifference to harm to the individual, which in turn leads to human rights abuses. This illustrates a basic concept of social influence: the organizations' practice of tolerating harm becomes the indifference norm that is institutionalized in international commerce—even where the norm includes human rights violations. Once institutionalized, even individuals in developing countries who took no part in the crafting of the rules feel the impact of the powerful organizations' indifference norm.

This is moral imperialism: human rights violations flow from the powerful organizations' worldwide imposition of their own Northern conceptual framework. To be sure, the most concrete example of moral imperialism is the conquering army that imposes its culture on the vanquished. Typically, the existence of such an army assumes a conquering nation-state complete with some form of traditional government. The model I suggest is not necessarily as intentional, and is based on commerce instead of arms, but its power is just as effective. However, it is not enough to describe a wrong; my goal is also to propose a solution.

Because international commerce's destructive norm is woven into the fabric of prevailing legal traditions and commercial practice, it will be hard to reverse. Nevertheless, a concerted effort can reverse the existing norm that ignores individual harm and thus permits human rights violations. In order to structure this reversal, we first must understand the conceptual underpinnings and practical reality of the existing norm: the values inherent in the North's existing, dominant theoretical framework that the supranational organizations and MNEs have imposed on individuals in the developing world. The second major task is to consider the structures within the international commercial community that can be expanded to support and stabilize a new norm that attenuates harm to individuals and respects human rights. The essential function of the expanded structures will be to promote dialogue not just between the currently active participants in the international commercial community, but also between the most vulnerable and the most powerful members of that community.

THE CONCEPTUAL NEOCLASSICAL AND SOCIOLOGICAL FRAMEWORK: INDIVIDUAL HARM AND HUMAN RIGHTS VIOLATIONS

Since the 1980s, the dominant conceptual underpinning for the Northern commercial norm has been the law and economics school, joined more recently by a sociological perspective. Neither framework is value-neutral. The law and economics perspective has adopted a cramped, neoclassical interpretation of Adam Smith's "invisible hand"[4] that ignores harm to the individual. The more recent discourse of social influence[5] also ultimately ignores harm to the individual. Although they start from very different points, both the law and economics and the sociological perspectives unabashedly focus any concern about harm on the societal, not the individual level. The two dominant frameworks for analysis perceive those affected by commerce as a vast, undifferentiated mass. This focus tolerates human rights violations by both quasi-public and private international organizations.

The law and economics tradition took its major theme from one aspect of neoclassical economics. The starting point is that individuals in society behave in accordance with their own self-interest. The end point is that the aggregated self-interested behavior of all participants in society will result in a benefit to society.[6] What is a benefit to the individual is defined by the individual.

To the neoclassical lawyer-economist the individual reveals preferences by exchanging value in order to achieve the desired result. A person contracts for, and pays for, an object, or even an opportunity to work in decent conditions. The payment can be either in the form of cash or a good in barter; clearly, it can be in the form of labor. If enough individuals pay for a safe workplace, society's work environments will be clean and decent. Thus, the persons who would otherwise have engaged in abusive employment practices will have been paid to provide those clean and decent work conditions. The lawyer-economist concludes that all individuals, and thus all society, will have benefited.

Conversely, if a person behaves opportunistically, that is, abuses another person's relative vulnerability in a deceptive and wholly self-regarding manner,[7] the exchange between the two parties does not, and cannot, reveal true preferences. The lawyer-economist complains that the opportunistic person has benefited at the expense of another, and therefore society has been harmed. After all, a person who acts opportunistically may acquire a good or service that another person values more, leading to an inefficient result that effects a misallocation that in turn is a cost to society. The focus is not on the harm to the vulnerable individual who accepted the transaction with the opportunist; rather, the focus is on harm to society. Thus, the lawyer-economist starts with benefit to the individual, proceeds to societal benefit by aggregating individual benefits, and concludes with harm to society from private actors' inefficient actions. What is missing is concern for harm to the individual.

More recently, sociology has begun to challenge the influence of economics on legal thought. The purpose of the sociological perspective is to consider the context in which people interrelate. Consequently, context—including the parties' relative power as they transact business—is central to the sociologist as distinguished from the lawyer-economist.

Sociology's point of departure is a broad overview of society as a whole. Thus, for example, sociology has considered the importance of division of labor to the evolution of modern society.[8] The focus is not on any particular individual, but rather on the synergistic changes in relationships that result from specialization. A sociological analysis of even the highly individualistic nature of U.S. culture still does not zero in on the individual but rather on the resulting harm to, and disintegration of, the social fabric.[9]

The sociologist's point of departure is society, not the individual, and thus he or she is immediately concerned with benefit to society rather than to the individual. Any consideration of harm is also at the societal level. Thus, for the sociologist as for the lawyer-economist, what is lost in the shuffle is an interest in and appreciation for harm to the individual.

The rhetoric of human rights discourse helps contextualize this discussion, but for these purposes it is useful to divide the rights into three generations: first, or civil and political; second, or social and economic; and third, or collective or cultural.

The law and economics perspective, with its celebration of the individual as the source of benefit to society, espouses a "first-generation"[10] human rights analysis. The government is urged not to interfere with civil and political rights, such as its citizens' freedom of expression, although the more libertarian law and economics perspective would be suspicious of any government intervention and would even protect workers' freedom to form a union. Because second-generation rights presume a need for government protection of social and economic rights, they are conceptually inconsistent with the neoclassical law and economics perspectives focus on benefit derived by the individual from private contracts.

In contrast, the sociological perspective focuses on the benefits and harm to society, rather than to the individual; an emphasis more consistent with the so-called "second-generation" human rights that focus on social and economic issues, such as the right to basic education and healthcare. Because of concerns about market failure, these rights are best protected through affirmative government—societal—actions, rather than by reliance on individual acts. However, the risk inherent in this sociological perspective is that the attempted cure at the societal level can create significant harm to individuals. Mass dismissals of workers as a by-product of attempts to correct social ills is an example of this phenomenon.

Thus, the protection of first- and second-generation rights stumbles on the law and economics and the sociological perspectives' studied ignorance of harm to individuals. What is missing, moreover, is support for the "third-generation" human rights—for transborder, collective rights such as the preservation of cultures and prohibitions against forced migrations, and even the right to peace. The law and economics perspective is unsuited because of its focus on benefits to the individual: harm to society is a by-product of private parties' failure to negotiate according to their preferences. The sociological perspective provides better underpinnings because its focus on society is essentially a sensibility of the collective. However, the final step in the analysis of even the third-generation rights is an acknowledgment of individual human misery. The right may be collective, but it is one specific individual at a time who is forcibly relocated, just as it is one person at a time who cannot speak freely or is not educated. Neither the law and economics nor the sociological perspective adopts this focus.

THE REALITY: INDIVIDUAL HARM AND HUMAN RIGHTS ABUSES BY QUASI-PUBLIC AND PRIVATE ORGANIZATIONS

The conceptual underpinnings of both the law and economics and the sociological approaches inform existing practical efforts to structure transnational commercial transactions which, in reality, also ignore both harm to the individual and human rights abuses. The players in the international commercial community, those who dominate international commercial transactions, are the quasi-public supranational organizations and the private MNEs. The former include international financial institutions such as the IMF and the World Bank, and organizations whose focus has been more on operational aspects of commerce such as the World Trade Organization (WTO) and even the International Labor Organization (ILO). The MNEs include companies such as Nike.

The MNEs and supranational organizations other than the ILO are fundamentally grounded in the law and economics perspective. They address first-generation rights and, in a more limited and clumsy fashion, second-generation rights as well. Even the ILO, although more sociological in its perspective and increasingly adept at considering first- and second-generation rights, fails to emphasize third-generation rights. None of these organizations recognizes harm to the individual.

The original purposes of the IMF and World Bank were very different. After World War II, the victorious countries formed the IMF for the purpose of avoiding the monetary instability that some believed had been a contributing cause of the war. Monetary stability in turn would spur the growth of trade. The purpose of the World Bank, in contrast, was to provide loans for the postwar reconstruction and development of its nation-members; that is why it is officially the "International Bank for Reconstruction and Development." Since their formation, however, the focus of these two organizations has converged on lending for the purpose of development. Interestingly, this new purpose draws them into the murky waters of conditionality, and conditionality has resulted in harm to the individual.

In its simplest form, conditionality means that the quasi-public supranational organizations provide benefits desired by the developing nations only if the latter abide by certain conditions. Thus, if the developing nations are to receive technical advice and loan assistance from the IMF, they must engage in structural reforms that the IMF asserts will lead to a sustained balance of payments equilibrium, including reforms that improve the efficiency and quality of capital investments.[11] Similarly, the borrower must address reform requests prior to receiving a World Bank loan.[12]

These reforms demanded by the IMF and the World Bank fall in the neoliberal law and economics mold. That is to say, the IMF and World

Bank propose reforms based on the theory that an appropriate structure—that in reality is in a Western or Northern model—will affect the behavior of individuals as they pursue their self-interest. For example, these supranational organizations insist on specific interest rates and on the devaluation of currency that in turn will affect the country's imports and exports. A higher interest rate will attract capital; a devalued currency will encourage exports. Thus, the economists from the supranational organizations are influencing decisions that have a profound impact on people living in the same region as the loan recipients. And these economists exert their influence by dealing with the economists of the host country, not with its political leaders,[13] let alone with the individuals ultimately affected. The influential economists—even those within the developing country—are far removed from the political process; these individuals thus have no voice.

Individuals are harmed in the process. While the international financial institutions assert their support for first-generation rights within the borrower countries, these institutions fail to support such rights in their own interaction with those countries. Conditionality means that the host country's economic elite, together with the international financial institution, dictates what that country's policies will be. In order to satisfy the IMF's vision of economic equilibrium, for example, unemployment in South Korea rose dramatically in 1998 despite a lack of social or economic safety nets.[14] The top-down imposition of those policies by supranational organizations that focus on finance reflect both the neoclassical economic insensitivity to individual harm evinced by the lawyer-economists and the resulting insensitivity to human rights abuses.

That same perspective also dominates other highly influential supranational organizations, including those that focus more on trade. The WTO, whose purpose is to liberalize trade, that is, to reduce trade barriers between and among nations, takes the neoclassical route too, but for different ends. The elimination of trade barriers allows the entire trading world to benefit from the concept of comparative advantage; each member country will focus on the product or service that it is relatively most efficient at producing. The first head of the WTO predicted in 1994 that by 2005 the world economy would enjoy an aggregate annual income gain of U.S.$510 billion due to efficiencies attributable to the WTO.[15]

Five years later, the WTO's critics complained that, as the organization continues to focus on the elimination of barriers, it fails to consider the impact on the people in developing nations. For example, the WTO could identify developing countries' low labor standards as a form of forbidden subsidy: from a manufacturer's perspective, allowing low standards is similar to a government subsidizing better working conditions. If low standards are a prohibited subsidy, the WTO permits the affected developed countries to retaliate by erecting barriers against goods from the developing country. The developing countries will then no longer be able to benefit from the competitive advantage inherent in low wages.[16] The developed countries insist that some labor standards are consistent with the trade liberalization that raises all boats; the developing countries retort that, instead, labor standards are protectionist barriers imposed for the benefit of developed-country trade.

This discussion is contentious and will have a profound impact on individuals in developing countries. Nevertheless, the WTO's constitutive documents do not address labor standards directly. It is a discussion that occurs amidst accusations that the WTO derives its support from business elites within each member country and thus is profoundly undemocratic and, consequently, opposes first-generation rights. Further, although there is provision for some preferential treatment of developing countries, the WTO's general insensitivity to the effects of high labor standards demanded by developed countries is arguably an indifference to second-generation rights. Since the developed countries are economically more powerful, they will inflict disproportionate harm on the developing country and all its residents. It is not clear whether the WTO will ultimately deem low standards to be a subsidy, but we do know that any action by the WTO to reduce developing countries' competitiveness also reduces their ability to preserve and enhance their economy, and thus their ability to protect their citizens. Especially if the developing country has a relatively democratic political system, to limit that country's autonomy is insensitive not only to the infliction of harm, but also to the harmed individual.[17] The WTO, operating at the national level, is at best unconscious of its impact on individuals.

The major supranational organization in this arena of commercial transactions, and the one that is the least thoroughly captured by the neoclassical model, is the ILO. Of all the quasi-public organizations mentioned up to this point, the ILO's structure is unique: its decision-making body is not composed entirely of government representatives. Instead, the ILO has a tripartite configuration: members are nations, but their representatives are chosen by three different interest groups, namely, employers, labor, and the government. The ILO has consciously and strategically sought to consider the impact on the host nations of the agreements it sponsors. The ILO's relatively sociological perspective reflects a sensitivity both to first-generation rights, in particular the right to free association, and to second-generation rights such as education. However, champions of human rights have criticized even the ILO as lagging behind certain national efforts in the protection of workers, specifically of indigenous workers—the individuals on the ground.[18] This also underscores the fact that third-generation rights relating to cultures, for example, are still not a focus.

Not unlike the quasi-public supranational organizations, MNEs can also inflict harm on individuals. Critics of MNEs have targeted Nike, alleging that it causes workers in developing countries to be underpaid relative to the United States, and that it then sells the resulting products in the United States and other developed countries as expensive luxury items. They further argue that Nike, therefore, is abusing those workers. It has been violating first-generation rights by seeking to avoid free association into unions, and second-generation rights by not assisting the workers to obtain healthcare and education. Third-generation rights are not even mentioned.

Pressure to reduce these violations has come from many different sources: from consumer groups, from the U.S. government where the president has "jawboned" leaders in the garment industry to generate standards through an industry organization, and from supranational organizations such as the ILO. In response to this combined pressure, including consumer demand for attention to working conditions even overseas, MNEs have sought to come to an understanding with those exerting the pressure, and have begun to adopt codes of conduct for themselves and their foreign suppliers. Unfortunately, the MNEs' ostensibly corrective efforts have, in practice, also inflicted devastating harm to individuals. The consequences of these efforts have included mass dismissals of suppliers' workers located in developing countries—persons with no legitimate alternative source of income.[19] That the MNEs harm individuals is, again, entirely consistent with the neoclassical perspective. It is true that some of the harm may be inadvertent, and some MNEs have begun to address second-generation rights such as education. Nevertheless, in the main the MNEs' perspective reflects a general lack of readiness to focus on helping workers enjoy their first- and second-generation rights.

Thus, except for the ILO, both the quasi-public and the private organizations all apply a neoclassical analysis. The ILO's perspective is more sociological. In each case, these organizations fail to focus on harm to the individual. That is the norm to which each of these organizations adheres, and which they reinforce by their adherence. This norm reflects moral imperialism: it imposes its values by lionizing the transaction-parties' exchange even at the expense of affected bystanders, or by focusing only on the impersonal, societal level. While there is varying but generally weak attention to first- and second-generation rights, there is minimal attention to third-generation human rights. If the injured collective at the center of third-generation rights was large enough to approximate the whole of society, perhaps at least the sociological perspective would recognize the harm that the collective suffers. Instead, the collective is considered to be more like an individual than a full society, and neither perspective focuses on injury to the collective.

AVOIDING HARM TO THE INDIVIDUAL: THE IMPORTANCE OF THE LOCAL

The challenge is to reverse the norm and to recognize harm to the individual. The task admittedly will be difficult: the existing norm is honored in many varied international commercial settings and has a well-established theoretical justification, although it does facilitate human rights abuses.

The current system supports the existing norm. For example, critics of the IMF, World Bank, and WTO accuse these organizations of not recognizing the effects they have on individuals. Similarly, the MNEs adopt codes of conduct, such as codes against child labor that when imposed on suppliers result in the mass firing of child workers.[20] The MNEs do not appreciate in time what those affected could have explained. Thus, it is critical that a corrective system drive these organizations to engage the individuals who may be harmed in dialogue, consciously and with intention.

In order to design a system to attenuate harm, it is not sufficient, for two reasons, simply to speak of human rights violations as harm. First, it is possible to have harm that is not a human rights violation. Second, although a human rights violation would indeed reflect harm, it is possible to have the same act viewed as a human rights abuse by the developing country but not by the developed country—or vice versa. Thus, one approach to this question of defining "harm" is to ask whose definition should rule.

The definition of harm invokes the classic universalism-relativism debate. If there are values, such as certain human rights, that are universal, the quasi-public supranational organizations and private MNEs can claim that their neoclassical values are universal. Or perhaps no values are universal: they vary from culture to culture, and it is meaningless to qualify some values as better than others. For example, perhaps no children should work. Or perhaps children must be allowed to work because their families will starve without their income.

It is famously difficult to parse this universalism-relativism debate and the failure to do so will have consequences. The quasi-public and private organizations have not negotiated in a meaningful way with the affected individuals; thus the neoclassical perspective cannot seriously suggest that an ostensible agreement between those organizations and individuals is a true exchange that reflects the latters' preferences.[21] Nevertheless, if these organizations decide that their values are universal, they will simply apply them. The universalist perspective is well-suited to organizations powerful enough to act unilaterally. The other end of the spectrum, relativism, creates its own dangers. Relativism can paralyze: if no culture can judge the values of another, there is no appropriate action for these organizations to take.

This is where the point of perspective may offer a solution. We already know that the quasi-public or private organization can articulate its perspective. If we consult the affected individual to ascertain what that person considers to be harm, to be a violation of human rights, we will open the other half of the dialogue. By this dialogue, we will take the first step in attenuating the moral imperialism of the North. We will create an environment designed to minimize devastating consequences that have in the past resulted not only from an indifference to human rights, but also from an insensitive, neoclassical attempt to support the first-generation rights of free expression and free association and second-generation social and economic rights. This same environment would also intentionally enhance cultural norms.

STRUCTURE AND THE INDIVIDUAL'S VOICE AS SUPPORT FOR THE NONHARM NORM AND HUMAN RIGHTS

How do we open this dialogue? Each individual does have a voice; however, each organization, public and private, must also hear that voice. The powerful must learn to hear the voice of the vulnerable. One way to achieve this result is to see people differently, that is, to see them as agents of and active participants in democracy, not merely as its passive recipients. The quasi-public and private organizations would no longer impose their norm unilaterally. Instead, they would engage in a dialogue with those who are affected.

One way to change perspective is to impose a structure that reorients the hegemonic point of view. That is the most aggressive method of norm-entrepreneurship. In the context of labor abuse, the WTO, World Bank, and IMF seem unsuited to the role because, structurally and functionally, they respond directly to governments, not to workers. To be sure, these three supranational organizations and their affiliates can have direct and indirect impact on private enterprise. For example, national governments bring disputes growing out of private enterprise before the WTO; affiliates of the World Bank do lend to private entities; banks do piggyback on IMF loans. However, the direct focus of these organizations is not on individuals: their approach is heavily dependent on neoclassical theory, and thus their support of even first-generation rights is unreliable.

On the other hand, the ILO's tripartite governance structure makes it relatively responsive to workers; the structure institutionally supports the ILO's articulated purpose of protecting workers' rights.[22] Indeed, the constitutive documentation of the ILO expressly recognizes that freedom from want will exist only when representatives of workers and employers engage in free discussion and democratic decision making with representatives of governments.[23] However, the ILO's sociological perspective does not instinctively focus on individuals, and even its tripartite structure does not adequately correct this failing. Indeed, a basic criticism of the ILO has been that its worker-representatives are labor organizations, which definitionally do not support unorganized workers—and most workers in developing countries are unorganized.

In order to protect the rights of individual workers more effectively, the ILO has been one of the early proponents of nongovernmental organizations (NGOs) as interpreters for the individuals on the ground, organized or not. This formulation permits the enhancement of all rights, including even the third-generation rights' championing of indigenous culture. However, the ILO recognizes that the strategy is only as good as the relevant NGOs, and their quality is uneven. Some NGOs have insufficient funds and staffing for a given task. Further, this weakness is even more salient because NGOs are essentially self-selected and the ILO does not formally investigate or certify a person or group who offers assistance, although the ILO can decide whether to credit the information.

The ILO structure deserves to be more fully realized and formalized in order to consider the impact on workers most effectively. A structure that magnifies the voice of the vulnerable worker can help impose a discipline on the MNEs that have, until recently, been driven to draft and implement codes only by their neoclassical sense of self-interest. The ILO's promulgation of conventions and the adjustment of its structure to include NGOs affects the MNEs. Specifically, it influences MNEs to behave as though they were moving toward the more sociological perspective of the ILO, as the ILO itself shifts its attention to the magnification of the individual worker's voice. That is, the ILO will be helping to shift the MNEs' norms toward a behavior that, at least ostensibly, consciously seeks to take into account harm to the individual. In its turn, this shift will help emphasize all generations of human rights.

This analysis also applies to the other quasi-public organizations such as the IMF, World Bank, and WTO. The structures of these organizations should increasingly mandate that they elicit voices that have been silenced. The organizations should be required to listen before imposing conditions that purport to stabilize an economy by requiring higher interest rates, or before defining impermissible subsidies to include non-Western labor standards. Despite the caveats noted above about NGOs, the efforts of the World Bank and more recently of the IMF to include NGOs may be a first step toward reconfiguring the quasi-public organizations' structures. In time, the norm may change so that the structures will no longer be necessary to support the no-harm behavior. The new norm favorable to human rights would then be in place. However, until that time the structures would attenuate the North's moral imperialism by supporting respect for the affected individuals.

CONCLUSION

Dialogue is necessary to commerce; arguably commerce is itself a form of dialogue. However, it is a dialogue that can operate between equals without concern for those outside the direct conversation, or it can occur despite a fundamental inequality of power. Thus, quasi-public organizations tolerate the violation of the rights of workers in developing countries, and MNEs of developed countries reflexively violate those rights. In neither case do any of these organizations focus on the impact of their acts or omissions on the persons affected by their behavior.

The solution is to construct a structure or series of structures that encourage a true dialogue, whereby all these organizations are forced to listen. Most of the established quasi-public supranational organizations, such as the IMF, World Bank, or WTO are not geared to such listening. The ILO, with its tripartite governance scheme and its early and persistent support of NGOs, provides a good starting point for a system that encourages listening. This influence can also be brought to bear on MNEs.

The challenge is to develop a structure that undermines moral imperialism by protecting the individual—by protecting human rights. Such a structure would work to modify the existing destructive norm of the international commercial community by forcing the quasi-public and private organizations to discuss their policies with those they affect. To this end, the structure would support first- and second-generation rights such as freedom of association and a right to education, and would be designed to explore respect for third-generation collective rights.

NOTES

1. *See* Harold J. Berman, *The Law of International Commercial Transactions (Lex Mercatoria)*, 2 J. Int'l Disp. Resol. 235–237, 243 (1988).

2. Mark Weisbrot, *Globalization for Whom?* 31 Cornell Int'l L.J. 647 (1998).

3. U.S. Department of Labor, Bureau of International Labor Affairs, *The Apparel Industry and Codes of Conduct: A Solution to the International Child Labor Problem?* (last modified on Oct. 1996), <http://dol.gov/ilab/public/media/reports/iclp/apparel/1c.htm> at 7.

4. Adam Smith, *An Inquiry into the Nature and Causes of the Wealth of Nations* 423 (1937).

5. John C. Turner, *Social Influence* 3, 35 (1991).

6. Richard A. Posner, *Economic Analysis of Law* 23 (4th ed. 1992).

7. Oliver E. Williamson, *The Economic Institutions of Capitalism: Firms, Markets, Relational Contracting* 47 (1985).

8. Emile Durkheim, *Division of Labor in Society* 68–87 (W. D. Hall trans. 1984).

9. Robert N. Bellah et al., *Habits of the Heart* 27–51 (1985).

10. For a discussion of all three generations of human rights, *see* Berta Esperanza Hernández-Truyol, *Women's Rights as Human Rights—Rules, Realities and the Role of Culture: A Formula for Reform*, 21 Brooklyn J. Int'l L. 622, n.53 (1996).

11. Erik Denters, *Law and Policy of IMF Conditionality* 127–28 (1996).

12. John D. Ciorciari, *A Prospective Enlargement of the Roles of the Bretton Woods Financial Institutions in International Peace Operations*, 22 Fordham Int'l L.J. 341 (1998).

13. Anne Orford, *Locating the International: Military and Monetary Interventions after the Cold War*, 38 Harv. L. Rev. 468 (1997).

14. Wiesbrot, *supra* note 2, at 646.

15. Paul Lewis, *Top International Trade Official Urges U.S. to Approve Accord*, N.Y. Times, Nov. 22, 1994, at A20.

16. Frances Lee Ansley, *Rethinking Law in Globalization Labor Markets*, 1 U. Pa. J. Lab. and Employment L. 411 (1998).

17. Amartya Sen, *Development as Freedom* 151 (1999).

18. *Final Report on the Study on Treaties, Agreements and Other Constructive Arrangements between States and Indigenous Populations*, UN ESCOR, Hum. Rts. Comm., 51st Sess., Prov. Agenda Item 7, UN Doc. E/CN.4/Sub.2/1999/20 (1999) at ¶¶ 47–48.

19. U.S. Department of Labor, *supra* note 3, at 7.

20. *Id.*

21. Richard S. Markovits, *Duncan's Do Nots: Cost-Benefit Analysis and the Determination of Legal Entitlements*, 36 Stanford L. Rev. 1176–77, 1194 (1984).

22. Declaration of Philadelphia, Art. I(d), incorporated into the ILO Constitution by the latter document's Art. 1(1).

23. *Id.*

9

Rerouting the Race to the Bottom?

Transnational Corporations, Labor Practice Codes of Conduct, and Workers' Right to Organize— The Case of Nike, Inc.

Tim Connor

In this industry, the only reason to change is because someone has got a great cattle prod that keeps jabbing you in the rear end. . . .
—Bud Konheim, President of U.S. apparel
firm Nicole Miller[1]

UNTIL APRIL 2000 the founder and CEO of Nike, Inc., Philip Knight, enjoyed a close relationship with the University of Oregon. The university had named its library after him and another building after his father. For his part he had donated more than U.S.$50 million to the school and was expected to give a further U.S.$30 million to expand the campus sports stadium. The relationship deteriorated sharply on April 14 when Knight learned that his alma mater had decided to join the Workers' Rights Consortium (WRC), an organization established by student activists and unions to monitor factory conditions in the production of collegiate licensed apparel by Nike and other companies. Knight announced that "the bonds of trust, which allowed me to give at a high level, have been shredded" and that he would be making "no further donations of any kind" to the university. He criticized the WRC as a misguided attempt "to bring apparel jobs back to the U.S." Instead he praised the Fair Labor Association (FLA), another monitoring organization established by a coalition of corporations (including Nike)

166

and human, consumer, and labor rights groups.[2] In the same month Nike cancelled planned sponsorships with Brown and Michigan universities, two other campuses that had joined the WRC. Not only were the company's actions condemned by the student activists who supported the WRC and publicly criticized by the noncorporate groups involved in the FLA, but they also sparked vigorous debate in the press.

The Nike episode is a small indicator of the intensity of the debate over labor practice codes of conduct. Such codes have arisen in response to the concerns of a growing international antisweatshop network of unions and consumer, student, and activist groups. These groups commonly argue that the globalization of the world economy is forcing the governments of countries with few other comparative advantages to engage in a "race to the bottom" in which they compete for investment by suppressing workers' human rights, particularly their rights to organize and bargain collectively. Some groups involved in this movement are seeking to enhance workers' power to respond to the mobility of transnational corporations by seeking to build transnational alliances between unions. These initiatives are in turn often frustrated by the suppression of workers' right to organize at the local level.

It has become "something of an orthodoxy" to describe the power relationship between workers involved in the global competition for low-skilled manufacturing jobs and the transnational corporations in the market for their labor in terms of the "race to the bottom" thesis.[3] Critics note that labor costs are never the sole factor influencing investment decisions and in many cases they make a very limited contribution to explaining the geography of production. In many industries "Just in Time" management techniques make proximity to markets significantly more important than labor costs in determining where production occurs.[4] Nonetheless, where production is labor intensive and demand is predictable, the mobility of capital exercises a powerful constraint on workers' ability to assert their rights. Such production is increasingly taking place in low-income countries, often in especially created Export Processing Zones (EPZs), in which the suppression of workers' rights in order to attract investment is usually particularly vigorous.

Since the mid-nineties a number of economic geographers have explored ways in which workers might develop international alliances to effectively challenge the mobility and power of capital. One scholar rejects the representation of transnational corporations (TNCs) as monolithic, all-powerful organizations and depicts them instead as sites of conflict and instability in which decisions regarding resource allocation can be influenced by a variety of forces, including worker solidarity.[5] Others consider the growth of internationalism amongst unions as a potential means of responding to the mobility of TNCs and criticize the literature for failing to recognize the role workers play in shaping the geography of international investment.[6] Similar ideas are being promoted within the field of labor studies and within the union movement itself.[7]

Not surprisingly, most studies of transnational organizing have been of industries in which production is relatively capital intensive. In labor-intensive industries, such as apparel, in which production is relatively mobile, it is very difficult for workers to build unions at the factory level, let alone engage in transnational solidarity. One writer considers the broader internationalism of the antisweatshop movement which involves workers, human rights groups, consumer and shareholder groups, and other civil society organizations working together in campaigns for the protection of workers' rights. She documents an extensive six-year consumer and shareholder campaign by U.S. labor rights groups which persuaded the Phillips Van Heusen company to recognize a union at the Camisas Modernas factory, making it the only factory in Guatemala's apparel-for-export sector with a collective bargaining agreement.[8] However, using campaign pressure alone to persuade companies to recognize particular unions in particular factories is a haphazard and piecemeal means of promoting labor standards, and represents a considerable drain on activist resources for limited and often temporary benefits. Less than two years after the collective agreement was signed at Camisas Modernas, Phillips Van Heusen closed the factory, claiming that it was a business decision necessitated by the loss of a key shirt customer.

In light of the various perspectives on globalization and labor, this essay considers the potential of codes of conduct which engage civil society groups to advance the protection of union rights. This work is a case study of the three codes that most strongly intersect with the debate on Nike's labor practices: Nike's own code, the FLA's code, and the WRC's. While only a minority of companies has adopted such codes, and even fewer have monitoring systems in place to ensure adherence, corporations like Nike are finding that a growing global civil society movement is in no mood to allow credibility with regard to labor rights and other social issues to be easily bought. Equally, activists are encountering strong resistance to the independent and rigorous monitoring of corporate labor practices.

THE GROWTH IN LABOR PRACTICE CODES

Codes of conduct offer the promise of corporations agreeing to put their own resources into protecting labor standards in exchange for greater credibility with consumers. Codes are regulatory instruments, voluntarily established by nonstate actors. As private arrangements, a company is not subject to state sanctions if it breaches a code. Although various attempts to codify sets of labor and other standards for TNCs have been made since the middle of the twentieth century, the latest wave of interest in labor practice codes began in the early 1990s in response to antisweatshop campaigns and has grown with the antisweatshop movement.

Codes can be broadly categorized in terms of the actors involved, with those codes which are most influenced by human rights and labor groups tending both to be more rigorous in the demands they make of companies and to have greater difficulty in attracting corporate involvement. The most common codes, however, are those developed by companies themselves or by industry associations. These tend to be the least credible, particularly in the area of union rights. In a survey of 121 company codes collected by the Investor Responsibility Research Center, it was found that only 18 made any reference to the right of freedom of association, and only 12 referred to the right to organize and bargain collectively.[9]

The codes developed by unions and nongovernment organizations (NGOs) are far more credible but are struggling to obtain corporate cooperation. In some cases unions and human rights groups have persuaded city councils, universities, sporting associations, and other institutions to include codes in their buying or licensing policies. While this has so far proved the most successful means of promoting these codes, Nike's response to the WRC is indicative of the strength of the industry reaction against these requirements. In the face of this reaction, institutions have not always been willing to demand credible monitoring of adherence to their codes. Finally, a handful of codes have been (or are in the process of being) negotiated between companies, NGOs, and/or unions. In some cases these codes have been initiated or are supported by national governments, as is the case with the Fair Labor Association in the United States and the Ethical Trading Initiative in the United Kingdom. The credibility of these codes is questionable, but they have managed to achieve a degree of corporate cooperation.

CODES VERSUS LAWS?

Even writers who see potential in regulatory mechanisms negotiated by nonstate actors recognize the considerable dangers inherent in this approach.[10] Such negotiations are not outside or above capitalism, but rather represent "another area where the dilemmas, contradictions and antagonisms of capitalism," including its dependence on the "market-mediated exploitation of wage labor," are expressed.[11] Considerable power differentials exist between the representatives of corporations and those of workers, and there may be a need for state intervention to provide material and symbolic support to the workers or to adapt legislated regulatory regimes in order to enhance workers' bargaining power at the negotiating table. Crises of legitimacy can also arise owing to the problematic relationship between NGOs or unions involved in negotiating codes and those workers whose interests and identities they are supposed to represent. This is particularly the case where unions and NGOs from industrialized nations seek to negotiate on behalf of workers from industrializing countries.[12]

Other theorists see codes and other nonstate regulatory initiatives as poor alternatives to state regulation. Critics of codes argue that labor standards, human rights, and environmental concerns are public rather than private matters and that nonstate initiatives are ill-equipped to protect them.[13] They note that a plethora of inconsistent voluntary initiatives is confusing for consumers, that the percentage of TNCs who participate in voluntary codes is small, and that the percentage willing to subject their participation to independent verification is even smaller.[14] The most common form of verification is that of "auditing," a practice that has been criticized for functioning as a substitute for democracy, transforming public accountability into an "expert" activity the processes and results of which are commonly concealed on the grounds of "commercial confidentiality."

The growth in codes of conduct need not, however, undermine the development of legislative measures. If a sufficient number of TNCs can be persuaded to abide by credible codes, corporate opposition to state regulation may be undermined and divided. Arguably if TNCs are united in their opposition to greater legal regulation of their international activities, the substantial resources they can devote to lobbying and public relations campaigns makes legal reform unlikely in any event. If campaign pressure can induce some TNCs to be part of code initiatives which effectively promote workers' rights, then the opposition of those particular companies to legal regulation might be diminished. They may even come to see it as being in their interest that other TNCs are legally required to keep to the same standards to which they "voluntarily" subscribe. Alternatively, failure to establish effective codes may increase the demand for more public responses to the issues, and lessons learned from these experiments might be applied to state initiatives which themselves are far from immune to regulatory failure. Activists in the United States and Europe involved in pushing companies to adopt more effective codes are also promoting legislative and parliamentary proposals geared to achieving the same ends. Given the small proportion of transnational corporations willing to submit their production to jointly negotiated codes, in the long term it is likely that the contribution of codes to promoting labor standards will depend on their role in the development of legislated responses to the issues.

NIKE AND CODES

A. The Nike Campaign

Most of the corporations that have agreed to multistakeholder codes have been those targeted by antisweatshop campaigns. Of these, Nike has been subject to the most intense public pressure. The international campaign to persuade Nike to improve its labor policies was initiated in the late 1980s by the then coordinator of the AFL-CIO's solidarity office in Jakarta (Jeff Ballinger) and a small group of Indonesian NGOs. Over the course of the 1990s the campaign grew to become one of the key drivers of the international antisweatshop movement. As of July 2000 a loose international network of some forty organizations has worked on the campaign and is in regular contact via a confidential e-mail list to discuss the campaign's progress and future direction.

Representatives of unions from North America, Europe, South Korea, and Australia work together with labor rights NGOs, development organizations, and religious and student groups from Asia, Australia, Europe, Latin America, and North America.

Although difficult to measure, indications are that the campaign has had significant success in raising awareness of the issue amongst consumers in the key markets of North America and Europe. Mainstream media interest in the issue has been considerable, and interest expressed via e-mail and the Internet is strong and growing. More than three hundred thousand people have signed petitions or campaign postcards to Nike, calling on the company to allow independent monitoring of its factories. During 1997 and 1998 there were three "international days of action," with the most successful involving demonstrations in ninety-five cities in twelve countries. In a May 1998 speech to the U.S. National Press Club, Nike's CEO Phil Knight acknowledged that "the Nike product has become synonymous with slave wages, forced overtime and arbitrary abuse."[15]

B. Nike's Code and Monitoring System

Initially Nike argued that it could not be held responsible for labor abuses because it contracted out all its production.[16] By June 2000 the company was claiming to have "the industry's most elaborate system of internal and external monitoring."[17] In 1992 Nike established a labor practices code which, at that stage, made no mention of union rights and left it up to suppliers themselves to report on code compliance. Nike did claim that there was at least one member of its own staff in every factory whose responsibilities included checking that the code was being observed.

However, monitoring by Nike's own staff did little to alleviate public criticism. Thus, in 1994 the company moved to employ the auditing firm Ernst and Young—replaced in 1998 by PriceWaterhouseCoopers (PWC)—to monitor each factory on an annual basis. In 1997 the process of monitoring by Nike's own staff was formalized into what the company calls SHAPE audits, which are conducted by a staff person in each factory on a quarterly basis.[18] In a small proportion of Nike contract factories, workers are interviewed by researchers from local universities or local research organizations. But to the extent that Nike and the groups involved have been willing to make their methodology public, these programs do not appear to investigate whether workers' union rights are protected.[19]

C. The Fair Labor Association

In August 1996 the then U.S. Secretary of Labor, Robert Reich, convinced a number of U.S. apparel and footwear companies, trade unions, and NGOs to form the White House Apparel Industry Partnership (AIP or Partnership), an organization whose mission was to negotiate a code to promote humane working conditions in the United States and overseas. In April 1997 the Partnership agreed to a Workplace Code of Conduct and the companies still involved became the initial signatories. The code included rights to freedom of association and collective bargaining and Nike adjusted its own code to include these rights. The Partnership also agreed on some principles of monitoring, but it took until November 1998, an additional eighteen months of "difficult" negotiations,[20] before a subgroup of the Partnership comprised of four of the companies (Liz Claiborne, Nike, Patagonia, and Reebok International) and four of the human rights groups (the International Labor Rights Fund, the Lawyers Committee for Human Rights, the Robert F. Kennedy Memorial Centre for Human Rights, and the National Consumers League) negotiated a preliminary agreement on a charter document for the Fair Labor Association (FLA) to oversee monitoring of the code. The religious and union groups involved in the AIP rejected the proposed monitoring system as too weak and pulled out of the process.

Efforts to recruit more companies have had some success and participation by U.S. universities has also increased FLA's membership. Beginning in 1997 a remarkably popular student movement across the United States successfully used sit-ins, "knit-ins," and demonstrations to pressure many university administrations to agree to relatively strong policies regarding the production of goods that carry university logos. Nike, which has many millions of dollars tied up in university contracts, responded by calling on universities to join the FLA. This call was remarkably successful and by March 2000, one hundred thirty-five U.S. universities had joined. The FLA has also responded to criticism about the lack of representation by Asian, Latin American, and African workers by establishing an NGO representative council, which includes labor rights groups and unions from Cambodia, Guatemala, Indonesia, Malaysia, Pakistan, and Taiwan.[21]

D. The Workers' Rights Consortium

The WRC was formed by the main U.S. student antisweatshop group, United Students against Sweatshops (USAS) in cooperation with U.S. unions, academics, and other groups with whom they work. USAS rejects the FLA on account of its lack of transparency, its failure to protect workers' right to a living wage, the lack of independence of the FLA monitoring system, and the small percentage of factories that will be independently monitored each year. The student group has been campaigning to persuade university administrators to leave the FLA and join the WRC. As of April 2000 when the WRC held its founding conference forty-four schools had joined and by the following month the number had grown to fifty-one. The WRC has also established an advisory council, with significant representation by trade unionists and labor rights activists from Asia, Latin America, and Africa.[22]

CODES AND WORKERS' RIGHT TO ORGANIZE

What are the relative merits of these three codes in protecting workers' right to freedom of association? The relevant issues can be broadly grouped into three categories: the nature and extent of the rights which each code purports to protect; the systems put in place to verify the effectiveness of that protection; and the grievance procedures made available to workers if they believe their rights are being infringed.

A. Rights Protected

Only a minority of corporate codes of conduct refer to international labor standards and many differ from or contradict international labor law.[23] The AIP code and (since 1997) Nike's own code require that employers recognize and respect workers' rights to freedom of association and collective bargaining. The FLA "Benchmarks and Guidance" document indicates that these rights will be interpreted in light of the relevant International Labor Organization (ILO) jurisprudence. The WRC code is also phrased in language that is in line with ILO conventions.

A key concern of activists and workers is that companies might respond to industrial collective action by moving production from unionized to nonunionized factories. Nike has a strong policy stance on this issue. In a September 1998 interview, Nike's Director of Labor Practices insisted that the company would never move production away from a factory because its workers were taking collective action, arguing that other factors are much more significant in determining where to locate production.[24] However, the company has failed to respond to allegations by its critics that it ceased ordering from particular factories in Thailand and Indonesia following industrial collective action. Both the FLA and the WRC regard moving production from unionized factories to nonunion locations as noncompliance with their codes.

The challenge lies in determining whether worker activism was the cause of the drop in orders. Such a determination is likely to be easy when there has been a direct threat that unionization will lead to loss of production but extremely difficult in other cases, particularly in the apparel industry, where ordering relationships are in any case often highly unstable. The task would be made easier by requiring companies to report, regularly and publicly, the level of orders they have made to each of their suppliers. Such an approach would at least give workers, unions, or NGOs evidence to argue to the monitoring body and to the public that the company may be punishing factories which are the sites of union activity. At this stage neither the FLA nor the WRC requires full disclosure of orders either publicly or confidentially to the monitoring body.

A related danger is that companies may use a supplier's failure to comply with code requirements on union rights as a justification for ending the business relationship and moving production to a factory where workers are not trying to organize. Workers' knowledge that reporting problems at their factory may result in a loss of orders and jobs may create a "perverse incentive" not to report.[25] It is not yet clear what process the FLA will require companies to follow before ending relationships with contractors who fail to comply with the code. During the AIP negotiations, representatives from the clothing union (UNITE) pushed for the code to specify that in such situations companies may only drop a contractor as a last resort, but the companies resisted this.[26] The WRC code explicitly prohibits companies from "cutting and running" when labor abuses are discovered, but again, proving motivation for relocation is a challenge.[27]

A considerable proportion of Nike's apparel and footwear (and that of other companies in the industry) is produced in countries or industrial zones where the right to organize is circumscribed by law,[28] effectively undermining the union rights of Nike workers in those jurisdictions and in others which are in competition with them for investment. Where it is illegal to organize, Nike claims it seeks to establish "parallel means of workers expressing views and concerns to management and means by which grievances can be addressed . . . [including] worker-management committees [and] worker-management periodic open meetings." But the company has declined to indicate either in which factories these committees are operating or whether workers' representatives on these committees are elected by the workers themselves.[29] According to students sent by Nike to observe its monitoring program, PWC monitors do not ask workers about their union rights if contract factories are located in Export Processing Zones where organizing is illegal.[30]

The question of what is expected of factories located in areas where it is illegal to organize has been a highly contentious issue within the AIP and FLA and is yet to be clearly resolved. Leaks to the press revealed that the labor and human rights groups in the AIP initially called on the companies to withdraw production from China because it restricted union rights, but the companies refused to do so.[31] In an October 1998 interview one of the UNITE representatives who at that stage was still involved in AIP negotiations, argued that in such cases companies should either breach laws preventing the right to organize or leave the country.[32]

The FLA charter document (released in November 1998) acknowledges that in some countries implementing the AIP code is "problematic" but it maintains that companies still have an obligation to "tak[e] steps to ensure that employees have the ability to exercise these rights without fear of discrimination or punishment." What steps are required, and what is expected of companies if governments intervene to prevent workers from exercising these rights, remains unclear. For certain countries the FLA will issue "special country guidelines" for participating companies which should help clarify what is expected, although the relevant decision-making process ensures that companies on the FLA board will have considerable power to veto country guidelines which they regard as unacceptable.[33]

The WRC code also confirms that monitored companies should seek full compliance with the code even where there is a conflict with local law or practice, and prohibits cooperation with state authorities in the suppression of workers' right to organize. It goes further than the FLA in requiring that licensing agreements not be renewed in countries where it is deemed impossible to meet the code's standards or where progress toward the implementation of those standards is not being made.[34]

B. How Is Each Code Monitored?

As the monitoring programs to be overseen by the FLA and the WRC are yet to be implemented, it is appropriate to defer a thorough examination of them until empirical evidence becomes available. But some comment on the design of each is possible.

The aspect of the FLA program most conducive to protecting workers' union rights is the apt and detailed methodology required of external monitors; the weaknesses relate to the way those monitors are selected, the lack of full transparency in their reporting, and the length of time between external monitoring visits. Participating companies select "independent external" monitors from a pool of monitors accredited by the FLA. One critic argues that such an arrangement renders monitors "neither independent nor external," because "third-party agents, operating for profit and paid by the MNCs they are charged with monitoring, are subject to . . . vested interest problems." Researchers have recognized that in an ideal system "independent" monitors would not be selected and paid by the companies whose performance they are monitoring, but have argued that if companies were not willing to accept such a system, then one in which monitors were accredited and overseen by a group like the FLA (which includes significant representation of human rights groups) would be an acceptable and workable compromise.[35] While the FLA's accreditation requirements for independent monitors and its monitoring benchmark and guidance document are relatively stringent, there are still grounds for concern that companies wary of having to deal with a unionized workforce may act in bad faith and seek to employ independent monitors who have the skills to pass the accreditation procedures but are not motivated to investigate rigorously whether workers' union rights are being protected. Because the FLA will not conduct any factory investigations on its own and will not make the addresses of factories monitored public, it will be difficult for independent researchers to verify how rigorously an FLA-accredited monitor has performed an audit. Hence if an investigation has been poorly conducted, it will only become apparent to FLA staff if the paperwork appears unacceptable or else a local group makes a formal complaint to the FLA about the factory.

Perhaps a more significant limitation is the infrequency of monitoring visits under the FLA's external monitoring program. Up to 15 percent of a participating company's suppliers may be "de minimis" facilities which are exempt from monitoring altogether.[36] Only 10 percent of the remaining facilities must be externally monitored each year[37] and the participating company has some influence over which factories are likely to be monitored. If a factory has successfully passed an external monitoring audit recently, the owner can be reasonably confident that the facility will not be subject to independent external monitoring again for something in the order of ten years.

The WRC is a more recent phenomenon than the FLA and so less has been finalized. Its primary focus is not on monitoring but rather on working with local unions and nongovernment organizations to inform workers of the existence and content of the WRC code, establishing grievance procedures that are accessible to workers, and investigating any complaints that workers make. The organization has a strong commitment to transparency. Thus, companies will be required to release not only the addresses of each factory, contractor, and subcontractor but also all objective measures of working conditions covered by the code.[38] There is a danger that the WRC's focus on working with local NGOs and unions might encourage companies to move production to countries like China where independent organizations are illegal, but this needs to be weighed against the requirement that production be withdrawn from countries where it is deemed impossible to meet the WRC code standards.

CONCLUSION

A 2000 opinion piece on Nike's response to the WRC entitled "Knight Is Right" criticized the WRC's connections with "protectionist" U.S. unions who wanted to "trash multinationals." The piece praised the FLA for demonstrating that the "best way to create global governance . . . when there is no global government is to build coalitions, in which enlightened companies, consumers and social activists work together to forge their own rules and enforcement mechanisms."[39] This article demonstrates the considerable dangers when "third way" theories of governance are translated simplistically in public policy debate (and in public policy itself). Detailed analysis of the codes which most strongly intersect with the debate on Nike's labor practices indicates that labor codes and monitoring systems negotiated between corporations and civil society actors are not desirable per se, but rather reflect the particular context in which they are developed and the relative negotiating power of each of the parties involved.

The FLA monitoring program represents an important advance in the individual self-regulatory efforts of companies like Nike, but its ability to adequately protect workers' right to organize will be undermined by the reluctance of the companies involved to withdraw investment from a country if protecting workers' union rights there proves impossible, by the questionable independence of the monitors it will supervise from the corporations they are monitoring, and by the limited proportion of participating companies' factories which will be independently monitored each year. No serious analysis of the WRC's approach could conclude that it is protectionist. The Consortium's focus on working with local labor rights groups to ensure that workers are aware of their rights and are able to access reliable and independent complaint mechanisms if those rights are infringed has considerable potential to assist those workers in exercising their union rights.

It will be a challenge for those student activists, unionists, and university administrators who support the WRC to ensure that the strength of corporate opposition does not derail the process altogether. Only a small minority of TNCs are currently participating in jointly negotiated voluntary monitoring initiatives like that of the FLA, and even fewer have subjected their production to activist codes that are independent of corporate influence like the WRC's. Whether these developments form part of a process toward effective international regulation of labor standards depends substantially on whether the international antisweatshop movement, which has utilized new information technology to build broad international alliances between unions and other civil society organizations, is able to maintain its momentum and build the capacity to significantly influence policy decisions on a global scale.

NOTES

This essay draws on audiotaped research interviews with key individuals involved in the development of labor practices codes of conduct. I conducted these interviews in North America, Europe, and Asia between September and December 1998.

1. *The Sweatshop Quandary: Corporate Responsibility on the Global Frontier* 11 (P. Varley ed. 1998).

2. These quotations are taken from Knight's statement on his company's website. *See* P. H. Knight, *Statement from Nike Founder and CEO Philip H. Knight regarding the University of Oregon* (last visited June 19, 2000), <http://www .nikebiz.com/labor/>.

3. Wills characterizes Tilly, Hobsbawm, Beynon, and Hudson; Storper and Walker; and Burawoy and Korten as examples of writers who take this view. J. Wills, *Taking on the CosmoCorps? Experiments in Transnational Labor Organization*, 74 Econ. Geography 111 (1998).

4. E. Schoenberger, *The Cultural Crisis of the Firm* 63–75 (1997).

5. J. K. Gibson-Graham, *The End of Capitalism (as We Knew It): A Feminist Critique of Political Economy* (1996).

6. A. Herod, *The Practice of International Labor Solidarity and the Geography of the Global Economy*, 71 Econ. Geography 341 (1995).

7. A. Breitenfellner, *Global Unionism: A Potential Player*, 13 Int'l Labor Rev. 531 (1997).

8. R. Johns, *Bridging the Gap between Class and Space: U.S. Worker Solidarity with Guatemala*, 74 Econ. Geography 252 (1998).

9. *See The Sweatshop Quandary, supra* note 1, at 423.

10. B. Jessop, *The Rise of Governance and the Risks of Failure: The Case of Economic Development*, 155 Int'l Soc. Sci. J. 29, 37 (1998).

11. *Id.* at 39.

12. *Id.*

13. R. J. Liubicic, *Corporate Codes of Conduct and Product Labeling Schemes: The Limits and Possibilities of Promoting International Labor Rights through Private Initiatives*, 30 L. and Pol'y Int'l Bus. 111 (1998).

14. P. Utting, *Business Responsibility for Social Development* (2000); J. Diller, *A Social Conscience in the Global Marketplace? Labor Dimensions of Codes of Conduct, Social Labelling and Investor Initiatives*, 138 Int'l Labor Rev. 99 (1999).

15. D. Lamb, *Job Opportunity or Exploitation? To Vietnam's Impoverished, a $65-a-Month Position at a Nike Factory Is a Prize*, L.A. Times, Apr. 18, 1999, at 1 (Record ed.).

16. J. Burns, *Hitting the Wall: Nike and International Labor Practices* 5 (Research Report, Harvard Business School 2000).

17. *See Nike in China* (last visited June 19, 2000), <http://www.nikebiz.com/media/n_nikeinchina.shtml>.

18. SHAPE stands for Safety, Health, Attitude of Management, People, and Environment. *See Labor Practices Timeline* (last visited July 10, 2000), <http://nikebiz.com/labor/time2.shtml>.

19. The Global Alliance for Workers and Communities is involved in an "assessment of worker/community needs" in twenty-one of Nike's more than six hundred suppliers. According to Kevin Quigley, director of Global Alliance, it will not be monitoring the protection of workers' right to organize. Interview with K. Quigley (June 1, 2000).

20. *See* P. J. Harvey, *Nike's Certification No Means Guaranteed*, Financial Times, Feb. 2, 1999, at 16.

21. In 1998 Women Working Worldwide (a small NGO based in the United Kingdom) conducted a research exercise involving consultation with women factory workers from Bangladesh, India, Sri Lanka, Pakistan, the Philippines, and Indonesia regarding their attitude to codes. The importance of workers being consulted during the development of codes emerged as a strong theme. A. Hale, *Women Workers and Codes of Conduct—Preliminary Research and Consultation Exercise* 3 (1998).

22. *Worker Rights Consortium Members and Endorsers as of May 10, 2000* (last visited June 8, 2000), <http://www.workersrights.org/ members.html>.

23. Diller, *supra* note 14.

24. Interview with D. Kidd, Nike's Director of Labor Practices (Sept. 29, 1998).

25. *See Worker Rights Consortium for the Enforcement of University Licensing Codes of Conduct* (last visited June 8, 2000), <http://www.workersrights.org/detailed_outline.doc>.

26. Interview with A. Hoffman, UNITE representative at AIP (Oct. 2, 1998).

27. The WRC code states that "when abusive conditions at a particular worksite are exposed to public view, the licensee company has an obligation to use its leverage to correct conditions—and not to 'cut and run' from that site." *Worker Rights*, *supra* note 25.

28. In China, where as of June 2000 Nike had ordering relationships with some fifty-nine factories, unions independent of the official government union are implicitly outlawed by Article 13 of the 1992 Trade Union Law, and the National Security Law allows workers to be detained and imprisoned or sent to forced labor camps for independent union activity. *See Nikebiz | labor | factory grid* (last visited June 6, 2000), <http://www.nikeBiz.com/labor/fact_grid.shtml>; *Annual Survey of Trade Union Rights* (last visited Jan. 20, 2000), <http://www2.icftu.org/displaydocument.asp?Index=990916876&Language=EN>.

29. *See* T. Connor, *Meeting and Subsequent Email Dialogue between Tim Connor of NikeWatch and Maria Eitel, Nike's Vice President of Corporate Responsibility*

(last visited July 1, 2000), <http://www.caa.org.au/campaigns/nike/email .html>. Interviews with workers from the WDI Supercap factory in China conducted by the Hong Kong Christian Industrial Committee in November 1999 indicated that in that factory the "workers' committee" is selected by management. A. Kwan, *Nike, Show Workers That Your Commitment to Human Rights Is Genuine* (last visited June 6, 2000), <http://www.cic.org.hk/ce_00feb.htm>.

30. S. Chakravarty, *Nike Student Monitoring Report, Bangladesh and Indonesia* (last visited Jan. 25, 2002), <http://www.nikebiz.com/labor/reports/stud9_1 .stml> at 9.

31. S. Greenhouse, *A New Approach to Eliminating Sweatshops*, N.Y. Times, Apr. 13, 1997.

32. "The companies should say to the workers—'The government says you don't have the right [to organize a union], as far as we are concerned you do. . . . [I]f you want to elect representatives we'll meet with them.' If the state takes action [against the union], the company should refuse to cooperate and should protest, publicly and loudly. . . . If all else fails the company should get out of there. A company gets certified or not certified on the basis of meeting the code. If you're operating in a country where it's impossible to meet the code, you should get out of there." Interview with A. Hoffman, UNITE representative at AIP (Oct. 2, 1998).

33. The adoption of special country guidelines is one of a number of FLA decisions which must be made by "super majority" vote. Such votes require the approval of at least two-thirds of all the industry members and at least two-thirds of all the Labor/NGO Members of the FLA Board. *FLA Charter Agreement* (amended June 1999) (last visited June 6, 2000), <http://www.fairlabor.org/ html/amendctr.html>.

34. *Worker Rights, supra* note 25.

35. Interview with P. Harvey, Executive Director of International Labor Rights Fund (Oct. 1, 1998); interview with J. Silk (Oct. 6, 2000).

36. De Minimis facilities are defined as factories in which the participating company operates for less than six months of a twenty-four-month period, or which produces less than 10 percent of the participating company's overall annual production. *See FLA Charter, supra* note 33.

37. This can be increased to 15 percent or reduced to 5 percent by the agreement of two-thirds of the NGO representatives and two-thirds of the corporate representatives on the FLA Board. *See id.*

38. Interview with M. Roeper, WRC coordinator (June 25, 2000).

39. T. L. Friedman, *Foreign Affairs: Knight Is Right*, N.Y. Times, June 20, 2000, at A25.

10

Both Work and Violence

Prostitution and Human Rights

Berta Esperanza Hernández-Truyol and Jane E. Larson

I. DOMINANT FRAMEWORKS

For more than a century the legal status of prostitution has been an un-
settled issue in nations throughout the world, and particularly in the
West. Before that time, in both common and civil law systems, prostitution was regarded as immoral but not consistently treated as a serious
offense against the law. Beginning in the late nineteenth century, however, the moral debate over prostitution shifted to the legal arena. All aspects of prostitution became the subject of legal reform in Western
countries, and that debate was carried from domestic politics to the
emerging arena of international law. This resulted in the adoption of the
international agreements and conventions aimed at eradicating the
cross-boundary trade in human sexual labor (known as trafficking) and
condemning prostitution as a practice akin to slavery. These international agreements rested upon at least a symbolic consensus that, according to the 1949 Convention for the Suppression of the Traffic in Persons, "prostitution and . . . traffic in persons for the purposes of prostitution are incompatible with the dignity and worth of the human
person."[1] In short, prostitution became a human rights violation to be
abolished.

After decades during which this abolitionist position prevailed, arguments for the tolerance or legitimation of adult, voluntary prostitution are newly alive in international fora, as well as within some national legal systems. Although the United Nations ratified abolitionist
language in the 1979 Convention on the Elimination of All Forms of

Discrimination against Women (CEDAW or Women's Convention), the body appears in recent years to be moving toward acceptance of a distinction between voluntary and forced prostitution, and hence a position that may tolerate some forms of prostitution and trafficking as acceptable by human rights standards. For example, notwithstanding CEDAW's abolitionist language and the 1949 Convention's position that all prostitution is compelled, the Platform for Action adopted at Beijing in 1995 condemns only forced prostitution. Similarly, the Declaration on Violence against Women approved by the United Nations in 1993 includes only "trafficking in women and forced prostitution."[2] The UN Special Rapporteur on Violence against Women observed in 1994, "Some women become prostitutes through 'rational choice,' others become prostitutes as a result of coercion, deception or economic enslavement."[3] This is quite a departure from the 1983 report of the UN Special Rapporteur on the Suppression of the Traffic in Persons and the Exploitation of the Prostitution of Others, which not only recognized all prostitution as inconsistent with human dignity, but expressly provided that "even when prostitution seems to have been chosen freely, it is actually the result of coercion."[4]

In the fight to retain the international commitment to abolish or, alternatively, to change course toward tolerance or legitimation of voluntary prostitution and trafficking, advocates seek to deploy human rights principles to these competing ends. The abolitionist position treats all prostitution as a human rights violation, specifically a form of slavery or an institutionalized practice of sexual violence and gender inequality. Abolitionists invoke the international conventions against trafficking in human beings and slavery, conventions for the protection of the rights of women and children, evolving standards concerning violence against women, and basic human rights instruments.[5] Although there is nothing in this position that necessarily opposes the amelioration of conditions in the sex trade, abolitionists have been wary of any compromise with prostitution or trafficking. Their position is that prostitution must be condemned uncompromisingly, like slavery or torture, and never equated with acceptable practices like work or with legitimating ideas like consent and choice. Legally and politically this translates into a refusal to distinguish consensual prostitution and voluntary immigration for sex work from forced prostitution and trafficking.

The opposing argument for tolerance or legitimation is that some prostitution and trafficking (adult, voluntary) is a free choice by an autonomous individual often made out of economic necessity. Respect for women's self-determination requires respect for female sexual choices. Advocates of this position invoke the human rights to work and to self-determination guaranteed by basic human rights instruments, as well as labor rights.[6] Advocates of this position also argue forcibly that prostitutes are harmed by limits on their freedom to market their resources, and urge that women be allowed to use their own bodies and labor to their greatest personal advantage, especially when they have few other economic opportunities and their need is great. This economic need argument grows more compelling in a globalizing economy as modernization, competition, structural reform, and international trading rules disrupt traditional household and social organizations, diminish government investment in social welfare, and drive down wages. This global context leaves many more women alone with children to support and with even fewer viable economic opportunities.

Advocates of this position may seek to legalize and fully legitimize prostitution as a job like any other, appropriately subjected to the labor protections offered all workers but to no other special rules, or simply seek to decriminalize and deregulate prostitution and allow political and economic forces outside the state to determine the status and meaning of sex work. Even some antitrafficking organizations adopt the distinction between voluntary and forced prostitution. The Global Alliance against Trafficking in Women (GAATW) demands that the international antitrafficking instruments distinguish between the traffic in persons and forced prostitution, which are "manifestations of violence against women . . . [and] a violation of the right to self determination," and "respect for the self determination of adult persons who are voluntarily engaged in prostitution."[7]

Thus, mutually exclusive frameworks for understanding prostitution—one that characterizes it as violence and one that treats it as work—dominate the current human rights debate. In this essay we argue that these seemingly irreconcilable positions can be negotiated in new ways that create common ground for law and policy. Accepting that prostitution can be a choice and a means for economic sustenance does not necessarily lead to the conclusion that the response must be legalization. To the contrary, if we look to the intersection of human and labor rights, we find moral frameworks and legal tools for resisting forms of work that harm the worker, that re-create colonial relationships, and that endanger the interests of labor as a political class. The crucial analytic move is our observation that sexual labor, like other forms of work, can be exploited. Arguing from such a perspective, we contend that prostitution is indeed chosen as a form of work in many instances, but it is an exploitative form of labor to be resisted and ultimately abolished. We urge the use of the international labor rights framework as the appropriate context within which to address prostitution and trafficking. This constitutes a significant reframing of the terms of the current debate.

This essay proposes to treat adult prostitution[8] as an exploitative form of labor analogous to sweatshop labor or child labor, and subject to the same legal and political pressures for abolishment. The development of this argument is connected with and strengthens growing political movements to address the conditions of child labor, indentured and bonded labor, and sweatshop labor. These exploitative forms of labor may conform to national law, but they bring home with force that some labor rights are human rights and should be enforced as such. Although the mechanisms within the human rights regime for the enforcement of labor rights are currently weaker than for civil and political rights, the recognition of labor as part of the fabric of fundamental rights represents the political as well as legal future of human rights. We contend that the problems of prostitution and the related issue of trafficking are important arenas within which such a synthesis needs to be developed.

II. CRITICAL PERSPECTIVES

In political debate, as the range of acceptable policy responses narrows, the converging policy orthodoxies begin to coalesce into dominant frameworks or "discourses" about the nature and meaning of the problem at hand. The dominant frameworks in the current debate on prostitution seek to give prostitution a single, unified, or "essential" meaning, whether as violence or work. These characterizations powerfully influence perceptions, allowing us to see some alternatives as viable while obscuring or discrediting others. Although the ongoing conflict between the violence and work frameworks means that there remains some imaginative space in this debate, the conflict has also shaped these discourses into mutually exclusive positions, concealing the partiality of each and denying the complexities of the social world each seeks to represent.

To create more room to think and to move in the debate, we undertake first to redescribe prostitution and trafficking as a set of social relations without preemptively "summing up" their nature and meaning. We begin, therefore, with a critical demography of prostitution. Prostitution is not an abstract exchange between undifferentiated and interchangeable individuals, but a relationship between social specifics implicating differences in power, status, and value. Prostitutes labor under different conditions, both in the prostitution enterprise and vis-à-vis their location in society. These social realities must be specified, identifying both the contradictions and variance of prostitution's meanings and experiences, and the broader commonalities that structure the practice. This demography reveals prostitution to be a social practice marked by an enduring division of roles based on gender, age, race, and ethnicity.

Having mapped out the players and their locations, we then consider these social relations through the light of critical feminist and race theories, analytic lenses that give meaning to gendered and raced relations. The picture that emerges is in some ways consistent and in some ways dissonant with the dominant violence and work discourses. Importantly, we conclude that prostitution is not an idea or an institution of an essential or singular character. It is a social practice that contains confounding elements of choice and coercion, autonomy and violence, freedom and oppression, opportunity and exploitation. As such, prostitution and trafficking can be *both* a choice of work and a danger to human dignity, suggesting that the effort to capture their complexity by either analogy fails.

A. A Critical Demography of Prostitution

The social relationship of prostitution today, and in the known past, consists to a marked degree of adult male patrons of adult females, and of male and female child prostitutes. Adult males dominate the profit centers of the trade in pimping and trafficking, and receive the surplus of pleasure created by the sexual exchange. In a minority of cases adult male homosexuals and transvestites provide sexual service, but this does not change the gender pattern; they too service male patrons and their role is often feminine.[9] Female patrons of male prostitutes are not unknown, but the rarity of the arrangement is its most notable characteristic.

Prostitution in the United States has marked racial and ethnic divisions. White men comprise most of the patron class and nonwhite women a disproportionate part of the workers.[10] Although in this country the majority of prostituted women are white, in the inner city the percentages of African Americans and Latinas increases to more than half. A study of New York City streetwalkers found that half were black, one quarter Latinas, and only one quarter white.[11] In addition, perhaps confirming historical patterns and cultural tropes that portray women of color as sexually accessible and desirable, zoning regulations usually permit sex businesses such as strip clubs and massage parlors in minority neighborhoods.

Prostitution is an exchange marked by other asymmetries of social power and status. Data from the United States indicate that sex workers, in addition to being mostly female and disproportionately of color, tend to be poor, young, uneducated, lacking economic stability, drug-and/or alcohol-dependent, survivors of sexual abuse, and at high risk for violent crime. As such, prostitutes are ripe for exploitation, degradation, and subjugation—locations that confirm their vulnerability and disempower them in dealing with the more powerful customer and business interests who profit from their labor.

In the United States females begin in prostitution young, at age sixteen years or younger, with some estimates of the average age of entry at fourteen years. One study of streetwalkers in San Francisco found that prostitutes' current ages typically ranged between fifteen and thirty years, with most being in the late teens or early twenties.[12] Early entry is also correlated with limited education; the same study found that streetwalkers had an average of a tenth- or eleventh-grade education.[13] Significantly, a majority of adult prostitutes (between 60 and 70 percent) were sexually abused as children.[14]

In the international arena both the concerns and the statistics are much the same. For example, the End Child Prostitution in Asian Tourism Organisation (ECPAT) estimates that some 1 million children are working as prostitutes in South and Southeast Asia.[15] Here too sex workers are similarly exposed to violence from customers, pimps, and boyfriends; the health risks are high; and the economic rewards are reaped mostly by the managers, pimps, or brothels and not by the workers themselves.

Although this is only a sketch, the demography suggests that any analysis of prostitution must deal with it as a social practice marked by an enduring division of roles based on gender, age, race, and ethnicity. In such structurally unequal exchanges, we might predict that relations of inequality are practiced and reinforced. To understand the social relationships that prostitution creates, we turn to feminist and critical race theories. Feminist theory asks about the impact and meaning of the practice of prostitution on women. We ask the woman question at both an individual and group level, analyzing the consequences of the practice on prostituted women in all their varied and various locations, as well as on the collective of women as a gender class. Our second analytical resource is critical race theory, in particular critical race feminism, which looks to the intersection of race, sex, and gender, and latcrit theory, which proposes the indivisibility of identity components for personhood.

B. The Woman Question

Different strands of feminism view prostitution differently, reflecting the fractured nature of the dominant violence versus work positions of the international debate. Radical feminists critique the objectification of women and the subordinate location of women in society, family, and state. This critique condemns prostitution as being part of and contributing to patriarchy, the pervasive male-female hierarchy found across cultures and throughout history. Sexuality is analyzed as one root of gender inequality as well as a practice of subjugation directed at women. Prostitution cannot be "just another job" from this perspective; rather, prostitution graphically exemplifies men's domination of women, expressing the traditional male prerogative of sexual access to, and power over, women's bodies. One commentator has said that "[p]rostitution isn't like anything else. Rather, everything else is like prostitution because it is the model for women's condition."[16] Scholars argue further that prostitution functions as a paradigm for degeneracy, identifying appropriate objects for contempt and punishment. By revealing the abased nature of woman, prostitution justifies her second-class citizenship. This judgment of degeneracy in turn supports other social inequalities beyond gender, such as class, disability, race, and sexuality.[17]

Although there is nothing in the radical feminist position that necessarily opposes law reform to ameliorate conditions in the sex industry, abolitionists have been wary of legalization or regulation because they believe the state must not legitimate or sustain prostitution in any way. Most often radical feminists advocate partial decriminalization of the prostitute's conduct and continued criminalization of patrons as well as those (other than the prostitute) who profit from the trade, such as the recruiter, the trafficker, the pimp, the brothel keeper, and the like.

"Prosex" feminists regard prostitution as a marker of sexual freedom; rather than subjugate women, prostitution liberates them. Identifying herself as a "Postporn Modernist," activist Annie Sprinkle, who went into prostitution because she needed money, says she "loved" her first job in a massage parlor, particularly having sex with johns she found repulsive.[18] She celebrates sex as "the nourishing, lifegiving force."[19] Sprinkle says she experienced "love" even in her brief sexual encounters with johns. Although she admits that some johns were disrespectful and abusive, Sprinkle maintains that "mostly [she] came out a winner," and blames herself (that is, the prostitute) for "any exploitation that occurred."[20]

A related position advocates for the rights of sex workers *as workers*, linking the legal treatment of prostitution to the regulation of women's economic positions and opportunities more broadly. Anne McClintock argues that some opposition to prostitution comes from the economic power it gives to women: "Society demonizes sex workers because they demand more money than women should, for services men expect for free."[21] Feminists who adopt the "sex work" perspective see prostitution as indistinguishable from other forms of labor in which the body is used, such as housecleaning, but as more profitable than other jobs available to poor women. Wendy Chapkis compares sex work to the category of "emotional labor," activities and jobs for which care and feeling are required, commodified, and commercialized, such as airline service work, acting, psychotherapy, massage, or childcare.[22] Martha Nussbaum claims that stigmatization is the only thing that meaningfully distinguishes prostitution from these other practices by which we lawfully sell bodily services for money.[23] If prostitution work is just another type of bodily labor, sex work feminists claim that the radical critique of prostitution is hypocritical: women lawfully sell their bodies for money in other trades, and women also "sell" sex in the context of lawful intimate relationships in which they receive things of value in exchange for sex.

Prosex and sex work feminists favor the decriminalization and deregulation of prostitution, as both have negative consequences for women; indeed, some argue that it is criminalization and regulation (and not prostitution) that "institutionalizes male domination and social control over women."[24] Some prostitutes' rights groups go further to endorse legalization, or removal of all laws penalizing women and youth in prostitution, as well as lifting criminal sanctions from all participants in the business, including pimps and patrons. Taking this position, COYOTE/the National Task Force on Prostitution and the International Committee for Prostitutes' Rights contend that prostitution must be fully legitimated in law, policy, and attitude.

Interestingly, both the feminist critics and the defenders of prostitution agree on one point: prostitution is one of women's best economic options. Radical feminist Catharine MacKinnon observes, "Aside from modeling (with which it has much in common) hooking is the only job for which women as a group are paid more than men."[25] Prosex feminist Anne McClintock similarly observes, "The sex worker cocks a snook at Johnson's famous edict that 'on the chastity of women all property in the world depends'—demanding, and generally getting, better money for her services than the average, male, white-collar worker."[26] Asking the woman question leads us to inquire why access to the sexual body is the most valuable resource a woman possesses, notwithstanding the other human capabilities and attributes she shares with men. Some argue that the explanation is women's unjust exclusion from other economic opportunities. But the disparity in value is absolute as well as relative: the disparity holds in nations and social strata where women enjoy substantially equal access to occupations and labor markets, and not only where women's employment options are deeply constrained by law or custom.

Thus the gendered demography of prostitution is revealed not to be incidental but constitutive. From a human rights perspective, where social location is determined significantly by sex and gender, the free choice of individuals is relevant but not determinative of the justice and dignity of that location. Critical feminist analysis shows the existence of a human rights issue which needs further exploration in light of the specific guarantees and values of the human rights system.

Beyond asking the woman question, we ask the race and ethnicity question. This is not a question that can be considered separately from the woman question. Moreover, it is a multidimensional question that takes into account related issues of class and nationality. The race and ethnicity question asks whether and how women and other members of minority groups are especially affected by the practices of prostitution and trafficking, and also how cultural ideologies about race, nationality, and ethnicity intersect with those about sex and gender in shaping the commercial sex industry, including its globalized labor market. For example, in the United States prostitution is both a racially integrated and a racially segregated arena of social relations: whites deal freely and regularly with nonwhites in the sex trade, but there is little exchange of roles; whites dominate the class of buyers and nonwhites are disproportionately represented in the class of sellers. Thus the race question not only asks about the consequences of prostitution on women of color in particular, but also about the sex of race.

History provides evidence of an enduring connection of race and ethnicity to prostitution. In the ancient world prostitutes were often slaves, foreigners, or both. So too in medieval Europe, prostitutes were often foreign women. Closer to home, there is a nexus between prostitution and race-based slavery in the United States by which white men claimed sexual rights to black female slaves; such women were not protected by the laws against rape, and status as property made the enslaved woman accessible to satisfy the sexual desires or needs of her masters or to increase his stock of slaves. The status of enslavement thus worked like the transfer of money in today's commodified prostitution, serving as a substitute for the woman's subjective consent to the sex. Patricia Hill Collins traces the sexualized and eroticized representations of African American women throughout U.S. history, linking these images, the display and sale of slaves at the auction block, and the current sexual objectification of African American women.[27] Within this history the nonwhite woman is positioned as sexually exotic and available; at the same time, she is a subordinate who may be treated in ways that privileged women need not accept. Hill Collins theorizes that the myth of the black prostitute is one justification for social control over black women and legitimizes rape and other forms of sexual violence directed against black women.[28]

This linkage of race and ethnicity to prostitution is not limited to the United States. In fact, even in the Netherlands, a society historically open to prostitution, the "local" trade has gone global. "From the estimated 20,000 prostitutes in Amsterdam, half of the windows used for prostitution . . . are rented out to non-European women."[29] The women being brought to the Netherlands to work as prostitutes are mainly from Southeast Asia, South America, and certain parts of Africa.[30] In such a global labor market, the question of nationality is a crucial determinant of a prostitute's vulnerability to abuse. Lack of identity papers, status as an undocumented migrant, and isolation from family, language, and culture mark out women trafficked across national borders as sexual labor for greater exploitation and harm.

Other historical realities also link prostitution and race in other parts of the world. For instance, it was the U.S. military's demand for sex entertainment as an outlet for its soldiers that created the sex industry in the areas around its military bases in Asia. Similarly, the Japanese military forcibly captured thousands of Korean women and forced them to serve as prostitutes to the Japanese troops during World War II. Today, a sex tourism industry thrives throughout Asia that brings men from developed countries, mostly Western, to countries where they can buy the sexual services of exotic others.

The racialization of the sex industry raises both woman and race questions that cannot be ignored in debating how prostitution and trafficking should be treated in the human rights construct. As with sex and gender, where social location is determined significantly by race and ethnicity, the free choice of individuals is relevant but not determinative of the justice and dignity of that location. Critical race analysis thus signals additional human rights issues to be further explored.

Together, these critical analyses reveal prostitution to be what Christine Overall terms "an inherent asymmetrical exchange," in which "the disadvantaged sell services to those who are more privileged."[31] Overall argues that the structural asymmetries of prostitution "provide the context [for] other forms of asymmetry, all of them with important implications for [prostitution's] moral assessment." We seek to assess the practices of prostitution and trafficking from within the moral and legal framework of the human rights regime.

III. THE RIGHT TO WORK VERSUS HUMAN RIGHTS: A FALSE DICHOTOMY

We have argued that the dominant frameworks of the current debate about prostitution are falsely polarized. One side maintains that the right to work and the right of self-determination include the right to sell access to one's body as a sexual servant for a limited period of time, the parallel of wage labor. The other side equates prostitution with slavery, a sale of one's self that denies humanness and strips one of dignity, affronting the foundational concerns, goals, and ideals of the human rights system. Our view is that this dichotomization closes off the analysis necessary to understand prostitution's social nature, each pole denying part of the meaning and experience of the practice.

In addition, we argue in the following section that these partial and polarized categorizations conflict with the human rights construct, which is built upon the interdependence and indivisibility of the multiple attributes and identities that make human beings proper subjects for dignified, respectful, and just treatment under international law principles. Specifically, to juxtapose a human right to work with the prohibition against slavery misunderstands the human rights system as it exists. To be sure, the right to work is a human right. But so too are workers endowed with human rights to resist work that endangers their dignity and humanity. We must therefore consider prostitution in a holistic manner, replacing an either-or approach with a both-and approach. Such a new paradigm is necessary because, as will be shown below, prostitution can be *both* a choice of work and a violation of human dignity.

A. The Human Rights Idea

International human rights are those predicates to life as human beings. They are fundamental, inviolable, interdependent, indivisible, and inalienable rights. Human rights are moral, social, religious, and political rights that concern the respect and dignity associated with personhood, with a human being's identity. Their foundation is the individual's status qua individual, and the dignity and justice owed based solely upon that status.

The origins of human rights are traced to religion, to natural law, and to contemporary moral values. This natural law basis protects "rights to which all human beings have been entitled since time immemorial and to which they will continue to be entitled as long as humanity survives."[32] These natural rights differ from positive rights in that they are inalienable; states can neither give them nor take them away. Although the concept of human rights is a historically modern one, it is universally applicable at least in principle.

World War II and the condemnation of Nazi atrocities are the watershed events for the change of the status of individuals in international law. But the identification of certain human rights as intrinsic to life as human beings occurred earlier. What we presently know as the human rights to life, liberty, and equality—rights pertinent to the prostitution debate, and particularly to the abolitionist claim that prostitution violates bodily integrity and dignity—were conceived in the last decades of the eighteenth century in conjunction with the rise of classical liberal political philosophies and the establishment of democratic forms of government. Throughout the nineteenth and early twentieth centuries, states entered into an increasing number of treaties with the purpose of protecting the rights of minority groups, that is, persons of a different race, religion, or language from the majority group within a state. In addition to these "minority treaties," other important developments were the treaties aimed at abolishing slavery and the slave trade.[33] Subsequent treaties further prohibited the trafficking of women and children.[34]

The real internationalization of individual rights, however, occurred after World War II. Following the signing of the UN Charter in 1945, international action concentrated on providing comprehensive protection for individuals against all forms of injustice regardless of whether the abuse or injustice was committed by a foreign sovereign or the individuals' own state of nationality.[35] The Universal Declaration, unanimously adopted on November 10, 1948,[36] is a comprehensive document addressing not only civil and political rights, but also economic, social, and cultural rights. Included in the Universal Declaration's protections of civil and political rights are the prohibition of slavery, inhuman treatment, arbitrary arrest, and arbitrary interference with privacy, as well as a broad, nondiscrimination provision that mandates equality on the grounds of race, color, sex, language, religion, political or other opinion, national or social origin, property, birth, or other status. Of the social, economic, and cultural rights, the Universal Declaration recognizes the rights to social security, full employment, fair working conditions, an adequate standard of living, education, and participation in the cultural life of the community.[37] Although debate about the legal status of the Universal Declaration is ongoing, many scholars consider it to have the status of *jus cogens*—norms from which no derogation is permitted.

A covenant to codify the protection of *all* the rights contained in the Universal Declaration was attempted and failed because of disagreements lodged by developed countries as to whether the social, economic, and cultural rights were as relevant or appropriate to the liberal conception of human rights as the civil and political rights of individuals. Western states maintained that social, economic, and cultural rights—those on which the prosex and sex work advocates rely for the claim of a right to choose sexual labor—were aspirational goals rather than "rights," as the attainment thereof was dependent upon economic resources, theory, and ideology. Consequently, Western states found it inappropriate to frame such rights as binding legal obligations. The different viewpoints resulted in the drafting of two documents—the ICCPR and the Economic Covenant—as opposed to only one covenant, to manifest the rights presented in the Declaration. Just as states are bound only by those treaties that they have ratified, unless particular norms contained in those treaties are binding as custom, the bifurcation of the covenants also imposed divergent obligations.

Based on this history of conflict among states, human rights generally are grouped into civil and political rights (the so-called first-generation rights) and social, economic, and cultural rights (the so-called second-generation rights). Yet the premise of the Universal Declaration is that all rights are indivisible and interdependent. Indeed, it is this indivisibility and interdependence of human rights—specifically the right to work and the rights to dignity and to bodily integrity—upon which we rely in rejecting the dichotomization of prostitution and trafficking as "either" an economic right "or" the violation of a civil right.

Significantly, first—and second—generation rights explicitly coexist in the Race Convention and the Women's Convention, instruments we consider essential to the human rights analysis of prostitution and trafficking. The Race Convention's definition of racial discrimination (and hence of race) is "any distinction, exclusion, restriction or preference based on race, colour, descent, or national or ethnic origin which has the effect of nullifying or impairing the recognition, enjoyment or exercise, on an equal footing, of human rights and fundamental freedoms in the political, economic, social, cultural or any other field of public life."[38] This definition assists us in asking the race question of prostitution by forcing consideration of whether the historical locations of women of color influence the practice.

Similarly, the Women's Convention, beyond expressly requiring states to "suppress all forms of traffic[king] in women and exploitation of prostitution of women," identifies sex discrimination as "any distinction, exclusion or restriction made on the basis of sex that has the effect or purpose of impairing or nullifying the recognition, enjoyment or exercise by women, irrespective of their marital status, on a basis of equality of men and women, of human rights and fundamental freedoms in the political, economic, social, cultural, civil or any other field of public life."[39] The convention recognizes that customs and practices can constitute sex discrimination, and in this regard is a useful tool with which to examine the practice of prostitution with respect to its effects not only on prostituted women themselves, but on women generally, in civil and public life, at home and at the workplace, in government and in the marketplace.

B. The Labor Rights Idea

Finally, it is imperative to locate labor rights as human rights. The International Labour Organization (ILO) is the primary international organization focusing on labor rights. Its predecessor, the International Labour Office, was formed as part of the post–World War I concern for individual human rights as reflected in several programs of the League of Nations (the predecessor to the United Nations).

The International Labour Office, which focused on individual welfare, was established by the Treaty of Versailles "to abolish the 'injustice, hardship and privation' which workers suffered and to guarantee 'fair and humane conditions of labour.'"[40] In furthering that goal, it launched numerous programs including a series of treaties that set standards for what we now identify as social and economic rights. These included conventions setting standards for minimum working conditions, including minimum working age, hours of work, time for rest, protection for sickness and accident, provision of old age insurance, and prohibition against discrimination in employment. It also included treaties dealing with freedom of association, the right to organize trade unions, forced labor, and related matters.

Not all the purposes of the International Labour Office were wholly driven by benevolence toward workers. For example, the West's support of the improvement of working conditions was at least partly fueled by the desire to stop the spread of socialism. Similarly, states were interested in the conditions of labor in nations with which they competed in trade in order to ensure control over production (particularly labor) costs and thereby retain a competitive position in international markets.

The successor organization, the ILO, has broadened and continues to pursue the idea that the right to work in proper working conditions is a human right. The ILO's existence and purpose reinforce the integration of economic rights into the human rights framework. The ILO's 1998 Declaration of Fundamental Principles and Rights at Work identifies five fundamental or "core" human rights related to labor that have universal applicability at all times, in all countries regardless of their level of economic development, and in all employment relationships. These include: (1) freedom of association, (2) right to organize and bargain collectively, (3) prohibition of forced labor, (4) elimination of exploitative forms of child labor, and (5) nondiscrimination in employment and occupation.[41]

The mix of national interest and altruism continues today in this emerging conception of labor rights as human rights. The current interest in labor rights as part of human rights is due in part to perceived competitive advantage that can be derived from low labor standards in a global economy: "Long hours of work, low wages, child labor, and poor working conditions are said to be a type of 'social dumping' or 'unfair subsidy' permitting developing countries or newly industrializing countries to market goods at a low price on the international market."[42] So too the practice of outsourcing labor—of shifting the production of goods offshore to countries with low wages, vulnerable and unorganized workforces, and poor working conditions—is now common among multinational companies producing for domestic markets in developed countries. The misery of and political mobilization against child labor and sweatshop conditions are counterpoints to our analysis of prostitution and trafficking within the human rights model.

IV. SEXUAL LABOR IN A HUMAN RIGHTS FRAMEWORK

There are three arguments for the eventual abolition of prostitution and trafficking from within the "labor rights as human rights" framework. First, the conditions faced by sex workers throughout the world indicate that prostitution is a practice that cannot be performed without an unacceptable degree of danger and degradation to the individual worker. Conditions vary, and sometimes dramatically so, but in every setting prostitution creates an environment in which women and youth are at great risk of being harmed through private violence, exposure to disease and other health risks, psychological diminishment and abuse, and economic exploitation. As such, the practice violates the worker's rights at the intersection of labor and human rights, including the specific rights to dignity, bodily integrity, physical and mental health, and freedom from violence.

Second, rather than advance self-determination or liberation, or confirm women's autonomy, the sex industry is a practice of colonization. Although proponents of sex workers rely heavily on the rhetoric of autonomy, the social reality of prostitution with respect both to its settings and players reveals that it is exploitative of laborers, reflecting two of the West's great embarrassments: its colonial heritage and its depraved history of slavery.

Further, the practice of prostitution harms the collective interests of women as the principal class of sexual labor. Within the broad context of the varied arrangements through which sex is exchanged between males and females, the commercial sex trade undermines other more protective and regulated arrangements, arrangements that fundamentally determine women's status and well-being in every society. And finally, prostitution undermines the rights of self-determination and the bodily integrity of women as a class by derogating the importance of female consent.

A. Prostitution Injures the Human Rights of Individual Women as Sex Workers

The working conditions of the sex industry vary importantly from site to site, and from nation to nation. The empirical task of documenting working conditions across the globe and in the wide range of arrangements within which prostitutes operate is daunting. These social, economic, and cultural differences alter the meaning and experience of prostitution from space to space. We emphasize again that there is no singular, universal, or essential meaning of the practice across history, culture, and location in the global economy. Yet respect for this variance cannot stand in the way of recognizing commonalities among people—including among workers—sufficient to allow us to begin to move toward generalizable principles of human rights, including labor rights. The fundamental human rights to bodily security and integrity, to dignity and honor, to association with others in order to make community, and to labor without exploitation and oppression are grounded in the common attributes and interests of human beings, and hence are of universal application in every social context and location.

Although there are set ideas as to what a prostitute is, different categories exist, none of which encompasses a homogeneous group but among which differences emerge. At the lowest end are the streetwalkers, which in the United States are predominantly poor women and women of color, representing approximately 20 percent of the prostitutes.[43] Significantly, most teen prostitutes fall in this category, comprising about 20 percent of the streetwalkers.[44] Streetwalkers are like day laborers who congregate in public places in order to advertise their availability, and who work on a casual basis for different employers as work becomes available. The casual nature of the employment relationship makes conditions difficult to monitor, and workers are easily exploited and abused. In studies in the United States, the average street prostitute had sex with a stranger four times a day, amounting to more than a thousand sexual encounters with nonintimates each year.[45] Streetwalkers typically perform in covert settings, including the john's car, a secluded public place like an alley, park, or hallway, and sometimes a hotel room. Streetwalkers have a limited ability to screen customers or, given their covert workplaces, to protect themselves from abuse; as a consequence they encounter high levels of violence from customers, being raped and beaten by customers in far greater numbers than are other women and children through domestic violence and child abuse.[46]

One protective mechanism is to work with a pimp or manager. Frequently the earnings of prostitutes are controlled by pimps, echoing systems of debt bondage as well as the control over a wife's wages granted a husband under the system of coverture. Pimps may also directly confine or restrain the movements of the prostitute, including by routine assault, or do so indirectly by threats to children or child custody, the withholding of a passport or threats of deportation, or exploitation of disability in the form of illness or addiction. There are almost no parallels to these kinds of abusive control in lawful employments, even in other types of low-paid, low-status work.

The next category, making up approximately 25 percent of prostitutes, is the call girl—the elite among the sex workers. Call girls work out of hotels or apartments and claim a steady, well-paying client base. They have more personal security, more selectivity in clients, higher earnings, and more comfortable physical work environments. Call girls are also more likely to be self-employed and to retain control over their own earnings. Even so, call girls report fears about health dangers, including sexually transmitted diseases, running afoul of the law and thus risking their businesses, and physical safety concerns.

Between the extremes of streetwalker and call girl are two other categories: escort services and in-house prostitutes. Escort services, a notch below call girls, provide dates for male customers. The escorts work in customers' homes, hotels, or business entertainment settings. The fourth category, in-house prostitutes, is made up of women working in brothels, massage parlors, or other establishments serving as a cover for prostitution. Often these workers are recruited through personal ads promising economic benefits; often they are trafficked internationally. Throughout the world brothel prostitution is correlated with a greater incidence of organized exploitation such as slavelike working conditions, debt bondage, confinement, and the use of threat, blackmail, and physical abuse to control prostitutes.

Some aspects of the working conditions of prostitutes are directly related to criminalization in countries like the United States, and so could be addressed by decriminalization or legalization. Without question, illegality drives much of the industry into the shadows, shielding business practices from scrutiny under ordinary legal standards. Criminalization has also led to widespread police corruption and the sexual abuse of prostitutes. And because the trade is stigmatized and unlawful, workers are de facto (if not de jure) denied the protection of the laws against sexual assault, battery, fraud, and even murder. But it is naive to believe that it is the laws that criminalize prostitution and not also the nature of the work itself and the social relations it creates that make prostitutes vulnerable to coercion, abuse, and exploitation.

When we take one step further and consider the evidence offered earlier of the health and safety risks of prostitution, the lower socioeconomic location and educational attainment of prostitutes, the prevalence of drug dependency, and the young age of entry, whether there exists for all prostitutes a true choice to labor under these substandard working conditions is reasonably to be questioned. But it is the substance of the working conditions and not the worker's choice to endure them that is the determinative question within our "labor rights as human rights" framework. Choice does not have the legitimizing power in the labor relationship that it has in other private relations. Acknowledging the power of economic duress, labor laws protect workers even where the worker may freely have contracted for sub-standard working conditions and wages.

B. Prostitution Injures Sex Workers Because It Is a Postcolonial Colonizing Enterprise

Beyond focusing on individual rights, a human rights perspective on prostitution also interrogates how the practice of prostitution affects social relations. A labor-sensitive human rights perspective on prostitution focuses on the dynamics of the labor environment. Such scrutiny unearths the power relations between the social actors and reveals the power imbalances that govern such interactions. Specifically, the character of the relationship between the individuals involved in an arrangement for the exchange of sex for money is of a colonial nature as it is an engagement marked by domination, subordination, and exploitation. As such the relationship violates the human rights of dignity, autonomy, and equality of the individual sex worker. Using such a framework shows the colonizing consequences of the power dynamics between the laborer and the purchaser of services in the prostitution exchange and helps unpack the reasons why prostitution is an undesirable form of labor: prostitution is a suspect institution because it re-creates a colonial relationship.

Although self-determination is the international norm both for persons and states, and colonialism is officially over, prostitution effectively creates a postcolonial colonized regime. Prostituted women are a symbol of the ongoing claim of the first world to extract the resources—human and otherwise—of the third world. Sex travelers—both those who travel seeking sexual marketplaces and those who migrate in order to provide sexual services—exemplify this analysis. The logic of the international trafficking in women for prostitution is to provide a "foreign" labor force for use in the domestic sex industry. Sex tourism too is driven by the desire of mostly men with money for leisure travel to visit foreign sex markets. Both international flows of people—migration for sex work and sex adventurism—are fueled by poverty, sexism, and racism, all of which create a situation of unequal bargaining power and vulnerability. "There is an international political economy of sex here, as sex tourism and the relations between clients and prostitutes mirror relations of domination, subordination and exploitation between first and third worlds."[47]

The sex industry, be it in the international scene or within national borders, re/presents colonial rule and power in the relations it establishes. In the international sphere, men, rich and mostly from core states, claim their privilege over women, poor, colored, and mostly from peripheral states; within domestic borders, men, white, moneyed, and mostly from suburbia (the first world), travel to the inner city and claim their privilege over women, poor, colored, and mostly from the inner city (the third world within the first world).

Sexual domination is often used as a metaphor for and privilege of other forms of domination, including colonization. Dominant group men expected sexual access to colonized women, while their states worked to construct and reproduce racialized orders and boundaries. While now formally dismantled, these colonial relations live on in racialized power differences and continuing, sometimes intensifying, relations of dominance, subordination, and exploitation.[48]

Thus are relations between master and servant, colonizer and colonized restated in the relation between patron and prostitute—all in supposedly postcolonial times.

C. Prostitution Injures the Collective Interests of Women

Finally, the practice of prostitution harms the collective interests of women as the principal class of sexual labor, and also undermines the sexual autonomy of women as a class.

We define sexual labor as the class of persons whose economic and social status depends upon establishing and maintaining relationships within which they exchange sexual services for other things of value. The status of women throughout the world remains closely tied to marital, intimate, and familial relationships organized around the exchange and/or control of female sexuality. Despite the recognition of separate female personhood and citizenship, including in the human rights regime, and notwithstanding the liberal desire to free women from such personal dependencies and reshape them as an autonomous and self-actualizing individual, these arrangements remain crucial to women's well-being and status everywhere. Where the arrangements hold, their terms establish women's health, wealth, social standing, and identity; where the arrangements falter or are disrupted, women suffer along many measures of well-being.

Sex workers have long been seen as a moral danger to traditional sexual values and gender norms, but not as a danger to any other group of workers. This is because the competition among women as providers of sexual services tends to be disguised within "nonmarket" frames as love, marriage, personal intimacy, or custom and tradition. By racializing, commodifying, depersonalizing, and colonizing sexual access, the commercial sex trade undermines these other more protective and regulated social relations through which men and women exchange sex.

To appreciate this perhaps unfamiliar argument about competition within the market for sexual labor, consider the parallel example of child labor. One reason for restricting child labor in both national and international contexts is the moral concern for the well-being of the vulnerable worker based on the belief that children cannot defend their own interests in the marketplace. (We have made an argument similar to this in our claims that the inequalities in bargaining power between prostitutes and other players in the sex industry lead to exploitative and dangerous working conditions.) However, there is also an argument that exploited workers injure the interests of labor as a class by bidding down wages and working conditions. Because employers are able to make unjust labor contracts with children, child labor has the indirect effect of driving down wages and working conditions for adult workers. This is the argument made for the inclusion of labor standards in international trading agreements. In the 1920s, the constitution of the ILO recognized the effects of inhumane labor standards on economic competition between nations, which in turn stifles national efforts to heighten worker protections: "[T]he failure of any nation to adopt humane conditions of labor is an obstacle in the way of other nations which desire to improve the conditions in their own countries."[49]

If inhumane labor standards undermine fair dealing between nations, the same must be said of its effects on the competition between workers in the same labor market. This explains, for example, why organized labor has taken the lead in the international antisweatshop movement. When factory workers held in slavelike conditions compete in the labor market with other workers, labor's interests as a class are impaired by the wages and working conditions the sweatshop worker endures.

We do not argue in this essay that marriage and other intimate heterosexual unions, or that family more generally, are ideal institutions from the standpoint of women's claims to dignity and equality. Yet prevailing standards of treatment in these noncommercial sexual relationships are higher than in commercial sexual relationships, and are enforced both by law and custom in every society. Arguably this is why prostitutes still find a market for their labor despite the widespread sexual availability of women who will consent to sex without pay, and may even offer greater value in sincerity, reciprocity, and passion. The sex worker finds a market because she—a gendered and racialized she—agrees to be used by men in ways unacceptable by standards that prevail elsewhere. In this sense prostitutes are like informal sector labor. Informal sector workers make their willingness to forgo minimum wages and decent health and safety standards into a bargaining chip that makes them a cheaper, more "flexible," and hence more attractive labor force.

The accessibility of some women for indiscriminate sexual use by men—be it voluntarily or involuntarily given—also injures the interests of women as a gender class, entirely apart from their interests as labor market competitors. The availability of sex workers confirms the social expectation that women *should be* accessible to men for their unilateral satisfaction of desire, an expectation that ignores what women want from sex. The prostitution exchange does not require mutual sexual desire; instead, a prostitute's need for money substitutes for her desire to have sex with the patron. Thus prostitution can be defined as a social relationship in which men's money speaks louder than women's desire. Where men control more money than women, which describes the economic position of the class of women as compared to the class of men everywhere and throughout known history, this substitution of money for consent negates any meaningful notion that women control their own sexuality or that females have an equal right to consent to sexual connection.

In sum, the coercive, unsafe, degrading environmental reality of the prostitution exchange cannot be reconciled with women's human rights to race and sex equality, to physical and mental health, to autonomy, dignity, security and self-determination. Indeed, it cannot be reconciled even with international labor standards that require safe and nondiscriminatory working conditions, that limit working hours, and that prohibit the exploitation of child labor. Further, selling a body for sex has broad societal implications and consequences; the industry has a colonizing effect on women across races, ethnicities, nationalities, and classes.

V. PROSTITUTION AS AN ILLEGAL LABOR CONTRACT

An international labor movement may respond to oppressive labor conditions by advocating reform, but labor may also seek to eliminate work that it deems inhumane, irremediably dangerous, or antagonistic to the interests of workers as a class. This is the approach that international bodies like the ILO and organized labor have taken to other exploitative labor arrangements, such as slave labor, child labor, and sweatshop labor. We suggest it is also the appropriate approach to take with respect to prostitution and trafficking. Commercial sex harms the individual sex worker; re-creates the colonial orderings of domination, subordination, and exploitation between persons and groups; endangers the interests of women as the class of sexual labor; and undermines female sexual autonomy. It should eventually be abolished.

We propose to treat prostitution like other forms of exploitative labor such as slave labor, child labor, and sweatshop labor. These are illegal labor arrangements for which the law holds the employer (in sex work, this includes the patron, the pimp, and all business interests) and not the worker responsible. At the level of domestic law, this approach would translate into the following regime:

1. Anyone who makes an arrangement for prostitution would be penalized like the employer who seeks to employ workers who are underage, in unsafe working conditions, or at below minimum wage rates.
2. Unlike the current treatment of prostitutes as criminals in some nations (like the United States), the worker employed in violation of labor laws would not be punished or stigmatized, even if the goal of the law is abolition of the worker's job.
3. Prostitutes could thus turn to the legal system to demand payment for work performed under an illegal contract, could protest harsh working conditions or violence by reporting to legal authorities, and could organize to defend their collective interests without suffering legal penalty, even though their employment would remain illegal and the state's goal would be its ultimate abolition. No longer would they be forced underground or into the shadows.

At the international level, this approach would translate into the following regime:

1. States and nonstate actors, including intergovernmental organizations (IGOs), nongovernmental organizations (NGOs), and multinational enterprises (MNEs) would agree (in appropriate form) that women have rights to equality, health, safety, dignity, autonomy, and self-determination—rights that are threatened by the practice of prostitution.
   A. In establishing a regime to combat prostitution, the parties would recognize that
      (1) economic coercion is not tantamount to consent;
      (2) there is no clearly defined line between forced and voluntary sex work, particularly when economic coercion is considered; and
      (3) given the prevalent problem of child prostitution (just as generally a problem exists with exploitative child labor), a minimum age of consent ought to be established.
   B. In establishing a regime to combat prostitution, the parties would agree to explore globalization, private industry, and how state programs and international programs work together to subordinate women, and to seek remedies for the root causes of such subordination.
   C. In establishing a regime to eradicate prostitution, the parties would agree to identify local practices, such as customs and cultural tropes, that contribute to or define women's subordinated location in society and to work together to eradicate those practices.
2. States would agree to pass regulations to promote the equality of women and to eradicate practices harmful to women, specifically prostitution. In so doing, as at the national level, states would agree to penalize those who make arrangements for prostitution in a manner similar to the penalizing of those who engage in illegal labor practices such as employment of underage workers, unsafe working conditions, or below minimum wage pay. The workers employed in violation of the labor laws would not be punished or stigmatized. The workers could demand payment for work performed under the illegal contract, seek

protection against poor working conditions or violence, and organize to defend their collective interests.

3. Systems of cooperation and reporting would be established in which states, working together with NGOs and IGOs, study and establish the root causes of prostitution and the role and impact of women's economic inequality, and develop programs that empower women economically so that prostitution is not the most viable source of sustenance. In this regard, the development policies of IGOs would be scrutinized so as to unearth and restructure any linkages between programs and the ongoing economic subordination of women.

VI. CONCLUSION

A commitment to the abolition of prostitution can be reconciled with an analysis of prostitution as sex work, revealing new strategies for legal reform both at the national and international levels. Cast as an issue of exploitative labor, we can address the contradictions of prostitution's continued existence in the face of commitments to the equality of persons, to self-determination, and to an end to sexual violence without further oppressing sex workers through legal strategies like criminalization.

NOTES

1. Convention for the Suppression of the Traffic in Persons and the Exploitation of the Prostitution of Others, G.A. Res. 317(IV), Dec. 2, 1949, art. 20.

2. E/CN.6/WG.2/1992/L.3 at art. 2(b) (approved by the General Assembly 1993).

3. *Report of the Special Rapporteur on Violence against Women*, E/CN.4/1995/42, UN Economic and Social Council, Commission on Human Rights, Nov. 22, 1994.

4. UN Doc. E/1983/7 at para 23 (1983).

5. Documents that create human rights obligations that are pertinent to this essay are the Universal Declaration of Human Rights, Dec. 10, 1948, U.N.G.A. Res. 217 [hereinafter Universal Declaration]; the International Covenant on Civil and Political Rights, G.A. Res. 2200, 999 U.N.T.S. 171 (adopted by the U.N.G.A. on Dec. 16, 1996, entered into force Mar. 23, 1976, rat-

ified by the United States June 8, 1992) [hereinafter ICCPR]; the Covenant on Social, Cultural and Economic Rights, 993 U.N.T.S. 3, *annexed to* U.N.G.A. 2200 (adopted by the U.N.G.A. on Dec. 16, 1966, entered into force Jan. 3, 1976) [hereinafter Economic Convention]; Convention on the Elimination of All Forms of Discrimination against Women, U.N.G.A. Res. 280, 19 I.L.M. 33 (1980) (adopted by the U.N.G.A. on December 18, 1979, entered into force Sept. 3, 1981) [hereinafter Women's Convention]; and the Convention on the Elimination of All Forms of Racial Discrimination, 660 U.N.T.S. 195 (opened for signature Mar. 7, 1966, entered into force Jan. 4, 1969) [hereinafter Race Convention].

6. *See supra* note 5.

7. Jo Doezema, "Forced to Choose: Beyond the Voluntary v. Forced Prostitution Debate," in *Global Sex Workers: Rights, Resistance, and Redefinition* 34, 38 (Kamala Kempadoo and Jo Doezema eds. 1998) (describing the GAATW position).

8. We confine ourselves in this essay to adult prostitution and do not address the distinct moral problem of child prostitution.

9. *See A Vindication of the Rights of Whores* 27 (Gail Pheterson ed. 1989).

10. For the racial demographics of prostitution in the United States, *see* D. Kelly Weisberg, *Children of the Night: A Study of Adolescent Prostitution* 87–88 (1985).

11. *See* R. Barri Flowers, *The Prostitution of Women and Girls* 20–21 (1998).

12. See Elizabeth Bernstein, *What's Wrong with Prostitution? What's Right with Sex Work? Comparing Markets in Female Sexual Labor*, 10 Hastings Women's L.J. 91, 102 (1999).

13. *Id.*

14. *See* Mimi Silbert and Ayala Pines, *Entrance into Prostitution*, 13 Youth and Soc'y 471, 479 (1982) (finding that 60 to 70 percent of prostitutes were sexually abused in childhood).

15. Jan Jindy Pettman, *Worlding Women: A Feminist International Politics* 199 (1996).

16. Evelina Giobbe, "Confronting the Liberal Lies about Prostitution," in *The Sexual Liberals and the Attack on Feminism* 67, 76 (Dorchen Leidholdt and Janice G. Raymond eds. 1990).

17. Beverly Balos and Mary Louise Fellows, *A Matter of Prostitution: Becoming Respectable*, 74 N.Y.U. L. Rev. 1220 (1999).

18. Sheila Jeffreys, *The Idea of Prostitution* 86 (1998) (citing Andrea Juno, interview with Annie Sprinkle, *Angry Women* (1991)).

19. "We embrace our genitals as part, not separate, from our spirits. We utilise sexually explicit words, pictures and performances to communicate our ideas and emotions. We denounce sexual censorship as anti-art and inhuman. We empower ourselves by this attitude of sex-positivism. And with this love for our sexual selves we have fun, heal the world and endure." *Id.* at 23.

20. *Id*. at 28.

21. Anne McClintock, *Sex Workers and Sex Work: Introduction*, 37 Soc. Text 1 (1993).

22. *See* Wendy Chapkis, *Live Sex Acts: Performing Erotic Labor* (1997).

23. *See* Martha C. Nussbaum, *"Whether from Reason or Prejudice": Taking Money for Bodily Services*, 27 J. Legal Stud. 693, 701, 707, 709 (1998).

24. Carlin Meyer, *Decriminalizing Prostitution: Liberation or Dehumanization?*, 1 Cardozo Women's L. J. 105 (1993).

25. Catharine A. MacKinnon, *Feminism Unmodified: Discourses on Life and Law* 21, 24–25 (1987); *see also* Nora V. Demleitner, *Forced Prostitution: Naming an International Offense*, 18 Fordham Int'l L. J. 163, 187 (1994) ("frequently women can make more money as prostitutes than in any other line of employment").

26. McClintock, *supra* note 21, at 1.

27. Patricia Hill Collins, *Black Feminist Thought: Knowledge, Consciousness, and the Politics of Empowerment* 143–46 (2nd ed. 2000).

28. *Id*. at 145–47; *see also* Balos and Fellows, *supra* note 17, at 1220.

29. Sheila Jeffreys, *The Idea of Prostitution* 310 (1998).

30. *See* Claire Sterk-Elifson and Carole A. Campbell, "The Netherlands," in *Prostitution: An International Handbook on Trends, Problems, and Policies* 194–95 (Nanette J. Davis ed. 1993).

31. Christine Overall, *What's Wrong with Prostitution? Evaluating Sex Work*, 17 Signs 715, 717 (1992).

32. Louis B. Sohn, *The New International Law: Protection of the Rights of Individuals Rather than States*, 32 Am. U. L. Rev. 1, 17 (1982).

33. These include the 1926 Slavery Convention, 46 Stat. 2183, T.S. No. 778, 60 L.N.T.S. 253 (concluded Sept. 25, 1926, entered into force Mar. 9, 1927, entered into force for the United States Mar. 1, 1929), and the 1956 Supplementary Convention on the Abolition of Slavery, the Slave Trade, and Institutions and Practices Similar to Slavery, 18 U.S.T. 3201, T.I.A.S. No. 6418, 266 U.N.T.S. 3 (concluded Sept. 7, 1956, entered into force Apr. 30, 1957, entered into force for the United States Dec. 6, 1967).

34. *See* International Convention for the Suppression of the Traffic in Women and Children, 60 U.N.T.S. 416 (1923), and the 1947 Protocol, 53 U.N.T.S. 13.

35. *See generally* Michael Akehurst, *A Modern Introduction to International Law* 75–76 (5th ed. 1984).

36. It is important to note that there were eight abstentions: Byelorussia, Czechoslovakia, Poland, Saudi Arabia, Ukraine, USSR, Union of South Africa, and Yugoslavia. The communist states that had abstained from signing the Universal Declaration in 1948 accepted the Declaration in the Final Act of the Conference on Security and Co-Operation in Europe (CSCE) in Helsinki in 1975.

37. *See* Akehurst, *supra* note 35, at 76; Universal Declaration, *supra* note 5,

passim; see also Louis B. Sohn and Thomas Buerengenthal, *International Protection of Human Rights* 516 (1973).

38. Race Convention, *supra* note 5, at art. 1(1).

39. Women's Convention, *supra* note 5, at art. 1.

40. Virginia Leary, "Lessons from the Experience of the International Labour Organisation," in *The United Nations and Human Rights: A Critical Appraisal* 580, 582 (Philip Alston ed. 1992).

41. International Labor Organization, Declaration on Fundamental Principles and Rights at Work (last visited June 28, 2000), <http://www.ilo.org/public/english/standards/relm/ilc/ilc86/com-dtxt.htm>.

42. Virginia A. Leary, "The Paradox of Workers' Rights as Human Rights," in *Human Rights, Labor Rights, and International Trade* 21, 27 (Lance A. Compa and Stephen F. Diamond eds. 1996).

43. *See* Ann M. Lucas, *Race, Class, Gender and Deviancy: The Criminalization of Prostitution*, 10 Berkeley Women's L. J. 47, 48–49 (1995).

44. *See* Flowers, *supra* note 11, at 18.

45. *See* Matthew Freund et al., *Sexual Behavior of Resident Street Prostitutes with Their Clients in Camden, New Jersey*, 26 J. Sex Res. 460, 465 (1989) (average of slightly more than four customers per day).

46. For violence, child abuse, and the rape of prostitutes, *see* Mimi Silbert and Ayala Pines, *Occupational Hazards of Street Prostitutes*, 8 Crim. Just. and Behav. 387, 397 (1981) (70 percent raped by customers and 65 percent beaten by customers).

47. Pettman, *supra* note 15, at 196.

48. *Id.* at 198.

49. Constitution of the International Labor Organization, 62 Stat. 3485, T.I.A.S. no. 1868, 15 U.N.T.S. 35, amended by 7 U.S.T. 245, T.I.A.S. no. 3500, 191 U.N.T.S. 143 (1953), 14 U.S.T. 1039, T.I.A.S. no. 5041, 466 U.N.T.S. (1962), U.S.T. 3253, T.I.A.S. no. 7987 (1972).

11

Policing the Boundaries of Truth in Narratives

Elizabeth Fakazis

IN THE 1960s, media research, both in the United States and abroad, linked imperialism—"a system of exploitative control of people and resources"—to culture. Researchers, heavily influenced by Althusser, Gramsci, and the Frankfurt School, began to analyze the effects of "cultural imperialism," or the extensive exportation of Western, mainly American, mass media corporations, products, and technology, on recipient cultures.

Early research focused primarily on the "sender" and "creator" of the media messages and products as the powerful, active, controlling agent; and on the monolithic and leveling influence of Western mass culture. But by the late 1970s and early 1980s, researchers complicated the cultural imperialism theory by recognizing the existence of "local elites who acted as relays in transmitting global culture at the local level; recognizing that audiences are not passive recipients of media messages but can appropriate cultural products or create oppositional readings; and recognizing that a theory of global media needs to take into account the interplay between powerful global economic structures and less powerful local 'audiences.'"[1]

Cultural imperialism and its critique facilitate the understanding of moral imperialism as a system of exploitation and control that functions by defining and imposing a particular morality. Studying imperialism unveils the use of economic and human resources by dominant groups to produce and impose a particular narrative of truth on "others"— whether those "others" reside within or outside one's national borders.

Moral imperialism and its related concepts of borders and exportation explain the struggle of subgroups within journalism to control what counts as truth in nonfiction narratives and what technologies are capable of producing it. The 1984 "scandal" of Alastair Reid, a writer for the *New Yorker*, depicts an instance of one who found himself caught, used, and abused by competing factions in the national debate about what constitutes truth.

ALASTAIR REID AT THE PILLORY

In December 1961, the *New Yorker* magazine published veteran writer Alastair Reid's "Letter from Barcelona" in which he described a "small, flyblown bar by the harbor" that was "a favorite haunt of mine for some years because of its buoyant clientele." Reid described how he stopped in the bar to watch a televised speech given by Francisco Franco, and used the rest of the letter to convey, through description and dialogue, the mood of the country under "the little Generalisimo."

Twenty-five years later, the "small, flyblown bar" came back to haunt him. In 1984 Reid found himself and his letter the subject of a front-page article in the *Wall Street Journal*.[2] The article, written by a young reporter who had attended a Yale writing seminar at which Reid had spoken, revealed that the flyblown bar had, in fact, been closed by the time Reid decided to use it as the setting for his story, and that he had taken conversations recorded in several different times and places and compressed them into one. "Whether the bar existed or not was irrelevant to what I was after," Reid was quoted as saying. "If one wants to write about Spain, the facts won't get you anywhere." Nonetheless, the article was constructed as an exposé—with the *Wall Street Journal* reporter revealing behind-the-scenes wrongdoings by a prominent writer and his prestigious publication, both of which had breached the public trust.

The article triggered responses that appeared in the *New York Times, Newsweek, Time*, the *New Republic*, and in other newspapers and magazines across the country. Journalists and cultural critics publicly castigated or defended Reid and his narrative methods. Reid became a pawn in two discursive struggles raging within the journalism profession and in the culture at large: the intensifying battle for the right to delineate and define what counts as truth in journalism, and to sanction certain reporting and writing practices as capable of producing that truth while discrediting others. That Reid continues to be used in the defense against postmodern assaults on traditional notions of truth by critics within and outside the profession serves as a point of departure in the exploration of the propriety of imposing normative standards of truth.

Reid is, of course, just one of many writers since the early 1980s whose credibility has been challenged on the grounds that their stories stray from the facts. Journalism has been the most intense and public hunt for inaccuracy and dubious storytelling methods but scrutiny has also snared nonfiction novels (*Eye for an Eye, M*), memoirs (*Angela's Ashes, I Rigoberta Menchu*), history (*The Return of Martin Guerre*), biography (*Dutch*), fictional novels that appropriate historical documents and figures (*Hitler's Niece, The Hours*), and movies (*JFK, Malcolm X*), to name just a few. While the hunt falls along somewhat predictable political lines (with conservatives chasing after a receding commitment to straightforward notions of truth, and liberals chasing after larger meaning), an unusual convergence has occurred between journalists, who tend to be left-of-center, and social conservatives.

Much of the public debate centers around the quest to determine the factual accuracy of stories, to discover how "true" they really are. The dominant discourse claims to safeguard the American public from narrative lies, and to ensure that journalists live up to the responsibility of a free press in a democracy: the responsibility to tell the truth unstintingly, without fear or favor. It equates the production of journalistic truth with the methods of daily newspaper journalism, which include reliance on official sources, use of quotes to communicate opinion or controversial information, reliance on verifiable fact, invisibility of the individual author—in short, all the methods that have been judged capable of producing the objective report. Yet in practice the label "journalism" has been historically and consistently applied to a much wider range of narrative types, practices, and ideologies, some of which have only recently been conceptualized as problematic.

Public commentary on Alastair Reid presents an opportunity to scrutinize the discourses that attempt to define his work and his identity, and to define the concept of truth in journalism and nonfiction writing. These discourses attempt to produce, in part, a moral understanding of truth; they evaluate Reid and his stories based on a specific interpretation of the moral imperative that journalists must always tell the "truth." Official discourses normalize certain types of knowledge by precluding other forms, by distinguishing the normal from the pathological, the good from the delinquent, the true from the false.

REDEFINING ALASTAIR REID

Michel Foucault challenged the notion of absolute truth by drawing attention to the way our understanding of truth changes historically, and how competing truths can coexist, each with its own rationality. Instead of discovering or producing absolute truth, Foucault describes and critically analyzes our continual desire for a single truth. He asks which truths, at any given period, come to predominate and how? One of Foucault's tasks is to expose "the historical specificity—the sheer fact that things could have been otherwise—of what we seem to know today with such certainty."[3] Foucault's theories and methods directly influence the study of the Reid case—controversy as a struggle to legitimate certain knowledges while subjugating others.

Subjugated knowledges are "those blocs of historical knowledge which were present but disguised," and "whole sets of knowledges that have been disqualified as inadequate to their task."[4] Journalists whose methods rest on an assumption of objective and universal truth often reject the reality that Reid's own methods were, until recently, unproblematic. Reid's knowledge that his particular writing practices are legitimate, common, and capable of producing narrative truth, runs like an undercurrent through the dominant discourse of journalism.

By demonstrating that what normatively counts as truth is always the result of specific, authorized techniques, Foucault interrogates the value of these techniques and the truths they produce. For example, Foucault challenged the notion of fixed or universal truth when he investigated the case of a nineteenth-century hermaphrodite, Herculine Barbin.[5] He showed how the medical and psychiatric sciences created two categories of sex for each individual, and the consequent difficulties they have faced with the reality of cases that do not easily fit into the established categories—like hermaphroditism.

Reid's writing can be seen as a literary hermaphrodite, not fitting easily into any of the official generic categories of literature: it does not seem to be wholly journalism as narrowly defined, nor does it seem to be wholly fiction or nonfiction. The dominant discourse does not provide the tools that would allow an easy categorization of Reid's writing, to know how to think about it, or how to evaluate it. As a result, there have been two responses to the conceptual conundrum: attempts to normalize it by creating a third generic category capable of explaining this work and answering the criticism that has been leveled against it; and attempts to discredit it as a valuable form of literature or as a legitimate form of nonfiction in general and journalism in particular.

With Reid, we can observe how the methods, values, and beliefs represented by his work are being redefined as subjugated or marginal knowledges, inadequate to the task of producing journalistic truth. Like the discourse of Foucault's other marginal characters—the madman, the patient, and the delinquent—Reid and writers like him hold knowledges about themselves and their work that diverge from categories that have been set up by dominant discourses. As a result, proponents of alternative approaches have become what one critic has described as unruly—as opposed to well-tempered—subjects, in need of being reformed or contained.

A TALE OF TRANSGRESSION

Joanne Lipman, a reporter who had attended a writing seminar in which Reid had spoken, wrote the *Wall Street Journal* article that made Reid and his narrative methods national news and subsequently interviewed him about how he constructed his *New Yorker* stories. Her article, and the ones that followed, were written as a morality play—at the center of which was an ostensible challenge to power, with the good journalists exposing the hidden transgressions of a distinguished writer and his prominent publication, and forcing them (the writer and the magazine) publicly to acknowledge their sins and repent. The articles drew on a moral vocabulary of dark and light, the hidden and the exposed. A reporter for *Time* magazine wrote that when Reid "admitted last week that he had indulged repeatedly in such sleight-of-hand, he prompted a well-deserved storm of criticism and an apology from the prestigious and generally scrupulous New Yorker."[6] A *New York Times* reporter described how the *Journal* had "uncovered this story," while others talked about the "revelations" and "disclosures" of Mr. Reid's "unorthodox journalistic techniques," and credited Lipman with bringing them "to light in a front page article."

Lipman, the "young reporter," thus emerges as the agent fulfilling the mythical role of every journalist, acting as the energetic and vigilant watchdog in pursuit of the truth, exposing the hidden abuses of government, business, even the Fourth Estate itself. In doing so, the watchdog was reproducing the normative by insisting on a singular, rigidly objective, decontextualized truth. Reid and his narrative techniques, on the other hand, emerge as the villains operating along the shady boundaries of the profession, where fact and fiction begin to lose their reassuring distinction. Reid-the-villain spoke his truth to power and revealed a subjectivity that is usually suppressed or concealed.

Reid was portrayed as a fallen journalist who had succumbed to the temptation to tamper with the facts by creating an imaginary setting for his story and compressing dozens of conversations into one. A great moral divide was erected between Reid and most other journalists. Unlike Reid, who took the easy way out, "most reporters labor hard to find perfect anecdotes and quotes to drive home the points they want to make," Time assured its readers.[7] A New York Times reporter said that Reid had "described departures from factual reporting that would violate the practices of most respected newspapers and magazines."[8] Another reporter writing for Time said, "Such fabrications however faithful they may seem to the spirit of a reporter's observations, are violations of the ethics of the craft." In fact, they were such egregious violations that the editor of the Los Angeles Times was quoted as saying he would dismiss a reporter for behavior like Reid's. "It is an indulgence we cannot afford in this business."[9]

What exactly is it that the business cannot afford, and just what business is he talking about? A reporter for the San Diego Union-Tribune provides an answer: "What's at stake here is the very heart of journalism." "If a newspaper says something happened, its readers should be able to assume something happened."[10] Another reporter warned of the dangerous potential for descent into chaos that Reid represented: "Any departure from fact is the first step on a slippery slope toward unbelievability."[11] Such a descent would present readers "with a dilemma: can they assume what they read is true?"[12]

The journalists who discredited Reid were discursively defending their own credibility and that of the American press by associating their reporting and writing methods with the production of unambiguous, objective truth. They were reacting, in part, to a series of media scandals that had plagued newspapers in the early 1980s and from which news organizations were still reeling. The most symbolically significant of these scandals involved Janet Cooke, a reporter for the *Washington Post* who, in the fall of 1980, fabricated a front-page news story about an eight-year-old heroin addict named Jimmy. The story won the Pulitzer Prize, journalism's most coveted award, and the *Post* had to return the prize when Cooke's fabrications were discovered. The scandal was highly publicized in the national press and it became a critical event that journalists used to reflect publicly on the foundations of their authority, and to organize the boundaries of what constitutes legitimate practice within the profession. Journalists turned their critical eye on themselves, explaining within the pages of their newspapers and magazines their triumphs and their mistakes. Turning the spotlight on the performance of individual journalists and news organizations became one tactic for repairing the news media's damaged self-esteem and credibility. Journalists began to publicly police each other, looking for and exposing ethical lapses and departures from fact, and trying to bring a generic purity to journalism by narrowing down the types of stories that could legitimately be called journalism. This process was quintessentially imperialistic as it imposed a normative standard of truth.

News journalists attempted to gain control over the meaning of journalism by associating it firmly and predominantly with the practices and narrative styles associated with the production of daily news. A representative example of this discursive strategy appears in a *Time* article which ascribed Reid's fundamental error to "assuming that large truth is the province of journalism in the first place. The business of journalism is to present facts accurately—Mr. Reid notwithstanding. Those seeking something larger are advised to look elsewhere." Journalism "rarely sees the larger truth of a story because reporters are usually chasing quite small elements of information." The *Time* reporter gave as an example the way news media usually treat wars, like the British invasion of the Falkland Islands, or chronic conditions like poverty that lack drama. He wrote,

> No one really knows anything about the Falkland Islands other than the war that gave it momentary celebrity—nothing about the people in the aftermath of the war, their concerns, isolation, or their true relationship to Argentina and Britain. . . . Journalism tends to focus on the poor when the poor make news, usually dramatic news. . . . It is not

journalism's ordinary business to deal with the unstartling normalities of life. . . . If one asks, then, where the larger truth is to be sought, the answer is where it has always been: in history, poetry, art, nature, education, conversations. . . . If people cannot rely on the news for facts, however, then journalism has no business for being.[13]

The *Time* reporter's version of journalism confines the genre to news, even though the label has historically been applied to a much wider range of narrative forms. Throughout the history of modern journalism in the United States there has been a tension between the straightforward factual reporting of news, and stories about real people and events that do not adhere to newswriting conventions. For a long time, this tension was manageable and even creative. But in the 1960s a group of journalists emerged who politicized journalism's central tension and created a profound ideological rift. These "new journalists," working individually and from different literary traditions (from realism to metafiction), sent postmodernism, with all its uncertainty, hurtling through journalism's barricaded door.

JOURNALISM'S COMPETING TRADITIONS

Reid belongs to a long line of writers who have self-identified or been identified as "journalists," but who have been doing work that is very different in purpose, content, and form from daily newspaper reporting. "Literary journalism" consists of nonfiction writing about current events—the "stuff of journalism," such as crime, politics, sports, and celebrity culture, that does not follow the conventions of newspaper reporting but has at its disposal a wider range of narrative tools. It has been defined as nonfiction writing that aims to communicate just the kinds of things that the *Time* reporter said fell outside the purview of journalism: the larger truth behind the facts, the normalities of everyday life, the aftermath of events, the human relationships and motivations that fuel a "story," even the interrogation of truth itself.

The tension between newspaper reporting and literary journalism was not always as intense as it is today: writers like Reid would not always have been classified so easily as transgressive. Journalists working from the 1890s throughout the 1920s saw themselves partly as scientists "uncovering the economic and political facts of industrial life more boldly, more clearly, and more realistically than anyone had done before," and partly as artists whose job it was to tell a compelling and persuasive story.[14] The key to persuasion was developing one's power of observation to "write a newspaper story, magazine article, or novel that was photographically true to life," and developing one's power of imagination to write a story that "sparkled."[15] Newspapers "took it for granted that there was no contradiction between the facts and the color" of a story, and that "the good reporter should be alert to both."[16]

Historically there has existed an understanding of the need to convey information both accurately and in an interesting way. "[A] reporter with sparkle would be forgiven inaccuracy, just as a reliable reporter would be forgiven a moderate degree of dullness in his style, but . . . the combination of reliability and sparkle was the recipe for professional success."[17] A reporter could use "his imagination to create images he had not witnessed and had no direct testimony about" as long as the imaginative writing was limited to "non-essential parts of an article. . . . Truth in essentials, imagination in non-essentials, is considered a legitimate rule of action in every office. The paramount object was to make an interesting story."[18]

Reid, then, was caught up in historical conditions that made it possible for Lipman to define what Reid did as transgressive, on the grounds that he had violated factual truth and deceived readers, and could therefore be considered a legitimate subject for a front-page news story. These conditions are recent. As chronicled in a history of the *New Yorker*, the lines between fiction and nonfiction have long been blurry. But modern conventions of newswriting began to solidify, and there was great public discussion about the limits of newspaper journalism and the possibilities of a form of writing that merged aspects of journalism with aspects of the realistic novel. A writer for the *Atlantic* recognized the fluidity of truth and facts, stating that "while most daily journalism had no life beyond the immediate facts reported, occasionally there emerged a 'poet reporter' whose writing had the power to 'make a day last forever.'"[19] Thus a challenge to a uniform way of reporting—to absolute normativity—emerged.

It is out of this literary journalism tradition that Reid wrote his "Letter from Barcelona." Despite his eventual public admission that "he had long regarded his inventions as an error," there is ample evidence suggesting that he never regarded what he did as wrong or deceptive. He, like other nonfiction writers before him, although perhaps not so many after him, talked openly and publicly of creating composite characters, compressing several conversations into one, and locating conversations that had occurred in disparate places into one setting in their stories.

The reporter who "exposed" Reid did not have to dig very far to get the information she needed to fulfill her watchdog role—she only had to listen to Reid freely talking about his work. Once "exposed," Reid defended himself by insisting that he never wrote with the intention to deceive or falsify, but to clarify. He explained that he had created several composite scenes in his stories about Spain, distilling things he had seen and heard in different places. He made a clear distinction between stories that demand absolute reporting of fact and those that do not. As Reid told Lipman, "I lived in Spain. . . . I spoke the language. I was reporting on the mood of this country. This was not invalidated by the fact that the bar is or isn't there."

Other writers agreed. As one writer said in coming to Reid's defense: "I don't know where you go off the scale here, but it doesn't sound to me as if Alastair Reid went off any scale of reader deception." Other writers also subscribed to "creative journalism." In one *New Yorker* piece, for instance, Paul Brodeur detailed a fishing trip with two Indians. According to the piece, the party caught two fish in a cove; in truth, Mr. Brodeur says, the fish were caught in separate coves but he consolidated the event "for reasons of economy." "That kind of economy and selection of detail," Brodeur added, "goes on all the time." Another *New Yorker* writer said, "If you're having a conversation with somebody on an airplane and you want to make it a train because it's better for the piece, I don't see that it's all that dreadful." And William F. Buckley, Jr., was quoted as saying he was not "personally offended by the disclosures because I never had the sensation that I'd been taken" and because "the rearrangements appeared to be merely atmospheric."

For example, in the 1940s Joseph Mitchell, a *New Yorker* writer who was (and is) identified as a journalist and as one of the nation's best nonfiction writers, wrote a three-part series profiling "a man identified in the opening of the first as 'a tough Scotch-Irishman I know, Mr. Hugh G. Flood, a retired house-wrecking contractor, aged ninety-three.'"[20] The author did not reveal that Mr. Flood was not a real person until his author's note in a 1948, in a book publishing the "profiles" which described Mr. Flood as a composite of men who worked at or spent time around the Fulton Fish Market. Interestingly, after the Mr. Flood profile first appeared, "several people went looking for the old fellow in the fish market." When Mr. Flood could not be found, "the newspapers said nothing, even though several editors knew Mr. Flood was a composite."[21]

One explanation for the newspapers' silence regarding Mr. Flood, and other characters like him, may be that literary journalism before the 1960s was not perceived by reporters as directly or profoundly threatening, and it was not framed as a radical attack on the ideological foundations of the profession. But the public discourse became politically charged in the 1960s with the advent of the New Journalism— a literary movement that many reporters and cultural critics have turned into a scapegoat for all of contemporary journalism's shortcomings. The news articles reporting on Reid castigated the New Journalism and asserted its decline as a discredited writing practice. Various challenges to this form emerged, including the following: "altering facts to achieve a dramatic narrative,"[22] the "novelization" of information, "the arranging of information into a new, more readable package, with facts presented not necessarily as they were but as they would appear most interesting,"[23] and "the notion of elastic truth."[24] Reid was described as a fan of this discredited literary form, in stark contrast to "most" reporters.

THE NEW JOURNALISM

The New Journalists of the 1960s rebelled against the objective, rigidly formulaic style of writing that came to define journalism following World War II. Journalists in the late nineteenth and early twentieth centuries believed in external facts, and had faith in their ability to discern and communicate the meaning inherent in those facts to their readers. But their faith quickly crumbled as they witnessed how propaganda and the nascent business of public relations could take solid facts and make them malleable. Journalists began to doubt their old standards. Facts alone are not absolute; "the facts of modern life do not spontaneously take a shape in which they can be known. They must be given a shape by somebody."[25] And that somebody was not always to be trusted. Journalists responded to their crisis of faith by acknowledging that subjectivity was a factor in reporting. Newspapers began using bylines to identify the individual writer of a story, and tagging news stories with the labels "interpretation," and "analysis."[26] They also responded by trying to shackle subjectivity and keep it safely confined. The primary restraining mechanism became the profession's appropriation of the scientific ideal of objectivity, "an ideology of the distrust of the self," designed to protect journalism from subjectivity and its dangerous consequences.

In order to protect themselves from attacks on their credibility and from the often devastating effects of libel suits, journalists translated the abstract, ideal concept of objectivity into practical rules and procedures or strategic rituals designed to protect journalists from the risks of their trade. An objective, credible news story became one that presented "both sides" of an issue, allowed expert sources to voice opinions within quotation marks, presented verifiable and verified facts, and spoke in an institutional third-person voice. The writer's subjectivity in gathering information and writing the story was to be kept firmly at bay, and journalistic truth became associated with the type of knowledge produced when journalists followed the rules.

It was these strategic rituals and this narrowing definition of journalism and journalistic truth that Tom Wolfe, Norman Mailer, Truman Capote, and other writers of the 1960s who became associated with the New Journalism openly challenged. The symbolic birth of New Journalism came with the 1965 publication of Capote's *In Cold Blood*, and of Tom Wolfe's *Kandy Kolored Tangerine Flake Streamline Baby*. *In Cold Blood* was Capote's narrative of the murder in Holcomb, Kansas, of a family of four, who had been killed in their beds as they slept. For Capote, the Holcomb case provided a perfect subject for writing "a true account of an actual murder case" without adhering to the rigid form of the typical news story. Capote wished to push the boundaries of journalism without transgressing the boundaries of reality. "It seemed to me," he said, "that journalism, reportage, could be forced to yield a serious new art form: the non-fiction novel."[27]

A few years later, Tom Wolfe pronounced himself the pioneer of a new journalism that incorporated the best techniques available to both reporters and novelists. Wolfe wrote about politics, celebrities, and popular culture in a very personal, committed, and energetic style, punctuated by outrageous commas, exclamation points, and question marks that refused to be confined to the end of a sentence.

Other writers followed. Norman Mailer caused a stir with his non-fiction novels, *Armies of the Night* and *The Executioner's Song*, in which he belligerently placed himself, as the subjective consciousness shaping a nonfiction narrative, at the center of the text. Gay Talese and Joan Didion also took as their subject "the stuff of journalism" and used the "techniques of fiction" to bring their subject matter to life, and to give it meaning. In the process, these writers liberated the concept of journalistic truth from the confines of objectivity. And the genie has yet to return to the bottle.

These new journalists rebelled against "the straightjacket of straight reporting,"[28] and directly challenged the assumptions of newspaper journalism regarding the relationship between representation and reality. They argued that the conventional style of newswriting was superficial, bereft of meaning, even dishonest. They demonstrated that journalism's procedural rules could not be relied upon to produce "truth," but were in and of themselves manipulative and deceptive because they denied the reporter's inescapable subjectivity. "[T]he problem with conventional journalism is that it refuses to acknowledge the creative nature of its news, instead concealing the structuring mechanisms of its organizational mind behind masks of objectivity and fact."[29] The new journalists sought to redefine journalistic truth by grounding it in an acknowledged and celebrated subjectivity that liberated the journalist's personal voice and challenged the fundamental assumptions that allowed for the separation of fact from fiction. This challenge to the concept of truth occurred within the cultural and political climate of the 1960s, when faith in institutions was shattered, when people were encouraged to defy convention, when the existence of different realities was acknowledged.

REDEEMING A RENEGADE FORM

Just as in earlier times the novel had to battle Puritan strictures against "falsehoods" and an elite disdain for popular amusements, so has nonfiction in more recent times had to battle the sense that it is inherently inferior to fiction. The development of this notion dates to the late nineteenth century, when "literature" came to mean "a privileged realm of works embodying timeless truths and transcendent values," a Romantic notion developed to separate true art from vulgar quasi-industrial cultural products like vaudeville, the serialized novel, and journalism.[30] Art for art's sake was deemed of greater value than art as commodity, and aesthetic criteria were developed that could separate high art from mass culture. Nonfiction was removed as a contender for inclusion in the exclusive literary club because it was concerned with external events instead of its own aesthetic form, with the particular instead of the universal, the ephemeral instead of the timeless.

Since the 1970s, critics have largely overcome this disposition against nonfiction by either rejecting the assumptions and value systems inherent in theories that created the categories of literature and nonliterature; or by attempting to prove that forms of nonfiction that were dismissed in the past are indeed literary—that they do conform to the same aesthetic criteria and engage the same aesthetic concerns as other members of the club. The majority of critics writing about literary journalism are engaged in the latter: other critics reject the practice of incorporating some works into the canon while judging others not worthy of inclusion on aesthetic principles. They remind us that the process of canonization is a gatekeeping process that determines which texts will be preserved. The academy, some critics urge, needs to value nonfictional, popular texts for "the complex political and historical issues they raise."[31]

The debate over the merits of literary journalism is a metaphor for the explorations of truth commenced by Foucault. In journalism the questions address how journalists can write compelling stories that allow them to express their individual subjectivity without doing violence to a journalist's primary social function. These are the same questions about the relationship between truth and representation that are haunting professional journalists, anthropologists, historians, sociologists, and other social scientists studying cultures and analyzing cultural tropes.

The newspaper articles written to discredit Reid and the groups and values he has come to represent are connected to broader, continuing attempts to stem postmodern challenges to traditional Western notions of objectivity to truth. In June 1999 an entire issue of the *American Enterprise* was devoted to exposing our growing public culture of lying—and journalists, as well as academics, politicians, and lawyers figured prominently.[32] Professionals were called to task for passing over reliable, straight-and-narrow facts in pursuit of vague, fuzzy notions of "larger truths"—notions promulgated by the new journalists from whence they migrated, infecting the entire public sphere.

CONCLUSION

Reid and his writing practices have been defined as transgressive only recently in the history of American journalism, and they have been so defined on the grounds that they violated journalism's moral and civic obligation to tell the truth. Journalism's main genre is daily news, and the democratic, civic function of news—to enable responsible citizenship by making available accurate information and to protect the public by exposing abuses of power—depends on the truthfulness of its content. Most journalists understand that the legal privileges and protections they are afforded under the Constitution demand in turn a responsibility to meet their civic obligations. It therefore becomes very important for news journalists to promulgate as unambiguous and consistent an understanding of truth as possible—and to enforce highly regulated procedures for its production. Writers like Reid are perceived as threatening because they treat the boundary separating fact from fiction as highly malleable and permeable—and they introduce within the rubric of journalism narrative practices that deviate from those associated with objectivity, which has been regarded as the most reliable technology of truth.

News journalists defending themselves against Reid are trying to figure out how to negotiate truth and representation in a world where objectivity is no longer available as a taken-for-granted method or ideology. Nonfiction—especially works classified as book-length "journalism"—has become the "defacto literature of our time."[33] American book clubs and magazines have turned to nonfiction as their staple, and cultural and academic critics have taken it up as worthy of serious study, believing that "nonfiction reportage has taken over many of the rhetorical responsibilities of other genres in recent American culture."[34] Nonfiction has joined fabulation as "one of the primary alternatives in contemporary discourse to the narrative conventions of the traditional novel."[35]

If nonfiction is indeed the literature of our time, then we need to figure out ways to keep it vital—to figure out principles and practices that can enable news to fulfill its democratic function, and writers and readers to conceptually accommodate creative nonfiction stories and novels that can venture beyond the scope of news reporting so that we can learn something about the Falklands "other than the war that gave them momentary celebrity." Should the dominant discourse prevail, for the duration of its prevalence we will be forced to live through a literary age incapable of generating anything but the most banal and hegemonic truths. The imposition of a highly specific and rigid method that may or may not work well for one genre (daily news) on the whole of nonfiction creates an illusion of truth that will only obscure the significance of human experience and reality.

NOTES

1. For a critique of cultural imperialism theory, *see Communication and Class Struggle, 1 Capitalism, Imperialism* (A. Mattelart and S. Siegelaub eds. 1979). For audience reception theory, *see, e.g.*, J. Fiske, *Television Culture* (1987).

2. Joanne Lipman, *At the New Yorker, Editor and a Writer Differ on the Facts*, Wall St. J., June 18, 1984, at 1.

3. Alec McHoul and Wendy Grace, *A Foucault Primer: Discourse, Power and the Subject* (1993); Michel Foucault, *Questions of Method: An Interview with Michel Foucault*, 8 Ideology and Consciousness 3–14 (1981).

4. Michel Foucault, *Power/Knowledge: Selected Interviews and Other Writings 1972–77* 81–82 (1980).

5. Michel Foucault, *Herculine Barbin* (1980).

6. William Henry III, *Embroidering the Facts*, Time, July 2, 1984, at 66.

7. *Id.*

8. Maureen Dowd, *A Writer for the New Yorker Says He Created Composites in Reports*, N.Y. Times, June 19, 1984, at A1.

9. Henry, *supra* note 6, at 66.

10. Alfred JaCoby, *Just When You Thought . . .* , Union-Tribune, July 2, 1984, at B10.

11. Henry, *supra* note 9, at 66.

12. JaCoby, *supra* note 10, at B10.

13. Roger Rosenblatt, *Journalism and the Larger Truth*, Time, July 2, 1984, at 88.

14. Michael Schudson, *Discovering the News: A Social History of American Newspapers* 71 (1978).

15. *Id.* at 73.

16. *Id.* at 79.

17. *Id.*

18. *Id.*

19. *See* Thomas Connery, *A Sourcebook of American Literary Journalism* 16 (1992). In 1937, Edwin H. Ford distinguished between straight news, or "a simple record of routine events of everyday life," and "writing articles of 'literary insight' in which the newspaper writer tries to 'make the reader hear, feel and

see' by using 'an approach somewhat similar to that of the novelist, short-story writer, and the poet.'" *Id.* (quoting Edwin H. Ford, *The Art and Craft of the Literary Journalist* (1937)).

20. Ben Yagoda, *About Town: The New Yorker and the World It Made* 401 (2000).

21. Norman Sims, "Joseph Mitchell and The New Yorker Nonfiction Writers," in Connery, *supra* note 19, at 107.

22. Henry, *supra* note 6, at 66.

23. JaCoby, *supra* note 10, at B10.

24. Anonymous, *There at the New Yorker*, Newsweek, July 2, 1984, at 53.

25. Schudson, *supra* note 14, at 144.

26. *Id.* at 145.

27. George Plimpton, *The Story behind the Nonfiction Novel*, N.Y. Times Book Rev., Jan. 16, 1966, at 2.

28. Shelley Fisher Fishkin, *From Fact to Fiction: Journalism and Imaginative Writing in America* 9 (1985).

29. John Hellman, *Fables of Fact: The New Journalism as New Fiction* 4 (1981).

30. *See* Phyllis Frus, *The Politics and Poetics of Journalistic Narrative* (1994); Pierre Bourdieu, *The Field of Cultural Production* 113 (1993).

31. Frus, *supra* note 30, at xii.

32. *What Ever Happened to the Truth?* Am. Enterprise, May-June 1999.

33. Chris Anderson, *Style as Argument: Contemporary American Nonfiction* 2–3 (1989).

34. *Id.*

35. *Id.*

12

Imperial Knowledge

Science, Education, and Equity

Kathryn Scantlebury, Elizabeth McKinley, and Joce Jesson

> Imperialism is the practice, theory and attitudes of a dominating metropolitan center ruling a distant territory.[1]

> Empire is a formal or informal relationship in which one state controls the effective political sovereignty of another political society. It can be achieved by force, by political collaboration, by economic, social or cultural dependence. Imperialism is the process or policy of establishing or maintaining an empire.[2]

ALTHOUGH THIS BOOK has a legalistic bent, we are not lawyers. Nor are we "Americans." In the context of this book's most likely audience—students in U.S. classrooms—we are "outsiders." For one, while many of the authors in this collection are professors of law, sociology, or economics, we teach education. Not only are we all teacher educators, but we also identify as belonging to "down under." Kate is an Australian currently living in the United States, while Elizabeth and Joce live in Aotearoa[3] New Zealand. Our cultural backgrounds and identities are also diverse: Elizabeth is Maori,[4] Joce is Pakeha,[5] and Kate is white. The connecting thread is our commitment to feminism, and springing from that political agenda, we are activists through research, teaching, and advocacy for equity in education, specifically science education.

In Aotearoa New Zealand, Australia, and the United States, there is a movement to seek equity and excellence in science education. The

229

focus of equity is typically to increase the numbers of people from underrepresented groups (such as Aborigine, First Nations, African Americans, and the like) in science[6] and to improve their achievement, retention, and success compared to their white peers. Historically, the research addressing this issue is framed in terms of trying to help "outsiders" get into science. Researchers seek reasons, usually in the form of factors and/or attitudes originating in and confined to the excluded groups and individuals, to explain why particular groups have not gotten beyond compulsory schooling in science. This research suggests that certain groups are underrepresented in science for a variety of determinable factors and relatively constant reasons. It is a research approach that raises several questions. For example, how are ideas of equity constructed in science education? Might we be able to reconceptualize those ideas so that groups of people are not viewed as deficient, and the constituent parts of their identities, including race, class, and gender, do not reinforce each other in effecting their exclusion from the field of science? And how might we move society toward a commitment to implementing real change?

An example from the United States provides an illustrative example of the efforts involved in seeking to attain educational equity, particularly in science education. During the 1990s the National Science Foundation (NSF) in the United States provided multiyear, multimillion dollar grants to twenty-four states and the Commonwealth of Puerto Rico to improve the teaching and learning of mathematics and science. Although the NSF solicitation for the statewide systemic initiatives emphasized equity and quality science education for all students, few of the statewide initiatives focused on urban education.[7] Yet the need for reform is greatest in large urban districts which collectively educate 25 percent of school-age students, 35 percent of poor students, and just under half of all minority children.[8] Even with policy makers' best intentions to promote change, why did the initiatives that addressed issues of equity not find their way into the schools most in need of reform—large urban schools that educate large numbers of poor minority students? Furthermore, how do such events reflect an imperial past and contribute to the production of ongoing imperial relations? These events, and the questions that emerge from them, support a growing consensus in science education that the slogan "science for all" is rhetoric and that little is being done to make it a reality in the United States or other Western countries.[9]

This essay posits that science education remains inequitable because science and education are imperialistic entities, not unlike the position of the United States as a global colonizing force. In the next section, we will show how science education has worked to exclude Others from its discipline through its definition of what counts as knowledge. We argue that science education is fundamental to the connection between the individual and/or group and a global economy. The links among culture, the knowledge of Western science, and globalization have led to education policies being dominated by U.S. philosophies. We show how the current attempts to engage "underrepresented groups" in science education are not only inadequate but contribute to ongoing imperial relations. Finally, we review research into "forms of address"[10] in classrooms in an attempt to offer a more complex understanding of difference and pedagogy.

EDWARD SAID'S *ORIENTALISM* AND SCIENCE EDUCATION

From a postcolonial[11] perspective, science education can be read as a technology of colonialist subjection in two intrinsically interwoven ways. First, it reproduces the objectivity and rationality of science as normative by claiming that the values embodied in science itself are "universal." And second, it represents the colonized to themselves as inherently inferior beings. Edward Said's *Orientalism* (1978) fundamentally critiques the structures of colonialism, such as education or the disciplines of academia.[12] Said deconstructs a wide range of texts in order to question the West's assumptions about other societies and peoples, assumptions reflected in Western institutional structures and accepted at the individual, academic, and political levels. He argues that the "Orient" is constructed by and in relation to Western identity. Further, he suggests that the "Orient" and its subjects serve as a mirror image of what is inferior and alien or "the Other" for the West.

Said focuses on individual artifacts of culture, such as language, literature, history, and society. He defines these artifacts as great products of the creative or interpretive imagination. Simultaneously he shows them to be part of the relationship between culture and empire that shapes the social experience of those who are part of the imperial culture. Extrapolating from this idea, it has been argued that the development and maintenance of all cultures that have a colonial history requires the existence of another and competing alter ego, that is, an Other.

Education, including science education, is often used, consciously and unconsciously, as a vehicle to educate the wider population of and about the Other. A survey of policy texts will show that there are several ways in which curriculum documents, including textbooks and classroom resources, can represent a "politics of culture."[13] Curriculum policy is never a neutral assemblage of knowledge. Choosing the knowledge imparted in schools is not just about what to teach and what is worth learning. Schools are the mechanism through which society inculcates its values, standards, and expectations. For example, let us consider the question "what counts as science in science education?" In the United States, the National Science Education Standards (NSES) are used by science educators as a blueprint to guide them in deciding what science is of importance for children to learn.[14] However, Alberto Rodriguez has criticized the NSES because of its "discourse of invisibility" regarding ethnic, gender, and socioeconomic issues.[15] Rodriguez describes the NSES as ethnocentric because ethnic groups such as African Americans, Asian Americans, Latinas/os, and/or First Americans are collectively grouped together as "minorities," ignoring the fact that there are different equity issues for each of them. In Aotearoa New Zealand, the national science curricula incorporate the dominant Pakeha groups' knowledge but exclude most Maori knowledge as that which exists outside science and science education. The only knowledge in the science curricula that is recognizably Maori is tangential to the "real" science, that is, "Western" science, and is usually included to set the context for that "real" science. For example, the Maori practice of *hangi* (a way of cooking in the ground using heated stones and water) is included in science education only as a means of teaching about forms of energy, particularly heat conduction. The education excludes any teaching about the cultural significance of the practice. This inadequate (and incomplete) portrayal of Others is similar to the portrayal of minorities in the NSES. In both cases, the curricula determine what knowledge is worth teaching and learning about in school.

In Aotearoa New Zealand, knowledge is deeply embedded in the colonial framework of the British empire and actively works against knowledge from a Maori perspective, or even the development of an authentic Pakeha worldview. For example, "ecological imperialism"[16] led teachers and administrators to introduce and plant fauna from Britain, such as ivy, sweet peas, weeping willows, and primroses around schools in order to promote the goals of the science syllabus. Sycamore seeds were especially imported to provide winged seed specimens to "draw from nature."[17] What counts as knowledge, the ways in which it is organized, who is empowered to teach it, and what counts as appropriate evidence of having learned it, are all part of the ways in which dominance and subordination are reproduced in society.[18]

The knowledge imparted in schools acts as a source of identity because it represents the best that is known and thought in a culture.[19] This knowledge can disrupt the subjectivity of the colonial Other through syllabus content, the exclusion or absence of knowledge, by internalizing explanations from incomplete knowledge, and through the interpersonal interactions between student and teacher. When science knowledge from home is not recognized in the classroom, students quickly learn that these places represent two different forms of identity, particularly if there are cultural differences between them. Going to the coast to gather seafood, or gathering "weeds" from a garden or creek bed to feed a large family is different from gathering seafood to be observed and drawn. These are the lessons students learn from their science classes and field trips. They learn that knowledge gained at school is not about their experiences and who they are. For them to do well they must absorb "the lesson of the master." As a result, and if they have learned their lessons well, they will speak as if they were the imperial speaker rather than the colonial subject.

Paul Feyerabend has raised concerns about the cultural nature of science itself and in particular the connection between culture and Western knowledge.[20] This has become part of the science that is constructed as anthropology:

> And so a story is told that no indigenous person is likely to understand though it is a story not only about them, but about the way in which an initially ignorant stranger experienced their life. Using abstract categories we might say that the anthropologist transforms impressions into knowledge by saying that we at once realise how culture-dependent this so-called "knowledge" really is.[21]

The construction of science as imperial knowledge thus becomes the process of science education.

EDUCATION AND THE GLOBAL ECONOMY

Education across the board is subject to questioning on account of its imperial foundations. Calls for equity and achievement seek to reform mathematics and science education for all children. The focus, however, is either on the children or the schooling. Science education is of specific interest to us as it plays a particularly important role in the creation of a culture for a new world order, portrayed as the global economy. The NSF's education mission statement illustrates this role:

> The NSF's cohesive and comprehensive set of education and human resources activities addresses every level of education, including early career development. Stimulating quality science, mathematics, engineering, and technology (SMET) education is vitally important to ensuring a diverse, scientific and technical workforce, as well as a citizenry capable of mastering the scientific and technological concepts and skills needed by workplace, social, and home environments that are characterized by increasing technological sophistication.[22]

The science curriculum, that is, science education, thus promises riches and access to power, both for individuals and for countries. Mathematics, technology, and science education are linked together as an unexamined holy trinity of success. Nonetheless, neither the culture of the global economy nor the science on which it is based are examined as containing culture. Or, in the words of the NAS statement, science education is not about equity, it is about global competition:

> [C]oncerns regarding economic competitiveness stress [the] central importance of science and mathematics education that will allow us to keep pace with our global competitors.[23]

Science is there, in Said's words, as the "marker." Science marks the culture of the economic competitiveness of the Internet, of technology, of the entrepreneur, and of capitalism's values. It produces a rational objective system that is beyond dispute. Science holds out this promise of riches and the better life for all in the global economy. As the National Research Council observes, "Americans agree that our students urgently need better science education. But what should they be expected to know and be able to do? Can the same expectations be applied across our diverse society?"[24]

Statements like this seek to achieve standard scientific literacy for all citizens. Yet when these ideas are unpacked what we seem to have is what Marx called the law of Moses and "the profits" clothed in the cultural accoutrements of America. There will be winners in the economy because there are losers. Science education links its ideal competitive aims with those of the World Trade Organization (WTO). The opening up of China through the WTO is about creating a global economy by creating more markets in which to sell products. Everything in this economic system has a value that is related to a price. The culture being developed is thus a culture of the market commodity. The division between science and culture is rendered invisible because the culture of global success is transmitted through science.

Educational strategies for equity have at the first level focused on a changed pedagogy. The informal, home-based understanding of the natural world and of numbers is transformed through the formal context of the classroom. Through programs like the NSF, schools are now being urged to help students to make connections between their informal learning and the classroom. Programs that emphasize experiential learning are now being developed. These programs draw on the communities in which children live to help them go beyond textbooks and develop real understanding. We are in support of these aims. Yet the social divisions which segment these communities are being ignored, as is the purpose of newly focused science education.

It is insufficient to see education as simply the benign and neutral transmission of various aspects of the culture to form part of the curriculum. Rather, we critique the positive and negative consequences of both the process and the content of education. From a postcolonial perspective we have to focus on the imperialist creation of a culture and interrogate the impact of the transmission of knowledge of the constructed culture as normative truth.

SCIENCE EDUCATION, CULTURE, AND EQUITY

Recent debates in the field of science and culture have focused on the way that science education should respond to cultural diversity, especially the presence in science classrooms of non-Western, Indigenous, and other minority group learners. While some authors such as Ronald Good and Cathleen Loving have argued that because science is universal the concept of "multicultural science" is problematic,[25] other authors believe that Indigenous and other minority groups have their own knowledge that can contribute to scientific understandings and, hence, to science education.[26]

In the literature concerning culture, science, and science education, a number of avenues are currently being investigated regarding the participation and achievement of marginalized groups in science and science education. In particular, these studies tend to address issues of either knowledge or pedagogy. However, we find that both these avenues have tended to focus on the idea of "managing" the Other in the classroom through learning about the Other's "cultural knowledge and ways." This approach is not satisfactory as it fails to address the historical and social power relations that exist between social groups in classrooms and the consequences of these power relations on both the students' learning and on the body of knowledge that is taught.

A body of literature questioning "knowledge" in school science curricula and "what counts as knowledge" is starting to emerge in science education. It has the potential to question school science and science education. Indigenous populations, such as Maori in Aotearoa New Zealand and the Yupiaq in Alaska, or Aboriginal people in Australia see the school curricula as a potential means of revitalizing their language and/or of reproducing their cultural knowledge. Such changes also encourage them to question the cultural knowledge that constitutes the basis of current school curricula.

The literature surrounding "culturally relevant pedagogy" has been influential in the field of science education. Building upon the assumption that teachers possess a specific understanding of pedagogical issues, Ladson-Billings has suggested that successful teachers of African American students shared specific and unique characteristics:[27] these teachers provided a culturally relevant pedagogy for their students.

Culturally relevant pedagogy involves students in knowledge construction. Teachers have high expectations and academic standards for their students. As such, educators must engage students in a critique of society's racist, sexist, and elitist social structure. For African American students culturally relevant science pedagogy includes their construction of knowledge about science and its culture, as well as their development of the skills they need to succeed in this field of study. Culturally relevant science pedagogy acknowledges that scientific discourse, the enacted school science curriculum, and confidence in the ability to construct scientific knowledge may not be part of African American students' culture. Culturally relevant science teaching values the learner's experiential, as well as theoretical, knowledge. In this pedagogical approach, teachers assist students in transcending the cultural borders between their personal lives and school science.

Sherene Razack sounds a note of caution about the different perceptions of relations between dominant and subordinate groups and emphasizes that these are not unmarked by histories of oppression.[28] She argues that without history and social context, problems of communication come to be seen as "technical glitches." They are misunderstandings that arise because the parties are culturally, racially, physically, mentally, or sexually different. Moreover, without an understanding of how responses to subordinate groups are socially organized to sustain existing power arrangements, we cannot hope either to communicate across social hierarchies or work to eliminate them. The implication is that teachers from the dominant group can learn how to "manage" Others in the classroom according to some "cultural" rules. This technical approach is prevalent in education, that is, dealing with Others through a variety of pedagogical "tricks" such as cooperative learning, girl-friendly science, and the use of myths and legends for introductions to the "real" science. The pedagogical tricks infer that one just needs to "learn the culture" to intervene "appropriately" and accommodate culturally different or gender-specific styles of learning. It is thus the creation of the imperial Other.

What makes the "managed" approach inadequate is that its emphasis on cultural diversity often reduces itself to a superficial reading of differences. The pedagogical approach can reinforce an epistemological cornerstone of imperialism, namely, that the colonized possess a series of knowable characteristics that can be studied, known, and managed accordingly. This approach also carries the danger of limiting student experiences or inferring negative characteristics about student ability. However, it is important to note that culturally relevant pedagogy does emphasize the cultural context of teaching and learning.

FINAL THOUGHTS

Some recent postcolonial literature focuses on understanding the relationships and interactions between different groups. Cross-cultural interactions are traditionally ignored in the research regarding "underrepresented" groups in science education. Christine Sleeter argues that the adoption of "cross-cultural" strategies does little to ensure that white teachers in the United States will view their black and Asian students as capable of the same level of achievement and range of desires as their white students.[29] Alison Jones suggests that the call for "cross-cultural" dialogue in Aotearoa New Zealand is reassuring at this "postcolonial" juncture when Pakeha/Western cultural dominance is no longer taken for granted—it reassures subjugated groups that the dominant group (white/Pakeha) is part of a scene of redemption, not the unfashionable colonizer or oppressor in the textbooks. She continues, "Through being good, open, loveable partners in the liberal social economy we seek liberation, through hearing you, through your dialogue with us. Touched by your attention, we are included with you, and therefore cleaned from the taint of colonization and power that excludes."[30]

Furthermore, she argues that in an entanglement of benevolence, desire, and colonization, liberal and radical dominant groups (white/Pakeha) have to engage in learning their (and our) own histories and social privileges in relation to ethnic Others. This will require embracing positively an acceptance of ignorance of the Other. What such work has begun to show us all is that we must come to a better understanding of how our classrooms operate and at the same time be able to "view it from its own shadows."[31]

We end with a series of questions. Can we as educators be comfortable with straying into an alien but uncannily familiar shadow cast by ourselves about teaching and learning? Can we as educators afford not to subject ourselves to such cognitive disjunctures? Things have been happening behind the teacher's back for far too long. Can we bring ourselves to face them by turning our backs to the (en)light(enment)? Ellsworth suggests that in order to "turn our backs" we must reach out into other disciplines of knowledge and practice what is "foreign." This will "breach the circle of education in the name of becoming educated about what the field of education itself prevents us from thinking and seeing."[32] We are not talking about finding out about things and incorporating them into our understanding of teaching to make it more accurate. We are talking about tracing the limits of our knowing and breaching them from within. We are talking about subjecting science education to a scientific analysis.

NOTES

1. Edward W. Said, *Culture and Imperialism* 9 (1994).
2. Michael Doyle, *Empires* 45 (1986).
3. Maori name for New Zealand.
4. Indigenous peoples of Aotearoa New Zealand.
5. Name given to non-Maori of mainly European descent.
6. Science in this context refers to science and science education.
7. *See generally* Thomas B. Corcoran et al., *The SSIs and Professional Development for Teachers* (1998).
8. Pew Charitable Trust, *Quality Counts: The Urban Challenge, Public Education in Fifty States*, Educ. Wk. (1998).
9. Eva Krugley-Smolska, *Cultural Influences in Science Education*, 17 Int'l J. Sci. Educ. 45 (Jan. 1995); Leslie Jones, "Science Education for All? Examining Connections/Disconnection between Theory and Classroom Practice and Finally Moving This Idea from Rhetoric toward Reality," "MS," symposium presented at the National Association of Research in Science Teaching, 2000.
10. Elizabeth Ellsworth, *Teaching Positions* (1997).
11. We use the term postcolonial in this essay because it implies a discursive formation of identity and representation—a condition of being postcolonial. At the same time, it embodies a strategy. Postcolonial is the time after a colony gained independence—a legal decolonization—and implies some formal break. However, for all former colonies of an empire this link usually continues in one, or both, of two forms. One is that of an imperial artefact. For example, England's Privy Council is still Aotearoa New Zealand's highest court. The second is the cultural and political domination left behind, often reflected in the practices, minds, and institutions of the former colony.
12. Edward W. Said, *Orientalism* (1978).
13. Michael Apple, *Culture, Politics and Education* (1996).
14. As curricular decisions are a local, not a national responsibility, there is no consensus across the United States's sixteen thousand school districts as to what science knowledge is and what should be taught.
15. Alberto J. Rodriguez, *The Dangerous Discourse of Invisibility: A Critique of the National Research Council's National Science Education Standards*, 34 J. Res. in Sci. Teaching 19–37 (1997).
16. Alfred W. Crosby, *Ecological Imperialism: The Biological Expansion of Europe 900–1900* (1986).

17. Joce Jesson, "New Zealand Science Curriculum and the British Connection," in SAME Papers (B. Bell ed. 1991).

18. *See* Apple, *supra* note 13.

19. *See* Said, *supra* note 1, at xiii.

20. Paul K. Feyerabend, *Three Dialogues on Knowledge* (1991).

21. *Id.* at 143.

22. *See* National Science Foundation, <http://www.nsf.gov> [hereinafter NSF].

23. *See* National Research Council, *National Science Education Standards* 1 (1996) [hereinafter NRC].

24. *See id.* at 4.

25. Ronald Good, *Comments on Multicultural Science Education*, 79(3) Sci. Educ. 335–36 (1995); Cathleen Loving, *Comment on "Multiculturalism, Universalism, and Science Education,"* 79(3) Sci. Educ. 341–48 (1995).

26. *See, e.g.*, Michael Christie, *Aboriginal Science for the Ecologically Sustainable Future*, 37 Australian Sci. Tchrs. J. 26–31 (1991).

27. Gloria Ladson-Billings, *The Dreamkeepers: Successful Teachers of African American Children* (1994).

28. Sherene H. Razack, *Looking White People in the Eye* (1998).

29. Christine Sleeter, "How White People Construct Race," in *Race, Identity and Representation in Education* 157–71 (McCarthy et al. eds. 1993).

30. Alison Jones, *The Limits of Cross-Cultural Dialogue: Pedagogy, Desire, and Absolution in the Classroom*, 29 Educ. Theory 299–316, 314 (Summer 1999).

31. *See* Ellsworth, *supra* note 10, at 194.

32. *See id.* at 195.

13

U.S. Policy on "Female Genital Mutilation"

*Threat of Economic Pressure Internationally,
Enactment of Criminal Sanctions at Home*

Holly Maguigan

SURGERIES ON FEMALE genitalia have been performed for at least twenty-five hundred years. Today they occur routinely in forty countries—in Africa, in the southern part of the Arabian Peninsula, and, to a smaller degree, in India, Pakistan, Malaysia, and Indonesia.[1] The World Health Organization estimates that 130 million women and girls have been subjected, at ages ranging from infancy to adulthood, to some form of female genital cutting.

Drawing on the experiences of the twenty-eight African countries in which the surgeries are routine, Amnesty International's Zan-Akologo described the reasons for the endurance of the practice:

> Though there are no laws that make female circumcision obligatory, the social pressure on women is enormous. In most cases the women in these societies in Africa cooperate with the practice, and continue to force it on the next generation of girls. These women are dependent on men, and therefore they have no alternative but to fall in line with the custom. In those parts of Africa men are still the only ones who make decisions, and it is they who set the standards for women's conduct.[2]

U.S. government sources suggest that as many as 168,000 girls and women in the United States have had their genitals cut or are at risk for the procedures.[3] These are overwhelmingly immigrants or the first-generation daughters of immigrants. Since 1996, the U.S. Congress and the legislatures of fifteen states have passed laws against "female genital mutilation."[4] Most statutes are criminal only, although some have civil provisions.

The question addressed in this chapter is not whether efforts should be made to eliminate the practice. It is, rather, whether these new statutes provide the appropriate tools to combat female genital mutilation (FGM) here or in other countries. Particular attention will be paid to criminal anti-FGM laws. The problem with these statutes is not simply that they are unlikely to keep girls and women safe from the procedure. Rather, and more importantly, the problem is that they are virtually guaranteed to drive FGM underground and increase the danger to those on whom it is performed.

It should be noted at the outset that the surgeries themselves vary widely. The least invasive entail either ritual "nicking" or the removal of a small portion of the clitoris. Others involve removal of all or part of the clitoral tissue. In the most significant procedures, practitioners remove the clitoris and labia minora, incise the labia majora, and stitch together the labia majora to cover the urethral and vaginal openings (leaving a small opening for the passage of urine and menstrual blood).

Various forms of the first type of female surgery—removal of part of the clitoris—were performed in the United States and the United Kingdom until the 1950s, ostensibly for the purposes of improving female mental health, discouraging lesbianism, and reducing the incidence of masturbation. During those periods the procedures were deemed medical and were fully legal. Now that female genital cutting is identified in this country as the practice of immigrants, however, it has been criminalized.

Several terms are used to describe the procedures. The term "female genital mutilation [FGM]" is very common in the United States and used almost exclusively in its criminal context. Indeed, the very term expresses the disapprobation of the procedure. Isabelle Gunning urges the use of "female genital surgeries [FGS]" to reflect the variety of procedures performed.[5]

Nahid Toubia, a physician of Sudanese origin, and an activist in the United States and abroad who is opposed to the practice, uses both the terms "female genital mutilation" and "female circumcision" (although she notes that the practice is not analogous to male circumcision). The reasons for her choices are reflected in a statement issued by RAINBO

(Research, Action and Information Network for Bodily Integrity of Women), an international advocacy organization which she founded:

> Efforts to empower women cannot begin with using language that offends them. . . . We accept that the term female genital mutilation has been too widely used to be rolled back. In fact, we prefer to retain the term FGM at the policy level to remind everyone of the effect of this practice on girls and women. However, we advocate the use of the term female circumcision when dealing with affected individuals, parents, or other community members. . . . It is important that we respect the feelings and beliefs of individuals even as we inform them of facts contrary to these beliefs.[6]

The decision to call the practice FGM for pragmatic and policy reasons, but to refer to it as FC in outreach and education efforts, reflects RAINBO's awareness of the complexity confronting opponents of the practice. It points to the need to choose one's strategy carefully.

INTERNATIONAL EFFORTS AND THE ROLE OF U.S. ECONOMIC POLICIES

In this country, many legislators and policy makers, including feminists, seem not to have taken into account the reasons for which parents, mainly mothers, decide on the procedure for their daughters. Some observers describe the difficulty of convincing a mother not to make this decision as part of the wider problem confronting activists working to eradicate various forms of violence against women and their daughters: women are complicit in their own oppression and that of their children. Tracy Higgins has explained the problem this way:

> The practice of female genital surgery poses a particularly difficult practical and theoretical problem for feminists, in that it is at once physically dangerous, deeply threatening to Western norms of female sexuality, reflective of patriarchal regulation of women's sexuality and, at the same time, performed by women on women and girls.[7]

It is important to recognize the reasons why a woman might perceive that keeping up tradition is in her daughter's best interest. The surgery is often seen as a rite of passage, the means of achieving cleanliness and beauty, a necessary precondition to marriage, a mark of identity and status, and necessary to a woman's full participation in the life of the community. Nahid Toubia has described the phenomenon this way:

> Cultural identity is of paramount importance to everyone. Defending that identity becomes especially important when the group has faced colonialism (as in Africa), when immigrants are faced with a stronger majority culture, and when change does not favor those holding social power (that is, men). Female circumcision is part of the socialization of girls into acceptable womanhood . . . [and is] the physical marking of the marriageability of women.[8]

Many mothers are motivated by the belief that the procedures are required by their religions, including Islam and Christianity. The fact that genital surgeries are not mandated by the official tenets of any organized religion is less important than the reality that many Christian and Islamic religious leaders and adherents, as well as those of some traditional African religions, believe that a woman who has not undergone the procedure is "unclean."

Opponents of the procedure will succeed when they design strategies which recognize the powerful reasons underlying a woman's decision to impose it on her daughters. The success of grassroots, religious, and government-led efforts in some of the countries where the procedure has been practiced widely is instructive about the sorts of strategies which may work in other such countries as well as in immigrant communities in the United States.

In Kenya, for instance, where FGM/FC is a rite of puberty, an alternative coming-of-age ceremony was designed by activists who report that in 1998 eleven hundred Kenyan girls received counseling, without physical circumcision, in a program called "Circumcise with Words." Practices are more varied in Ethiopia, where in different cultures the procedure ranges from partial to complete excision and is performed at ages varying between seven days and sixteen years. There, government- and UNICEF-sponsored radio broadcasts and women's meetings have been effective in convincing women to band together to withstand traditional pressures to excise their daughters.

Local organizing has been credited with reducing the incidence of the practice in Senegal, where an NGO educational effort begun in one village in 1991 has now resulted in 148 communities' publicly renouncing FGM/FC. A multidisciplinary group in Mali—including Muslim leaders who have issued a statement that FGM is not mentioned in the Koran and that a decision not to practice excision is no sin—plans intervention strategies in schools and university-based educational fora.[9]

The relationship of the United States to these efforts in other countries poses a particular conundrum for anti-FGM/FC activists. Many applaud the provision of economic support to local NGOs, like the one in Senegal, just as they do the funding provided by other Western and Northern countries.[10] (An analogous requirement of domestic educational efforts is the relatively noncontroversial provision of the federal Female Genital Mutilation Act. It mandates outreach and education by the Secretary of Health and Human Services but does not provide or require funding for those efforts. It is not, therefore, likely to be implemented soon.)

More problematic than affirmative funding to NGOs is the Act's threat to withhold essential disaster and humanitarian aid. A noncriminal portion of the FGMA applies to that category of aid to other countries. Section 579(a) requires that, as of 1999, the Secretary of the Treasury oppose new or continued funding to countries receiving U.S. loans and other funds (through USAID, monies contributed by the United States to the World Bank, and various NGOs) if those countries have a known history of the practice of female genital mutilation and have not taken steps to implement educational programs designed to prevent the practice.

The section containing the threat to withhold this aid was enacted in 1996, effective in 1998, and by its terms required the withholding of aid by 1999. Some critics of Senegal's January 1999 enactment of a criminal prohibition of FGM/FC suggest that it acted in response to the implied pressure of Section 579(a). They said that their own criminal statute was passed not as part of a real effort to end FGM/FC, but "only to please American sensitivities." These observers praised the work of FGM/FC opponents in Sudan and Egypt who "favour education over criminalisation."[11] Another commentator, on the other hand, sees the Senegalese criminal law as the direct and positive outgrowth of NGO activity in local communities (a product, therefore, of affirmative aid from U.S. agencies rather than of the threat to withhold monies). Still another, who opposes this extraterritorial application of U.S. pressure, says that the authorized economic sanctions have yet to be invoked in practice because the Clinton Administration found the language too vague to implement.[12]

WHY DOMESTIC CRIMINAL SANCTIONS WILL MAKE THE PRACTICE MORE DANGEROUS IN THE UNITED STATES

Resorting to criminal sanctions, while failing to appropriate funds for education and outreach, is the product of a total failure to learn from the lessons of other Western and Northern countries that have attempted to curb the practice through criminal justice methods. While many countries, including some which have long performed the surgeries, have enacted criminal statutes, the experience of two European nations is particularly useful to the United States as a basis for predicting the outcome here.[13]

In France female genital surgeries have been the subject of prosecution under general assault (rather than specially defined) statutes since 1983. In the twenty-six cases brought to trial, twenty-five convictions have been obtained. Those convicted were rarely the practitioners, because families declined to identify them. The majority of defendants convicted and sentenced were mothers of the affected girls. The high conviction rate masks the fact that these prosecutions have been counterproductive from the perspective of the safety of at-risk girls and women. Rather than stop it, they have driven the practice underground. Some parents return to their countries of origin to have the operation performed. Others remain in France but are discouraged from seeking medical treatment for life-threatening complications after the procedures.[14]

In the United Kingdom, a special criminal ban against FGM, the Prohibition of Female Circumcision Act, was enacted in 1985. (It was supplemented by the Children's Act of 1989, which provided specifically that FGM is child abuse.) The penalty for performing, aiding, or "procuring" the procedure is imprisonment for up to five years. Healthcare personnel are required to report instances of FGM to law enforcement. There have been no prosecutions to date.

Critics of the Female Circumcision Act assert that public dissemination of information about penalties has had the same result in Britain as the history of prosecutions has had in France. The Act has discouraged parents from seeking the necessary medical attention for their postoperative daughters:

> Some health care workers have derided efforts to eradicate the practice through legal measures. They fear criminalization has, perversely, made FGM an even greater health hazard.[15]

In the United States, there is every reason to predict that resort to a criminal justice "solution" will have the same discouraging impact on parents' seeking medical treatment to protect the health of their postoperative daughters. They will learn about the possibility of prosecution in the same ways as their counterparts in France and the United Kingdom: the existence of the criminal statutes is discussed in the media (and even people not fluent in the language of the print or broadcast press have friends who will translate); healthcare professionals issue warnings during visits for other purposes; activists publicize the existence of the prohibitions; and word of mouth carries the information further into communities.[16] In addition, in this country one of the civil provisions of the Female Genital Mutilation Act requires INS officials to inform immigrants, at their ports of entry, that permitting the procedure will subject them to prosecution.

Criminal sanctions alone rarely deter effectively. Without the support of the relevant communities, they are unlikely to persuade people to change (as oppose to hide) their patterns of behavior. Immigrant anti-FGM/FC activists are divided on the question of whether criminalization will prove an effective tool in their campaigns. For instance, Meserak "Mimi" Ramsey, an immigrant from Ethiopia who is now an organizer throughout the United States, was instrumental in obtaining the passage of the California criminal statute. On the other hand, Nahid Toubia, who founded RAINBO in response to many years of experience treating excised women and girls in the Sudan, opposes punishing the practice as a crime.

There is not much basis in U.S. history (as opposed to that of France and Britain) for predicting who is correct. The popular press and legal literature contain reference to only one prosecution in this country, and the discussion which followed it was marked by anger. In 1986 in DeKalb County, Georgia, a nurse who had immigrated from Somalia was charged with assault. The allegation was that she had excised the genitals of her two-year-old niece. The defendant was acquitted because the prosecution failed to prove that she was the one who had performed the procedure. There was a swift and negative response from the Somali community in Atlanta to the decision to prosecute:

> "The Somali woman doesn't need an alien woman telling her how to treat her private parts," says Samme Warsame, founder of the Somali Relief Adjustment Organization, Inc., in Atlanta. "The decision must come from the Somalis."[17]

While prosecution under general assault statutes is a bad tool for changing behavior, special anti-FGM laws are even more likely to provoke anger and fear. At least it can be said that an assault prosecution is the enforcement of a law which applies to all people living in the jurisdiction in question. The special federal and state laws, on the other hand, are aimed at immigrants. First and most obviously, legislators have selected for particularized treatment a practice which could be prosecuted under the assault and child-endangerment laws of all jurisdictions.

Second, evidence of cultural beliefs, while not constituting a separate "cultural defense" anywhere in this country, is admissible and relevant in a trial under general laws. It makes sense both as a policy and as an evidentiary matter that a judge or jury should hear the reasons for which a parent would consent to the procedure and have the benefit of evidence that the defendant did not have a criminal intention to "disfigure" or "maim" her daughter (disfigurement and maiming or their equivalents are elements of the offense of assault)—even if the result is that the defendant is convicted and the cultural background evidence is only used at sentencing.

Cultural evidence appears to be specifically excluded by the terms of the federal and most special state statutes. They contain the language, "In applying [the defense that the procedure is necessary and performed by a licensed medical practitioner] no account shall be taken of the effect on the person on whom the operation is to be performed of any belief on the part of that person, or any other person, that the operation is required as a matter of custom or ritual." It is unusual for a criminal law to include, in addition to definitions of the offense (and sometimes of possible defenses) a prohibition of the types of evidence or issues which a judge or jury may take into account.

The implications of the special laws go beyond the issues of specially defined criminal acts and the exclusion of types of evidence. Of particular concern is the fact that the Federal Sentencing Guidelines mandate a sentence of imprisonment of up to five years after conviction under the FGMA. The sentence actually imposed on a person with no criminal history will range from thirty-three to fifty-seven months, depending on whether the person stood trial or entered a plea of guilty.[18] Most of the states' special laws similarly require sentences of imprisonment. They deny a judge discretion to put a parent on probation after conviction. (In France, many postconviction sentences were probationary ones.) All, of course, permit the conviction of parents (and, as has been the case in France, most of those prosecuted will be mothers) on a theory of accessorial liability. Some specifically make it a crime for a parent to consent to the procedure.

Because most of those convicted will be immigrants, in addition to mandatory incarceration they will face the certainty of deportation if and when their convictions come to the attention of the Immigration and Naturalization Service. At least one state's anti-FGM provisions include, *within the criminal statute*, a mandate for reports to the INS whenever a defendant is thought to be an immigrant. Colorado's statute provides, "If the district attorney having jurisdiction over a case arising under this paragraph . . . has a reasonable belief that any person arrested or charged pursuant to this paragraph . . . is not a citizen or national of the United States, the district attorney shall report such information to the immigration and naturalization service in an expeditious manner."[19]

The deportation or removability provisions of the Illegal Immigration Reform and Immigrant Responsibility Act (IIRIRA) apply to lawful permanent residents as well as those with less secure status.[20] These provisions guarantee the removal of any immigrant convicted of a crime of violence, a crime of child abuse, or a crime of moral turpitude committed within five years of admission to the United States and punishable by a year in prison.

As if these threats—at both the state and national levels—were not enough to discourage parents from seeking medical help when their daughters require it after a procedure, some statutes make clear the danger of such an effort: healthcare personnel are required to report instances of FGM to law enforcement. In addition, they prohibit any medical cooperation with compromises between the traditional practice and a more moderate version. Most, by their terms, make criminal even a minor ritual version of the surgeries as well as reinfibulation of a woman after childbirth.[21]

CONCLUSION

The issue is not whether female genital cutting is an acceptable form of violence against women and girls. It is not. The question is the utility of resort to prosecution instead of, or even as preliminary to, organizing and education efforts like the ones that have been successful in other countries. A real problem with the anti-FGM criminal legislation is that it is likely to terrorize immigrants. For those who lack legal status in this country, it will only add to the reasons that prevent them from seeking medical help. Even lawful permanent residents who may otherwise avail themselves of services without that level of fear, face certain removal from the United States if convicted. If people in this country are genuinely concerned about the safety of at-risk girls, the correct approach cannot involve threatening their parents with imprisonment and deportation.

NOTES

1. Solita Sarwono, *Females Who Are Circumcised Suffer Throughout Their Lives,* Jakarta Post, Apr. 23, 2000, *available at* 2000 WL 4788174.

2. Daphna Lewy-Yanovitz, *A Conspiracy of Silence: Amnesty International Is Fighting the Practice of Female Genital Mutilation in Africa and Elsewhere,* Ha'aretz, Apr. 3, 2000, *available at* 2000 WL 7219340.

3. Wanda K. Jones, Jack Smith Burney, Jr., and Kieke Lynne Wilcox, "Female Genital Mutilation/Female Circumcision: Who Is at Risk in the U.S.?" *U.S. Department of Health and Human Services,* 9/19/97 Pub. Health Rep. 368, Vol. 112, No. 5 (reporting on 1996 estimates by the Department of Health and Human Services, derived from a 1990 report by the Centers for Disease Control and Prevention).

4. See 18 U.S.C. §116(a) (1999) (the federal Female Genital Mutilation Act). The following states have enacted similar criminal statutes: California, Colorado, Delaware, Illinois, Maryland, Minnesota, New York, North Dakota, Oregon, Rhode Island, Tennessee, Texas, West Virginia, and Wisconsin. For a chart comparing the provisions of the various enactments as of 1999, *see* Holly Maguigan, *Will Prosecutions for "Female Genital Mutilation" Stop the Practice in the U.S.?,* 8 Temp. Pol. and Civ. Rts. L. Rev. 391, 415 (1999).

5. *See, e.g.*, Isabelle R. Gunning, *Arrogant Perception, World-Travelling and Multicultural Feminism: The Case of Female Genital Surgeries*, 23 Colum. Hum. Rts. L. Rev. 189 (1992).

6. Jones, Burney, and Wilcox, *supra* note 3 (quoting RAINBO website)(citations omitted).

7. Tracy E. Higgins, *Anti-Essentialism, Relativism, and Human Rights*, 19 Harv. Women's L.J. 89, n.89 (1996).

8. *See* Nahid Toubia, *Female Genital Mutilation: A Call for Global Action* (1993).

9. The Kenyan experience is described by John Mwaura, *Female Circumcision Alternative Gains Support*, Africa News Service, Jan. 7, 1999, *available at* 1999 WL 7543523. For the educational efforts in Ethiopia, see Hadera Tesfay, *In Ethiopia, Women Say No to Female Genital Mutilation*, UNICEF Information Feature (visited Jul. 26, 1996), <http://www.unicef.org/features/feat176.htm>.

10. *See* Theresa Lora, "Discrimination against Women," Testimony before the House Committee on International Relations, Congressional Testimony, May 3, 2000, *available at* 2000 WL 19303171; Brian Kenety, *NGOs Applaud Trade Deal Linking Health, Development*, Inter Press Service, May 24, 2000.

11. *Female Genital Mutilation: Is It Crime or Culture? Banning the Practice May Not Be the Best Way of Ending It*, Economist, Feb. 13, 1999, at 45.

12. Antonia Kirkland, *Female Genital Mutilation and the United States Vote at International Financial Institutions*, 20 Women's Rts. L. Rep. 147, 152 (1999).

13. For a chart describing, as of 1999, the criminal prohibitions of twenty-four countries, *see* Maguigan, *supra* note 4, at 418.

14. *See* Bronwyn Winter, *Women, the Law, and Cultural Relativism in France: The Case of Excision*, 19 Signs 939 (1994).

15. Carol M. Messito, *Regulating Rites: Legal Responses to Female Genital Mutilation in the West*, 16 In the Public Interest 33, 54 (1997–98).

16. *See, e.g.*, Winter, *supra* note 14 (on the French experience).

17. Nina Schuyler, *Cultural Defense: Equality or Anarchy?* 1 San Francisco Wkly., Sept. 25, 1991; *see also* Jane Hansen and Deborah Scroggins, *Female Circumcision: U.S., Georgia Forced to Face Medical, Legal Issues*, Atlanta J. and Const., Nov. 15, 1992, at A1.

18. The U.S. Sentencing Commission has not yet designated guidelines for the sentence after conviction of Section 116. The sentence range available to judges will be that for the statute most analogous, aggravated assault.

19. Co. Stat. Ann. § 18-6-401 (West 2000).

20. *See* Illegal Immigration Reform and Immigrant Responsibility Act of 1996, Pub. L. No. 104–208, 110 Stat. 3009.

21. L. Amede Obiora, *Bridges and Barricades: Rethinking Polemics and Intransigence in the Campaign against Female Circumcision*, 47 Case West. L. Rev. 275 (1997).

PART III

COLLECTIVE AND GROUP RIGHTS

14

Bridging False Divides

Toward a Transnational Politics of Gender

R. W. Perry and L. Amede Obiora

AT THE TURN of the millennium, in many parts of the world political ideas and positions identified with feminism still routinely arouse resistance, even outrage. Such reactions derive from the long history of gender moralizing in the discourses of Western colonial expansion. In nineteenth-century British debates around the practice of *sati* in India (as well as numerous other gendered practices elsewhere in colonized regions), the agenda of rescuing nonwhite women from nonwhite men and from the backwardness of non-Western cultures played an important role in justifying imperialism. According to Sir Henry Maine in 1861, the status of women in any society, when compared to the condition of women in Maine's own Victorian England, provided a measure of that country's level of civilization. In Jules Verne's 1873 whizbang novel of technological progress, *Around the World in Eighty Days*, the French futurist author depicted a moment of high drama and romantic interest when his protagonist, the Victorian English gentleman Phileas Fogg, rescues Aouda, an Indian princess, from death on the flames of a funeral pyre. This image of Western reason, morality, and technology arriving to save a brown woman from the barbarity of the culture into which she had the misfortune to be born was repeated in various versions of Western modernization-as-redemption narratives set in Asia, Africa, and the indigenous Americas.[1]

Such narratives have been enduring and influential. Advocacy by local, non-Western women of reforms identified as feminist is viewed as pandering to outside pressures and as a betrayal of local cultural norms of gender propriety and indigenous gender relations. Reformist endeavors are construed as direct threats to the autonomy of local communities, indeed even as indirect continuations of colonial hegemony. Such reactions raise a number of pressing questions. Foremost among them are, first, the question of what feminism is—whether it is necessarily a purely Western entity; and second, the question of the authenticity of the local, that is, of what constitutes an external versus an internal influence.

In order to advance the prospects for a transnational, multicultural gender politics, this essay argues for a reconceptualized, integrated human-rights platform. Employing the example of the stereotyping of African women in global gender rights discourse, we address the dilemma of rights integration—specifically, how to appropriate universal human rights notions to further the diverse interests of all women in concrete local contexts.

AFRICAN WOMEN IN GLOBAL GENDER RIGHTS DISCOURSE: A CAUTIONARY TALE

Tribalism and globalism are the two axial principles of our time that present two alternate and opposing paths to a global future.[2] One implication is that to escape the backwardness insinuated in the very term tribalism, all local social formations must henceforth necessarily be expressed and regulated through the interventions of global networks. Many feminist campaigns for the reform of local gender relations through the framework of international human rights discourse exemplify this pattern. Such contemporary campaigns are a continuation of decades of Western, non-Western, and transnational feminist struggles to expose gender inequities to normative scrutiny. With the intensification of global cosmopolitanism from the 1980s onward, local gender relations have increasingly been scrutinized in dialogue with alternative modes of being.[3] The ubiquitous descriptions of traditional patriarchal forms in Africa exemplify the failure of universalizing human rights discourse to contextualize adequately the phenomena of which it speaks.

Beginning in the colonial era, reform initiatives to advance the rights of African women have frequently invoked an image of the African continent as the silhouette of a woman carrying a heavy burden on her head and back.[4] We would reinterpret this long-standing icon of female subordination in Africa by suggesting that, upon closer examination, a viewer might equally well be struck by the fine precision with which this African Everywoman balances her burden, for perhaps there is more to her balancing act than meets the eye. In a great many African countries, women's socioeconomic productivity is not only central to the national economy, but also enables women to meet their families' needs, to augment other household earnings, and to provide stability for their communities. These enormous contributions have largely gone unreckoned by critics, as has the central economic position and leverage of women in local African communities.

Now, to an increasing extent, African women are gaining recognition for their contributions; indeed, they are being recognized as protagonists of a quite different sort of narrative about Africa. The convergence of historical circumstances which is now reconstituting the political economy of contemporary African states presents an opportunity both to mitigate gender inequities and to reconceive gender-role differences as constitutive of local social and economic formations. Indeed, for today's much-ballyhooed African Renaissance to mature from the stuff of media sound bites into a concrete reality for all Africans, explicit attention must be given to the material conditions of women in all dimensions of their lives.

To further this reconceptualization of the position of African women within both African and transnational gender politics, we question representations of gender that ignore the central role of both local history and contemporary global restructuring in creating existing gender systems.[5] One hears much of the complicated construction of personhood and the specific positions of individual men and women in African communities. Yet what we do know does not suggest that African communities have been devoid of protective resources for women. Even where gender-related inequities are pervasive, they are not necessarily regarded as unproblematic—it is not as though individuals have an unconstrained prerogative in the local moral economy to perpetrate them.

Similarly, gender consciousness is never static, but rather is constantly produced and transformed in everyday experience. Nevertheless, reductionist accounts of African women's lives remain insufficiently challenged. We would hardly deny that women in Africa and elsewhere are subject to myriad disadvantages imposed by virtue of their gender. Yet the unidimensional nature of these accounts, in particular those found in many feminist texts, reenacts the invisibility of African women. Especially in the rural regions of Africa, where it is clear that women constitute the backbone of the economy, such accounts simply rehearse African women's lack of agency. In striving to buttress its case for gender equity, international feminist scholarship has tended to flatten the specificities and meanings of women's lived experiences. The ignorant reductionism of such accounts surely predates contemporary feminism, but it has taken on a new force in global feminist rights discourse.

The abundant evidence that African women have been constrained and disenfranchised by gender-biased policies and practices does not negate the fact that they have been neither mute nor invisible in the course of history. Accounts that focus solely on the evils of a putatively universal patriarchy without attending to women's agency and to everyday forms of resistance are no longer defensible even as polemics.[6] Patriarchy is neither total nor totalizing. It could not be so. To imagine otherwise is to erase a long history of resistance by women. The representation of African women as passive victims of patriarchal structures serves to naturalize its own narrative. If women were indeed so passive, then there would be no hope for gender reform. The actual experiences of women now and in the past are evidence of the need for an alternative to standard accounts of the "powerlessness of African women." Moreover, in conceptualizing the situation of women, a great deal hinges on how one conceptualizes power.

In one revealing anecdote some Western feminists went to Nigeria to film a documentary on a market women's village organization. On arrival in the village they encountered a woman selling goods by the roadside. The visitors' only contacts prior to arriving at the village were academics. When the time for the meeting came, the turnout was very low. The visitors subsequently found that their academic contacts had neglected to go through local channels to mobilize the women in question. To make amends, the visitors were introduced to the recognized leader of the market women. They were amazed to recognize that this was the same woman they had encountered earlier in the street. She assured them that she would do her best to gather her associates. At the rescheduled meeting, the venue was filled to capacity. Months of planning and advertising had failed to achieve what this single woman accomplished in hours without even the advantage of telephones. Despite the political marginalization of such women, theirs is the street-level reality with which one must reckon. How do they fit into existing config-urations of power? What accounts for their erasure in feminist under-standings of the structures and negotiations of power in gender rela-tions? Does this blindness to alternate realities reinforce the status quo and its limits? How can such stereotyped representations be resisted, while nevertheless opposing the realities of gender inequities?

The task of challenging gender exclusion may require illuminating the little-known experiences and struggles of women—without accept-ing their subordination as an immutable eternal essence of African val-ues and philosophies.[7] Lessons can be drawn from attending to the ways in which women understand their own life circumstances and how they translate these circumstances into critique and resistance to gender conflicts.[8] Histories of various specific claims by women pro-vide insight into alternate understandings of women's positions in so-cial life. Rather than naturalizing power relations and homogenizing complex layers of gender experience under universalizing narratives of patriarchal oppression, one might rather consider how women articu-late issues in their own terms in order to comprehend the diversity of actual gender beliefs and practices.

In the state of near emergency that exists in many parts of Africa today, women's efforts to revivify local traditions of self-reliance and to forge informal networks for mutual support in daily struggles for sub-sistence, sustenance, and self-affirmation shows the commitment of many women to assert agency and control over their own lives.[9] In some places, women have challenged policies of exclusion by organiz-ing cooperative associations for a wide range of purposes ranging from rendering mutual aid or disbursing rotating credit for small enterprises to caucuses for leveraging political influence. In other instances, women have aggressively "made war" to remedy injustice.

Numerous writings have described militant acts of protest by women against their marginalization by colonial and other governing structures. One enduring example of such counterhegemonic action by African women is what has come to be known as the Aba Women's War of 1929, in which Igbo women forced British administrators to address their grievances. The colonial administration had imposed a head tax upon Igbo men. Not only did this tax indicate a misunderstanding of the gendered division of economic activity in Igbo land, but the British were also stunned when they confronted violent protest from Igbo women. For it was upon women, as the primary economic actors of households, that the burden of the tax fell most harshly. Indeed, so strong was the women's protest, and so intransigent were they, that the British found themselves having to relent in their tax scheme after they were confronted with the consequences of putting down an uprising of women with brutal force.[10]

This women's rebellion was not an isolated incident, but was an expression of a long tradition among Igbo women of voicing and protesting their grievances. The women mobilized such widespread indignation among the entire population because the Igbo retained a vivid sense of the world they perceived under threat by external governance. They were experiencing changes that had only just begun to take place, and they were determined to contest the rapid transformations that were being externally imposed. Yet contemporary feminist writings would suggest that such resistance by African women is a thing of the past and that the condition of the current generation of African women is one of relentless subordination. In our view, such a conclusion is flawed for two reasons. One, it is a premature conclusion, and two, lessons to be gleaned from the past are valuable in evaluating contemporary struggles.

How is gender inequity justified in contemporary African societies? How do African women perceive these issues? Are there competing discourses? Are women today responding to official containment strategies specifically directed at them and to the conditions and failures of governance in many parts of Africa? How are they reacting to the consequences of structural adjustment measures and other impositions of state power? Are they the helpless victims of unrelieved patriarchal oppression, or are they also agents engaged in processes of change and attempting to negotiate the terms of their existence, however severe the constraints they face? To the extent that these women appear more disaffected today than in the past, could this be alternately read as a measure of their exclusion and/or as a passive form of resistance?

Can African women's apparent agitation-fatigue be transformed into something more progressive? How do they combine a culture of criticism and opposition with the virtues of praise-singing to devise an alternate paradigm for gender critique? How can traditional forms of women's networks be harnessed to channel political dissent and to facilitate reforms seeking to effect more equitable social arrangements? How can one grasp women's particular relations to structures of power and their perceptions of shifting gender hierarchies?

Rather than focusing solely on apparent conflicts between so-called feminist and so-called indigenous worldviews without also attending to the relationships between, across, and among these views, campaigns for gender equity might be advanced by seeking, from within indigenous African cultures, legitimation of alternate, culturally embedded frameworks of understanding. There are numerous reasons, not the least of them political expediency, for reconceptualizing gender-rights discourse as it is applied to Africa and other non-Western and postcolonial contexts. For example, more adequate consideration can be accorded to those indigenous women's organizations that have long fought for goals akin to those now being advanced by feminists working for women's rights within a global human rights paradigm.

It will thus be helpful to frame ideas of gender equity as an engagement within local frameworks of understanding and political action, instead of attempting to propagate them in a missionary fashion.[11] The international women's rights movement did not invent the idea of gender equity, nor was it simply manufactured from thin air in Paris, London, or New York. Notions of equity have always been part of the material lives and situated experiences of women in their everyday struggles.

Because it is impossible to understand gender relations independent of the contexts in which they take place, it is important to explore the insights that can be gleaned from local historical studies. Such analysis allows us to understand the complex dynamics of how social relationships are constructed through the perception of differences and how particular state structures and agencies act to construct gendered subjects.

HUMAN RIGHTS, GENDER RIGHTS: PARTICULAR INTERVENTIONS OF A UNIVERSAL PROJECT

Human rights advocates have long cautioned that the interdependence of rights must be recognized. Yet a world of finite resources compels choices and prioritizations. In 1966, the United Nations passed the so-called International Bill of Rights comprised of both the International Covenant on Civil and Political Rights and the International Covenant on Economic, Social and Cultural Rights as different and complementary aspects of the same international campaign. While the covenants are two separate instruments, the rights they articulate must be recognized as interdependent. Experience shows the counterproductivity of focusing on one of these covenants to the exclusion of the other. The increasing trend, especially with the attenuation of ideological biases associated with the Cold War, to give greater deference to international human rights norms and ideals for political and socioeconomic participation has highlighted the problems of hierarchically prioritizing human rights.

The International Covenant on Economic, Social and Cultural Rights offers little clarity as to precisely what constitutes a violation of the rights that it was intended to protect. Indeed, the Covenant remains a largely aspirational document, to the extent that it articulates rights without any real means for their enforcement. Fundamental social, economic, and cultural concerns were recognized as rights under public international law in the 1966 Covenant. Yet it is less clear how to define them or how to enforce them. In this regard, it is quite unlike the International Covenant on Civil and Political Rights which provides for specific remedies and sanctions for infractions. This not simply an academic issue, because it has increasingly been acknowledged that civil and political rights are contingent upon the guarantee of a modicum of social, economic, and cultural rights. How then do we create a strategy that recognizes the interdependence of both categories of rights? Specifically concerning gender equity, the central question is how we appropriate human rights principles to advance the interests of women, especially those of non-Western women.

With the increasing ascendence of international human rights regimes, what are the prospects for translating human rights principles to local gender politics? What would it mean to ensure human security for women—civil and political as well as social, economic, and cultural—as part of an international rights agenda? As an illustration of this question, picture a shabby market square in the outskirts of Kampala where a number of women eke out a living in very difficult circumstances. At the same time, the international development community is pushing a new "flavor-of-the-month"—say, domestic violence prevention. Thus, the development agencies will fund NGOs to conduct a domestic violence awareness campaign and these NGOs make their best effort to devise culturally appropriate posters for this campaign. NGO representatives then invite market women to attend a training session and are appalled by their poor rate of attendance.

Worse still, the NGO workers receive reports that their posters have been converted into peanut wrappers by the market women. It would be easy to dismiss this response as evidence of apathetic disengagement. However, it would be more productive to examine the women's response for lessons about how to maximize the benefits of such well-meaning gender-focused interventions.

Closer scrutiny of this vignette suggests that what might be mistaken for the market women's apathy might actually be a poignant commentary on the flaws of the approach. The market women's reaction suggests that poverty may be the most important causal factor in gender violence. How then do we address poverty, without giving up on measures to palliate its harshest effects such as domestic abuse? It is here that we see the significance of the principle that human rights are interdependent on one another.

Official commitments to gender equity are often undermined by ambiguous role definitions and by the low ranking of the agencies involved. Some of the agencies are structured not as sectoral ministries, but as cross-sectoral monitors. This has proven to be both a strength and a weakness. The absence of a mandate for implementation often diminishes these agencies' fiscal allocation, which in turn compromises their clout and their ability to influence, let alone to coordinate, issues in other sectors. The adverse consequences of such budgetary constraints most sharply hamper the formation of political will to effect change, for it makes little sense to agitate for rights which, even if won, will lack any concrete impact because of lack of resources.

A radical strategy for eradicating gender violence would incorporate an agenda which foregrounds education, health, and income generation for women. A coherent and integrated legal outreach strategy would approach the law as one element of an outcome-determinative context by emphasizing the social, economic, cultural, civil, and political rights of the beneficiaries, as articulated by the human rights agenda. Considered in its totality, this sort of rights agenda offers a starting point for coherent policy and for the strategic sequencing of complementary measures which address the many faces of gender-based discrimination. More importantly, it is now beyond dispute that the impact of such rights is undermined if they are pursued without similarly safeguarding the basic social and economic prerequisites for human dignity. Amidst findings about the increasing feminization of poverty, it is instructive that international development practitioners long committed to traditional concepts of economic growth now recognize the necessity of empowering women for effective citizenship. The goal of advancing women's economic viability is now seen as inextricably intertwined with the prospects for their meaningful political participation. The importance of integrating gender considerations into routine economic and sector development operations is reflected in the often-heard criticisms of merely nominal, symbolic deference to these principles in strategy formulation, rather than implementing specific projects to actualize the goal of improving women's access to vital assets and public goods.

Gender-disaggregated empirical data show that the economic deprivation and vulnerability of women in Africa, as elsewhere, is the root of their vulnerability to domestic violence and other gender-specific forms of abuse. Even in emerging African democracies, political and economic development reflects ongoing patterns of male privilege attributable to enduring patrilineal structures and to other cultural biases; many women end up devoid of assets which could have enabled them to compete for employment or entrepeneurial opportunities in the general economy. The unequal opportunities for participation in the labor market increase the likelihood of women being regarded as economic liabilities by their families and communities. This in turn renders them even more vulnerable to prejudice and abuse. Further, economic dependency severely limits the exit options of many women who are trapped in difficult marriages. The prevalence of such economic constraints on women's mobility risks reducing divorce-reform initiatives to little more than symbolic gestures.

Although it is widely acknowledged that economic empowerment is key to reducing women's vulnerability, it would be misguided to assume that economic empowerment by itself will eliminate gender discrimination.[12] There is much empirical evidence to show that economically autonomous women can still fall victim to gender-biased abuse. Thus, a need exists for a functioning legal framework to protect women's interests. Although the relationship between economic autonomy and the sociopolitical empowerment of women is not simply a linear function, promoting economic growth opportunities for women does promise compelling payoffs. This combination of efficiency, equity, and antipoverty rationales reinforces the argument for a systematic strategy to address deeply embedded prejudices.

Abundant empirical evidence demonstrates a causal link between poverty and gender conflict in Africa and elsewhere. Unfortunately, from these facts the literature has drawn inferences for economic development that tend to portray African women solely as victims of structural and cultural violence; these are inferences that obscure women's potential role as socially adept agents of change. Enhancing women's access to capital and educational assets not only reduces their vulnerability, but it also holds out the possibility for broad-based socioeconomic growth. Research and experience have shown that women's economic activities can greatly expand the gross domestic product. Further, ameliorating gender inequity has intergenerational benefits. Alleviating the impediments to women's economic participation improves the general well-being of their households, raises women's social and political status, contributes to effective and equitable growth and governance, and triggers other desirable cultural and sociostructural advances.

The benefits are even greater when economic prosperity initiatives for women are coupled with efforts to enhance their political participation. It is clear to the present generation of African women that their concern for meaningful economic participation and social equity cannot be separated from their prospects for political empowerment and representation. Since the end of the Cold War, it has been commonplace to advance both normative and empirical arguments in favor of a model of Western liberal democracy as a fundamental precondition for a good society. Such claims for the virtues of liberal democracy coincide with a widespread explosion of popular agitation for expanded political participation.

With the rapid expansion of communications media and the dispersal of ideas that characterize the contemporary era of globalization, many population groups in Africa and around the world are organizing around democratic ideals in the name of social justice. Encouraged by a vision of a reciprocal relation between participatory governance and social welfare, a wide variety of groups and individuals have invoked the ideals of self-determination. With the new and rapidly evolving models for international cooperation and commerce in the post–Cold War era, liberal democratic ideas and values have had a strong market appeal. There has emerged a collective expectation that political governance should be consensual and actively participatory.

International donors and institutional lenders now insist on participatory politics and democratic institutions. This accompanies structural adjustment programs of economic stabilization and liberalization as a precondition for grants and loans. Alongside growing global and popular pressures for political reform, this prioritization of political pluralism offers a strong impetus for at least the appearance of democratic reforms. There has been an emerging global consensus for the expansion of democracy, specifically for an ideal democracy grounded in a civil society that transcends class and communal divisions. Previously weak civic associations that had lacked solidarity and continuity have found new life and now aspire to participate in the consolidation of democratic rule. Mobilized and empowered under the umbrella of civic organizations, numerous groups—students, churches, trade unions, civil servants, market women's associations, and similar grassroots networks—are insisting on democratic accountability, the inclusion of diverse interests, social reforms, and political renewal. These groups are at the same time drawing direct connections between chronic economic and political malaise and the tenuousness of governance structures.

CONCLUSION

The slight presence of African women in institutional politics is reflected in their low participation as party executives, in elected offices, and as political appointees. For women, the promise of democracy as a guard against state and communal inequities cannot be realized in the face of arrangements that reaffirm patriarchal privilege. The ideals of electoral politics do not exhaust the need to confront enduring gender inequality and to vindicate the substantive rights of women. In spite of the underrepresentation of women in formal politics—or rather because of it—the processes and outcomes of policy making have special significance in the perpetuation of the postcolonial state as a gendered hierarchy. Hence, a heightened understanding of the gendered dimensions of politics and of the political dimensions of gender in (re)constitutive programs of rights is needed. Yet it is striking that the globalizing vision of advancing democracy in Africa and elsewhere in the postcolonial world is still a vision that represents the local beneficiaries of democratic rights, most of all the female population, as the passive recipients of an internationally dispensed largesse rather than as active participants in the reshaping of the social, political, economic—and yes, the gendered—conditions under which they live.

NOTES

1. *See* Inderpal Grewal, *Home and Harem: Nation, Gender, Empire, and the Cultures of Travel* (1996); Lata Mani, *Contentious Traditions: The Debate on Sati on Colonial India, 1780–1833* (1998).

2. *See* Benjamin Barber, *Jihad vs. McWorld* (1995); Daniel Patrick Moynihan, *Pandemonium: Ethnicity in International Politics* (1993).

3. Anthony Giddens, "Living in a Post-Traditional Society," in *Reflexive Modernization: Politics, Tradition and Aesthetics in the Modern Social Order* 56, 105–6 (Ulrich Beck, Anthony Giddens, and Scott Lash eds. 1994).

4. Most notably, Winwood Reed, critically discussed in L. Amede Obiora, *Bridges and Barricades: Rethinking Polemics and Intransigence in the Campaign against Female Circumcision*, 47 Case West. L. Rev. 275 (1997) [hereinafter Obiora, *Bridges*].

5. *See* L. Amede Obiora, *Reclaiming a Heritage of Resistance, Excavating an Alternate Gender Critique Paradigm*, 26 Syracuse J. Int'l Law and Com. 203 (1999).

6. Other scholars have described the complex dynamics and mutually reinforcing nature of power and resistance. *See, e.g.*, James C. Scott, *Weapons of the Weak: Everyday Forms of Resistance* (1985).

7. This approach is bound to underscore some of the historical processes which have transformed gender ideologies and expectations in Africa. For more discussions, see L. Amede Obiora, *New Wine, Old Skin: (En)Gaging Nationalism, Traditionalism and Gender Relations*, 28 Indiana L. Rev. 3 (1995); Simi Afonja, *Reconsidering African Customary Law*, 18 Legal Stud. F. 217 (1993).

8. Karen B. Warren, "Introduction: Revealing Conflicts Cross Cultures and Disciplines in Warren," in Karen B. Warren, *The Violence Within* (1993).

9. *See generally* Simi Afonja, *Changing Modes of Production and the Sexual Divisions of Labour among the Yoruba*, 22 Nigerian J. Econ. and Soc. Stud. 85 (1988); Jane Guyer and Pauline Peters, *Introduction, Conceptualizing the Household: Issues of Theory and Policy in Africa*, 18 Dev. and Change 197 (1987).

10. Judith Van Allen, "Aba Riots" or Igbo "Women's War"? Ideology, Stratification, and the Invisibility of Women, in *Women in Africa: Studies in Social and Economic Change* 59 (Nancy Hafkin and Edna Bay eds. 1976); Judith Van Allen, *"Sitting on a Man": Colonialism and the Lost Political Institutions of Igbo Women*, 6 Canadian J. African Stud. 165 (1972).

11. *See* L. Amede Obiora, *Symbolic Episode in the Quest for Environmental Protection*, 21 Hum. Rts. Q. 464 (1999); L. Amede Obiora, *Reconstituted*

Consonants: The Reach of a Common Core, 21 Hastings Int'l and Comp. L. Rev. 921 (1998).

12. While rigorous analysis of gender issues in the context of poverty assessments emphasizes the improvement of social indicators, a wide range of gender-disaggregated data point up the continuing need to redress asymmetries in access to basic services and infrastructure. Indeed, the underdevelopment of these is an issue that transcends gender considerations. But there is objective evidence to suggest that women are particularly vulnerable to disadvantage and that gender disparities may well be intensifying in the face of economic restructuring.

15

Membership Denied

*An Outsider's Story of Subordination and
Subjugation under U.S. Colonialism*

Ediberto Román

IT IS POSSIBLE to imagine that in the not-too-distant future the
United States may want to "redefine the American landscape by eliminating the foreign drain on the economy." To that end it might seek to
enact a law the purpose of which, ostensibly, will be to end the dependency created by past colonial regimes. The law might apply to natives of Puerto Rico, Guam, the U.S. Virgin Islands, the Federated States
of Micronesia, the Northern Mariana Islands, Palau, American Samoa,
and the Marshall Islands. For well over a century island peoples in
these Pacific and Caribbean islands have lived under the American flag,
have been protected by the U.S. military, and have received billions of
dollars in economic aid. However, many Americans believe these persons are not true members of our body politic because they speak different languages and embrace different cultures.

In order to cease the drain on its economy, the United States could
use the plenary powers granted to Congress under Article IV of the U.S.
Constitution to strip the populations of such dependencies of their U.S.
citizenship and nationality status. In addition, the United States could
terminate all economic aid and military support. In order to prevent a
mass exodus from among the over 3.5 million citizens or nationals of
the dependencies to the U.S. mainland, the law could also strip the inhabitants' rights to relocate to the United States.

To be sure, such actions by the U.S. Congress would unquestionably confer the unfettered sovereignty many such dependencies have
accused the United States of denying them. The problem is that these

new would-be sovereigns currently do not have the economic independence necessary to survive, let alone thrive, without U.S. aid. As former dependencies they lack the basic tools of diplomatic survival, military forces, and international alliances. Their woes are further augmented by their lack of sufficient credit, which makes capital investment and World Bank assistance unfeasible. The anticipated instability could lead multinational corporations to terminate all relationships with these states. Such acts would in turn produce a scarcity of goods that would threaten fundamental human needs such as medical supplies and food.

In reality, the people of the U.S. possessions have always been forgotten, underrepresented, and disenfranchised. The peoples themselves never chose to be part of America; rather, they were, and have always been, treated as booty of war. These territories are not states because they were never given the chance to become states; they are just territories populated by persons perceived to be aliens because of their different languages and cultures.

I. THE REALITY OF THE U.S. COLONIAL EXPERIENCE

Americans typically do not associate colonialism with the United States. In truth, the United States is the world's greatest colonial power. Thus, the suggested possibility of the United States stripping many of its subjects of their citizenship is intended to highlight one of the potential consequences of American colonialism. It also underscores the alien subjugation of millions of American citizens and nationals that goes virtually unmentioned in American academic and political discourse. The U.S. colonial experience is in fact one of the most effective and complete examples of hegemony in modern history. By unveiling this dark secret, this essay unpacks the tools used to perpetuate colonialism, and the half-truths, self-denial, and unwitting complicity that followed.

Such indictment of American colonialism echoes John Milton's sententious maxim that "neither man nor angel can discern hypocrisy—the only evil that walks invisible, except to God alone, by His permissible will through heaven and earth."[1] Efren Rivera-Ramos observed that "the colonial[ist] and imperial[ist] have not paid their score.... [For this reason] [w]e must take stock of the nostalgia for empire, as well as the anger and resentment it provokes in those who were ruled, and we must try to look carefully and integrally at the culture that nurtured the sentiment, rationale, and above all the imagination of empire."[2] I extend Rivera-Ramos's observation by proposing that the postcolonial discourse is a myth. There is nothing "post" in the U.S. colonial discourse—for the imperialism that began in the late nineteenth century, although artfully concealed, thrives today.

Examining America's overseas conquests illustrates how this country has repeatedly used the hegemonic tools of citizenship, international status, economic dependency, and American idealism to convince its citizens, the international community, and the conquered that its relationship with the conquered peoples is not a colonial one. The United States uses three hegemonic tools to mask its imperial rule. First, it has persuaded the conquered and the international community of the colonies' membership in the community of nations—of their independence amid sovereignty—through the use of such labels as statutory citizen and national. Next, the United States has found approval for its fictitious grant of autonomy through the use of such thinly veiled euphemisms for colony as "commonwealth status," "federated states," and "free association." The third hegemonic tool is the use of economic dependence on U.S. public or private investment, coupled with a democratic rhetoric, in order to produce a need-based desire for association.

These tools have convinced the conquered that they are free, full-fledged members of the U.S. body politic. The reality, however, is dramatically different. A conquered, dependent people despite the ostensible status conferred upon them by the United States, they continue to lack *independence, sovereignty,* and *equal* status as citizens. Far from being full citizens, they are second-class nationals whose status can be stripped by the United States as a colonial power.

II. COLONIALISM

In order to reveal the hegemonic tools used by the United States to mask the reality of colonialism, it is necessary to examine the nature of the practice. Jurgen Osterhammel defines colonialism as a "relationship of domination between an indigenous or forcibly imported majority and a minority of foreign invaders."[3] He describes the relationship as one where the fundamental decisions affecting the lives of the colonized people are made and determined in a distant metropolis pursuant to the colonial rulers' interests. Thus the term colony, which stems from colonialism but is not necessarily present in every colonial undertaking, is a new political organization created by invasion and cultural domination.

The international community has recognized this view of colonialism through the "salt water theory," which defines a colony as one separated from its ruling country by a body of salt water. UN General Assembly Resolution 1541 adopted the "salt water theory" by defining a dependent territory as a "territory, which is geographically separate and is distinct ethnically and/or culturally from the country administrating it."[4] This definition demonstrates the international community's assessment that unlike independent countries, colonies are possessions of the parent country. Colonies have no separate statehood or sovereignty. Thus "[t]he parent state alone . . . possesses [the] international personality and has the capacity to exercise international rights and duties."[5] The parent state may bestow upon its colony a degree of internal and possibly even external autonomy. However, such privileges do not eradicate the colonial relationship because they exist only at the will of the parent state.

III. THE MIRAGE OF MEMBERSHIP

The traditional response to the characterization of the colonial impetus of the United States is to shift the emphasis from the creation of empire to the "choices" made by the conquered. This "colonialism by consent" defense contends that the conquered are not subjugated, because they have, by act or omission, accepted the conquest. But as Antonio Gramsci has pointed out, the consent of the conquered does not justify their subordination. Rather, subordination is merely a by-product of psychological domination which, coupled with the lack of political and economic autonomy fostered by the conqueror, annihilates the subjugated peoples' ability to consent to the conquest. Gramsci's observation is significant because the international community has used the colonialism by consent defense to reconcile colonialism with the right to self-determination.

The idea (or excuse) of consent is particularly important to the

United States because in 1917, under the leadership of President Woodrow Wilson, the United States committed itself to the international recognition of the right to self-determination. This commitment established a tension between the empire that the United States had established as a result of the Spanish American War in 1898 and its international proclamations. The inconsistency led to the use of hegemony centered on a "strictly electoral version of democracy, in which the important thing is that the colonial people be given the 'opportunity to exercise their right to choose.'"[6] This so-called procedural right to self-determination embraces imperialism because it reduces the right to simply a formal manifestation of consent, irrespective of the circumstances under which a state gives such consent. In order to prevent this perversion it is necessary to look beyond the method of consent and examine the circumstances surrounding that consent.

To this end we must examine the narrative that has crippled and obscured the right to self-determination for so long. Many still believe

> that to be American, a person did not have to be any particular national, linguistic, religious, or ethnic background. All he[/she] had to do was commit himself [/herself] to the political ideology centered on the abstract ideals of liberty, equality, and republicanism. Thus the universalist ideological character of American nationality meant that it was open to anyone who willed to become an American.[7]

However, inclusion in the U.S. body politic is not as ecumenical as that vision would have it. To the contrary, American citizenship has historically been used as a tool with which to include Caucasians and exclude African Americans, Indians, and other nonwhites from the polity. In contrast, internationally, the label of "citizen" has served the purpose of creating a quasi-status—or at least the illusion of membership—that pacifies both the conquered and the international community.

Traditionally, the label "citizen" has been "applicable only to a person who is endowed with full political and civil rights in the body politic of the state."[8] The label thus carries a sense of belonging and fosters concessions in the name of shared national identity. However, in the case of the U.S. island dependencies the hegemonic creations of "citizen" and "national" are a deviation from this general understanding of citizenship. Instead, the form of U.S. citizenship held by natives of island dependencies is evidence of U.S. hypocrisy—the status has facilitated a piecemeal application of the Constitution, and conflicts with the very foundation of U.S. national ideology.

For example, although the inhabitants of Puerto Rico were granted citizenship in 1917 pursuant to the Jones Act, unlike their brethren on the mainland these Americans are not full or equal citizens entitled to participate in the U.S. national political process, are not entitled to the full protection of the Constitution, and can be stripped of their status at any time by simple congressional fiat. Inhabitants of the unincorporated territory of Guam have been granted a similar form of American citizenship. As a possession of the United States the island can be "bought, sold, or traded by the federal government."[9] The unincorporated territory of American Samoa has received even less; as nationals they have even fewer rights. These creations of citizenship were necessary because they "allowed the United States to expand its empire without being constitutionally compelled to accept as citizens populations that might be part of an 'uncivilized race.'"[10]

Significantly, this policy toward the territories did not change with the emphasis on self-determination that preceded World War II. In fact, the U.S. "policy" toward Micronesia continues to be blatantly imperialist. Initially the United Nations approved the complete and total domination of Micronesia by the United States. But once Micronesia became the only remaining trusteeship in the world, the United States masked the colonial reality by creating the concept of Free Association. This new hegemonic tool, like citizenship status and commonwealth status, turned on procedural self-determination. It successfully veils Micronesia's complete political and economic dependency on the United States by highlighting the inhabitants' "free" choice to remain associated. The brief introduction of these hegemonic tools facilitates the tracking of their role in the formation and maintenance of the U.S. colonial empire.

IV. POST–SPANISH AMERICAN WAR COLONIALIST ENDEAVORS

The end of the Spanish American War marked the emergence of the United States as a colonial power. The Treaty of Peace in Paris of 1898, which culminated in the acquisition of Guam, the Philippines, and Puerto Rico, marks the inception of U.S. overseas colonialism.

A. Puerto Rico

In the case of Puerto Rico the illusion of self-rule began shortly after the conquest. In the earliest stage, Puerto Ricans were led to consider U.S. military rule as a transitional period toward eventual incorporation. This belief was shaped by comments such as that of General Nelson A. Miles, the military overseer of the territory, who pledged in 1898 to protect the Puerto Rican people, promote prosperity, and bestow "the immunities and blessings of the liberal institutions of the [U.S.] Government" upon the inhabitants.[11] This illusion of political progression was strengthened by the replacement of the military government by a civilian colonial government. But on the mainland, subsequent Supreme Court decisions clarified Puerto Rico's true fate. In 1901 in *DeLima v. Bidwell* the Court set the stage for the piecemeal application of the Constitution by holding that the entire U.S. Constitution did not apply to Puerto Rico. The Court then proceeded to create the classifications of "incorporated" and "organized." These classifications created a colonial hierarchy based on the potential of eventual incorporation. Justice Brown, however, revealed the true intent of these classifications by noting that the Court's affirmation of the plenary power of Congress was necessary in order to prevent the automatic grant of citizenship to the inhabitants of the territories.[12]

The line of cases that followed further developed the hierarchy through the incorporation doctrine, which holds that all the rights and privileges of the Constitution applied to incorporated territories, while only "fundamental" constitutional rights applied to the residents of unincorporated territories. In *Downs v. Bidwell* in 1901 the Supreme Court found that Puerto Rico was not worthy of eventual "membership" and thus only entitled to fundamental constitutional rights.[13]

The need to conceal this outsider status and the use of citizenship as a hegemonic tool led to the passage of the Jones Act in 1917. This act was a concession that responded to the xenophobic fear that full incorporation of Puerto Rico would darken the American Frontier. By creating a three-branch system, establishing a Bill of Rights, and granting the inhabitants a diluted version of U.S. citizenship, the act sought to mitigate the appearance of a colonial relationship between the United States and Puerto Rico.[14] However, the act only resulted in the illusion of incorporation: statutory citizens cannot vote for president and vice president and they lack the right to congressional representation—both central characteristics of U.S. citizenship. In addition, the power given to Puerto Rico to self-govern was largely illusory. As stated in the Jones Act, "[a]ll laws enacted by the Legislature of Porto Rico[15] shall be reported to the Congress of the United States . . . which hereby reserves the power and authority to annul the same."[16]

In 1943, the illusion of membership had still not evolved into true incorporation into the U.S. body politic. The Puerto Rican legislature responded by demanding that Congress terminate "the colonial system of government" once and for all.[17] After decades of U.S. congressional and executive committees and studies, the United States denied Puerto Rico the options of independence or statehood. With the help of influential Puerto Rican leaders the colonial relationship was masked by the creation of commonwealth status. This compromise afforded Puerto Ricans only limited local control but to this day maintains the less-than-equal status necessary to the survival of the U.S. empire. Currently the use by the United States of the island of Vieques for U.S. Navy bombing against the will of the Puerto Rican people has highlighted the colonial nature of commonwealth status.

B. Guam

As inhabitants of an unincorporated territory, the people of Guam do not possess even the modicum of local autonomy brought by Puerto Rico's anomalous commonwealth status. Instead they live in a state akin to the naked colonialism of centuries past. Guam, like Puerto Rico, was ceded to the United States in the Treaty of Peace in Paris. Since then the United States has maintained absolute and plenary power over Guam via the territorial clause of the Constitution.

Before it was transferred to the Department of the Interior, for over fifty years the territory was subject to absolute rule by the Department of the Navy. Yet this modification procured very little for the Guamanians because the Organic Act of 1950 only established a local government structure and granted citizenship. Like other territorial legislation, it failed to provide autonomy because it maintained the trappings of foreign control. For example, like Puerto Ricans the Guamanians are unable to participate in presidential elections and are only entitled to elect a nonvoting representative who exercises a lobbyist-like role in

Congress. The lack of representation of the people of Guam was further heightened by the U.S. Supreme Court's dissolution of the Guamanian Supreme Court in 1977.

The absolute control of the United States has so inhibited the Guamanians' quest for autonomy that, like the other territories, their only option has been compromise. Believing that the hegemonic creation of commonwealth status would procure greater autonomy, the Guamanians presently aspire to a status similar to that of Puerto Rico. However, despite the establishment of a Commission on Self-Determination, even their request for the form of autonomy afforded by commonwealth status has been ignored.

C. American Samoa

In 1900 American Samoa became an unincorporated territory of the United States. As a result of Japanese activity in the Pacific, the United States instituted absolute military control over the island. In 1951, however, a presidential executive order transferred authority from the Department of the Navy to the Department of the Interior. The newly formed civilian government, like those of the other territories, while "American in appearance . . . [was and remains] illusory."[18] For example, the Samoan legislative enactments are nothing more than recommendations to the governor that have no binding authority. The use of hegemonic tools to create the illusion of autonomy is further revealed by the power of the Secretary of the Department of the Interior to appoint virtually every member of the Samoan government.[19]

Like the other unorganized and unincorporated territories, under the series of Supreme Court cases decided between 1920 and 1923 referred to as the Insular Cases, the residents of Samoa are only entitled to the fundamental rights of the U.S. Constitution.[20] The political quest for autonomy in American Samoa is further debilitated by its lack of economic viability. Currently, private industry consists of only two canneries that employ 28 percent of the total workforce. The territory's economy is driven by its largest employer, the U.S.-subsidized civilian government. Given these economic and political realities, it is not surprising that, like the other territories, American Samoa desires to remain in close association with the United States.

D. U.S. Virgin Islands

In 1916, the United States bought St. Thomas, St. John, and St. Croix from Denmark for 25 million dollars. The citizens of Denmark approved the sale by plebiscite but the inhabitants of the islands were never consulted. The reason for the U.S. purchase and the subsequent naval administration was its need to monitor German activity in the Atlantic Ocean. In 1917, Congress provided the islands with an organic act establishing a civilian government that replaced the Department of the Navy's direct control. Like the other territorial possessions, the civilian government—which included a judicial system, a bicameral legislature, and a governor appointed by the President of the United States—created a status that served to mask the true colonial nature of the relationship.

Following the creation of a "municipal council" for each main island, for example, the inhabitants were allowed to hold their first constitutional convention in 1964. Given the limited bargaining power of the islanders the convention merely sought a locally elected governor, an abolition of the veto power of the United States over local legislation, and the right to participate in U.S. presidential elections. In response, Congress enacted the Elective Governor Act of 1968, which provided a governor by general election and eliminated the U.S. president's right to veto local legislation. However, as an unincorporated territory governed by the Territorial Clause of the Constitution, the inhabitants of the U.S. Virgin Islands continued to be guaranteed only fundamental rights and a nonvoting delegate to the U.S. Congress. They do not participate in U.S. presidential elections.

In 1993, like the other territories, the people of the Virgin Islands voted in a status referendum to maintain the relationship with the United States which they had described at their constitutional convention as being premised on territorial autonomy.

V. POST–WORLD WAR II CONQUESTS IN THE PACIFIC

Since the end of World War II, the United States has maintained a uniquely hegemonic relationship with a group of islands in the Pacific known as Micronesia. This island group is comprised of three archipelagoes: the Marianas, the Carolines, and the Marshall Islands. The area presently consists of the Republic of Palau, the Commonwealth of the

Northern Marianas, the Marshall Islands, and the Federated States of Micronesia. These new nations were once part of the U.S.-administrated Trust Territory of the Pacific. Today, their ties with the United States are, irrespective of UN recognition, far from severed. And yet their lack of autonomy has received little attention. The kinship, as one commentator recently observed, was driven by the United States's determination that "the islanders, because of their color and culture, [were] too backward to rule themselves."[21] This attitude, although presently concealed by the hegemonic labels of "free association" and "commonwealth," is a current example of the United States's disregard of the right to self-determination.

A. The Trust Territory of the Pacific

Following World War I the League of Nations established a mandate system that classified the level of self-determination available to the once colonial possessions of the defeated parties. Falling within the paradigm of the mandate system the people of Micronesia were "not yet able to stand by themselves under the strenuous conditions of the modern world."[22] Micronesia was subsequently entrusted to Japanese administration. Believing that the attack on Pearl Harbor had been devised in the Marshall Islands, the United States entered World War II with the intent of neutralizing this security threat.

The establishment of UN trusteeships replaced the League of Nations mandate system and led to the administration of Micronesia by the United States. The trusteeship was preferred to the mandate system because it circumvented the pre–World War II colonial language. By definition the trust was not a colonial possession because a trusteeship never technically became U.S. territory. The provisions of the trust theoretically created a form of stewardship based on the zealous duty of the United States to democratize the so-called natives.

B. The Marshall Islands, the Northern Marianas, and the "Federated" States of Micronesia

One of the most dramatic examples of the complete dominion over "foreign" territory by the United States is the nuclear testing that the latter conducted on the Marshall Islands. It demonstrates that the interests of the United States in Micronesia were essentially strategic.

For example, in the summer of 1946, prior to the establishment of the trusteeship, the Atomic Energy Commission (AEC) commenced "Operation Crossroads," which consisted of experiments in nuclear fission at the Marshall Islands' Bikini Atoll.

Following the ratification of the Trusteeship Agreement, the AEC revealed its selection of the Marshall Islands' Eniwetok Atoll as a site for further nuclear detonation. In 1958, after sixty-seven nuclear devices had been exploded in Bikini and Eniwetok, international pressure succeeded in terminating the testing of nuclear armaments on the atolls. The tests conducted in the Marshall Islands, however, like the naval bombarding in Vieques, Puerto Rico, are classic examples of colonialism, as the United States "could not conduct [the tests] on the United States mainland 'with [a] the requisite degree of safety.'"[23]

The colonial domination of the United States, however, was not limited to the use of certain atolls. In fact, it dominated every aspect of life in Micronesia. For instance, against the will of the peoples that constitute Micronesia and notwithstanding cultural dissimilarities, the United States sought to create a unified international status for the variety of countries and peoples. This determination was especially insulting in light of the Northern Marianas' desire to be unified with Guam. Despite their democratically articulated plea to "be incorporated into the United States of America either as a possession or as a territory . . . [and to] attain American citizenship,"[24] the United States ignored the plebiscite because it was contrary to its interests.

In the 1960s the United States silenced the islanders by providing economic aid instead of autonomy. This response contradicted the purpose of U.S. stewardship which was to provide the inhabitants with the tools of democracy so that they could exercise sovereignty. Emulating the efforts of Puerto Rico and the other territories, the Micronesian Congress responded by petitioning President Johnson to consult them when assessing the political future of Micronesia. The U.S. Congress established a Future Political Status Commission to identify and report on the political options available to Micronesia. The second of two reports prepared by the commission recommended that Micronesia become self-governing and freely associated with the United States, or alternatively that it become "independent."[25] In 1969, notwithstanding the commission's recommendation, the United States offered Micronesia territory status. The Congress of Micronesia rejected the offer as well as the possibility of commonwealth status.

The "options" of the United States were based on the reality that the people of Micronesia "have no alternative between abysmal poverty in independence and being steamrolled into something they do not want."[26] The United States had successfully made the islands economic dependencies, thereby facilitating its continual presence. Then, in light of its previous territorial experiences, the United States proceeded to provide a modicum of autonomy by allowing the territories to organize governments and establish constitutions. These actions facilitated and secured the subsequent "choice" of association under the hegemonic labels of freely associated states and commonwealths.

Therefore, it came as no surprise when in 1986 the United States signed and implemented a Compact of Free Association with the Federated States of Micronesia—states that sought to appease the United States by establishing a unified statelike federation similar to what the United States had initially envisioned for Micronesia. The Republic of the Marshall Islands also signed a Compact of Free Association absolving the United States of further liability for nuclear testing in exchange for economic aid.[27] As temporary unilateral treaties, these compacts grant the United States exclusive military use of each territory in exchange for economic aid and the promise of economic viability. Notwithstanding their unequal bargaining power, the compacts with Micronesia were approved by the United Nations as autonomous determinations.[28]

Irrespective of the United Nation's acceptance of these creations, the territories, because of their limited local control, are still effectively possessions of the United States.

C. The Republic of Palau

The extent of the cloaked dominion of the islands by the United States is demonstrated by the struggle between the United States and the Republic of Palau. Although the United States declared that it had completed negotiations with the Republic of Palau in 1982, the Compact of Free Association with Palau was not actually implemented until 1994. The delay was a result of the conflict that existed between the Compact and Palau's Constitution. When, like the other territories, the inhabitants of Palau were given permission to establish a constitution, they approved the world's first nuclear-free constitution. This constitution required a plebiscite, approved by 75 percent of registered voters, in order to authorize any "use, testing, storage or disposal of nuclear, toxic chemical, gas, or biological weapons intended for use in warfare" within Palau.[29] Such a democratic mandate was problematic for the United States because it conflicted with the provisions of the Compact which granted the United States categorical authority over the defense and security of Palau.

Cognizant of this conflict, the United States objected to this clause of the Palauan Constitution along with another clause which prevented foreign ownership of land and the exercise of eminent domain powers prior to the constitution's approval. While the Palauan constitutional legislature, the ConCon, was still working on the constitution, U.S. Ambassador Rosenblatt sent the following cable:

> [t]he United States has made clear that any prohibition against nuclear or conventional weapons, to which U.S. cannot agree in the Compact, would leave the U.S. warships and aircrafts from transiting Palau either in time of peace or war. We urge that this proposal be dropped (as was done in the Marshall Islands). . . . Unless deleted or amended, the proposed language would create problems of the utmost gravity for the U.S.[30]

Notwithstanding this threat, 92 percent of the Palauan electorate approved the Constitution. The United States reiterated that the nuclear clause of the Compact was nonnegotiable. The approval process for the Compact was set in motion and the first of seven U.S.-funded plebiscites took place in 1983. Two lawsuits, a fiscal emergency, two assassinations, and one suicide later the final version of the Compact was approved.[31] It provided that in return for unfettered access to the islands the United States would provide for the defense and security of Palau. The Compact took effect on October 1, 1994 and allows the United States to transit nuclear waste and weapons within Palau by suspending the conflicting Palauan constitutional provisions for fifteen years in return for 517 million dollars in economic aid.

VI. CONCLUSION

Notwithstanding the post–World War II international movement that condemned colonization and embraced every state's right to self-determination and sovereignty, this noble aspiration is not yet a reality. The United States deploys myths about the independent status of its colonies by using terms such as commonwealth, unincorporated territory, and associated territory. Far from promoting independence, the United States today is a major colonial power that has denied true independence to Puerto Rico, Guam, the U.S. Virgin Islands, the Federated States of Micronesia, the Northern Mariana Islands, Palau, American Samoa, and the Marshall Islands. As the example of Puerto Rico suggests, these islands are convenient political and military outposts. The peoples of these islands have never achieved independence or sovereign status. Indeed, they have even been granted a form of U.S. citizenship. However, such citizenship is second-class, not full U.S. citizenship. Many in the United States believe that these island peoples are not true members of our body politic because of their different language and cultures. Thus, because they are economically dependent on the United States, the latter's relationship to the islands and their populations is one of colonialism—a subordinated relationship that persists amidst the rhetoric of independence, sovereignty, and self-determination.

NOTES

1. John Milton, *The Complete Poems of John Milton: Paradise Lost, Book III* 152 (Harvard Classics ed. 1980).

2. Frantz Fanon, *The Wretched of the Earth* 78 (C. Farrington trans. 1965).

3. Juren Osterhammel, *Colonialism* 16 (1997).

4. G.A. Res. 1541, UN GAOR, 15th Sess., Supp. No. 16, p.2, UN doc. A14684 (1960).

5. Robert D. Jennings and Arthur Watts, *Oppenheim's International Law* 275–76 (9th ed. 1993).

6. Efren Rivera-Ramos, *Self-Determination and Decolonization in the Society of the Modern Colonial Welfare State* 122 (1999).

7. Peter J. Spiro, *The Citizenship Dilemma*, 51 Stan. L. Rev. 597, 601 (1999).

8. Green Haywood Hackworth, *Digest of International Law* 1 (1942).

9. H.R. 1720–01 (1993).

10. Ediberto Román, *The Alien-Citizen Paradox and Other Consequences of U.S. Colonialism*, 26 Fla. St. U. L. Rev. 1, 23 (1998).

11. Office of the Commonwealth of Puerto Rico, *Documents on the Constitutional History of Puerto Rico* 55 (1964).

12. *Id.*

13. For the Supreme Court's articulation of fundamental rights *see Torres v. Puerto Rico*, 442 U.S. 465, 474 (1979) (the Fourth Amendment applies to Puerto Rico); the Due Process Clause, *Calero-Toledo v. Pearson Yacht Leasing Co.*, 416 U.S. 663, 668 n.5 (1974); the Equal Protection Clause, *Examining Bd. of Eng'rs, Architects, and Surveyors v. Flores de Otero*, 426 U.S. 572, 601 (1976) (holding that the Equal Protection Clause applies to the inhabitants of Puerto Rico).

14. *See* Jones Act, Ch 145, §§ 12, 26–27, 39 Stat. 951, 955–61 (1917). Under the Jones Act, the governor was still appointed by the president, but the House of Delegates and Executive Council were replaced by a Senate and House of Representatives elected by popular vote.

15. In 1900, Congress changed the name of Puerto Rico, which in Spanish means rich port, to Porto Rico. The blunder took thirty years to correct.

16. Jones Act §§ 34, 39.

17. *Autonomy Is Asked in Puerto Rico Vote*, N.Y. Times, Feb. 11, 1943, at 6.

18. James R. Thornbury, *A Time for Change in the South Pacific*, 67 Rev. Jur. U.P.R. 1099 (1998).

19. *See* King v. Morton, 520 F.2d 1140, 1159 (D.C. Cir. 1975).

20. For a lengthier discussion on the Insular Cases, *see, e.g.*, Daniel E. Hall, *Curfews, Culture, and Custom in American Samoa: An Analytical Map for Applying the U.S. Constitution to U.S. Territories*, 2 Asian-Pacific L. and Pol'y J. 69, 78–87 (2001).

21. 137 Cong. Rec. E871–01 (quoting Doug J. Swanson and Ed Timms, *American Empire: The U.S. Territories*, Honolulu Star Bulletin and Advertiser, Sept. 23, 1990).

22. League of Nations Covenant, art. 22.

23. D. Michael Green, *America's Strategic Trusteeship Dilemma: Its Humanitarian Obligations*, 9 Tex. Int'l L.J. 19, 34 (1974).

24. *UN Trusteeship Report of 1951* 18 (Annex 1).

25. Lisabeth A. McKibben, *The Political Relationship between the United States and Pacific Entities: The Path to Self-Government in the Northern Mariana Islands, Palau and Guam*, 31 Harv. Int. L J. 257, 270 (1990).

26. Gary F. Quigg, *Coming of Age in Micronesia*, 47 For. Aff. 493, 508 (1969).

27. *See* Arthur John Armstrong and Howard Loomis Hills, *The Negotiations for the Future Political Status of Micronesia (1980–1984)*, 78 Am. J. Int'l L. 484, 485 (1984).

28. 135 Cong. Rec. H9626–03, H9628.

29. Republic of Palau Constitution of 1979 (effective Jan. 1, 1981), art. II, § 3.

30. *Gibbons v. Salii*, No. 8–86 (Sup. Ct. Palau, App. Div. Sept. 17, 1986), at 341.

31. *See Gibbons v. Remeliik*, 1 Republic of Palau Intrm. 80, 81 (No. 67–83) (Palau Sup. Ct. Trial Div., Aug. 6, 1983).

16

The Moral High Ground?

The Relevance of International Law to Remedying Racial Discrimination in U.S. Immigration Laws

Kevin R. Johnson

THE UNITED STATES has had a deeply disturbing history of racial violence and discrimination. Well-documented episodes include the enslavement of African Americans, the genocide of the Native American peoples, and the horrible violence against persons of Mexican and Asian ancestry. This discriminatory legacy continues to affect modern social life in this country. At the same time, the U.S. government is quick to criticize human rights abuses in other countries, especially those involving racial or ethnic discrimination. Indeed, the U.S. Department of State issues an annual report on human rights conditions in other countries that purports to document such discrimination. Long criticized for slanting the facts to serve foreign policy ends, these reports establish the official position of the U.S. government on discrimination, and human rights generally, around the world.

Sadly enough, racial discrimination traditionally has been a central feature of U.S. immigration laws, which historically have been designed and enforced to limit the immigration of the particular pariahs of the day. Racist milestones of U.S. immigration history include the infamous Chinese exclusion acts of the 1880s that effectively prohibited Chinese immigration until well into the twentieth century, the notorious national origins quota system in place from 1924 to 1965 that limited the number of immigrants from southern and eastern Europe to the United States, and various modes of discriminatory border enforcement against Mexican immigrants. Similarly, from the country's first naturalization law until 1952, only "white" immigrants could become citizens. Much of this immigration law and policy, and more, violated international law.

Today, "[t]he nondiscrimination ideal has been firmly embedded and elaborated in major international legal instruments, such as the United Nations Charter, the Universal Declaration of Human Rights, the International Human Rights Covenants, and the International Covention on the Elimination of All Forms of Racial Discrimination."[1] Modern U.S. immigration law and policy, however, fails in important respects to meet this laudatory nondiscrimination goal.

The conventional wisdom among legal scholars is that the last vestiges of invidious discrimination have been removed from U.S. immigration laws. Importantly, the Immigration Act of 1965 eliminated the national origins quota system and adopted a facially neutral admission scheme focusing on family reunification and employment-related immigration. True, consistent with the nondiscrimination norm popularized during the civil rights era of the 1960s, the end of formal discrimination represented a much-heralded and necessary change in the law. However, the rosy view that discrimination is a thing of the past minimizes the significance of the discrimination that survives in the *operation* and *enforcement* of modern U.S. immigration law. The waning years of the twentieth century were chock-full of examples.

The interdiction and repatriation of Haitian, Chinese, and Cubans fleeing their homelands immediately come to mind. Greatly enhanced enforcement of the southern border of the United States with Mexico, contributes to increasing reports of human rights abuses which, not coincidentally, are directed at people viewed as racially different. Importantly, the nitty-gritty of the modern, facially neutral immigration laws, such as per country ceilings, diversity visas, the public charge exclusion ground, and a variety of removal grounds, has an unquestionable racial impact.[2] The racial concerns implicated by immigration law and policy emerged in the public debate in the 1990s, which not infrequently resorted to race-based arguments for restricting immigration.[3]

Thus, while the U.S. government eagerly criticizes discrimination by nonallied nations, especially sworn enemies, it allows sophisticated racial discrimination to remain in its own immigration laws. What explains the dichotomy between the international preachings of the United States and its domestic immigration practices? Part of the answer involves the long, often unfortunate, history of race relations in this country, which has a continuing impact on American society. As a nation, the United States has exhibited a troubling lack of commitment to complying with international law prohibiting racial discrimination. This is consistent with the nation's failure to enforce domestic law prohibiting racial discrimination and its narrow conception of the constraints imposed on it by international law generally.

U.S. immigration and immigrant law and policy at times have violated, and in many instances continue to violate, a variety of covenants barring racial discrimination.[4] Divergent perspectives on equality help explain why U.S. law often fails to meet its obligations under international law. International law tends to approach "equality . . . from a broader perspective than the one that courts in the United States are willing to accept. At the international level, the formal equality embedded in the concept of equality of opportunity, gives way to de facto equality or equality of outcome."[5] Consequently, although the facial neutrality of the immigration laws satisfies U.S. constitutional norms and popular sensibilities, the disparate racial impact of these laws raises red flags under international law.

Importantly, the U.S. failure to comply with international law is not limited to immigration matters. For example, in 1992 in *United States v. Alvarez-Machain*,[6] the U.S. Supreme Court found that, although a kidnapping by federal agents of a Mexican citizen in Mexico violated customary international law, it did not run afoul of the extradition treaty between the United States and Mexico and thus did not preclude a U.S. criminal prosecution. A less well-known episode occurred during World War II when the U.S. government interned Japanese Peruvians, who were forcibly removed from Peru in violation of international law, with that government's assistance.[7]

U.S. courts not infrequently have rejected arguments based on international law. In the best of circumstances, courts have utilized international law to rationalize decisions, or offered it as an afterthought to buttress a conclusion. In essence, contrary to constitutional mandate, international law is viewed and applied as the law of last resort, not the supreme law of the land. This suggests that we should be circumspect about the efficacy of international law as a means for convincing the courts to remedy discrimination in the United States. However, international law can serve—and, in fact, has served—as an important tool for policy makers and political activists seeking to reform domestic law.

In analyzing this topic, this chapter brings together two distinct strands of emerging scholarship. First, as the twentieth century came to a close, legal scholars increasingly used critical theory as a tool for analyzing immigration law and policy. Second, we have seen increased scholarly attention to international human rights law as a constraint on domestic immigration and immigrant policy. This chapter considers how the U.S. courts have treated international law in interpreting immigration laws. It analyzes compliance with international law by the European Union nations in their immigration and nationality laws and discusses the relevance of international law to ending racial discrimination in domestic immigration laws.

I. U.S. IMMIGRATION LAW AND POLICY'S ERRATIC ADHERENCE TO INTERNATIONAL LAW

A fundamental premise of U.S. immigration law is that the nation has virtually unlimited sovereign power to control its borders. The Supreme Court expressly relied on international law as the rationale justifying this power. Based on notions of territorial sovereignty, the Court in the infamous Chinese exclusion cases helped create the much-maligned "plenary power doctrine" under which the substantive content of U.S. immigration laws remains almost wholly immune from meaningful constitutional scrutiny and judicial review.[8]

Forcefully challenging this starting point, modern commentators claim that international law, in fact, constrains national sovereign power to limit immigration.[9] Many international treaties binding on the United States restrict state prerogative in the treatment of immigrants and refugees. Nonetheless, U.S. immigration law for the most part remains premised on the proposition that the nation possesses unfettered power to regulate immigration. As a result, U.S. immigration law remains resistant to reform efforts based on international law.

Asylum and Refugees

Consider adherence by the United States to international refugee law. The Supreme Court's 1987 decision in *Immigration & Naturalization Service v. Cardoza-Fonseca*[10] offers important guidance on the burden on asylum applicants seeking to prove that they fled their homelands because of a "well-founded fear of persecution on account of . . . political opinion," a legal requirement rooted in the United Nations Convention Relating to the Status of Refugees and the United Nations Protocol Relating to the Status of Refugees.[11] Besides considering the text, language, and structure of domestic immigration laws, the Court relied on international law as *supporting* its interpretation of the evidentiary burden on an asylum applicant. The Court explained its reliance by stating that "[i]f one thing is clear from the legislative history of the new definition of 'refugee,' . . . it was that one of Congress' primary purposes was to bring United States refugee law into compliance with" the United Nations Protocol. In looking to international law, the Court carefully evaluated the language of the treaty, the history of the definition of "refugee" under international law, and even the United Nations High Commissioner for Refugees' *Handbook for Procedures and Criteria for Determining Refugee Status.* After so doing, the Court concluded that the evidentiary standard was more generous than that advocated by the Immigration and Naturalization Service. *Cardoza-Fonseca* arguably represents the highwater mark in the U.S. Supreme Court's asylum jurisprudence, and its adherence to international law in an immigration case.

Compare the alleged devotion to international law, at least in a supporting role to bolster the Supreme Court's reasoning, in *Cardoza-Fonseca* with the wholesale failure to consider international law in the 1992 case *Immigration & Naturalization Service v. Elias-Zacarias.*[12] In that case, the Court focused myopically on the plain language of the domestic law and held that a Guatemalan teenager who fled forced recruitment by the guerrillas had failed to establish a well-founded fear of persecution on account of political opinion. The Court's stringent interpretation of the law flies in the face of the flexible approach advocated by authoritative international sources. In that vein, the Court ignored the pleas of the United Nations High Commissioner for Refugees, the Lawyers Committee for Human Rights, and the American Jewish Committee, that international law dictated a different result. Consistent with the *Elias-Zacarias* approach, the Supreme Court in the 1999 decision of *INS v. Aguirre-Aguirre* rejected the proposed interpretation by the United Nations High Commissioner on Refugees of a provision of the U.S. asylum laws based on the Refugee Convention and reversed a lower court finding that a Guatemalan political activist was eligible for asylum.[13]

Unfortunately, the inconsistency between *Cardoza-Fonseca* and *Elias-*

Zacarias reveals the weakness of the United States's commitment to international refugee law. Decisions like *Cardoza-Fonseca* may well represent the exceptions that prove the rule exemplified by *Elias-Zacarias*. In *Cardoza-Fonseca*, even though the Court arguably strived to comply with international law, it appeared to reach its conclusion based on the statutory language and legislative history before resorting to international law as secondary support for its conclusion. In *Elias-Zacarias*, on the other hand, it reached its conclusion based solely on the statute and left it at that. In both cases, however, the Court's interpretation of the statute, not international law, dictated the result.

There are other well-known instances of the courts, including the Supreme Court, failing to adhere to international law in immigration and refugee matters. The infamous 1993 Haitian interdiction and repatriation case, *Sale v. Haitian Centers Council, Inc.*, is perhaps the best-known example.[14] In a policy adopted by the first Bush Administration and continued by President Clinton, the U.S. Coast Guard interdicted some Haitians on the high seas and returned them to Haiti, a country that was at the time in the throes of a violent political upheaval, without any effort to determine whether any of the persons being returned had a bona fide claim of persecution. On behalf of the Haitians, Harold Koh claimed that the policy violated the *nonrefoulement* provisions of Article 33 of the United Nations Convention Relating to the Status of Refugees, which bars return of persons to a country where they face a well-founded fear of persecution on account of political opinion. The United Nations High Commissioner for Refugees, the Lawyers' Committee for Human Rights, the Association of the Bar of the City of New York, the International Human Rights Law Group, the American Jewish Committee, the Anti-Defamation League, and Amnesty International all filed *amicus curiae* briefs emphasizing that the U.S. policy of Haitian interdiction and repatriation violated international law. Nevertheless, the Court refused to disturb the president's policy choice. Rejecting powerful arguments based on international law, the Court emphasized that a variety of sources "solidly support[] our reluctance to interpret Article 33 to impose obligations on the contracting parties that are broader than the text commands. We do not read that text to apply to aliens interdicted on the high seas."[15]

The Haitian interdiction case is centrally important to any discussion of race and U.S. immigration laws. Many factors obviously came into play in the government's controversial policy decision, such as U.S.

foreign policy interests, fears of a mass migration, and the health and safety of Haitian immigrants. However, domestic concerns about a mass migration of *black* refugees to the United States inevitably affected the policy choice and contributed to the U.S. government's harsh policy judgment. Notably, few elements of the American public raised much of a fuss at the inhumane policy directed at the black, poor, culturally different Haitians.[16]

The precedent-setting Haitian interdiction case continues to have an adverse impact on refugees of color. In fact, it encouraged the United States to initiate aggressive actions to stop certain groups of refugees from reaching this country. Not long after the Supreme Court's vindication of the Haitian policy, the U.S. government began interdicting Chinese ships and returning Chinese persons to their homeland. Similarly, in the summer of 1999, the Coast Guard used force to halt Cubans attempting to make it by boat to the shores of south Florida. Law created in the Haitian interdiction case inevitably motivated and legitimated this policy. If the Cubans made it to shore, they would have the right to a hearing on their asylum claims; if stopped before touching ground, they—like the interdicted Haitians—could be returned immediately to Cuba.

II. INDEFINITE DETENTION

Another example of the U.S. government's failure to abide by international law in immigration-related matters concerns the detention of noncitizens. In the 1995 *en banc* decision of the court of appeals in *Barrera-Echavarria v. Rison,*[17] the Immigration and Naturalization Service detained a Cuban national who came to the United States in 1980 on the Mariel Boatlift and had been ordered to be returned to Cuba because of criminal convictions for which he had served his sentence. The Cuban government refused to accept Barrera-Echavarria and he faced the prospect of indefinite detention, which he contended violated international law. Upholding the detention, the court emphasized that "[i]nternational law can be binding upon the United States in domestic courts. . . . *It is well-settled, however, that international law controls only 'where there is no treaty, and no controlling executive or legislative act or judicial decision.'"*[18] According to the court, because domestic law permitted the detention, it was legal.

The inconsistency in the United States's adherence to international law can be seen by comparing *Barrera-Echavarria* with the 1981 court of appeals decision in *Rodriguez-Fernandez v. Wilkinson*.[19] In *Rodriguez-Fernandez*, the court invalidated the indefinite detention of a Cuban noncitizen based, in part, on international law principles. Even in *Rodriguez-Fernandez*, however, the international law argument was more of an afterthought than the foundation for the court's decision. Importantly, *Rodriguez-Fernandez* was the exception in this line of cases, until the Supreme Court in 2001 delivered the final word and, without resort to international law, concluded that the U.S. government lacked the statutory authority to detain noncitizens indefinitely.[20]

Historical examples abound of the violation of international law principles in immigration and immigrant cases involving persons of color. For example, the Supreme Court upheld the Chinese exclusion laws in the nineteenth century despite the fact that the Burlingame Treaty of 1868 barred such restrictions.[21] Similarly, the anti-Japanese "alien land laws" popular in many western states in the first half of the twentieth century, and generally upheld by the courts, violated international law.[22] Race matters effectively trump international law, such that race often prevails over the requirements of domestic law.

The pattern reflected in these cases supports the proposition that international law often is rejected as binding authority or used simply to rationalize conclusions already reached by the courts. This observation may be limited to immigration and refugee cases, instances in which immigrants (often, in these times, racial minorities) have few domestic supporters and in which few legal or political checks are in place on the acts of Congress or the Executive Branch. That limitation, however, is far from self-evident.

III. IMMIGRATION LAW AND INTERNATIONAL LAW IN OTHER NATIONS

The previous section focused on the failure of the United States to adhere to international law in immigration matters. This record must be placed in its proper context, specifically by acknowledging that other Western nations treat immigrants, and international law, in ways strikingly similar to the way that the United States does. Moreover, international law has been limited in its scope and commitment to refugees, the most revered and protected group of immigrants, and even more limited in its protection of the rights of ordinary immigrants. Critics of the international refugee law regime press for improvements. One respected observer contends that the Western nations embraced the United Nations Convention Relating to the Status of Refugees, which focuses on protecting persons fleeing the deprivation of political rights respected in liberal democracies, because it provided them with but another foreign policy tool to condemn Eastern bloc nations during the Cold War.[23] In another vein, similar to the critique of the international refugee law regime as failing to protect the rights of refugees, human rights scholars and Critical Race Feminists forcefully contend that international human rights law has failed to adequately protect the rights of women,[24] who, it is estimated, comprise 80 percent of the displaced persons worldwide.

The breadth and depth of criticism suggests a deeper problem with international law. In the domestic setting, we worry about biases in lawmaking and enforcement. International law warrants similar concerns. One would expect that treaties entered into by national actors would further perceived national, not necessarily immigrant and refugee, interests. Evolving practices that shape the formation of customary international law follow a similar trajectory. One would expect that provincial concerns would affect the law and its enforcement, particularly when those tasks are left to national governments.

For these reasons, it should not be surprising that other Western nations, like the United States, have spotty records in adhering to international law, flawed as it may be, in the immigration realm. The European Union (EU) has been criticized for creating a "Fortress Europe," facilitating migration among skilled workers and professionals within the EU but greatly restricting the migration of low-skilled workers from outside the member nations. As a precondition to allowing labor migration *within* the EU, controls restricting migration from *outside* the Union became a priority. In the name of curbing asylum abuse and in the exercise of their sovereign powers, EU nations have taken affirmative steps in ways inconsistent with international law to prevent refugees from crossing their borders. In addition, the EU concept of citizenship ensures that Turks, to use a well-known example, are second-class residents, not citizens. Unfortunately, the well-documented increase in xenophobia in Europe during the 1990s may well be tied to the emergence of "Fortress Europe."[25] The tightening of borders to exclude migrants from outside the EU might well have exacerbated the disdain for the groups being excluded.

Interestingly, the migration provisions of the various EU treaties have proven difficult to enforce and resulted in unforeseen consequences. Indeed, the EU has experienced significant difficulties in ensuring labor migration among EU nations, even though the countries themselves agreed to such migration. Resistance can be traced to the reluctance of national governments to cede sovereignty over immigration controls.

Domestic immigration and naturalization laws in EU nations arguably violate international law. Until recent changes in the law, Germany, for example, long adhered to a strict *jus sanguinis* (citizenship by descent) concept of citizenship, which ensured that groups of persons without German ancestry who had been born and had lived in the country for decades and whose ancestors had lived in Germany, could not become citizens.[26] In France, discrimination against immigrants, particularly Arabs, has fueled recent restrictive changes in French immigration laws. Spain, whose rapid industrialization is partly attributable to low-wage labor provided by undocumented immigration from Morocco, for years had laws that offered virtually no legal protections to Moroccan workers and effectively facilitated their exploitation by employers.

All this suggests that, similar to the United States, other nations fear relinquishing sovereign power over immigration matters. Concern over migration exceeds that generated by the trade of goods. Immigrants often are viewed as a threat to a nation's cultural and racial composition and, indeed, to an entire way of life. International law seeking to change immigration and refugee policy cannot ignore such national resistance, but must anticipate and address it.

IV. THE RELEVANCE OF INTERNATIONAL LAW TO RACIAL DISCRIMINATION IN DOMESTIC IMMIGRATION LAWS

The first two sections of this chapter may reasonably lead one to question the ability of international law to curb racial discrimination in national immigration law. As we have seen, to this point nations have failed to exhibit a durable commitment to international refugee law norms. Domestic exigencies, which often implicate national sovereignty, foreign policy, and domestic political issues, influence immigration policy more than international norms.

As legal thinkers from the Legal Realists to the Critical Legal Scholars have emphasized, the power of the rule of law is often exaggerated.[27] The United States does not always comply with its own domestic laws, much less international law, when it comes to such controversial issues as civil rights and racial discrimination. Even those parts of U.S. immigration law that bar racial and national origin discrimination have proven difficult for the government to enforce.[28] The influence of race on the law and its enforcement in a country does not vary significantly depending on the body of law being enforced. Whether it be a local, state, or international law, one must worry about the influence of race in both the creation of the law and its implementation. Because law is both made and enforced by people, it reflects their biases, interests, and desires. "Given the international legal paradigm's implicit reliance on liberalism, there is much to learn from analyses of U.S. municipal law that demonstrates how liberal judicial process, and the substantive legal rules they apply, render issues of ethnicity less visible than they ought to be."[29]

Richard Delgado and Jean Stefancic expressed their skepticism as follows: "[T]here are no safe havens, no areas of law—not jurisprudence, not moral philosophy, not constitutional law, not international law—where one will be embraced, where one will find wholehearted allies."[30] Law requires societal commitment. Simply making new law, or new international law, absent more, will not change matters. This raises the broader question of "why do nations obey international law?"[31] Often, nations adhere to international law when it serves national interests, an essential insight into the limits of law.

Ultimately, "international norms relevant to U.S. immigration policy" face "the problem of weak enforcement mechanisms. The improbability of serious international repercussions for adopting even flagrantly illegal policies continues to breed cynicism and disregard for preserving the 'national honor' in the course of devising immigration policy."[32] Lax enforcement allows nations to proclaim that their laws prohibit discrimination and to condemn that occurring in other countries, when in fact there may be little real difference between the actual levels of discrimination among the nations.

International law, however, can prove to be important to efforts to change domestic immigration and refugee law and policy. Domestic conditions within nations greatly affect matters and, at times, the political process has been influenced by international law to the benefit of immigrants and refugees. Importantly, international law serves many functions besides simple enforcement in domestic and international tribunals. Indeed, it can be a tool for securing change in local policy. For example, advocates have employed the Convention against Torture and Other Cruel, Inhuman or Degrading Treatment or Punishment to push for improvements in the protections afforded refugees in the United States.[33] Although the Treaty of Guadalupe Hidalgo ending the U.S.-Mexican war in 1848 has encountered numerous enforcement difficulties, it has served as a rallying point for the Chicano/a community and its significance has been resurrected by Chicano/a Studies scholars calling for social change. Indeed, "Reies López Tijerina relied heavily on the Treaty in his highly-publicized fight [in the 1970s] to reclaim land for persons of Mexican ancestry in New Mexico."[34]

We should not discount "the discursive power of human rights claims to spark political action and change governmental conduct."[35] International law can be relied upon by activists to press for changes in domestic law and for social change more generally. The demise of apartheid in South Africa stands out as a shining success story of this type of strategy. The symbolic impact of the law, often highlighted by critical thinkers, can prove to be an invaluable weapon in the arsenal for change. In this way, international law can be deployed to challenge discrimination in U.S. immigration and refugee law and policy.

CONCLUSION

The United States frequently claims a position of moral superiority in condemning racial discrimination in other countries. In the past, the most blatant examples of racial discrimination in U.S. society have been eliminated, in part for foreign policy reasons.[36] The nation, however, continues to experience serious racial discrimination, including in its immigration and refugee laws. Although the immigration laws are facially neutral, their operation unquestionably has a racial impact and the laws have been enforced in racially discriminatory ways.

What can be done? Domestic law has been ineffective. Why should we believe that international law will improve the treatment of immigrants and refugees? Under current circumstances, there are few indications that the courts will employ international law to remove racial discrimination from U.S. immigration laws. However, activists and policy makers may employ international law as a political lever to move domestic law toward enlightenment. International law may serve as a beacon of hope in the darkness of night.

NOTES

1. S. James Anaya, *The Capacity of International Law to Advance Ethnic or Nationality Rights Claims*, 75 Iowa L. Rev. 837, 837 (1990) (footnotes omitted).

2. *See, e.g.*, Tanya Katerí Hernández, *The Construction of Race and Class Buffers in the Structure of Immigration Controls and Laws*, 76 Oregon L. Rev. 731 (1997); Jan C. Ting, *"Other than a Chinaman": How U.S. Immigration Law Resulted from and Still Reflects a Policy of Excluding and Restricting Asian Immigration*, 4 Temp. Pol. and Civ. Rts. L. Rev. 301 (1995).

3. *See, e.g.*, Peter Brimelow, *Alien Nation: Common Sense about America's Immigration Disaster* (1995).

4. *See* Berta Esperanza Hernández-Truyol and Kimberly A. Johns, *Global Rights, Local Wrongs, and Legal Fixes: An International Human Rights Critique of Immigration and Welfare "Reform,"* 71 S. Cal. L. Rev. 547, 568–72 (1998).

5. Celina Romany, *Claiming a Global Identity: Latino/a Critical Scholarship and International Human Rights*, 28 U. Miami Inter-Am. L. Rev. 215, 216 (1997).

6. 504 U.S. 655 (1992).

7. *See* Natsu Taylor Saito, *Justice Held Hostage: U.S. Disregard for International Law in the World War II Internment of Japanese Peruvians—A Case Study*, 40 B.C. L. Rev. 275 (1998).

8. *See, e.g.*, Stephen H. Legomsky, *Immigration Law and the Principle of Plenary Congressional Power*, 1984 Supreme Court Rev. 255 (1984); Michael Scaperlanda, *Partial Membership: Aliens and the Constitutional Community*, 81 Iowa L. Rev. 707 (1996).

9. *See, e.g.*, James A. R. Nafziger, *The General Admission of Aliens under International Law*, 77 Am. J. Int'l L. 804 (1983); Michael Scaperlanda, *Polishing the Tarnished Golden Door*, 1993 Wis. L. Rev. 965 (1993).

10. 480 U.S. 421, 436 (1987).

11. *See* UN Convention Relating to the Status of Refugees, 189 U.N.T.S. 137 (1951); UN Convention Relating to the Status of Refugees, 606 U.N.T.S. 267 (1967). A related treaty, which the Immigration and Naturalization Service has made efforts to implement, is the Convention against Torture and Other Cruel, Inhuman or Degrading Treatment or Punishment, adopted Dec. 10, 1984, 23 I.L.M. 1027 (1984), 24 I.L.M. 535 (1985), which the United States ratified in 1994. *See Recent Actions regarding Treaties to Which the United States Is a Party*, 34 I.L.M.

590, 591 (1995). This treaty, generally speaking, bars the return of a noncitizen to a country where she faces torture. *See* Morton Sklar, *New Convention against Torture Procedures and Standards*, Immigr. Briefings, July 1999, at 1.

12. 502 U.S. 478 (1992); *see* Kevin R. Johnson, *Responding to the "Litigation Explosion": The Plain Meaning of Executive Branch Primacy over Immigration*, 71 N.C. L. Rev. 413, 461–72 (1993).

13. 526 U.S. 415 (1999).

14. 509 U.S. 155 (1993).

15. *Id.* at 187.

16. *See* Joyce A. Hughes and Linda R. Crane, *Haitians: Seeking Refuge in the United States*, 7 Geo. Immigr. L.J. 747 (1993); Kevin R. Johnson, *Judicial Acquiescence to the Executive Branch's Pursuit of Foreign Policy and Domestic Agendas in Immigration Matters: The Case of the Haitian Asylum-Seekers*, 7 Geo. Immigr. L.J. 1 (1993).

17. 44 F.3d 1441 (9th Cir.) (en banc), *cert. denied*, 516 U.S. 976 (1995).

18. *Id.* at 1450–51 (emphasis added) (quoting *The Paquete Habana*, 175 U.S. 677 (1900)); *see, e.g., Ho v. Greene*, 204 F.3d 1045 (10th Cir. 2000); *Guzman v. Tippy*, 130 F.3d 64, 66 (2d Cir. 1997); *Gisbert v. U.S. Attorney General*, 988 F.2d 1437, 1447–48 (5th Cir. 1993).

19. 654 F.2d 1382, 1388–89 (10th Cir. 1981). *See Ma v. Reno*, 208 F.3d 815, 830 (9th Cir. 2000), *aff'd sub nom; Zadvydas v. Davis*, 69 U.S.L.W. 4912 (Jun. 28, 2001) (relying on international law to support a similar conclusion reached on statutory and constitutional grounds).

20. *Zadvydas v. Davis*, 533 U.S. 678 (2001).

21. *See, e.g., Chae Chan Ping v. United States*, 130 U.S. 581, 589–603 (1889) (*Chinese Exclusion Case*).

22. *See Oyama v. California*, 332 U.S. 633, 673 (1948) (Murphy, J., concurring).

23. *See* James C. Hathaway, *A Reconsideration of the Underlying Premise of Refugee Law*, 31 Harv. Int'l L.J. 129 (1990).

24. *See, e.g.,* Jacqueline Greatbatch, *The Gender Difference: Feminist Critiques of Refugee Discourse*, 1 Int'l J. Refugee L. 518 (1989); Hope Lewis, *Global Intersections: Critical Race Feminist Human Rights and Inter/National Black Women*, 50 Me. L. Rev. 309 (1998).

25. *See generally New Xenophobia in Europe* (Bernd Baumgartl and Adrian Favell eds., 1995).

26. *See* Daniel Kanstroom, *Wer Sind Wir Wieder? Laws of Asylum, Immigration, and Citizenship in the Struggle for the Soul of the New Germany*, 18 Yale J. Int'l L. 155 (1993); Herbert Dittgen, "Volk Nation or Nation of Immigrants? The Current Debate about Immigration in Germany and United States in Comparative Perspective," in *Immigration, Citizenship, and the Welfare State in Germany and the United States* (Hermann Kurthen et al. eds., 1998).

27. *See generally* Karl N. Llewellyn, *The Bramble Bush* 5 (7th ed. 1981); *The Politics of Law: A Progressive Critique* (David Kairys ed., 1998).

28. *See, e.g.*, U.S. Commission on Immigration Reform, *U.S. Immigration Policy: Restoring Credibility* 52, 80 (1994); U.S. General Accounting Office, *Immigration Reform: Employer Sanctions and the Question of Discrimination* (1990); Cecelia M. Espenoza, *The Illusory Provisions of Sanctions: The Immigration Reform and Control Act of 1986*, 8 Geo. Immigr. L.J. 343, 347–48, 364–69, 381–83 (1994).

29. José E. Alvarez, *Crimes of States/Crimes of Hate: Lessons from Rwanda*, 24 Yale J. Int'l L. 365, 474 (1999).

30. Richard Delgado and Jean Stefancic, *Cosmopolitanism Inside Out: International Norms and the Struggle for Civil Rights and Local Justice*, 27 Conn. L. Rev. 773, 787 (1995).

31. *See* Harold Hongju Koh, *Why Do Nations Obey International Law?* 106 Yale L.J. 2599 (1997).

32. Joan Fitzpatrick and William McKay Bennett, *A Lion in the Path? The Influence of International Law on the Immigration Policy of the United States*, 70 Wash. L. Rev. 589, 608 (1995).

33. *See supra* note 11 (citing authority).

34. Kevin R. Johnson and George A. Martínez, *Crossover Dreams: The Roots of LatCrit Theory in Chicana/o Studies Activism and Scholarship*, 53 U. Miami L. Rev. 1143, 1148 (1999) (footnote omitted).

35. T. Alexander Aleinikoff, *Between National and Post-National: Membership in the United States*, 4 Mich. J. Race and Law 241, 254 (1999) (footnote omitted); *see* Harold Hongju Koh, *How Is International Human Rights Law Enforced?* 74 Ind. L.J. 1397 (1999).

36. *See, e.g.*, Mary L. Dudziak, *Desegregation as a Cold War Imperative*, 41 Stan. L. Rev. 61 (1988); *see also* Natsu Taylor Saito, *Crossing the Border: The Interdependence of Foreign Policy and Racial Justice in the United States*, 1 Yale Hum. Rts. and Dev. L.J. 53 (1998).

17

Indigenous Peoples' Human Rights in U.S. Courts

Eric K. Yamamoto, Carrie Ann Y. Shirota, and Jayna Kanani Kim

Americans are quick to condemn human rights violations in far corners of the world, such as Tibet, Kosovo, Jerusalem, China, South Africa and beyond. Yet all the while, within its own borders captive people still yearn to breathe free.

—Kehaulani Lum, "Native Hawaiians' Trail of Tears," *Chicago Tribune*, August 24, 1999

The time has come to create a mechanism for self-government for the Hawaiian people. The question of Hawaiian sovereignty and self-determination needs to be dealt with now.

—Mililani Trask before Congress on Hawaiian Sovereignty, 1990

"HIDDEN HAWAI'I." That is the name of the IMAX tourist film. Spectacular vistas seen only by helicopter. Craggy cliffs, cascading waterfalls, erupting volcanoes. Things the millions of yearly visitors, familiar with Waikiki beaches and hula dancers, rarely see. Yet there is another "Hidden Hawai'i" beyond the images of paradise. It is the compelling story about justice for Hawai'i's indigenous people told by Native Hawaiians themselves.[1]

Just over a hundred years ago, until 1898 Native Hawaiians were citizens of the sovereign Hawaiian nation. Then a small group of American businessmen tied to the sugar plantations, and some descendants of New England missionaries, overthrew the Hawaiian government with the armed support of the U.S. military. President Grover Cleveland investigated the overthrow and found it illegal. But in 1898, after Cleveland left office, the United States annexed Hawai'i as a territory through the Newlands Resolution.[2] In doing so, over the vehement objection of Queen Liliu'okalani and the protest of almost all indigenous Hawaiians, the United States confiscated two-thirds of Hawai'i's lands, including Pearl Harbor.[3] These lands are commonly referred to as "ceded lands" because the self-proclaimed Republic of Hawai'i ceded lands from the Kingdom of Hawai'i to the United States.

Americans in control banned the Hawaiian language and closed Hawaiian schools. As with many Native American tribes, Western diseases and the separation of Hawaiians from their homelands hastened an economic, cultural, and spiritual decline. So devastating was this decline that in 1920 Congress deemed Native Hawaiians a "dying race" and set aside 200,000 acres of "homelands" to resurrect Hawaiian life and culture.[4] But this program was so poorly (and sometimes corruptly) administered by the federal and later the state governments that non-Hawaiians ended up occupying most of the lands, while 20,000 Hawaiians jammed the homelands' waiting list. Hawaiians continue to be the group worst off in terms of poverty, illness, incarceration, and homelessness.

So Lehua Napoleon asks, "How is this possible . . . that I and many Hawaiians have yet to return to the land . . . [to] make right the original wrong, the illegal seizure of the Hawaiian Kingdom, the total annihilation of our religion, culture, language and lifestyle."[5] Many indigenous Hawaiians are frustrated and angry. And they have transformed that frustration and anger into a political movement. As 20 percent of the state's population, Native Hawaiians are in the midst of a momentous grassroots political struggle to regain control over some former Hawaiian lands and to establish self-governance. The banner is "Sovereignty": "Hawaiian sovereignty needs to be dealt with now."

Hawai'i's multiracial people, including those whose ancestors earlier immigrated from Japan, China, Korea, the Philippines, Samoa, and the continental United States, are taking Hawaiian justice claims seriously. So are the federal and state governments. At the behest of Congress, in 1993 President Clinton apologized to the Hawaiian people for the United States's pivotal role in the overthrow and asked for present-day reconciliation. To pursue this goal, in 1999 Attorney General Janet Reno and Interior Secretary Bruce Babbit appointed representatives from the U.S. Interior and Justice Departments to gather information and opinions from Hawaiians on issues such as the political "native" status of Hawai'i's indigenous people, land trust abuses, and compensation. The government not long ago stopped forty years of military practice-bombing of once populated Kaho'olawe Island; the island has been partially cleaned and turned over to the state for cultural reclamation by Hawaiians.

The state itself amended its constitution to establish the Office of Hawaiian Affairs (OHA) to represent Hawaiians. And OHA has asserted major claims (possibly over a billion dollars) concerning the state's long misuse of ceded lands held in trust for Hawaiians. Most striking, a "Hawaiian Renaissance" has invigorated this quest for justice with a rebirth of Hawaiian culture—hula dancing and ancient chanting, Hawaiian language, agriculture, environmental protection, communal dispute resolution, and spirituality.[6] While emanating from Native Hawaiian communities, this cultural rebirth has touched, and transformed, almost everyone in multiracial Hawai'i.

Unmistakably, this grassroots movement has rendered Hawai'i deeper and richer. It has also rendered Hawai'i more complex, because the Native Hawaiian self-determination movement and cultural rebirth also raise new questions: What form of self-governance? Some Hawaiians favor secession; many favor some form of nation-within-a-nation status, like American Indians; others look to the private corporation model of the Alaska Native. What form of control over land and water resources now held in trust by the state for the benefit of Native Hawaiians? And with what impact on Hawai'i's multiracial populace?[7]

I. INTRODUCTION

Native Hawaiians are asserting their rights to self-governance in the language of international human rights norms. In 1993, Haunani-Kay Trask, a leader in Ka Lahui Hawai'i, a major sovereignty group, charged the United States with committing human rights violations, including "(1) an arbitrary deprivation of our nationality; (2) an arbitrary deprivation of our lands; (3) a denial of self-determination as a people, including our aboriginal rights to our natural resources."[8] The 1993 Hawai'i State Legislature characterized the 1893 overthrow as having occurred "without the consent of the native Hawaiian people of the lawful Government of Hawaii *in violation of treaties* between [the United States and the Kingdom of Hawai'i] *and of international law*." [9] Also in 1993, in *Kealoha v. Hee*, Native Hawaiians filed suit against the Office of Hawaiian Affairs to forestall a $100 million settlement until the Hawaiian people could create a recognized sovereign entity to undertake negotiations.[10] The complaint asserted that the settlement would violate Hawaiians' right to self-determination protected under international law. A year later, Native American law professor James Anaya concluded that the Native Hawaiian people are "entitled to self-determination under international law."[11] In addition, at this time Hawaiian political leaders participated in the redrafting of the Declaration of Rights of Indigenous Peoples.

Yet, despite the strong articulation of Native Hawaiians' rights of self-determination under international law during the 1990s, recent Hawaiian claims to self-governance over land and cultural resources, filed in federal and state courts, have been framed without reference to international law and human rights. This raises questions about the role and strategic use of international human rights law in U.S. courts to address the concerns of America's indigenous peoples. This chapter explores these questions by briefly sketching the pertinent international human rights framework and then examining the ongoing Native Hawaiian rights case of *OHA v. Housing and Community Development Corporation*.[12] It closes with a brief comparative inquiry into the Japanese court's 1997 recognition of the international human rights of Japan's indigenous Ainu people.[13]

II. INTERNATIONAL HUMAN RIGHTS OVERVIEW

International law addresses relations between nations. Its foundational concepts are territorial sovereignty, national citizenship, and legal equality among nation-states. More recently, the rights of individuals which originally were protected only by their own governments or, through comity or agreement, by the governments of other nations, have also been protected in international law by international human rights norms.

The modern human rights regime posits that people have fundamental rights under international law, even against their own governments. In addition, that regime recognizes that other nations and certain international organizations can intervene in what would otherwise be a nation's domestic affairs in order to protect the targets of human rights abuses. Under this regime, human rights, while broadly conceived as indivisible, are nevertheless divided into three "generations": civil and political rights (first generation); social, economic, and cultural rights (second generation); and solidarity rights or collective rights (third generation).

III. NATIVE HAWAIIAN SELF-DETERMINATION

Native Hawaiian "ceded land" trust claims against the state are traceable to the State Constitution and the federal Admissions Act. *OHA v. Housing and Community Development Corporation of Hawai'i* contests the state's control over a million and a half acres of Native Hawaiian trust lands which many Native Hawaiians argue are essential to native cultural restoration and, ultimately, to Hawaiian sovereignty.

A. Nature of the Claims

In 1997, OHA, an agency created by the State Constitution to represent Hawaiians, filed a governmental breach of trust claim in state court. OHA, along with several of its beneficiaries, asserted that the sale of the fee title to the ceded lands violates the state's fiduciary responsibilities as trustee under the State Constitution and Admissions Act. International second- and third-generation human rights also implicitly form the basis of OHA's claims. OHA and the individual plaintiffs (hereafter collectively "OHA") accused the state of "illegally alienating ceded lands which came from the Kingdom of Hawai'i and the Hawaiian people to third persons who are not state entities and without regard for the claims of Hawaiians to those lands." For this reason, OHA sought to block sales "until the claims of [sovereignty restoration] of the Native Hawaiian people are addressed and resolved in a full and fair fashion."[14]

OHA's claims built upon government acknowledgments recited in Public Law 103-150, the 1993 "Hawaiian Apology Resolution," in which Congress acknowledged that the taking of Hawaiian lands was illegal according to international law. "The indigenous Hawaiian people in 1898 never directly relinquished their claims to their inherent sovereignty as a people or over their national [ceded] lands to the United States, either through their monarchy or through a plebiscite or referendum."[15] Congress also determined that it was "proper and timely" to "acknowledge the historic significance of the illegal overthrow of the Kingdom of Hawaii, to express its deep regret to the Hawaiian people."[16]

As expressed by Native Hawaiians, Hawaiian self-determination is inextricably tied to control over illegally taken ceded lands.[17] Native Hawaiians, like Native Americans, have a special, and in important respects, a spiritual connection to their homelands. The land, or 'aina, is the source of physical and spiritual sustenance; it structures communal relationships. For these reasons, traditionally Hawaiian land, water, and other natural resources were held in common, not owned individually.[18] They were nurtured through group stewardship, or malama 'aina. Without their homelands, Hawaiians can have no cultural or economic base. In turn, without a cultural and economic base, there can be no self-governance. Thus, the recognition of rights of self-governance is meaningless without the return of Hawaiian lands. Many Native Hawaiians therefore believe that the ceded lands controversy litigated in OHA is at the heart of their existence as a distinct people and their capacity to pursue group development on ancestral lands.

The struggle for control of ceded lands in OHA thus raises third-generation, or "solidarity" rights, including third-generation group rights to group self-determination, economic development, and a healthy environment. In addition, the Native Hawaiian claims in OHA also implicate second-generation (economic, social, and cultural) rights. Native Hawaiians remain the most socially and economically disadvantaged of the islands' population. They are overrepresented among welfare recipients and prison inmates, and underrepresented among high school and college graduates and professionals. Serious illness among Native Hawaiians is disproportionately high.

The continuing spiritual and cultural harm Native Hawaiians have suffered from their separation from the land, OHA asserted, could only be repaired through the restoration of a land base for Hawaiians, and the rejuvenation of Hawaiian culture.

> Many important lands have already been lost from this trust. Plaintiff's witnesses will demonstrate that the 'Aina, or land, is of crucial

importance to the Native Hawaiian People—to their culture, their religion, their economic self-sufficiency, their health and their sense of personal and community well-being. 'Aina is a living and vital part of the Native Hawaiian culture and tradition, and it is irreplaceable.[19]

Indeed, OHA's legal filings argued that Hawaiians will suffer irreparable harm from the sale of ceded lands because those sales would further erode the Hawaiian land trust and would diminish a primary foundation for Hawaiian self-determination—the homelands needed for housing, food, culture, and spirituality.

B. Selection of Domestic Law Framework

Second- and third-generation human rights highlight the international significance of OHA's claims. The claimants in *OHA*, however, employed a very narrow rights framework. First, the *OHA* complaint omitted reference to international human rights law and asserted only a state law breach of trust claim which invokes rights traditionally recognized by the American legal system: The state's "failure to exercise due care" in the discharge of its "fiduciary duties." Breach of trust claims, most often understood in the commercial context of money management, are ill-suited to address Native Hawaiian self-determination claims as they fail to embody the cultural, spiritual, and political experiences of indigenous Hawaiians.

Second, the *OHA* complaint did not refer to Hawaiian self-determination, even though self-determination appears to be at the center of the suit. The complaint and subsequent legal memoranda cited neither the International Covenant on Civil and Political Rights nor the United Nations Charter[20]—both treaties were ratified by the United States (although they are non-self-executing) and incorporate the right to self-determination.

A more expansive framework could have cast claims in the language of international human rights (self-determination), along with traditional domestic law claims (breach of trust). Indigenous peoples' assertions of claims within such an expanded framework would perform two functions: challenge the legitimacy of an "occupying" government's employment of its own established legal norms to decide the political and cultural rights of indigenous peoples, and provide a starting point for understanding how indigenous peoples might reinterpret or transform those established norms to reflect justice under their circumstances.

It is important to ask why in *OHA* the attorneys and activists, who were experienced in Hawaiian rights litigation and have asserted human rights claims in domestic courts before, avoided explicit international human rights claims, specifically the right of self-determination. Well-developed breach of trust doctrines based on domestic law have been the centerpiece of the federal government's Native American policies since the early twentieth century. Thus, one answer involves a strategic judgment by the OHA attorneys that this doctrine, extended to Native Hawaiians, would form the most promising body of substantive law for blocking the sale of ceded lands.[21] Furthermore, OHA attorneys perhaps also sensibly cast favorable glances at the Hawai'i Supreme Court which, in a series of recent cases interpreting the Hawai'i Constitution, recognized and then expanded Native Hawaiians' traditional and customary gathering rights over privately owned property.[22] This narrowly focused domestic law approach, however, came at a price—the loss of human rights norms and rhetoric and possible political support from international human rights and indigenous peoples' organizations.

IV. INDIGENOUS PEOPLES' HUMAN RIGHTS CLAIMS IN U.S. COURTS

OHA enables us to explore the additional dynamics that might have influenced indigenous claimants to bypass human rights arguments. Specifically, a question arises about the extent of U.S. courts' authority to interpret and apply cultural and economic group-based human rights norms to decide native peoples' claims relating to land and self-governance. In exploring this terrain it is also important to ask what might be the value to America's indigenous peoples of asserting human rights claims in U.S. courts, even if formal recognition and enforcement presently are unlikely. More generally, and from the vantage point of indigenous peoples, it is necessary to ascertain the political forces that influence how international human rights laws are developed, rhetorically framed, and institutionally enforced. In beginning this analysis the remainder of this essay offers a glimpse of the limits and potential of U.S. indigenous peoples' human rights claims in U.S. courts.

A. International Law in U.S. Courts

According to the U.S. Constitution, "treaties made . . . under the authority of the United States shall be the Supreme Law of the Land."[23] Because the plain language of the Constitution mandates the application of treaty-based international law, domestic courts are bound to enforce these international (usually commercial) laws. The U.S. Supreme Court has also recognized the enforceability of international customary law.[24]

Although also sourced in treatises and custom, the jurisprudential terrain differs markedly, however, for international human rights.[25] Civil and political, or "first-generation," human rights generally require governments to refrain from interfering with an individual's right to participate in civil society or the political process. The Universal Declaration of Human Rights (Universal Declaration)[26] and the International Covenant on Civil and Political Rights (ICCPR)[27] are the primary international instruments prescribing an individual's civil and political rights.

The ICCPR establishes a minimum standard of conduct for all participating governments. It recognizes the right of every person to life, liberty, and personal security; to privacy; to freedom from torture and cruel, inhuman, or degrading treatment or punishment; to immunity from arbitrary arrest; to freedom from slavery; to a fair trial; to recognition as a person before the law; to immunity from retroactive sentences; to freedom of thought, conscience, and religion; to freedom of opinion and expression; to liberty of movement and peaceful assembly; and to freedom of association.[28] These rights were deemed enforceable upon ratification of the ICCPR.

The United States ratified the ICCPR on June 8, 1992. Notably, it has been criticized for its "excessive" package of reservations—unilateral qualifications—that limit the legal effect of the ICCPR. For instance, the Lawyers Committee on Human Rights accused the United States of hypocrisy because "one set of rules applies to the United States and another set to the rest of the world."[29]

The primary international agreement that addresses second-generation (economic, social, and cultural) rights is the International Covenant on Economic, Social, and Cultural Rights (ICESCR).[30] The ICESCR proclaims a right to work; equal pay and protection against systemic unemployment, to formation of trade unions; to rest and leisure; to food, clothing, housing, and medical care; to social security, education, and participation in the cultural life of the community; and to the protection of scientific, literary, and artistic production. In contrast to first-generation rights, second-generation ICESCR rights are to be implemented "progressively," "to the maximum of [a country's] available resources."[31] The United States has yet to ratify the ICESCR.

First- and second-generation rights are individual rights; third-generation rights, on the other hand, are group rights. Although some disagreement exists about the full range of specific third-generation rights, there is general consensus about the principle that "[a]ll peoples have the right to self-determination":[32]

> All peoples have the rights of self-determination. By virtue of that right, they freely determine their political status and freely pursue their economic, social and cultural development.

The United States did not explicitly disavow the right of self-determination in ratifying the ICCPR. This may have been a strategic move to avoid futile acts likely to generate criticism because "self-determination has undoubtedly attained the status of a 'right' in international law."[33] But this "right" has been sharply limited. It has been recognized primarily in the context of the decolonization of acquired territories. Charter nations formally recognize the right of self-determination of colonized peoples on "foreign" soil. They have denied, however, and continue to deny, indigenous peoples' right of self-determination within their state boundaries. In response, indigenous peoples have demanded international legal recognition of their right to self-determination within state boundaries, locating this right in the United Nations Charter, the ICCPR, ICESCR, and in addition, the Draft Declaration on the Rights of Indigenous Peoples.

The Draft Declaration is significant in several respects. First, indigenous peoples, including Native Hawaiians, directly participated in drafting the Declaration—the first UN instrument so drafted. Second, the Declaration affirms basic international law by guaranteeing indigenous peoples "the right to the full and effective enjoyment of all human rights and fundamental freedoms recognized in the Charter of the United States, the Universal Declaration of Human Rights and international human rights law."[34] Third, the Declaration recognizes indigenous peoples' third-generation or collective rights, including the right to self-determination without limitation to state boundaries. Finally, the Declaration cannot typically achieve the status of international law. Unlike a treaty or covenant, the Declaration is not a formal instrument subject to ratification by, and binding upon, nation-states. (Its potential rhetorical, legal, and political value are discussed in the closing section.)

B. A Critique of the Human Rights Structure

The overall international human rights regime has appropriately been extolled for its articulation of progressive values and aspirational norms that transcend traditional national borders. The generational construct that divides human rights into three separate categories, however, has faced intense criticism. Implicit in this tiering is a hierarchical structure that places certain human rights ahead of others. Critics charge that this structure perpetuates the hegemony of powerful countries, particularly the United States. They contend that by recognizing only first-generation human rights, which mirror domestic rights already in place, the United States is authorized to intervene in recalcitrant countries' political affairs under the banner of human rights without risking "reverse intervention" in U.S. affairs. In effect, the United States has expanded its global power and enhanced its overall moral authority without risk of intervention.

The formal justification for the acceptance by the United States of first- but not second-generation rights does not address the "risk of intervention" issue. Rather, it focuses abstractly on the linkage of democracy to first-, and only to first-generation rights. The explanation starts with the premise that the right to vote, assemble, speak freely, worship, use the courts, own property, and contract are central to a living democracy and are consistent with the basic scheme of the U.S. Constitution and its plan for democratic governance. The assumption, then, is that democratically elected governments will likely ensure domestic protection of second- and third-generation rights.

By contrast, according to the formal explanation, second- and third-generation rights are not essential to democracy. They may even dilute it. Social, economic, and cultural rights, and especially rights to develop and self-determination, are group-oriented. They prescribe minimum standards of living for all, but do nothing to advance a democratic agenda for achieving those standards—hence the opposition by the United States of these rights as part of the fabric of state obligation.

This formal narrative, however, tells only a partial story, glossing over its ideological underpinnings. According to critics, those underpinnings are revealed by context: a commitment to continuing Western political and economic dominance. According to one observer, second-generation rights grew out of a "Socialist tradition. . . . [T]hey have developed in response to what some consider to be the excessive individualism of the first generation of rights and the impact of western capitalism and imperialism." Third-generation rights "grew out of the plight of the poorest two-thirds of the world, much of which were colonies of Western countries and which generally remain poor." These collective rights "reflect the emergence of Third World nationalism and its demand for global redistribution of power [and] wealth."[35] In assessing the challenges to the prevailing international human rights framework, then, the primary question is not only which rights are inherently human or democratic. The question is also which rights benefit dominant countries' political and economic agendas and their interests in economic globalization.

Critics respond to that question in the following manner. Economically, the United States encourages global capitalism. It remains staunchly antisocialist. Politically, the United States is the world's most powerful country. It encroaches, or threatens to encroach, on other countries' sovereignty when vital U.S. interests are at stake. Sometimes those interests are largely humanitarian—as in Kosovo. Other times the interests are driven by the political economy—as in Vietnam and, recently, Taiwan. Accepting first-generation human rights (albeit with reservations) confers moral authority. Blocking recognition of second-generation rights that address minimum living standards advances the interests of Western capitalism. Rejecting third-generation rights undermines the Third World's (including democratic governments') demands for a global redistribution of power and wealth.

Thus, the United States does not acknowledge rights to adequate food, shelter, medical care, or jobs or to economic development, cultural preservation, or self-governance. To do so would likely (1) undermine the expansion of Western capitalism and entail a redistribution of U.S. resources, domestically and internationally, and (2) allow other nations and its own citizenry to hold the United States accountable for its group-based human rights failings. Indeed, some conservative Americans have already labeled the second-generation ICESCR the "Covenant on Uneconomic, Socialist and Collective Rights."[36]

If the critique of the latent ideological underpinnings of the pre-vailing human rights regime holds, then for indigenous peoples still re-sisting forms of Western colonialism, the specter of possible "human rights imperialism" emerges. Does the imposition of Western human values on a non-Western tradition constitute a form of Western human rights imperialism? What about the interests of those who argue that they had little input in framing the formal human rights instruments and their ordering of interests and values?

In sum, according to critics, the nations most interested in main-taining dominant global economic positions help construct and perpet-uate a hegemonic three-tier hierarchy of human rights. The United States, for instance, recognizes first-generation rights, but only reluc-tantly, as revealed in its reservations to the ICCPR. By accepting these rights (in limited fashion) and then rejecting second- and third-genera-tion "socialist" rights, the United States can assert its commitment to human rights and legitimate its intervention in other nations' domestic affairs without the practical risk of reverse intervention or of "legiti-mate" demands for restructuring Western capitalism and redistributing wealth globally. At bottom, the United States garners the moral legiti-macy to police the global economy and democracy while avoiding any real international obligations for its own human rights violations. As Kehaulani Lum says in the epigraph to this chapter, "Americans are quick to condemn human rights violations in the far corners of the world . . . yet all the while, within its own borders, captive people yearn to breathe free."[37]

C. International Human Rights, U.S. Courts, and Native Hawaiians

Returning to *OHA*, these general critiques raise a specific question about the meaning and utility of the international human rights frame-work for Native Hawaiians and indeed for all indigenous peoples. Did the *OHA* attorneys and claimants eschew complementary international human rights claims because they believed that U.S. courts are unwill-ing to enforce, let alone recognize, second-and third-generation rights claims? Or might *OHA* attorneys have assessed that U.S. hegemony under the international human rights regime stacks the deck against the indigenous peoples of the United States, and therefore have refused to employ that regime in domestic courts to resist a latent form of "human rights imperialism"?

Or did *OHA* attorneys and claimants strategically decide that a lawsuit framed narrowly within a domestic law framework was simply politically prudent in light of forthcoming U.S.-Hawaiian reconciliation efforts? Pursuant to the Apology Resolution, in December 1999 federal officials from the Departments of Justice and Interior assured Native Hawaiians that those departments have the ability to establish a government-to-government relationship, similar to that with Native Americans. The officials, however, also said that they lacked the authority to give what most Native Hawaiian people who attended reconciliation meetings said they wanted: the restoration of a sovereign Hawaiian nation.[38] "We're undertaking a process under domestic law. . . . Greater self-determination or nation within a nation, that's the kind of dialogue we can have."[39]

All these considerations likely came into play. One of the attorneys in *OHA* stated that it was the strength of established domestic law (breach of trust) and the many problems with human rights claims (practical and ideological) that led him to prefer to exclude those claims from the litigation. Asserting human rights claims in state and federal courts was a "strategy tried and failed." "The U.S. plays up human rights elsewhere but refuses to enforce human rights at home. I'm concerned about condoning that set up."[40]

Nevertheless, might there have been process benefits from asserting human rights in U.S. courts, even in light of ideological concerns? In conclusion, this essay speculates about the potential strategic process benefits for indigenous peoples asserting human rights claims in domestic courts, even when substantive enforcement is unlikely, even in light of the ideological risks. First, as expressed by Native Hawaiians, the discourse of international human rights, including the rights stated in the Draft Declaration on the Rights of Indigenous Peoples, has enabled indigenous Hawaiians to frame and express their oppression in global terms as indigenous peoples.[41] This has helped connect their political struggle to other indigenous peoples, including the Maori of New Zealand (Aotearoa), Native Americans, and the Ainu of Japan.[42] Second, asserting human rights claims in domestic courts at times has provided indigenous peoples, like Native Americans, a public education forum and helped begin to get the mainstream public used to the idea of a group right to self-determination.

Third, asserting indigenous rights articulated in the Draft Declaration of Indigenous Human Rights and other international human rights instruments, even when rebuffed, has been a source of political education. It has enabled indigenous peoples to use the domestic courts, and the media and scholarly attention they receive, to help generate new policy narratives about the cultural, economic, and spiritual foundations of self-determination claims.

The recent *Nibutani Dam* decision illustrates the potential narrative-generating benefit of legal process even where "substantive" benefits are not realized. In its carefully crafted opinion, the Sapporo district court of Japan, citing human rights norms, detailed the substantial history of oppression of Japan's indigenous peoples. Although ultimately denying substantive relief on Japanese constitutional grounds, the court's lengthy opinion generated a compelling new narrative about the Ainu and the moral foundations of their cultural claims. That narrative has had an impact on emerging Ainu social justice efforts and on future legislative and executive policy initiatives.

Finally, asserting international human rights in domestic courts has enabled indigenous peoples to articulate aspirational norms in the form of rights claims for the purpose of building group solidarity and political movement. It has also potentially enabled Native Hawaiians, for example, to demand U.S. cooperation in light of those aspirations, particularly in light of current U.S. reconciliation overtures. Article 73 of the UN Charter mandates that "states having jurisdiction over non-self-governing territories have a sacred trust . . . to develop self-government, to take due account of the political aspirations of the peoples, and to assist them in the progressive development of their free political institutions, according to the particular circumstances of each territory and its people and their varying stages of development."[43]

In this light, the ongoing *OHA* case is a story in the here and now about advocates, lawyers, and organizations grappling to find the best legal approach to stopping the state's sale of Hawaiian lands, to block further erosion of a significant Hawaiian land trust. *OHA* might be recast as a story of an imagined future—a story of indigenous peoples' struggles to assess strategically the utility and value of third- and to some extent of second-generation human rights claims as part of a larger political movement toward self-governance and cultural reclamation in domestic courts generally inhospitable to those claims.

NOTES

1. Lilikala Kame'elehiwa, *Native Lands and Foreign Desires* (1992); Act of War (1993)(film documentary); Melody Kapilialoha MacKenzie, *Native Hawaiian Rights Handbook* (Melody K. MacKenzie ed., 1991); *He Alo/Face to Face: Hawaiian Voices on Sovereignty*, American Friends Service Committee—Hawai'i (1993).

2. Although the U.S. Senate failed to obtain the required two-thirds vote under the U.S. Constitution to ratify the Treaty of Annexation, the United States passed a joint resolution purporting to annex the Hawaiian Islands on July 7, 1898, and President McKinley signed it into law. Tom Coffman, *Nation Within: The Story of America's Annexation of the Nation of Hawai'i* (1998).

3. Members of Hui Aloha 'Aina (the Hawaiian Patriotic League) and Hui Kalai'aina (Hawaiian Political Party) gathered over 38,000 signatures out of a total Native Hawaiian population of about 40,000, vehemently opposing the Treaty of Annexation.

4. Hawaiian Homes Commission Act of 1920, 42 Stat. 108 (1921).

5. Eric K. Yamamoto, *Interracial Justice: Conflict and Reconciliation in Post-Civil Rights America* 7 (1999).

6. Interview with Brandon Kekoa Parades, hula choreographer and teacher (Nov. 15, 1999).

7. The Hawaiian sovereignty and self-determination movement has also been affected by the U.S. Supreme Court's recent decision, *Rice v. Cayetano*, 120 S.Ct. 1044 (2000). In *Rice* a white rancher challenged the Hawaiian-only voting requirement for the State Office of Hawaiian Affairs on grounds that the requirement constituted an impermissible racial preference (rather than a political act between government and native peoples). The Court agreed that the Fifteenth Amendment of the U.S. Constitution prohibited the voting limitation. Following the *Rice* case, another suit was filed seeking to invalidate all Hawaiian programs receiving government support, including OHA and the Hawaiian Homelands Trust Program, as well as certain Hawaiian customary rights guaranteed by the state constitution. *Barrett v. State of Hawaii*, Civ. No. 00-00645 (D. Haw., filed Oct. 3, 2000).

8. Haunani-Kay Trask, *From a Native Daughter* 27 (2nd ed. 1999).

9. 1993 Haw. Sess. Laws 359 (emphasis added).

10. First Amended Complaint, *Kealoha v. Hee*, Civ. No. 94-0188-01 (1st Cir. Haw., filed Feb. 2, 1994).

11. James Anaya, *The Native Hawaiian People and International Human Rights Law: Toward a Remedy for Past and Continuing Wrongs*, 28 Ga. L. Rev. 309, 324 (1994).

12. Civ. No. 94-4207-11 (1st Cir. Haw., filed July 14, 1995).

13. The Ainu, physically and culturally distinct from the Japanese majority, are the indigenous peoples of Japan. Like many indigenous peoples, the

Ainu have experienced a long history of social, political, and economic oppression at the hands of the dominant culture. The Japanese government unilaterally asserted political control over Ainu territory during the Meiji era without any treaties or formal agreements with the Ainu, and prohibited them from living according to their traditional culture. Teruki Tsunemoto, *Constitutional Protection of Indigenous Minorities*, Fifth World Congress, International Association of Constitutional Law, Jul. 13, 1999.

The "Hokkaido Former Aborigines Protection Law" of 1899, a government policy of assimilation heavily influenced by the U.S. General Allotment Act, had a devastating impact on the Ainu people. It forced them to assume the derogatory status of "former aborigines" and forbade the use of their own language or the observation of their own culture. The Ainu, traditionally a culture of hunters and gatherers, were relocated to homesteads, many barren, and forced into an unfamiliar agrarian lifestyle. Tsunemoto, *supra*.

In recent years, the Ainu have experienced a cultural and political renaissance. In 1997, the Japanese government officially recognized the status of the Ainu as an indigenous and minority people with a distinct culture through the enactment of the "Ainu Culture Promotion Law" designed to replace the 1899 law. However, although the law recognized the Ainu as a minority people with a distinct culture, it declined to endorse any special indigenous rights. *Id.*

That same year, the Ainu peoples' status was further advanced by an important judicial determination under international human rights law. *See Kayano v. Hokkaido Expropriation Committee* (The Nibutani Dam Decision), 38 I.L.M. 394 (1999) (trans. by Mark A. Levin) [hereinafter *Nibutani Dam*].

14. Plaintiffs' Memorandum in Opposition to Defendant State of Hawaii's Motion in Limine to Exclude Any Reference to Facts Related to 1893 to 1898 Provisional Government and the Overthrow of the Kingdom of Hawaii at 3, *OHA v. Housing and Community Development Corp.*, Civ. No. 94-4207-11 (HI Cir. Ct.). OHA also argues that according to ordinary property law the transfer of any of these lands is improper while Native Hawaiian claims remain unresolved because the state cannot transfer clear title. The state holds only "naked" title to these lands. *See* Order Denying State's Motion to Dismiss Certain Counts and for Partial Summary Judgment at 2, *OHA* (citing *State v. Zimrig*, 52 Haw. 472, 479 P.2d 202 (1970), *reh'g denied*, 52 Haw. 526, 479 P.2d 202 (1971)).

15. Joint Resolution to Acknowledge the 100th Anniversary of the January 17, 1893 Overthrow of the Kingdom of Hawai'i, Pub. L. 103-150, 107 Stat. 1510 (1993) [hereinafter Apology Resolution].

16. During the December 1999 U.S. Department of Interior's reconciliation hearings, held pursuant to the Apology Resolution, many Hawaiians demanded the return of Hawaiian lands to a Hawaiian nation. Pat Omandam, *Official: Hawaiian Independence Unlikely*, Honolulu Star Bulletin, Dec. 11, 1999.

17. Interview with Kehaulani Lum, reporter for Chicago Tribune (Jan. 10, 2000).

18. Lilikala Kame'elehiwa, *Native Lands and Foreign Desires* (1993).

19. Plaintiffs' Memorandum in Opposition at 9, *OHA*, Civ. No. 94-4207-11 (HI Cir. Ct.).

20. The UN Charter provides that one of the purposes of the United Nations is "to develop friendly relations among nations based on respect for the principle of equal rights and self-determination of peoples." UN Charter, art. 1, para. 2.

21. Interview with William Meheula, OHA counsel (Jan. 22, 1999).

22. *Public Access Shoreline Hawai'i v. City Planning Committee*, 79 Hawai'i 425, 903 P.2d 1246 (1995).

23. U.S. Const. art. VI, sec. 2.

24. *Paquete Habana*, 175 U.S. 677, 700 (1900). "International (customary) law is part of our law and must be ascertained and administered by the courts of justice of appropriate jurisdiction as often as questions of right depending upon it are duly presented for their determination." *Id.* at 700.

25. Frank Newman and David Weissbrodt, *International Human Rights: Law, Policy, and Process* 577 (2nd ed. 1996); Hans A. Linde, *Comments*, 18 Int'l Lawyer 77 (1984).

26. Universal Declaration on Human Rights, G.A. Res. 217A, UN Doc. A/180 (1948) [hereinafter Universal Declaration].

27. International Covenant on Civil and Political Rights, adopted Dec. 16, Annex to G.A. Res. 2200, 21st Sess., Supp. No. 16, at 52, UN Doc. A/6316 (1966) (entered into force Mar. 23, 1976) [hereinafter ICCPR].

28. Anne Paxton Watgley, *Newly Ratified International Human Rights Treaties and the Fight against Proposition 187*, 17 Chicano-Latino L. Rev. 88, 90.

29. Tony Evans, "Introduction: Power, Hegemony, and the Universalization of Human Rights," in *Human Rights Fifty Years On: A Reappraisal* 11 (Tony Evans ed. 1998)[hereinafter Evans, *Introduction*](citing Lawyers Committee for Human Rights, *Letter to Senator Clairborne Pell*, 14 Hum. Rts. L.J. 3–4 (1992)).

30. International Covenant on Economic, Social, and Cultural Rights, adopted Dec. 16, 1966, Annex to G.A. Res. 2200, 21st Sess., Supp. No. 16, at 49, at UN Doc. A/6316 (1966) (entered into force Jan. 3, 1976) [hereinafter ICESCR]. The ICESCR expands on provisions of the Universal Declaration. Regional agreements such as the American Convention on Human Rights and the American Declaration on the Rights and Duties of Man also recognize second-generation rights.

31. Newman and Weissbrodt, *supra* note 25; Philip Alston and Gerard Quinn, *The Nature and Scope of State Parties' Obligations under the International Covenant on Economic, Social and Cultural Rights*, 9 Hum. Rts. Q. 156, 157–92 (1987).

32. Other generally agreed upon third-generation rights include the right to development, the right to peace, and the right to a healthy environment. African Charter on Human and Peoples' Rights, June 26, 1981, OAU Doc. CAB/LEG/67/3/ Rev. 5, arts. 19–24 (entered into force Oct. 21, 1986), reprinted in 21 I.L.M. 58 (1982).

33. John Henriksen, *Implementation of the Right of Self-Determination of Indigenous Peoples within the Framework of Human Security*, UNESCO Conference on the Right to Self-Determination as a Contribution to Conflict Prevention, Nov. 1998, at 3.

34. UN Draft Declaration on the Rights of Indigenous Peoples, E/CN.4/Sub.2/1994/2/Add.1 of 20 April 1994 at pt. I, art. 1 [hereinafter Draft Declaration].

35. D. Neil Snarr, "Human Rights," in *Introducing Global Issues* 47–48 (M. Snarr and D. N. Snarr eds. 1998).

36. Philip Alston, *U.S. Ratification of the Covenant of Economic, Social and Cultural Rights: The Need for an Entirely New Strategy*, 84 Am. J. Int'l L. 365, 365–92 (1990).

37. Bartram S. Brown, *U.S. Objections to the Statute of the International Criminal Court: A Brief Response*, 31 N.Y.U. J. Int'l L. and Pol. 855 (1999); Robert A. Williams, Jr., *The American Indian in Western Legal Thought: The Discourses of Conquest* (1990).

38. According to federal officials at the Reconciliation Hearings, "there is nothing the President, Congress or any federal agency can do to allow Hawaii to secede from the union and be led by a native Hawaiian government, as some sovereignty advocates have advocated." Pat Omandam, *Official: Hawaiian Independence Unlikely*, Honolulu Star Bulletin, Dec. 11, 1999.

39. Jan TenBruggencate, *Restore the Kingdom—Reconciliation Talks Draw 200 Hawaiians on Kauai*, Honolulu Advertiser, Dec. 6, 1999.

40. Interview with William Meheula, OHA counsel (Jan. 20, 1999).

41. Trask, *supra* note 8.

42. In the *Nibutani Dam* decision, Ainu plaintiffs, farmers whose lands had been taken by the government for the construction of a massive dam and floodplain control project, sued under the ICCPR and the Constitution of Japan for revocation of the expropriation orders. 38 I.L.M. at 399. The plaintiffs argued that the lands over which the dam was built contained many sacred and historically important Ainu sites that would be irrevocably lost to the project. 38 I.L.M. at 410–14.

The plaintiffs argued that their cultural claims were entitled to enhanced consideration because of their special status as "ethnic minorities" under Article 27 of the ICCPR and the Japanese Constitution. ICCPR Article 27 provides: "In those States in which ethnic, religious or linguistic minorities exist persons belonging to such minorities shall not be denied the right, in community with the other members of their group, to enjoy their own culture, to profess and practise their own religion, or to use their own language." ICCPR, art. 27, U.N.T.S. No. 14668 (1976)(adopted by Japan along with other select international human rights laws in 1979 without significant reservations).

The Japanese district court agreed with the plaintiffs' arguments and ruled that the government had acted illegally by expropriating the lands without giving sufficient consideration to the cultural significance of the land to the Ainu. *Nibutani Dam*, 38 I.L.M. at 427. First, the court noted that Article 27 of the ICCPR only addressed protection of "minorities" and not indigenous rights, that is, rights of self-determination or political control. The court expanded its analysis of the ICCPR, however, stating:

> If one minority group lived in an area prior to being ruled over by a majority group, while another came to live in an area ruled over by a majority after consenting to the majority rule, it must be recognized that it is only natural that the distinct ethnic culture of the former group requires greater consideration. (38 I.L.M. at 419)

Using this legal framework, the court delved into the history and culture of the Ainu and concluded that they fit its definition of an "indigenous minority." 38 I.L.M. at 419–23. Its comprehensive recounting included an indictment of the various government policies involving the Ainu which resulted in "enormous social and economic devastation wrought by the rule of our country's majority members." 38 I.L.M. at 422.

Despite its ruling that the taking was illegal, the court ultimately dismissed the plaintiffs' claims. 38 I.L.M. at 428–29. The court applied a balancing test and determined that an injunction would not serve the public welfare. 38 I.L.M. at 428–29. Since almost a decade had passed between the original expropriation rulings and the court's decision, the dam had been completed and the disputed sites lost. *See* Mark A. Levin, *An Illegal Dam Still Stands: The Nibutani Dam Litigation and the Indigenous Status of the Ainu People of Northern Japan*, The University of Hawaii Center for Japanese Studies Fall Seminar Series, Oct. 15, 1999. (See note 13 for a brief account of Ainu history.)

43. UN Charter, art. 73.

18

Climate Change, Opinions, and Imagination

Toward a New Ethic of Curiosity

Mary Loring Lyndon

THE SPACE WE inhabit—the earth's ecosystem—consists of complex physical dynamics. Until recently we have taken their stability for granted. Ecological systems may change, however, and it seems that the industrial economies are affecting the global climate.

Consumption patterns, resource depletion, and pollution have been linked to this development. Mainstream economists hold that consumption and growth are the keys to wealth; wealth finances innovation, which responds to social problems, such as pollution and resource scarcity.[1] The prescription is plain: economies should grow by producing more goods and the resulting wealth will facilitate an improved quality of life, including reduced pollution. This effect will spread as more people and nations participate in the growth economy. Restricting consumption, therefore, is self-defeating.

There are cracks in the standard model, however. The signs of global environmental stress are growing clearer and wealth distribution is growing less even. Consumption is only one factor in these developments, but it is a crucial one. The United Nations has estimated that the richest 20 percent of the world's population now consumes six times more food, water, energy, oil, and minerals than our parents consumed twenty-five years ago. Twenty percent of the world's population consumes 80 percent of the resources.

Climate change has brought fossil fuel consumption to center stage. To much of the world, it appears hugely unfair that the fossil fuel stores of the earth, slowly banked over the millennia, are being used in one

320

moment by a radically consumerist culture. The comfort proffered by conventional Western economics, that this profligacy benefits everyone by leading to eventual wealth for all, seems overplayed, if not disingenuous. Looking at the bald consumption figures, charges of imperialism hit home.

We can shift our economic trajectory, but the technical and normative issues are substantial. We will need some level of consensus to manage the process. In the United States, conflicting opinions about the environment are so extreme that the different sides sometimes seem to come from different planets. One basic divide is between those who consider reducing consumption a necessary and viable policy goal and those who oppose it as too risky to the U.S. economy and its international competitive position. This conflict has been finessed for decades, with a vision of benign growth and green consumerism grafted onto the technological optimism of U.S. environmental policy. It seems increasingly clear, however, that consumption itself must be addressed. How to contain U.S.-style consumption is a core question which animates climate change politics.

This essay describes the background and dynamics of the climate change debate in the United States. It examines the competing conceptual frameworks which shape the discussion and explores ways to increase the opportunities for a useful exchange of views. It recommends, first, that environmental debates expressly consider the different ways in which people understand the world. Dialogue about the factual underpinnings of different "cosmologies" and identification of the values expressed in each perspective would help build consensus to support environmental action. Second, it suggests that we acknowledge and explore more openly the scientific and social uncertainties inherent in the effort to shift our economic agenda. Policy debates usually grind along, with each perspective repeating its certainties; meanwhile power and self-interest determine outcomes. Much of what is uttered is strategic rhetoric; thus an express commitment to consider what we do not know might take the dialogue to a new level.

CLIMATE CHANGE

"Greenhouse gases" (GHGs), especially carbon dioxide (CO_2), absorb heat radiated by the sun, trapping it in the earth's climate. As the atmospheric levels of such gases rise, the temperature may also rise. Over the past two centuries, human activities have emitted increasing amounts of GHGs into the atmosphere. Fossil fuel combustion is the chief human source of CO_2. Energy consumption by industrial, residential, and transportation uses in Northern countries accounts for a substantial portion of GHG emissions. While oceans, forests, and some land areas act as carbon sinks, trapping CO_2, these gases are released when conditions change, as when a tundra melts or forests are harvested.

The potential for "global warming" from industrial activity was identified over a century ago, but it received little attention until the 1980s. There is now a broad, though incomplete, scientific consensus that climate change is occurring and that human activity is probably a significant contributing factor; the degree, pace, and location of changes remain uncertain. Until recently, gradual effects were expected, with greater warming in the northern latitudes, but recent analyses of ancient ice cores suggest that large-scale change can occur quickly, in one or a few decades. If massive amounts of CO_2 were released from a melting tundra, for instance, this could accelerate warming and lead to the melting of substantial portions of the Antarctic ice cap. This in turn could cause a rise in the global sea level of as much as five to six meters. Worst-case scenarios cannot be dismissed, since the dimensions of the uncertainties are beyond our capacity to measure.[2] Even less drastic changes would seriously stress most social institutions and impose catastrophic burdens on low-lying and island nations.

The dissenting view on the science of climate change stresses that there is a great deal we do not fully understand. Some bases for questions include the current incomplete understanding of the role of water vapor, the simplicity of mathematical climate models relative to atmospheric dynamics, and questions about the accuracy of measurements used in the leading models. Climate is so complex that it is not hard to identify poorly understood but relevant factors. Yet most environmental problems are incompletely understood; the question is what to make of the uncertainties.

The United States is the world's largest energy consumer and also the largest emitter of GHGs, both by a wide margin. Its share of global carbon emissions, 23 percent, is close to its share of the Gross World Product, 26 percent, while its population is only 5 percent. China, the next largest contributor of GHGs, at 13 percent, has only 2 percent of the world's wealth, but 21 percent of the world's population.[3] Both countries rely heavily on domestic coal supplies for energy. China, Brazil, India, and other growing economies are also rapidly industrializing, emulating the wealthy nations' record of growth and consumption. Unless these new industrial economies pursue alternative development strategies, in a few decades and perhaps sooner, they may become larger emitters of GHGs than North America and Europe combined.

The 1992 United Nations Framework Convention on Climate Change (FCCC) established a working plan for an international response to climate change concerns. The 1990s yielded considerable study of the scientific, economic, and policy issues involved. In 1997 the Kyoto Protocol established emission reduction goals to be met by the wealthy industrialized countries by 2012. While these nations would start the process of GHG emissions reduction, the plan included procedures for adding other countries later.

Some critics have charged that the Kyoto Protocol set emissions targets so low and applied them to so few relevant economies, that even full compliance would have little effect on global GHG emissions. Others have argued that the reduction targets are too high and economically unrealistic. The leading argument of U.S. conservatives has been that the arrangement is unfair, as they claim that it assigns 48 percent of the reductions to the United States; they characterize the entire negotiation process as strategic behavior by cartels of nations jockeying for position in a post-Kyoto energy world.[4] In addition, some advocates have pointed to current scientific uncertainties and argue that we should not reduce emissions, but should use our resources to prepare to adapt to climate change.

Early in 2001 the Bush Administration repudiated the Kyoto plan. Conservatives in the United States proclaimed that the Protocol was never workable and that a new strategy should be developed. One wrote in the *Wall Street Journal* that the United States was well rid of the treaty and should "Go it alone!" However, many U.S. citizens and businesses have reacted negatively to the Bush Administration's peremptory move and its failure to propose viable alternatives. The Administration has advocated for increased fossil fuel production and reliance on nuclear power, but this is seen by many as a political response to a core Bush constituency.

At the same time, energy conservation has become a serious political topic after nearly three decades of absence from the legislative agenda. When global emissions data are configured to show countries in descending order of efficiency, it appears that the United States is the second least efficient. As much as one third of U.S. emissions might be cut using technologies which are currently available, though approaches to technology selection and financing vary widely.[5] In the past, industry representatives have frequently overestimated the costs of prospective environmental regulation; opportunities for savings and productivity gains have emerged during shifts to new technologies and this is likely to occur in any climate change program. While it is clear that a serious response to climate change will be quite costly, legislation to support conservation and alternative technologies is now being considered.

Even if the Kyoto Protocol survives, few nations will meet their emissions targets. The U.S. Department of Energy has predicted that international energy use will increase by 60 percent by 2020, compared to 1997. U.S. energy consumption has risen steadily through the 1990s, so that, unless changes are instituted soon, the original commitment by the United States to a 7 percent reduction below 1990 levels may amount to a 30 percent reduction by the year 2012. Still, barring a surprise from climate scientists, the problem is not going away. A decade of intense work yielded the Protocol, and it includes most of the arrangements which the Clinton Administration sought in order to ease the transition for the United States. At this writing the Protocol remains the only landmark on the landscape.

One aspect of the Protocol for which the Clinton Administration fought is the use of "flexibility mechanisms," particularly emissions trading. This approach would allow polluting firms to finance energy-efficient and carbon-capturing projects in other countries and receive domestic credits toward the emissions reduction goals. Trades between industrial and nonindustrial countries would be supervised and possibly arranged by a new agency, the Clean Development Mechanism.

The United States argued that allowing maximum flexibility would promote stability in the global economy and provide a market for new environmental technologies. At the same time, it would allow U.S. political leaders to present climate change as an economic opportunity for domestic firms and even as a form of aid to developing countries. The Protocol gives weaker economies more time to catch up before taking on GHG limits and also creates incentives for investment in "green development."

Another contested question has been the extent to which the expansion of carbon sinks, such as planting forests, should count toward meeting the Protocol's targets. The United States strongly favored treating carbon sinks as allowable mechanisms under the Protocol. However, most other parties, including Europe, objected, in part because carbon sinks are temporary and their carbon effects are hard to measure. Some also worry that the United States might achieve its Kyoto target exclusively by planting trees and purchasing emissions reductions abroad, especially cheap credits from Eastern Europe. However, the U.S. contribution to GHG emissions is so large and so much of it is from fossil fuel combustion that there will be no easy way out.

The European Union led the challenge to the U.S. insistence on maximum flexibility. The EU energy profile—including natural resources, energy use patterns, and fuel prices—is very different from that of the United States; also a number of European countries have already reduced their emissions during the 1990s and the EU will be able to treat all its members' emissions together, both of which are advantages if the Kyoto plan is followed. At the same time, the EU and others argue that substantial reliance on emissions trading and carbon sinks will blunt short-term incentives to conserve, effectively granting an extension of time to the U.S. culture of consumption. In the view of many, it is precisely the consumerist lifestyle of wealthy countries—especially the United States—which has triggered the climate's change.[6]

As the climate problem becomes more salient, however, challenges to U.S. fuel consumption are growing more intense, both within the United States and around the globe. It is not likely that other countries or even mainstream business and political leaders will turn their backs on the basic content of the FCCC and the Kyoto Protocol. After a period of ignoring calls for increased energy efficiency, in February 2002 the Bush Administration released a proposal to grant limited tax credits to encourage voluntary efficiencies. The debate continues as environmentalists, businesses, and legislators press for real reforms in U.S. energy consumption.

DEBATE

The climate change issue is recognized as "emblematic" by both the right and left, as it involves core questions of fairness, rationality, and power on which political groups differ. Sooner or later, the United States will have to address the difficult questions. How much reduction should the United States attempt and how fast? Who should pay for it and how? What kinds of economic and technological means should be used? There are a variety of proposals for GHG reduction programs, including some designed to counteract the regressive effect of emissions taxes, using rebates for residential and other basic energy uses. Each approach involves numerous factual and normative issues. The outcome of the climate change debate will profoundly affect the environment and economic equity. Moreover, the debate process will shape the way we make law and policy in the United States and at the global level.

The fragmented character of environmental debate in the United States stems in part from the great range of opinion among policy advocates. Three groups can be identified. On one side of the policy debate are environmentalists and environmental professionals, including many scientists and economists, and representatives of NGOs who are actively pressing for GHG reductions. They focus on the physical risks of climate change, its scale, and its irreversibility. Inordinate consumption, increasing extremes of poverty, and political disenfranchisement are integral aspects of the climate problem, in their view. Since climate change defies the expectations of past governing strategies, many in this group believe that the debate on climate change should be an occasion for restructuring the institutions which have led to it.[7] The evolution of ecological approaches to economics,[8] the experience of "development," and the inequities of the trade system lend support to the environmentalist critique of the current system.

In the middle, policy analysts attempt to accommodate concerns about climate change without fundamentally changing existing institutions. The climate change policy debate in the 1990s took place in this middle terrain and concerned present options: how can we redirect the wealthy economies and their newer copies into less destructive production and consumption patterns? Most in this middle group have been skeptical of the wisdom of taking dramatic action, but the more proactive voices have proposed laws to encourage immediate "no regrets" efficiencies.[9] Moderate environmentalists advocate dramatic action on climate change, but do not criticize the basic institutions of the U.S. economy.[10]

On the right the third perspective sees the basic direction of the economy as correct, needing only time and reduced interference in order to complete its project of wealth production and, eventually, appropriate distribution.[11] This group includes most of the petroleum industry.[12] Many consider climate change to be a myth manufactured by the left to legitimate a power grab, a last-ditch effort to stall the market's global expansion. Both the urgency of the left, with its use of the "hysterical subjunctive," and the elaboration of global bureaucracies by the middle are seen as opportunism.

These three groups continue to debate climate change options without much participation by the general public. Opinion polls show that most people share a basic desire to protect the global environment.[13] However, most U.S. citizens are apparently unaware of the issues, particularly the facts about global inequities in resource distribution. Data on wealth and consumption are not part of the news and when they are mentioned, they apparently are not easily absorbed. Many people no doubt believe that U.S. wealth is a happy accident which generally benefits everyone, as the U.S. economy is understood as the "engine" which generates prosperity for the rest of the world. Most also believe that the United States is a generous provider of aid to poor countries.[14] Thus when they hear that the Kyoto Protocol sets no emissions standards for developing countries, this seems unfair.

U.S. consumers are also vague about the costs of energy. Fuel efficiency in consumer vehicles has declined, but drivers seem not to mind. Gas at the pump is still relatively cheap. This price does not reflect all its costs, however. The International Center for Technology Assessment has asserted that gasoline costs the U.S. economy between $5.60 and $15.14 per gallon; the costs take the form of health and material damage from emissions, industry tax breaks, military protection for oil supplies, and other subsidies.[15]

The participants in the policy debate continue to repeat their positions. The Bush Administration's combative but empty-handed policy has led to greater contact between the left and the middle-opinion groups, but there is no apparent path toward consensus. The obstacles to dialogue on climate change are familiar. They include the limitations of available formats, particularly journalism,[16] the lack of interdisciplinary communication,[17] and the culture of technocratic management. These limit opportunities for discussion of normative issues and for consensus building. Ideas about the environment and society can also be limiting factors, particularly when they are not made explicit.

OPINION

Given their contrasting beliefs, different groups can be expected to assess the scientific signals of climate change differently and to organize different responses. To reach a consensus on action to reduce fuel consumption, we must identify and translate complex ideas from one belief system to another. The scope of the climate change discussion therefore should be expanded, to give greater attention to the premises of opinions and to possible paths toward reconciling them. Identifying the underlying assumptions—drawing cultural maps—may allow us to assess the actual extent of disagreement on climate change and consumption. Code words and assertions which signal allegiance and oppositions should be unpacked and examined, not just as an academic exercise but as part of the public debate.

A number of studies have charted the opposing cosmologies in environmental conflicts. One analysis in the early 1980s identified an emerging "new environmental paradigm" in contrast with the existing "dominant social paradigm."[18] The two differed on issues ranging from levels of faith in expertise to their valuation of public goods. The dominant view promotes economic growth as an unquestioned good and the best means to reduce poverty and inequality; the new paradigm holds that lifestyles with less consumption can be better than consumerist living and maintains that the market cannot manage ecosystems. These are familiar dividing lines, but it seems that both views have gotten stronger in the last two decades.

A more recent study focuses on climate change itself. It describes the debate as taking place in a policy space formed by three competing institutional voices. Each espouses a different root cause of environmental degradation: these are profligacy in resource use or excessive consumption; economic inefficiency (resulting from incorrect pricing or allocation of property rights); and population growth.[19] The voices describe varying myths of nature, principles of wealth distribution, experiences of social solidarity and of time, and notions of the appropriate bases for consent and liability.[20]

Understanding contrasting myths of nature may help to explain some of the key opinion differences on climate change. The notion of nature as benign and stable underpins much of modern economic thought, making the idea of global environmental disaster implausible. When Mr. Cheney describes coal as the United States's "most plentiful source of affordable energy" and claims that people who want to phase it out "deny reality," he is accepting the bounty of coal on its own terms; it would be wrong to waste this gift of coal by leaving it in the ground. In this cosmology, the risk of severe climate dislocation is much less real than the coal. However, a less confident myth of nature has a growing scientific foundation and would change the equation.[21]

The sense of the time available to respond to signs of climate change also varies among different perspectives. Temporal frameworks are linked to the relationship between the fairness of current wealth distribution and the adequacy of procedures for achieving equity.[22] To environmentalists, the current damage is salient and adequate remedial institutions are lacking. In contrast, mainstream economics holds that making wealth now will put later generations in the best position to provide for themselves through technological innovation. The mainstream and conservative perspectives tend to place less emphasis on the current impact of environmental damage on people and ecosystems.

Indeed, under the mainstream "resource management" approach to environmental policy, local people are largely invisible. This partial perspective yields inaccurate assessments of local environmental conditions. It also tends to lead to proposals such as Bruce Yandle's suggestion that "If global warming is beneficial for some countries but harmful to others, actions can be considered for accommodating migration and other remedies for negatively affected people as well as for the natural environment."[23] This suggestion may appear rational to conservatives and is framed in familiar cost-benefit terms; it also expresses the sense that we can let climate change happen and then fix its effects. We have time to work out a fair arrangement.

Maybe we have time, but much of the current evidence does not support this expectation. Moreover, on its face, weighing the continued unrestrained use of fossil fuels against the financial costs of relocating coastal peoples and nations around the globe seems an unacceptable indulgence. The people who will be most affected—island peoples, for instance—would surely object to the suggestion; however, outrage and its justifications are not on the agenda.

Some current analyses of environmental politics directly address the potential for collaboration and cross-fertilization among different perspectives. John Dryzek works with four general categories of environmental discourse—problem solving, sustainability, survivalism, and green radicalism.[24] He describes the basic entities which are recognized or constructed, assumptions about natural relationships, and key metaphors. Dryzek sees conceptual variety as a resource and identifies potential alliances among different perspectives. For instance, "green romanticism" addresses consumption directly, which other perspectives do not, by providing values such as thrift in purchasing and investing in natural resources. These values align the individual's daily life with a personal experience of nature. While this perspective has had considerable impact on U.S. culture, Dryzek suggests that "romantics" need to look to other perspectives for ways to be more effective politically and to identify practical steps toward changing existing consumerist institutions.

The possibility that one could learn from a "green" or "romantic" perspective is not credible to mainstream rationalists, let alone to conservatives. Mr. Cheney speaks to these groups when he describes conservation as possibly a "sign of personal virtue" but not a basis for policy, and promises to oppose any measures based on the idea that Americans now "live too well" or that people should "do more with less." In this scheme, opposing views are accorded no value; the dismissive characterization of anticonsumerist views attempts to neutralize the policy potential of conservation and nonpolluting energy.[25] However, less extreme views may find common ground on moral issues, particularly when religious, ethical, or democratic values are invoked.

Policy creates a field in which there are opportunities for careers in "expertise."[26] Participants in political debates rarely acknowledge uncertainty; indeed, political competition seems to encourage any assertion in place of a question. Conscious attention to the concepts underlying the different sides of the debate would expand the terrain of exchange. While we cannot expect that dialogue alone, even with extended discussion, will lead to easy resolution of oppositions or to compromise and coalition,[27] we surely expect too little of policy debate at the present time.

CURIOSITY

If we are to identify paths away from our current consumption patterns, policy debates will have to change. One option is to set up more inclusive and open settings for discussion. As Maarten Hajer suggests, a "societal inquiry" can explore complex problems like consumption and climate change in a formal but open-ended setting, drawing together all the relevant strands of reasoning and allowing extended interplay among viewpoints.[28] Such a context for dialogue would allow participants to understand and respond to the assumptions at the base of each position.

It would also reduce the availability of rhetorical evasion tactics. One tactic used very commonly is simple exaggeration and the denigration of opposing views, as in Mr. Cheney's treatment of anticonsumption arguments as merely "moral" and not practical. Another tactic, which Hajer calls "black boxing," is the discursive device which separates a key question from the debate and makes it appear "fixed, natural or essential," thus "steering away latently opposing forces."[29] Consumption and the consumer's right to cheap gasoline have long been unavailable for questioning in the United States; as a result, alternative transportation and energy strategies have not been presented to the public as feasible options.

The extended format of a "societal inquiry" would allow sustained attention to complex technical and social issues. It would also push dialogue past disagreement over the "facts" and allow for the evolution of new debate ethics. Orientation to debate is a genuine impediment to dialogue in the United States. "Stretching the facts," blind allegiance to familiar analytical frameworks, and consumer passivity are routine. The natural inclination to feel that one's views are right leads to rejection of alternative ideas. In climate and trade politics, secrecy and elitist decision making prevail in spite of the obvious truth that dissenters are making valid points that must eventually be addressed.

Openness to opposing views is already implicit in the very notion of debate, but it is a frail norm and, in practice, almost an anomaly. To strengthen communication, perhaps we can consider uncertainty in new ways, taking some lessons from disciplines which regularly deal with it. For instance, social scientists utilize "gaps and blinders" methods in their research, articulating the limitations of their techniques.[30] Formal approaches to decision making under conditions of uncertainty also expressly acknowledge uncertainties and incorporate them into risk analyses. Their final results are expressed with reference to the appropriate range of uncertainty.

In systems theory, only surprise qualifies as information, because only surprise tells you something you didn't know. At the same time, many things we experience as surprises are actually not so, since we have been unconsciously aware of them as if they were dwelling in our peripheral vision. An artist draws the negative space around a figure and a poet perceives the shadow cast by an image.

Uncertainty is often the result of the way a question is framed or the way earlier learning has been conducted. To a great extent, we know what we don't know, what we haven't looked at yet, what is implied by what we do know. This awareness—or "unawareness" in Beck's terms —is a realm to be explored and understood.[31] An environmental agenda based upon these principles would work from what we know about what we don't know, such as discontinuities and synergies, now considered beyond the capacities of our research and therefore largely ignored.[32] Turning our attention toward the edges of what we know, examining apparent mysteries, may provide us with the beginnings of new research and new dialogue.

An ethic or norm which embraces curiosity can be fostered in environmental debates. A deliberate pause in argument, intended to create the experience of a gap, could be a formal part of debate. Or positive arguments might be followed by questions, such as: could this be wrong? What are its weaknesses? These questions could become routine elements in the legal and journalistic coverage of environmental issues. Currently public figures assume they will not be pressed to speak on topics outside their own particular agendas. Thus, interviewers will not expect Mr. Cheney to discuss the downside of his energy plan or the future of solar, biomass, or other renewable energy sources.

Basic questions form the negative space around the climate change debate. What would our lives be like if we changed our approach to consumption? What social arrangements and technologies might we develop in order to change? Which pleasures and fears do we express in our current patterns and what would be released by change? For instance, are "green romantics" the only ones who are wearied by the physical weight of the materials we use up every week or is this feeling widely shared? While the prospect of reducing consumption might feel burdensome, the actual letting go of things might be pleasurable, even liberating. We have not explored the possibilities of consuming much less, except to the extent that we witness poverty within the consumption culture.

Acknowledging the uncertainties and remaining aware of them would allow the discussion to proceed to higher levels of sophistication. We need more than simple receptivity, however. We need to look for surprises. As things stand now, there is no express norm or process that encourages humility or curiosity, even when the debate is about issues of true enormity.

CONCLUSION

Climate change challenges our isolation and forces us to consider new ways of understanding each other. Yet in the climate change debate, people hold contradictory certitudes. These may actively define each group in contradistinction to the others. If this is so, deciding whose facts are right and whose are wrong may be inadequate or even off the point. Curiosity, then, should acknowledge uncertainty about the facts and should also be an exercise in the suspension of our existing ties, an imagining of other relationships beyond our daily contacts.

In Kafka's short story, "An Imperial Message," the emperor, dying in his palace, has whispered something to his guard; sitting at the window of his home, the narrator waits to receive the message; the emperor's guard pushes his way through the many gates of the palace and then through the throngs of the city, ever closer to delivering the message, but still immensely, impossibly far away.[33] In Kafka's parable, the narrator does not get up to go meet the messenger. Perhaps that would be unwise; it would be easy to choose a different path and miss him altogether. Instead, he waits alone, surrounded by an anonymous world.

Large-scale environmental threats change the familiar underlying social equations. If the earth's climate changes dramatically, as Ulrich Beck notes, there will be no "Other," as we will all be affected; this will put an end to "all of our carefully cultivated opportunities for distancing ourselves."[34] If we could sustain some awareness of the connections in time and space between our consumption and its effects on the rest of the world, we might find "unlikely" ways of connecting with new possibilities.

This prospect may be exactly what is being resisted, but it would be better to go meet it. Refusal to engage may be smart in the short term, but it insults those who will absorb the greatest impact of climate dislocations. And in the long term, delay closes off our options. The wisest and most moral posture must be to orient ourselves toward new economic and social possibilities.

NOTES

1. *See* Kenneth Arrow et al., *Economic Growth, Carrying Capacity, and the Environment,* 268 Science 520–21 (1995); K. J. Arrow et al., "Intertemporal Equity, Discounting, and Economic Efficiency," in *Climate Change 1995—Economic and Social Dimensions of Climate Change, Contribution of Working Group III to the Second Assessment Report of the Intergovernmental Panel on Climate Change* 125–44 (1995).

2. Donald Ludwig, Ray Hilborn, and Carl Walters, *Uncertainty, Resource Exploitation, and Conservation: Lessons from History,* 260 Science 17 (1993).

3. Worldwatch Institute, *State of the World 1997, A Worldwatch Institute Report on Progress toward a Sustainable Society* 8 (1997). Japan, with 2 percent of the population and a 17 percent share of the GWP, contributes 5 percent of carbon emissions. Russia, with 3 percent of the population and 2 percent of the GWP, contributes 7 percent of carbon emissions.

4. Bruce Yandle, *After Kyoto: A Global Scramble for Advantage,* IV Independent Review 19 (1999).

5. For discussion of short-term and long-range efficiency options, *see, e.g.,* Paul Hawken, Amory Lovins, and L. Hunter Lovins, *Natural Capitalism—Creating the Next Industrial Revolution* 241–59 (1999).

6. *See* Carmen G. Gonzalez, *Imperialism: An Environmental Justice Critique of Free Trade,* 78 Denv. U. L. Rev. 689 (2001), describing the environmental dynamics in current international politics.

7. *See* Maarten A. Hajer, *The Politics of Environmental Defense—Ecological Modernization and the Policy Process* (1995). For online resources, *see* the Climate Action Network, http://www.climatenetwork.org.

8. *See, e.g.,* Robert Costanza et al., *An Introduction to Ecological Economics* (1997); David W. Pearce and R. Kerry Turner, *Economics of Natural Resources and the Environment* (1990).

9. *See* Pew Center on Global Climate Change, http://www.pewclimate .org, and Resources for the Future, http://www.weathervane.rff.org.

10. *See* Timothy W. Luke, *Ecocritique—Contesting the Politics of Nature, Economy, and Culture* (1997).

11. *But see, e.g.,* James E. Krier and Clayton P. Gillette, *The Uneasy Case for Technological Optimism,* 84 Mich. L. Rev. 405 (1985).

12. *See, e.g.,* The Global Climate Coalition, <http://www.globalclimate.org>.

13. *See* D. E. Bloom, *International Public Opinion on the Environment,* 269 Science 354–58 (1995) (reporting that more than half of survey respondents in both industrial and developing countries agree that transnational environmental problems—acid rain, global warming, ozone depletion, species loss, and loss of rain forests—are very serious).

14. In 1995, the average U.S. citizen thought that foreign aid made up 26

percent of the federal budget and believed that 13 percent would be more reasonable; in fact all international affairs spending accounts for about 1 percent of the federal budget and aid accounts for 0.5 percent. *See The Reality of Aid, Eurostep and ICVA* (T. German and J. Randel eds. 1996).

15. Dallas Burtraw and Michael Toman, *The Benefits of Reduced Air Pollutants in the U.S. from Greenhouse Gas Mitigation Projects*, RFF (Resources for the Future) Climate Issue Brief #7 (Apr. 1998).

16. *See* Joshua Carliner, *The Corporate Planet—Ecology and Politics in the Age of Globalization* 168–96 (1997), and sources he cites on journalism and environmental public relations campaigns.

17. *See* Gretchen C. Daily and Brian H. Walker, Seeking the Great Transition, *Nature*, Jan. 20, 2000, at 243.

18. *See* Lester W. Milbrath, "The World Is Relearning Its Story about How the World Works," in *Environmental Politics in the International Arena* 21–39 (S. Kamaniecki ed. 1993).

19. *See* Asoka Bandarage, "Population and Development—Toward a Social Justice Agenda," in *Dangerous Intersections* 24–38 (1999).

20. *See* Steve Rayner, Elizabeth L. Malone, and Michael Thompson, "Equity Issues and Integrated Assessment," in *Fair Weather? Equity Concerns in Climate Change* (Ferenc L. Tóth ed. 1999).

21. For contemporary ecologists, stability is not a constant and there appear to be no consistent "factors tending toward homeostasis." Daniel B. Botkin, *Discordant Harmonies—A New Ecology for the Twenty-First Century* (1990).

22. *See, e.g.*, Robert C. Lind and Richard E. Schuler, "Equity and Discounting in Climate-Change Decisions," in *Economics and Policy Issues in Climate Change* 59, 60 (1998); *see also* Edith Brown Weiss, *In Fairness to Future Generations: International Law, Common Patrimony and Intergenerational Equity* (1989).

23. *See* Yandle, *supra* note 4, at 36.

24. John S. Dryzek, *The Politics of the Earth* (1997).

25. Conservatives active in the climate change arena are fond of the terms "neo-Malthusian" and "Luddite," but name-calling obscures the relevant issues. See the discussion of the "spiral of stereotypes" in William R. Freudenberg and Robert Gramling, *Oil in Troubled Waters—Perceptions, Politics, and the Battle over Offshore Drilling* 91–92, 97 (1994).

26. *See* Pierre Bourdieu, *On Television* (1996).

27. Majid Rahnema, "Participation," in *The Development Dictionary—A Guide to Knowledge as Power* 116–31 (Wolfgang Sachs ed. 1992).

28. Hajer, *supra* note 7, at 288–92.

29. *Id.* at 272.

30. *See* William R. Freudenberg, "Understanding the Socioeconomic and Political Settings," in *Tools to Aid Environmental Decision Making* 94, 107–18 (Virginia H. Dale and Mary R. English eds. 1999).

31. *See* Ulrich Beck, *World Risk Society* 109–33 (1999).

32. *See* Norman Myers, *Environmental Unknowns*, 269 Science 358 (1995); *see also Environmental Law and Ecological Responsibility—The Concept and Practice of Ecological Self-Organization* (Gunther Teubner, Lindsay Farmer, and Declan Murphy eds. 1994).

33. Franz Kafka, "An Imperial Message," in *Franz Kafka—The Complete Stories* (1946).

34. Beck, *supra* note 31, at 62.

19

Immigration, Poverty, and Transnationalism

The Changing Terms of Citizenship in a Global Economy

M. Patricia Fernández-Kelly

AT THE BEGINNING of the new millennium the world remains a patchwork quilt of contradictions. In some regions prosperity reigns as never before. In others, destitution and abandonment are fiercer than in any previous age. When millions of people work for giant corporations, others migrate to distant places in search of opportunity, and still others languish without employment throughout the globe, where is the locus of civic rights and responsibilities to be found? How is our concept of citizenship being transformed by the political and economic changes occurring around the world?

Globalization has rendered national boundaries increasingly porous from an economic point of view. Capital flows freely roam the world in search of profit; investors have become almost impervious to the demands of nation-states. However, the same is not true for labor. Workers remain subordinate to regulations affecting their ability to negotiate better working conditions and higher wages. This lack of labor mobility is reflected in the reality that although there are locations where large numbers of immigrants concentrate, fewer than 5 percent of the world's inhabitants move away from their places of birth.[1]

Globalization has had a profound impact in rich and poor countries. In the United States, for example, the relocation of industrial jobs overseas caused an epidemic of plant closings and the elimination of millions of jobs in the 1970s and 1980s.[2] In less developed countries like Mexico, fledgling attempts to strengthen autonomous industry gave way to a new emphasis on exportable manufactures. Governments in Asia, Latin America, and the Caribbean rushed to implement programs to attract foreign investment. Neoliberal policies like the North American Free Trade Agreement further contributed to regional economic integration during the last decade of the twentieth century.[3]

These economic changes have affected groups in rich and poor countries in disparate ways. The contrast between the capacity of capital to transcend international borders and the relative immobility of labor has implications for our understanding of citizenship. For professionals and those linked to the most advanced sectors of production, the global village is laden with opportunities. For others—the poor and racialized, the unskilled, especially women, and some immigrants—the prospects are bleak. The first group faces an expanded definition of citizenship made possible by access to material wealth, specialized information, and rapid transportation; the latter, confronting stagnant wages, dismantled or broken welfare programs, and growing exclusion from civic participation are only nominal citizens even in the wealthiest and most democratic country in the world.

Even among the more vulnerable populations, however, there are differences worth exploring. Three populations, distinguished by their specific relationship to structures of opportunity, have differing capacities to exercise or alter notions of citizenship: redundant workers, immigrants, and transnational communities. But, as shown below, all share the reality that economic factors define the limits of their entitlements and obligations.

THE URBAN POOR: GENDER, POVERTY, AND RACE IN THE AMERICAN GHETTO

The industrial restructuring that has resulted from globalization has had dire effects on the urban poor. While industrial restructuring revitalized the demand for immigrant workers, it also reduced the opportunities for blue-collar employment among African Americans,[4] as evidenced during the second half of the twentieth century in Baltimore which, together with Pittsburgh and Philadelphia, is one of the main centers of steel production in the nation. For example, in the 1970s, Bethlehem Steel, Baltimore's principal employer, hired upward of thirty-five thousand: two decades later that number had shrunk to eighty-five hundred. The effects of decline were visible throughout the urban landscape.

The period that witnessed the demise of steel production in Baltimore coincided with the accelerated arrival of migrants from the rural South—the Great Black Migration during which people moved north, chasing opportunities. Their influx provoked the departure of older residents—the descendants of Eastern European Jews, Germans, Irish, Polish, and Italians—to the Maryland suburbs. By 1989 more than half of the city's dwellers were African American; in the West Baltimore neighborhoods of Upton and Lower Park Heights the figure surpassed 95 percent. Shrinking opportunities, "white flight," and residential segregation resulted in the concentration of poverty in these neighborhoods and others like them.[5]

Consequently, a gaping disconnection from the larger society shaped life and identity in West Baltimore. Hardly anyone owns a home. Thousands live in publicly subsidized housing. Abandonment and arson are commonplace, evidenced by the large number of charred and boarded-up buildings that have become havens for drug dealers.[6] Business activity is puny, with the exception of the sprinkling of small food and liquor stores inherited by Korean entrepreneurs from an earlier cohort of Jewish merchants. Children can be seen everywhere—in the playgrounds of decrepit schools, running along the graffiti-laden walls, at the intersections where *crack* is sold—their laughter incongruous in the desolate landscape.

Significantly, in the urban ghetto the state penetrates the daily existence of individuals and families in diametrical contrast to its role in increasingly removing itself from the global economy. The police and a multitude of social workers, administrators of correctional facilities, the penal system, half-way houses, group homes, shelters, rehabilitative centers, and those ubiquitous, publicly funded researchers conducting yet another costly survey are ever present in the inner city. This totalistic presence of government illustrates a distorted embeddedness of the state in civil society in the age of global capitalism.

In the inner city, bureaucracies now occupy spaces left empty by the departure of productive capital, with unforeseen and grave consequences. One consequence is the increase of illicit economic activities, especially those related to the drug trade. Another is that from the moment of birth, inner-city children experience contact with the agents of control and beneficence. Because of the divided American tradition that sees poverty both as an affliction and a trespass, they are simultaneously the objects of compassion and mistrust. Over time, this has had an effect upon their sense of self, as well as on the way they envision their position in the larger society. While youngsters in more prosperous neighborhoods become acquainted with institutions that bestow a modicum of power, the children of poverty interact with public offices that unwittingly erode their sense of agency. As they grow older, those interactions influence their perception of their economic options and even the manner in which they address personal conflict.[7]

Furthermore, in its dealings with impoverished populations, the American state assumes positions that differ in terms of gender. Women and children are routinely monitored through programs that adminis-ter government largesse, encourage reproductive control, and protect children from negligence and abuse. Even prepubescent girls living in poverty encounter public agencies' vision of maternity, family life, and other related matters. On the other hand, by early adolescence boys are more likely to come face to face with the police and the correctional and court systems.

The combined effect of capitalist devolution, state omnipresence, and residential segregation also results in acute isolation, weakening the ties upon which individuals can rely to gain access to jobs, informa-tion, and other valuable assets.[8] For example, downtown Baltimore, with its aristocratic buildings, plazas, and monuments, is but a ten-minute drive away from Upton. Yet it is possible to grow into young adulthood in the Upton neighborhood without ever having crossed the limits of the ghetto. This isolation, exacerbated by racism and prejudice against, for example, those who live in public housing, diminishes the contacts and information available to black urban dwellers to enhance their socioeconomic opportunities.

The exceptional character of the experience in American inner cities explains the causes and consequences of specific behaviors such as the high rate of teenage pregnancies. Critics of welfare programs blame public policy and cultural pathologies for the looseness of sexual be-havior that they assume explains the large number of out-of-wedlock births in black neighborhoods. They are mistaken. Beyond the condem-nations and maudlin laments about "babies having babies" dwells the harsh logic of ghetto life. The stigma that haunts young and poor moth-ers is one of citizenship. For many girls and young women excluded from membership in the larger society, motherhood represents both a psychological substitute for and a deterrent to economic and political participation.[9] Poverty-stricken youths lacking other assets turn to their bodies to affirm their adult status. In contrast, more affluent youngsters rely on the material and symbolic resources placed at their disposal by their families to transition into maturity.[10]

Thus, the stigma attached to poor young women having children derives from the grudging concessions of parenting rights to those believed not to have earned them through their successful participation in the labor market. The underlying assumption is that all groups share equivalent means to enact and enjoy the prerogatives of citizenship. Therefore they should be measured by the same standards of responsibility. Yet such seemingly equitable treatment in terms of citizenship flies in the face of the historical inequalities and differentials of power stemming from class, gender, and race.

Speculating about rights and obligations without considering these critical issues does violence to the very meaning of citizenship. Nothing is more unjust than the application of equal measures, like those defining citizenship, to people who historically and circumstantially have been treated unequally. Individuals cannot effectuate rights and obligations independent of the groups to which they belong. For poor inner-city residents such as impoverished adolescent mothers effectively ejected from the labor market, the critical issue is their exclusion from opportunity and their lack of access to resources that make the notion of citizenship meaningful.[11]

IMMIGRANT LABOR AND INDUSTRIAL RESTRUCTURING

Contrary to the isolation and invisibility of the urban poor that resulted from global industrial restructuring, immigrants are increasingly visible in some of the most vibrant sectors of the economy. Propelled by the desire to improve their economic standing, or forced to leave their hometowns by political turmoil, immigrants and refugees judge their adoptive countries by the standards of lives left behind. For that reason, and because immigration has often taken place surreptitiously, making the undocumented, or insufficiently documented, vulnerable, they are more willing than citizens to accept low wages and harsh working conditions.

The public in advanced countries has been conditioned to believe that contemporary immigration stems from the desperate quest of third world peoples trying to escape poverty at home. In reality, it is not the poorest of the poor who migrate; the facts are vastly more complex. Two major forces rooted in the dynamics of capitalist expansion have driven contemporary immigration: first, the labor demands of first world economies and, second, the widespread diffusion in peripheral countries of standards of consumption and cultural patterns generated in advanced societies. Acute labor scarcities in rich nations include the dearth of industrial workers in Japan and deficits in certain professions like nursing and engineering in the United States. In some instances the scarcities arise from cultural expectations, as manifested by the resistance of native-born workers to accept low-paid and menial jobs commonly performed by migrants in the past.[12]

The flip side of the coin entails the effects of globalization on the supply of immigrants. The drive of multinational capital to expand markets in the periphery and simultaneously to take advantage of its reserves of labor has had important social consequences. Among them are the reconfiguration of popular culture and the introduction of new consumption standards bearing little relation to local wage levels. This imbues future immigrants with expectations of lives abroad, and increases their drive to close the gap between local realities and imported desires.

In effect, then, migration from poor to rich countries is driven by the requirements of capitalist accumulation. For example, the 1970s saw an emerging international division of labor in which direct production would all but disappear in advanced countries while poor nations would become the primary producers of exportable manufactures. The number of "high-tech" jobs requiring "symbolic skills" grew, especially in rich nations, and export-processing zones multiplied in the less developed world.[13] However, domestic manufacturing did not disappear from core countries like the United States. Instead, it was reorganized. The streamlining of operations, subcontracting, innovative marketing strategies, and the tapping of new labor pools enabled new sectors of production to expand.

Globalization has also altered the development strategies of poor countries, especially in Asia and Latin America. Responding to the changing conditions of international production and to the expansion of export-processing zones, less developed countries abandoned the import-substitution industrialization policies of the 1960s and 1970s in favor of liberal economic policies. As in the United States, this transformation paralleled the feminization of the labor force, with women playing a conspicuous role in the reconfiguration of the world economy and changing our definition of rights and responsibilities upon which citizenship is based.

Immigrant women have become the preferred bearers of labor for certain kinds of manufacturing in the changing U.S. economy. This reality, although markedly different from the experience of impoverished African Americans discussed in the prior section, underscores the importance of gender as a major factor in the allocation of power and resources. In the United States, the shift toward a services- and information-based economy brought about the expansion of technical and professional jobs but also the creation of an even larger number of jobs whose characteristics were formerly associated with female employment—temporality, low pay, and a paucity of benefits.

Developments in the electronics industry illustrate the process of change in U.S. manufacturing.[14] Despite major losses in actual and potential employment, electronics is still the fourth largest industry in the United States, and one of its fastest-growing economic sectors. Ethnographic research shows the conspicuous presence of women and immigrants in the lower echelons of electronics production,[15] as they are an affordable labor pool with low wage expectations and low unionization rates.

Small firms vulnerable in the industry and with a huge proportion of labor cost, hire cheap labor and are prone to be cited for labor code violations. Almost 60 percent of direct production workers in those plants are women and almost half are Hispanic.[16]

The large number of ethnic and immigrant women in the labor force requires us to consider their transition from being domestic to public actors. In the early stages of industrial capitalism, production rigidified the division between the labor market and the home, promoting gender definitions that bound women to the private sphere of family and unpaid work, and men to the public world of remunerated employment. While men acquired status as citizens on the basis of economic and political recognition, women's domestic contributions became invisible. As exemplified by the arduous struggle to gain the vote, women's claims to citizenship remained contested. Gradually, women have attained civic rights but their progress has been contingent on their contributions to the economy.

In light of the historical link between women's civic rights and economic participation, industrial restructuring has had an impact on gender demarcations. Globalization has altered the relationship between capital and labor, one built upon the premise that men are providers and women housewives. Industrial relocation has allowed employers to exploit large wage differentials abroad and elude workers' rising demands at home, the same process that is leading to new gender definitions while eroding old understandings of men as family providers and women as specialized domestic workers. In some respects, patriarchal mores and definitions remain unaltered. Men have been slow to assume responsibility for domestic chores, including childcare. Nevertheless, no longer are women's responsibilities confined to the home. Increasingly, the norm is represented by the case of Hispanics: women are expected to participate in paid employment.

The diffusion of feminist ideology and the women's movement since the 1970s have helped to propel and rationalize the growing participation of women in the labor force. More fundamentally, however, economic realities have conspired to trump political ideology by creating new demands for women as economic actors. Whether this will increase or diminish the capacity of both men and women to exercise citizenship rights and obligations remains uncertain, especially in light of the fact that women's desirability as economic actors is premised upon their willingness or need to accept low pay, low benefits, and low job security—all trappings of exploitation and second-class citizenship.

TRANSNATIONAL COMMUNITIES: A NEW ALTERNATIVE TO CITIZENSHIP?

Transnational communities are incipient but powerful forces that challenge the more visible manifestations of globalization, including the growing imbalance between capital and labor. They are born when a substantial number of individuals, sharing common characteristics, systematically engage in one or more transnational activities. Members are at least bilingual, move easily between different cultures, frequently maintain a residence in two countries, and pursue economic, political, and cultural interests that require a simultaneous presence at home and abroad. The end result of this process is the transformation of pioneering economic ventures into transnational networks densely woven across space by an increasing number of people who lead dual lives.

Robert Smith conveys the unique character of transnational com-

munities in his description of the reaction of the Ticuaní Potable Water
Committee upon learning that the much-awaited tubing had arrived
and, with it, the final solution to their town's water problem:

> They immediately made plans to inspect the newly installed equip-
> ment: On first sight, this is no more than an ordinary civic project. . . .
> Yet when we consider certain other aspects of the scene, the meaning
> becomes quite different. The Committee and I are not standing in Tic-
> uani [Puebla], but rather at a busy intersection in Brooklyn. . . . The
> Committee members are not simply going to the outskirts of the town
> to check the water tubes but rather they are headed to JFK airport for
> a Friday afternoon flight to Mexico City from which they will travel
> the five hours over land to their pueblo, consult with the authorities
> and contractors, and return by Monday afternoon to their jobs in New
> York City.[17]

This is an image of individuals transcending the borders between home
country and immigrant settlements in pursuit of civic action that
churches and private charities have joined, involving migrants in bina-
tional entrepreneurship.

Transnational enterprise would be unlikely if the conditions confronting today's immigrants were similar to those faced by their U.S.-
bound European predecessors at the turn of the century. By comparison, that earlier period featured two significant differences. First, a
plethora of relatively well-paying industry jobs militated against widespread entrepreneurial ventures and gave rise, over time, to stable
working-class communities. Most immigrants continue to work in low-
skilled menial occupations either in factories or, more typically, in services. Notwithstanding globalization, the decline of the manufacturing
economy has restricted their capacity to increase their earnings.

Second, in an earlier time costly and time-consuming long-distance
transportation made it prohibitive for ordinary migrants to span national divides on a regular basis. Today airplanes, telephones, fax ma-
chines, and electronic mail facilitate transnational contact and exchange. People from Latin America and the Caribbean—a growing
proportion of migrants to the United States—experience particular advantages because of their proximity and continued familiarity with
everything American. Immigrant communities, like the ones formed
by the Chinese in Monterey Park near Los Angeles and some towns in

El Salvador and the Dominican Republic, are examples of rampant transnationalism.[18]

Global capitalism has given rise to conditions and incentives to transnationalize labor. Capital's ability to relocate production from advanced to less developed countries, however, has dealt a severe blow to workers' organizations on both ends of the geopolitical spectrum.[19] In poor nations, the establishment of export-processing zones and the implementation of neoliberal policies thwarted workers' attempts to mobilize effectively. In rich countries like the United States, globalization brought about rapid declines in union membership even as average wages stagnated.[20] To counter the most flagrant effects of this process, government and private organizations attempted to create international trade unions and impose universal labor standards. Both efforts have been ineffective because the competitive realities of the modern world undermine fledgling class solidarity along national lines.[21]

At the local level, however, workers, whose economic activities across borders sustain the communities, have begun to create social networks that allow them, in a real sense, to be in two countries at the same time. More and more frequently, individuals live out a divided existence in which home—the place of community and personal validation—and workplace—the locus of subsistence and competition—are separated by international borders. This aspect of belonging to a larger society—albeit one that traverses national borders—is in stark contrast to the isolation and loss of community support experienced by inner-city dwellers in the United States. However, in their economic grounding, these transnational communities are no different from multinational corporations, except that they originate at the grassroots level and their actions are often informal.

Transnational communities promote activities that have a differing impact on individuals and the larger societies in which they occur.[22] Individual actors may be transnational with respect to some aspects of their lives and not others. They may earn their sustenance across borders but remain aloof from political participation in either country. They may be loyal to the institutions and mores of their country of destination but be emotionally dependent on religious or other cultural demands in their countries of origin. They may evenly divide their time between nations in order to finance small businesses in their hometowns. They may opt for dual citizenship to retain visibility and "voice" in two different political contexts. Capital's ability to transcend frontiers has been followed by a less noticed, but equally important, phenomenon entailing workers' strategies. For example, the entrepreneurial impulse in immigrants is not solely an effect of the new global order but also a way to upend some of its deleterious consequences, such as the limited remuneration and less than ideal labor conditions and opportunities available for them in the advanced world. By combining their new technological prowess with the mobilization of their social capital, former immigrant workers are able to imitate corporate entities by taking advantage of economic opportunities unequally distributed in space.

Nevertheless, the parallel between the strategies of dominant economic actors and immigrant entrepreneurs is only partial. While corporations rely primarily on their financial muscle to make such ventures feasible, immigrant entrepreneurs depend almost entirely on social capital.[23] The social networks that underlie such popular initiatives are constructed through a protracted and difficult process of adaptation to a foreign society. Significantly, this social capital is wholly lacking for the isolated urban poor, the redundant workers who are increasingly bound by state bureaucracies.

Once transnationalization starts, it acquires a cumulative character that expands not only in numbers but also in the quality of activities encompassed. Hence, while the original propeller of these activities may be economic, subsequent developments encompass political, social, and cultural events as well. For instance, many immigrant groups organize political committees to lobby the home government or to influence local municipalities on various issues. As a result governments have begun to perceive their expatriate communities not just as sources of remittances but also as a possible fountain of investments, entrepreneurial initiatives, markets, and political representation. Many have initiated or implemented policies to grant citizens abroad dual nationality to facilitate their political involvement at home. Seven of the ten countries sending the most immigrants to the United States between 1981 and 1986 now allow some form of dual citizenship.[24] This is in striking contrast to earlier times when emigrants were seen almost as defectors and when naturalization in a different country entailed the automatic loss of citizenship in the country of birth.

Third world governments' initiatives seek to reap economic and political benefits from expatriate communities. They range from a specialized ministry of government in Haiti and Mexico, the granting of dual citizenship and the right to vote in national elections in Colombia, and new legislation allowing the election of representatives of the diaspora to the national legislature in Colombia and the Dominican Republic. Mexico, Colombia, El Salvador, Guatemala, and the Dominican Republic have opened consulates in parts of the United States where their nationals are concentrated. Paradoxically, some states like Mexico promote the acquisition of U.S. citizenship or permanent residence as a strategy to establish a firm foothold beyond the Mexican border. In like fashion, some governments like El Salvador and Guatemala even support their citizens' claims to political asylum abroad, tacitly admitting to repression and persecution at home.

Despite states' efforts to retain ties with their expatriates, transnational migrants—particularly those who leave their countries partly due to frustration with corruption and negligent bureaucracies—are unwilling to proclaim their loyalty to the political elite of their countries of origin. In fact, transnational migrants may use the new opportunities offered by dual citizenship or the right to vote to express their dissatisfaction with the established political order. This, too, is in stark contrast to the political disempowerment of the urban poor.

While creating new opportunities for many who were formerly disempowered, this transborder fluidity raises the question of whether transnational communities pose a threat to traditional notions of citizenship. Do these arrangements prevent immigrants from assimilating into receiving societies and becoming true citizens? In any case, transnational communities liberate citizenship from the antiquated constraints of the nation-state. They may also afford vulnerable groups a degree of autonomy from capitalist exploitation by providing workers with new channels for subsistence and accumulation through commerce and entrepreneurship. Finally, transnational communities are constructing surprising alternatives to political participation within the nation-state and, in some cases, challenging entrenched structures of privilege.

CONCLUSION: NEW DIMENSIONS OF CITIZENSHIP IN THE AGE OF GLOBALIZATION

This essay has reviewed three populations that bear a distinctive relationship to the nation-state and, therefore, to notions of citizenship. The same processes that have brought about international economic integration have reshaped the nature of the experience for these groups distinguished in terms of gender, race, ethnicity, and physical location.

First, the forces of globalization are rendering superfluous the labor provided by large numbers of people situated in both advanced and less developed countries. Disconnection from the system of production marks the redundant worker, an emerging nonworking class for whom citizenship and its accompanying prerogatives become increasingly difficult to attain. Second, immigrants, as exemplified by Hispanic women in the California electronics industry, constitute a strategic class of laborers whose services are critical to the expansion of capitalist enterprise, especially in advanced countries, by lowering production costs. Immigrants bring to the foreground the economic advantages and disadvantages that result from power differentials related to citizen status. Finally, the same forces that have led to the growing integration of the world economic system drive transnational communities. This process, which is reconfiguring notions of citizenship, is not static but dialectic. Transnational networks maintain an opportunistic relationship vis-à-vis capitalism, taking advantage of interstices in the margins of hegemonic investments and state action. Transnationalization weakens the hegemony of corporate economic elites and domestic ruling classes, thereby strengthening everyone's citizenship claims. Yet it can also exacerbate inequalities between third world families and transplanted communities.

There is reason to be optimistic about the overall effects of globalization. The process of capitalist globalization is so broadly based and has generated such momentum as to continuously nourish its grassroots counterpart. It is there, at the grass roots, that the new frontier for mobilization in favor of justice and full citizenship for all resides.

NOTES

1. Aristide R. Zolberg, *The Next Waves: Migration Theory for a Changing World*, 23 Int'l Migration Rev. 403 (1989).

2. *See generally* Bennett Harrison, *Lean and Mean: The Changing Landscape of Corporate Power in the Age of Flexibility* (1994).

3. Robert L. Bach and Howard Brill, *Impact of IRCA on the U.S. Labor market and Economy. Report to the U.S. Department of Labor, Institute for Research on International Labor* (1991).

4. William J. Wilson, *The Truly Disadvantaged: The Inner City, the Underclass, and Public Policy* (1987).

5. Douglas S. Massey and Nancy A. Denton, *American Apartheid: Segregation and the Making of the Underclass* (1993) (offering the most thorough explanation of the causes behind urban poverty).

6. David Simon and Edward Burns, *The Corner: A Year in the Life of an Inner-City Neighborhood* (1998) (detailing the circumstances of addicted inner-city dwellers).

7. Patricia Fernández-Kelly, "International Development and Industrial Restructuring: The Case of Garment and Electronics Industries in Southern California," in *Instability and Change in the World Economy* 147 (Arthur MacEwan and William K. Tabb eds. 1995).

8. Mark Granovetter first articulated the well-known distinction between strong and weak social ties in the 1970s. According to him, strong ties are those developed within intimate circles formed by family and friends. They offer continuous interaction and exist by virtue of membership in a particular group. Weak ties, by contrast, are those established with individuals who are often outside the individual's primary group and with whom interaction is less frequent, but who can play a decisive role in making information and opportunities available.

9. Patricia Fernández-Kelly, "Social and Cultural Capital in the Urban Ghetto: Implications for the Economic Sociology of Immigration," in *The Economic Sociology of Immigration: Essays on Networks, Ethnicity, and Entrepreneurship* 213 (Alejandro Portes ed. 1995) (discussing factors that lead youngsters to value parenthood prematurely).

10. These processes include socialization characterized by actual or figurative interactions with the market, such as educational opportunity and extracurricular activity designed to provide them with the skills necessary to successfully function as economic actors. It is not surprising therefore that middle-class children correctly interpret pregnancy and premature parenthood as serious threats to future options.

11. Lack of space prevents me from expanding a complementary argument concerning black men whose capacity to behave and be treated as genuine citizens continues to be compromised by labor market exclusion and state surveillance.

12. Alejandro Portes and Luis E. Guarnizo, "Tropical Capitalists: U.S.-Bound Immigration and Small Enterprise Development in the Dominican Republic," in *Migration, Remittances, and Small Business Development: Mexico and Caribbean Basin Countries* 101 (Sergio Diaz-Briquets and Sydney Weintraub eds. 1991); Saskia Sassen and Alejandro Portes, *Miami: A New Global City?* 22 Contemporary Sociology 1 (1993).

13. Robert Reich, *The Work of Nations: Preparing Ourselves for 21st Century Capitalism* (1992).

14. Patricia Fernández-Kelly, *For We Are Sold, I and My People: Women and Industry in Mexico's Frontier* (1983) (basing discussion on research conducted with Saskia Sassen in the late 1980s regarding conditions surrounding Hispanic women in the electronics industry.

15. In southern California, one of the leading industrial centers in the world, fully 66 percent of the workforce in the large occupational category of "operators, fabricators and laborers" are ethnic minorities. Fifty-one percent of them are Hispanic females. Minority women comprise 71 percent of all machine operators, assemblers, and inspectors. Of these, Hispanic women make up 76 percent. Finally, ethnic minorities comprise 70 percent of all metal and plastic machine operators, a category of special relevance to the electronics industry. Hispanics form almost 80 percent of those workers. About 30 percent of workers employed in the southern California electronics industry are foreign-born Hispanics.

16. These employment statistics are striking in light of the demographic composition of the region. Slightly over 23 percent of the population in southern California is Hispanic, but 44 percent of direct production workers in electronics firms, and upward of 57 percent of those employed in small firms cited for labor code violations belong in the same ethnic group. These statistics are almost the reverse of those for African Americans in the same region. African Americans comprise 12 percent of the population of southern California but represent only 3 percent of direct production workers in electronics.

17. Robert C. Smith, *Los Ausentes Siempre Presentes: The Imagining, Making, and Politics of a Transnational Community between New York City and Ticuani, Puebla* (1992).

18. Min Zhou, *New York's Chinatown: The Socioeconomic Potential of an Urban Enclave* (1992); Min Zhou and Carl L. Bankston, "Entrepreneurship: An Alternative Path to Economic Mobility for Asian Americans," in *Asian American Almanac* (I. Natividad ed. 1994).

19. Patricia Fernández-Kelly, "The Future of Gender: Economic Transformation and Changing Definitions," in *Understanding Societies* (York Bradshaw and Joseph F. Healey eds. 2000).

20. *Id.* The tendency toward world economic integration has been a two-pronged process. From an economic point of view, it has contributed to the realization of profit through the reduction of production costs. As a political trend, it represents a massive realignment in the balance of power between capitalists and workers in favor of the former. *See also* Fernández-Kelly, *supra* note 7.

21. Alejandro Portes, "By-Passing the Rules: The Dialectics of Labour Standards and Informalization in Less Developed Countries," in *International Labour Standards and Economic Independence* 159 (W. Sensenberger and D. Campbell eds. 1994).

22. Peggy Levitt, *Transnational Migration and Development—A Case of Two for the Price of One?* Working paper #00-02-I. Center for Migration and Development, Princeton University, 2000.

23. Luis E. Guarnizo, "One Country in Two: Dominican-Owned Firms in the United States and the United States and the Dominican Republic" (1992) (unpublished dissertation on file with author).

24. *See* Levitt, *supra* note 22. Some seventy nations, including Canada, Italy, Israel, South Africa, and New Zealand, allow their citizens to retain or regain their citizenship or nationality after becoming naturalized in another nation.

20

Human Rights, Globalization, and Culture

Centering Personhood in International Narrative

Berta Esperanza Hernández-Truyol

AFTER WORLD WAR II, internationalism underwent dramatic transformation. As a response to Nazi war atrocities human beings, who up until then had been merely objects of international law, were recognized as subjects of international law. The human rights regime that emerged from this tragedy is a rich and complex one. Significantly, in reaching beyond the state and looking at individuals and their rights regardless of where they might be located, human rights law redefined the concept of sovereignty, that formerly omnipotent power of the state to do as it wished vis-à-vis its subjects everywhere, and with respect to everyone within its territorial borders. The idea of personhood unbounded by territorial lines or citizenship ties originated as a reaction against the sovereign abuse of unfettered power.

To be sure, the human rights system is not perfect; it is fraught with stresses that emerge from the diversity of the cultures, languages, and religions around the world, and it is plagued with contradictions that result from its ideological origins. Yet, despite its weaknesses, it has transformed international law.

Since the latter part of the twentieth century, internationalism has been undergoing another dramatic transformation: globalization—a powerful and dynamic force. Formerly distant places are as close as our fingertips—the stroke of a computer keyboard—or only as far as an airplane ride. While once it took much planning (including translations) and time—hours, days, months—to communicate with places at opposite ends of the globe, today we are increasingly using a single language (English) across our myriad borders, and communication takes only a matter of seconds. These conditions enable increasing familiarity with cultures, customs, and religions not long ago deemed obscure.

Globalization, like human rights norms, also transcends the state. It, too, is reconfiguring sovereignty, but far more than human rights, globalization blurs the public and private divides.[1] Powerful and rich transnational entities (TNEs), with book values far exceeding the gross national product of many states, are setting norms that apply across national boundaries. For example, the elision of private and public lines and functions is magnified by the proliferation of the so-called corporate codes of conduct for TNEs. In response to U.S. consumer outrage at the conditions of workers abroad who make soccer balls, athletic wear and other garments, and rugs, to name a few items made for Northern consumption, codes of conduct are being promulgated not by local governments, but by the TNEs themselves. Working conditions are so bad in some locations that they threaten the workers' personhood. However, it is the TNEs' self-interest in retaining market share and not concern for workers' well-being that is driving these codes.[2] And the codes' impact is felt by the workers—workers who have no formal voice in establishing the terms of the codes. Typically, workers are represented by nongovernmental organizations and not by direct votes or even by unions of which they chose to become members.

Whether the driving force is public or private, some halting attempts, ostensibly in support of the weak, are evident. Not everyone is sharing in the benefits of globalization, however. Simultaneously coexisting with any apparent progress is the stubborn persistence of poverty; hunger; illiteracy; war; disease; religious, national, ethnic, and racial hatreds and strife; and sex and gender subordination and marginalization. The technologically facilitated compression of time and space has increased our familiarity, but not always our comfort with, or tolerance of others.

In the midst of these transformations, how can peoples and cultures, especially those that are not dominant in the globalization explosion, be protected against oppression and even extinction? We can use the tool of human rights norms to effectively curb the possible deleterious consequences of globalization as well as to foster its positive aspects. Globalization exposes cultural fault lines, sometimes unearthing possible backlash forces that have the potential to harm minority cultures and those who are different or disempowered.

It is appropriate to move away from a purely economic notion of globalization and to adopt a version that puts a human face on it. Such a shift moves us toward a vision of human flourishing, a condition that requires the thriving of individuals and of members of larger communities—both of which are expressly protected by human rights norms. It is appropriate to develop a consensus model to resolve conflicts that are more likely to arise because of the *mondialisation* phenomenon. The process entails legitimate communications. The framework's design aims at obtaining the input of multiple relevant actors to negotiate, evaluate, and resolve existing tensions. The intent of this model is to provide an evaluative context for conversations about globalization, human rights, cultural practices, and individualism. Ultimately, this conceptual methodology serves to reveal the sources—structures of domination, whether cultural, national, ethnic, or racial—so that peaceful solutions accommodating cultural differences can be attained.

PERSONHOOD: THE HUMAN RIGHTS STRATEGY

The human rights ideal provides the foundational predicate for human flourishing. It recognizes and embraces the condition of human beings as free and equal in dignity and rights; it confirms that freedoms are to be enjoyed without discrimination on the bases of race, color, sex, language, religion, political or other opinion, national or social origin, property, and birth or other status. Life, liberty, and security of the person are assured, as are freedom of thought, conscience, and religion, and freedom of opinion and expression.[3] Moreover, the human needs for rest and leisure, the right to work, healthcare, an adequate standard of living including food and shelter, and social security are expressly recognized,[4] much as they were in Franklin D. Roosevelt's *Four Freedoms* speech. Finally, human rights norms also acknowledge the human need for community and express the right freely to participate in cultural life.[5]

Notwithstanding these broad protections, the human rights model ought not to be romanticized. The thriving international system reflects the contradictions of liberalism's roots in the late eighteenth century's political and social uprisings. These sought to identify impermissible governmental intrusions into individual rights, reflected in the American Declaration of Independence and the French Declaration of the *Droits de l'Homme* (Rights of Man). Ironically, this movement for individual freedom coexisted with the institution of slavery and with women's status as mere chattel. Moreover, the crafting of the human rights framework was constituted by the voice and position of a few powerful states claiming to speak for all states in promulgating universal, and universally binding, norms. There are Western assumptions, evaluations, and even institutional divisions operating within human rights norms. The construct reflects the deficiencies of liberal thinking and its origins with respect to sex, race, class, and community hierarchy. Consequently, "the language used to enact, enforce, describe or analyze [human rights] is not transparent, innocent, ahistorical or simply instrumental."[6]

Not surprisingly, the Western impetus to universalize these norms has faced strident opposition. In the early 1960s the new postcolonial states of the South were vocal in their resistance to the imposition of a process that they had neither started nor designed, structured, or defined. They rejected the Western-Northern assumptions of universality pervading the human rights model. The Western-Northern states were comfortable only with the negative rights construct, that is, the granting of individual rights to be free from governmental interference with respect to civil and political rights. In turn, the Western-Northern states resisted the recognition of positive rights concerning social, economic, and cultural matters, or the undertaking of obligations with respect to such positive rights. The new postcolonial states of the South, together with the then-second world, on the other hand, sought to prioritize collective, including economic, rights over individual ones. They claimed that an emphasis on civil and political rights simply gave the already powerful bourgeoisie power over the masses. The subordinated, these states argued, could be liberated only by the grant of social and economic rights.

Vestiges of the North-South, East-West, capitalism-socialism tensions persist. A prime example is the failed programs of aid which were destined for failure because they were envisioned, crafted, and imposed by core states on peripheral ones without any understanding of the various cultures, the needs of diverse peoples, or the problems in various and varied societies. Similarly, post–Cold War events reveal discord, in part due to economic instability and the attendant increase in nationalism, ethnic strife, cultural and religious differences, civil war, and human rights abuses.

A human rights strategy that centers personhood embraces the ideal of the indivisibility and interdependence of rights—the full panoply of human rights as envisioned in the Declaration: civil and political rights as well as social, economic, and cultural ones. These constitute the proverbial bundle of sticks that belongs to persons *because* they are human beings. Human flourishing requires humanity, dignity, and access to the means of basic survival; it is indivisibly connected not only to individual fulfillment, but also to membership and participation in our varied and various communities. A blueprint premised on dichotomies is structurally defective; human lives are constituted by interlocking communities. Liberal individualistic and communitarian traditions are not irreconcilable visions. Rather, they are interdependent and complementary dimensions of human existence. It is not contested that international human rights doctrine recognizes individual rights as well as cultural, social, religious, and linguistic liberties. Thus, international human rights principles are invaluable in interpreting and translating within, between, and among cultures, by creating a context that embraces the value of diverse peoples, speaking different languages, and from varying cultural traditions.

Contrary to this ideal, the culture of power universally imposes the visions of a few on everyone all the time. But as the new postcolonial states have asserted, universality should not mean that someone's culture is imposed on everyone else. Rather, universality should be a vehicle for building consensus, pluralism, and democracy. It should not be deployed to suppress or "other" differences. Universality is at its least appealing and most damnable when it is used as a sword to eviscerate traditional cultural practices, effectively to commit cultural genocide. Nonetheless, this does not mean that we cannot or should not universally condemn genocide—including cultural genocide—committed in the name of cosmopolitanism.

Conversely, relativism should not mean that we do not examine, critique, try to change, or even render outlaw some cultural practices. While the culture of power should not permit the dominant culture to effect erasures of traditional cultural practices, neither should the power of traditional culture be accepted as a shield to protect so-called traditional cultural practices that create, reinforce, and perpetuate the subordination, enslavement, or exclusion of individuals within their particular cultures.

And while we have acknowledged the human rights system's

flawed roots in liberalism, it is noteworthy that liberalism is an important paradigm for the personhood project. It is that very liberal language of rights that women, slaves, ethnic and racial minorities, and indigenous groups have adopted and utilized to clamor for their rights. Of course, we have to own up to the melange that constitutes liberalism. But does anticosmopolitan tribalism underly these new liberal claims for full personhood by former nonpersons? I think not. Indeed, part of the liberal claim is that we share space, not usurp it, at the global supper table.

GLOBALIZATION

In looking at that global supper table, it is important to define globalization—a widely used but seldom explained word. Globalization, for the personhood project, is the process by which movements of capital, information, and persons within and across national borders serve to influence local norms, traditions, processes of learning, the exchange of information and goods, and lifestyles. In studying the global, it is necessary also to analyze local movements to ascertain which objects and ideas result in cultural changes. It is important too that globalization not be synonymous with Westernization.

In light of such definition, to examine globalization and its consequences, it is apt to begin by reviewing the data recently described by Secretary General Kofi Annan as "astonishing facts"—facts that starkly reveal the disparate levels of human existence and provide a glimpse of the impact of globalization on personhood. The richest fifth of the world's people consume 86 percent of all goods and services, while the poorest fifth consumes just 1.3 percent; the three richest people in the world have assets that exceed the combined gross domestic product of the forty-eight least developed countries; and the world's two hundred twenty-five richest individuals, of whom sixty are *estado unidenses*, have a combined wealth equal to the annual income of the poorest 47 percent of the world's population; in the United States we spend $2 billion more a year ($8 billion total) on cosmetics than the estimated total needed to provide a basic education for everyone in the world; *estado unidenses* and Europeans spend $17 billion a year on pet food—$4 billion more than the estimated annual additional total needed to provide basic health and nutrition for everyone in the world; of the 4.4 billion people in developing countries, nearly three-fifths lack access to safe sewers, a third have no access to clean water, a quarter do not have adequate housing, and a fifth have no access to modern health services of any kind.[7]

Plainly, many in the global community are far from living in conditions minimally necessary for human thriving. This is particularly true for racial and ethnic minorities and women (particularly when they are also racial and ethnic minorities) within first world states, most people in third world states, and indigenous peoples in all states—North and South, East and West. All these populations are experiencing a widespread pattern of inequality in access to education, health, nutrition, and participation in the political and economic sphere.

These facts underscore the effects of globalization on a shrinking world—be it in the public or the private domains; they present novel issues in global governance. Kofi Annan's facts on poverty, work, consumption, and power confirm that the locations and geographies of hunger are as predictable as the locations of wealth. With globalization, persons, cultures, and capital are unbound from territorial borders; membership and immersion in more than one community or culture becomes the rule; and persons form multiple alliances that cross national, linguistic, and cultural borders.

Thus, human rights is a significant paradigm in the globalization discourse because regardless of location, human beings are entitled to experience and enjoy their human rights. A human rights lens on globalization moves personhood from the edges to the center of a globalization project that marks the expansion of an international civil society. The reason we need to focus on personhood is the very blurring of boundaries effected by globalization and the boundary crossings that human rights norms witness. Although at present it may be a contested space, it represents one where marginalized communities—within and without national territories—can gain both visibility and protections.

Such a changed vision of globalization could transform the emphasis on transnational capitalism which has become the new colonial model rapidly replacing the nation-state as the world's colonizing force, to a broader forum in which to evaluate economic justice. In this regard, Kofi Annan's facts show that the benefits of globalization that some of us so placidly enjoy are bypassing more than half the developing countries; they reveal global inequities. Money and power are concentrated in the hands of a sorry few. Certain cultures and cultural practices are still deemed normative—those old "civilized cultures" still embarrassingly embedded in article 38 of the Statute of the International Court of Justice[8]—and some, likely the uncivilized and savage as we have called African and indigenous traditions and laws, are deemed "outsider" cultures not worthy of a presence in the international imagination or life. Even within the rich-poor dichotomy, some are more so than others—there is a South within the South, just as there is a South within the North.

These actualities confirm the pervasive violence of (economic) power—the polarized concentration of money among a few at the expense of the many and of the earth itself; the power of cultural norms—often gendered, racialized, and classed; and the need to redefine the culture of violence to include more than the paradigm of physical invasion—be it at home or in war: the need to include violence perpetrated by the present and real, gendered, localized concentrations of money and power. So in our conversations about economic globalization, let us not forget the people.

CULTURE

Just as patterns of inequality persist, so do varied cultural practices that with globalization are traveling beyond their native geographies. While the international community is not likely to dispute the universality of the prohibition against genocide or torture, there are hugely contested areas regarding so-called cultural practices. For example, some, if not most, traditions and cultures still hide behind the shield of tradition and culture to subordinate women, racial, ethnic, and sexual minorities, and the poor. Although the subordination of the disempowered infects the North and the South, the East and the West, in different locations the expressions of subordination exhibit or reflect cultural or local particularities.

Consider some of the various forms of sex-based subordination. In the United States—considered by some as the quintessential North—women make less than men; in the South there are honor killings; in the West rapists are set free because sexual intercourse with a woman wearing jeans is deemed consensual: jeans are tight and difficult to take off;[9] and in the East medical doctors are starving and their patients are dying because as women they are no longer allowed to practice their professions. Every day female genital mutilation threatens the life and health of girls and the killing of lower castes in the East and of lesbians (and gays) in the West is an affront to the right to life. Good leaders are expelled and excluded from the boy scouts because they are gay; children work at trades that will cripple them for life—from soccer ball making, to carpet weaving, to prostitution. All these realities are violations of personhood—cultures and individuals notwithstanding.

Conversations about economic globalization have included the movement of *some* persons—the cosmopolitan who thrives on the diversity of culture. As Jeremy Waldron, a self-proclaimed cosmopolitan, says, "he refuses to think of himself as defined by his location or his ancestry or his citizenship or his language."[10] Rather, "he does not take his identity to be compromised when he learns Spanish, eats Chinese, wears clothes made in Korea, listens to arias by Verdi sung by a Maori princess on Japanese equipment, follows Ukranian politics and practices Buddhist meditation techniques."[11] Such a person is "a creature of modernity, conscious of living in a mixed-up world and having a mixed up self."[12] Mixed-up self he may be, but he still thinks about compromising his identity. Yet with the stroke of the same pen, Waldron decries communitarian excess as costly because it requires supporting dying cultures, customs, languages, and peoples.

This is a cynical and myopic view of cosmopolitanism. All that Waldron craves—his languages, his ethnic foods, the varied cultures—will be lost under his analysis: many of his favored cultures may well die if they are not somehow propped up; all cultures will end up being the same. Where will he get his meals, his music, his equipment, his enjoyment of politics, his voice? This construction of cosmopolitanism becomes but a reductionist exoticization of cultural tropes rather than an honest acceptance of the reality that cultural traditions are intertwined with human dignity.

However, the cosmopolitans are generally only the economic elite attached to the big industry money–economic globalization movement. In this group, we already see factual, if not de jure, dual citizenship—persons who live in New York City, Tokyo, Hong Kong, or Sao Paolo but carry passports from another place, travel in the Concorde and across continents, wear fancy designer suits, work incessantly on their identical laptops, and talk incessantly on their identical cell phones. The national differences so emphasized by the poor, the underprivileged, and the disempowered are subsumed here by the color of commerce. The cosmopolitans' allegiances are increasingly deterritorialized; their views and lifestyles increasingly homogenized.

But there are also low-level economic actors in the global economic marketplace who have a huge impact on cultural transmission and who bear the brunt of the pattern of inequality evidenced by globalization. Economic globalization stories should also chronicle them—transmigrations of labor, more frequently than not ethnic and national minorities, generally taken for granted in conversations about globalization.

The janitors whose job it is to clean the shiny financial centers' offices for their U.S., Arab, Swiss, Brazilian, Japanese, and German bosses inspire whole industries to support their cultural needs. These include ethnic grocery stores and restaurants (fetishized and appropriated by the cosmopolitan bosses as third world chic), and check-cashing, cash-sending, phone-card-selling stores where the laborers can send their hard-earned hard currency home—to their abroad home in any case, because they often go to another home in the inner city or distant suburbs where their kids, often born in the United States, speak English and go to school, and do homework, and wear GAP jeans and Levis, probably made in Mexico. Putting a human face on economic globalization would include the participation of the service workers and their unrecognized but observable presence in the marketplace as well as their impact thereon: the migration of customs, languages, and religious and cultural practices.

Globalization broadly reaches culture and markets, affecting civil, political, social, cultural, economic, and group rights, reconfiguring cultural tropes. Seldom can a person from the United States travel abroad and not see a McDonalds or Citibank or the GAP, which may make some of us feel more at home while abroad. Seldom can someone from the United States walk through a state or county fair or an art fair in the United States without seeing some form of performance of an "other" culture, often foreign, often indigenous, say a Peruvian representation, or wander through a U.S. city without seeing West African hairdressers, Korean grocers, or Chinese launderers.

The shrinking of the world, the CNNing of international relations, the pressure of codes of conduct, the visible shedding of real blood by real people in China, Italy, Cuba, Brazil, Sierra Leone, Bosnia, and East Timor is having a transformative impact on global society. The blurring of borders is having a similar effect. "European art" has been denationalized.

Europe's "national" artists are Portuguese and Swiss choreographers at home in Germany; Moroccan and Turkish songwriters in Amsterdam and Berlin; African, Japanese and Vietnamese writers and directors in England and France. . . . All the while, Dutch producers are organizing everywhere, cultural traders in the manner of their merchant forebears. . . . [S]o many artists from Central Europe, from Belgium to the Netherlands, have adopted the dreaded interloper of English to universalize their cultural experience.[13]

Globalization has redefined community. Cuban Americans or Ameri-Cubans see their communities as spanning that ninety-mile stretch between Key West and Havana—and this includes folks who have never been to Cuba. Puerto Ricans see their communities spanning New York City and *la isla*. Dominicans, Indians, and Pakistanis, to name a few, have similar transnational existences.

The movement caused by the denationalization of borders or deterritorialization of nations hybridizes cultures and traditions, often eliciting ugly backlashes—frequently expressed as a nationalistic-nativistic attempt to reterritorialize nations.[14] Such reactions bring to mind the vestiges of the polarization of the civil, political, cultural, social, and economic interests of various states. Consider the events surrounding two Northern leaders. During his time in office, President Clinton traveled north to Canada to inaugurate a U.S. embassy to celebrate the success of trade between the two countries. Amidst the celebratory spirit, the reaction of one nationalist group was cultural and resentful: "You are seeing the Americanization of Canada, no doubt about it,"[15] said a critic who may well be correct: since its entry into Canada in 1994, WalMart—almost as much a symbol of the U.S. as McDonalds, Citibank, and the GAP—has become Canada's largest retailer.

On a different occasion and on a different coast, former Prime Minister Margaret Thatcher proclaimed the superiority of British culture. "We are quite the best country in Europe," she said, noting that "[i]n my lifetime all the problems have come from mainland Europe, and all the solutions have come from the English-speaking nations across the world."[16]

Similarly and at the same time, during its reign of terror, the Taliban claimed to be imposing religious rule in Afghanistan, saying *they* had the answers, they were the true Islam. In an interesting twist, we also had Muslims claiming that the Taliban had Islam all wrong, that it "misused and distorted the principles of Islam in justifying their rule of terror, their suppression of human rights, and their politics of hate and drugs."[17] The popular repudiation of the Taliban version was plainly viewed around the globe when the Northern Alliance liberated Kabul. Men cut their beards and women shed their veils. All—men and women, young and old—again listened to music. Hence the reality is that there are dissenting views within Muslim communities as to the true boundaries of Islam.

Just who is right about Islam and about the superiority of the English-speaking world? These nationalistic reactions are unbecoming cultural consequences of globalization, and seek to reverse its course— closing boundaries not only across nations but also within nations and cultures, to effect an inversion of what becomes "outsider," and "othered" communities within foreign national territory.

Thus, with globalization the tensions between as well as within cultures are likely to grow, not to diminish. An imperial majority may seek to destroy minority cultural tropes for the sake of universality and civilization. Likewise, in the face of cultural assault, minority cultures may seek to entrench and enforce, both at home and abroad, cultural tropes that violate individual human rights—those of women or sexual minorities, for example—for the sake of preserving their cultural identity from majoritarian domination or subjugation. Pluralized participation and representation will safeguard against the "tyranny of the majority" and ensure both that the powerful do not use culture as a sword to eviscerate minority cultural traditions and that such traditions are not used as a shield against accountability for human rights abuses.

TOWARD A HUMAN RIGHTS GLOBALIZATION STRATEGY

Plainly, global movements require an environment in which we can preserve personhood, engender human flourishing, and advance the economic development of all the world actors. Globalization, culture, and human rights are linked. Human rights discourse can create the infrastructure of communication in the evaluation of the predicates of personhood. A communications process and substantive analysis that considers particularities serves to counterbalance the universalist nature of a paradigm that may raise questions of dominance, imperialism, and essentialism. An analytical framework in international conflict resolution or norm creation, evaluation, and enforcement requires an expanded focus on globalization that gives it a human face.

Globalization creates four basic geographies of tension: first, nation versus nation—struggling for cultural dominance or survival; second, a nation-TNE relationship that challenges the private-public divide and concepts of self-determination; third, nation versus outsider communities within its national borders; and fourth, the majority versus outsiders (or nonconformists) within their own communities—be these majority or outsider communities. In all these locations a human rights informed construct is useful for defining the parameters of personhood.

With respect to nation versus nation, we should reinforce the decolonization model of self-determination, sovereignty, and independence while recognizing the economic polarities of states. Engagements between states should reflect the interdependence of equals in which each has something to share in a relationship. A plain and common example is core states' need for labor and peripheral states' supply of labor. Such mutual engagement should take place within a human rights-respecting construct, not one in which either a state or its people is exploited by either public or private actors.

With respect to nation-TNE relations, as in the context of nation-nation relationships, it is imperative to scrutinize power dynamics. In these two contexts—nation vis-à-vis nation and TNE vis-à-vis nation—if money is allowed to become a substitute for self-determination the legitimizing force of ostensibly consensual relations is stripped away and the relations between the core state and the peripheral state or between the TNE and the peripheral nation become colonial in character, with the moneyed state or TNE being the colonizing force. Nations constrained by dire, unbearable economic need might not have the capacity to identify and defend their own, including their peoples', best interest vis-à-vis either of these powerful counterparts. If this is the case, then in a new world order dominated by economic power—whether concentrated in core nations or in TNEs—weaker nations need access to sources of power to resist economic abuse by powerful public or private entities. The structural source of such resistance lies in a reconstituted human rights construct and its realization depends on the proposed discursive methodology.

With respect to an outsider within alien national borders—whether the outsider is an individual or a whole community—one basic human rights issue is easily solved. The way a state treats its own citizens with respect to fundamental rights creates a basic threshold—a bottom line—of social benefits that it must grant to all those present within its borders. While this would arguably still permit, although not require, some differentiation between citizens and noncitizens, for example with respect to the vote, it would limit any differentiation that violates human dignity.

With respect to an individual minority dissenting within his or her minority community or a member of the majority who is a dissenter within his or her own culture, the human rights paradigm protects individuals from denial of personhood simply because they take a differently charted path. In all these contexts we need to navigate the potentially stormy relationship between group rights and individual rights. Identifying the different human rights interests at stake, the range of those interests, and balancing the competing interests (resolving existing tensions) in the context of social, economic, political, and individual circumstances will not be easy.

To be sure, it is impossible to foretell the virtually infinite issues or combination of issues that may emerge, and thus we cannot create a rigid system that will cater to every combination or permutation of future problems. Consequently, this proposal is meant to be flexible. The questions set out below simply provide guidelines that can serve as a methodological tool for building consensus.

First, it is important to establish the claim of right or of breach of right that is being made. That is, what is the norm in question? At this stage the origins of the norm must be scrutinized for legitimacy. Next, it is imperative to interrogate the circumstances purportedly giving rise to the claim. Once the factual underpinnings of the claims are established, it is necessary to examine who is claiming the alleged breach— is it a cultural insider or a cultural outsider; a member of the global power elite (public or private), or a member of a subordinate or disempowered group or nation? Similarly it is important to determine who is allegedly transgressing the right—is it a member of the culture or group, or is it an outsider to the culture or group?

This status of insider or outsider raises a relevant question of degree of harm and in some cases even "standing," to make a claim. To ascertain the affront of any particular action on either the individual right or group claim that might be in question, one may first ask what the impact is of enforcing the group norm as compared to the impact of protecting the individual right. Next, it is necessary to ascertain what the consequences are on the group of noncompliance with the norm; what is the level of intrusion of the group norm on individual freedoms (that is, is it deleterious to personhood); and what are the consequences of erosion of the norm on the community. With regard to the problematics presented by the erosion of the norm on community, for example, it is appropriate to inquire whether it is a minor or major effect. For instance, what happens if one person does not want to wear a veil? It is not likely that such failure will erode the cultural and religious norm. But what happens if, one by one, increasing numbers of persons decide not to wear the veil?

Here, the norm formation literature is relevant. For example, tipping point notions say that there will come a time when one additional person following or refusing to follow the norm will have an impact on the norm itself. At that juncture the difficult question arises of the propriety, desirability, or need for continuation of the norm for the survival of a culture. Here we must be ready to confront the possibility that some norms, indeed even some valued cultural norms, may well have to cede to an individual's dignity. Consider, in particular, those norms that are discriminatory on grounds proscribed by reformulated, nonimperialistic, and nonessentialist human rights precepts, and thus are deleterious to personhood.

It is important that the process of interrogation be a discursive one in which different views and interests are represented. In this model there is not one entity representing the "true, valid" norm. Rather, the process should be one in which the divergent concerns are presented and discussed by both proponents and opponents—believers and nonbelievers.

Given the existing power differences as plainly spelled out by Kofi Annan's "astonishing facts,"[18] and the need for a level playing field, it is clear that fair discursive exchanges will have to rely on the generosity of those in power. If the spirit is one of interdependence, the ostensible differentials may well balance out; if the spirit is one of colonialism, the differences may fatally taint the process.

This process provides a blueprint for the resolution of conflicts by placing at the center the preservation of personhood, which, as defined, includes both individualism and community. The model would apply to the concept of personhood processes that are quite familiar in the realm of economic globalization: negotiation, conciliation, and expert evaluation. As has become clear in the *mondialisation* process, all of us are individuals, as well as members of not just one but many interconnected and interdependent communities. All our varied locations are necessary for our enjoyment of personhood. Considering the realities of globalization, this methodology assists in the protection of all our passports.

NOTES

1. *See* Saskia Sassen, *Losing Control? Sovereignty in an Age of Globalization* 21–22 (1995) [hereinafter Sassen, *Losing Control?*].

2. Universal Declaration on Human Rights, G.A. Res. 217, U.N. GADR, 3rd Sess., Supp. No. 127, UN Doc. A/810 (1948); International Covenant on Civil and Political Rights, Dec. 16, 1966, 999 U.N.T.S. 3 (entered into force Mar. 23, 1976) [hereinafter ICCPR].

3. Universal Declaration, *supra* note 2; International Covenant on Economic, Social, and Cultural Rights, Dec. 16, 1966, 993 U.N.T.S. 3 (entered into force Jan. 3, 1976).

4. ICCPR, *supra* note 2, art. 276.

5. *See* Robert J. C. Young, *Colonial Desire: Hybridity in Theory, Culture and Race* 163 (1995).

6. For a more detailed analysis of the universalism-relativism dyad, *see* Guyora Binder, *Cultural Relativism and Cultural Imperialism in Human Rights Law*, 5 Buff. Hum. Rts. L. Rev. 211 (1999); Berta Esperanza Hernández-Truyol, *Women's Rights as Human Rights—Rules, Realities and the Role of Culture: A Formula for Reform*, 21 Brook. J. Int'l L. 605 (1996).

7. *See* UN Development Program, *Human Development Report 1998* (last visited on July 21, 2000), <http://www.undp.org/hdro/98.htm>; *see also* Barbara Crosette, *Kofi Annan's Astonishing Facts*, N.Y. Times, Feb. 27, 1998, at 4–16.

8. *See* Statute of the International Court of Justice, 59 Stat. 1055, T.S. No. 993, 3 Bevans 1179, signed June 26, 1945, at art. 38 (noting as a source of law "the general principles of law recognized by civilized nations").

9. An all-male-judge panel of an Italian appeals court threw out a rape charge against a man, stating that the female victim's jeans could not be removed "without the active help of the person wearing them," and consequently she could not possibly have been raped. *See "Jeans for Justice" Day Declared to Protest Italy's Jeans Rape Defense*, Agence France Presse, Apr. 21, 1999, http://www.expressindia.com/ie/daily/19990421/ige21029.html.

10. *See* Jeremy Waldron, *Minority Cultures and the Cosmopolitan Alternative*, 25 Mich. J. L. and Reform, 751, 754 (1992).

11. *See id.*

12. *See id.*

13. *See* David R. White, *New Europe '99: In the New World of Euro Arts*, N.Y. Times, Oct. 10, 1999, at 2–1.

14. *See* Saskia Sassen, *Globalization and Its Discontents: Essays on the New Mobility of People and Money* xxviii (1999).

15. *See* James Brooke, *Clinton Opens Embassy in Canada as Relations between Neighbors Remain Warm*, N.Y. Times, Oct. 9, 1999, <http://www.nytimes.com/library/world/americas/100999clinton-canada.html>.

16. *See* Warren Hoge, *Return of the Iron Lady*, N.Y. Times, Oct. 10, 1999, at 4–2.

17. *See* Naveed Iqbal, *Punish the Taliban*, N.Y. Times, Oct. 9, 1999, at 4–14.

18. Crosette, *supra* note 7.

About the Contributors

SUSAN MUSARRAT AKRAM is an Associate Professor at Boston University School of Law where she teaches and publishes on Immigration and Comparative Refugee Law. She is a graduate of the University of Michigan, Ann Arbor, the Georgetown University Law Center, and the Institut International des Droits de l'Homme, Strasbourg, France. She taught at Al-Quds University/Palestine School of Law, East Jerusalem, as a Fulbright Senior Scholar where she wrote recommendations for Palestinian refugees in light of the final status talks. She is a founding director of several immigration projects and the interim director of the Joint Voluntary Agency for resettlement of Iraqi refugees from refugee camps in Saudi Arabia after the Gulf War.

TIM CONNOR, an economic geographer and activist, is currently a doctoral student at the School of Geosciences in the University of Newcastle in Australia. His thesis on Corporate Codes of Conduct and workers' right to freedom of association uses Nike as a case study on codes. He has a Bachelor of Arts degree from the University of Sydney and a Bachelor of Laws degree from the University of New South Wales.

CLAIRE MOORE DICKERSON, Professor of Law and Arthur Dickson Scholar at Rutgers Law School-Newark, received her J.D. from Columbia University School of Law and an LL.M. in Taxation from New York University School of Law. She applies socioeconomic principles to business-related areas of the law in both the domestic and the international commercial arenas, with a particular focus on standards of performance. Before going into academia, Professor Dickerson was a partner in a New York-based international law firm, where she specialized in international commercial transactions and worked principally with French multinationals.

ELIZABETH FAKAZIS is completing a Ph.D. at Indiana University School of Journalism. Her dissertation analyzes the way journalists police the boundary between fact and fiction and work to maintain their authority as society's truth-tellers. She has taught courses on media and society, and newswriting. Her published work has appeared in the *Gainesville Sun*, the *Indianapolis Star*, and the *Columbia Missourian*.

M. PATRICIA FERNÁNDEZ-KELLY, a Ph.D. in Social Anthropology (Rutgers University), holds a joint position in the Office of Population Research and the Department of Sociology at Princeton University. Her research focuses on international development with special attention to gender, migration, and race and ethnicity. She has conducted extensive research on economic internationalization and women's employment in export-processing zones, including pioneer research on Mexico's *maquiladora* program. She coproduced the *Emmy* Award-winning documentary, *The Global Assembly Line* with filmmaker Lorraine Gray. She is the author and editor of numerous books, including *For We Are Sold, I and My People: Women and Industry in Mexico's Frontier*, and (with June Nash) of *Women, Men and the International Division of labor*.

CHRISTY GLEASON is a Program Coordinator at the Center for American Women and Politics at Rutgers, the State University of New Jersey. She received her B.A. in political science from American University and her J.D. from St. John's University School of Law. In her published work, she combines her experiences in politics and law, writing on issues of gender and sexuality discrimination, and the intersection of law and politics.

GIL GOTT is an Assistant Professor of International Studies at DePaul University in Chicago, Illinois, where he teaches international law, human rights, international organizations, migration, and racial and ethnic conflict. These are also areas in which he writes. Professor Gott holds a Ph.D. from the University of California at Berkeley, and a J.D. from the University of Illinois.

BEVERLY A. GREENE, Ph.D., ABPP, is a Professor of Psychology at St. John's University and a certified clinical psychologist. A Fellow of the American Psychological Association and six of its divisions, she is a Diplomate of the American Board of Professional Psychology in Clinical Psychology and serves as an Editorial Board member of numerous scholarly journals. She has served as founding coeditor of *Psychological Perspectives on Lesbian, Gay and Bisexual Issues* (Sage), a series of annual publications sponsored by Division 44 of APA. A recipient of numerous national awards for distinguished professional contributions and publications, she is coeditor of the recently published *Psychotherapy with African American Women: Innovations in Psychodynamic Perspectives and Practice.*

BERTA ESPERANZA HERNÁNDEZ-TRUYOL is the Levin, Mabie and Levin Professor of Law at the Levin College of Law and affiliate professor, Center for Women's Studies and Gender Research, University of Florida, where she teaches International Law and International Human Rights. Widely published in these areas, her scholarly focus is on issues of sex, race, ethnicity, language, and culture, and the intersection of these themes with immigration, as well as in the location of Latinas within the majority U.S. environment and within the Latina/o community. She has participated in the UN Conferences on Population, Social Development, and Women. She holds an LL.M. in International Legal Studies from New York University School of Law, a J.D. from Albany Law School of Union University, and an A.B. from Cornell University.

JOCE JESSON is a Principal Lecturer and the Director of Research Development at the Auckland College of Education. She teaches research methods, educational policy, and science education. Her doctoral study was on the changing nature and role of the New Zealand secondary education union, in relation to the state. She has a particular interest in the construction of Pakeha identity through education.

KEVIN R. JOHNSON is Associate Dean for Academic Affairs and Professor of Law and Chicana/o Studies at the University of California at Davis. He has written extensively on international migration, immigration law and policy, and civil rights, with a particular focus on Latinas and Latinos, including his recent book *How Did You Get to Be Mexican? A White/Brown Man's Search for Identity.* A graduate of Harvard Law School and the University of California at Berkeley, he clerked for the Honorable Stephen Reinhardt of the U.S. Court of Appeals for the Ninth Circuit in Los Angeles and has practiced law in San Francisco.

JAYNA KANANI KIM is a Staff Attorney at the Hawai'i Civil Rights Commission and a graduate of the William S. Richardson School of Law at the University of Hawai'i, 1999.

JANE E. LARSON is Professor of Law at the University of Wisconsin. She has written widely on issues of sexual regulation, including *Hard Bargains: The Politics of Sex*, with Linda R. Hirshman.

MARY LORING LYNDON, a graduate of Columbia University (J.S.D.), Northeastern University School of Law, and Manhattanville College, is a Professor of Law at St. John's University School of Law where she teaches Torts, Environmental Law, and Toxic Torts. Prior to joining the law faculty, Professor Lyndon practiced broadcasting and telecommunications law and later became an Assistant Attorney General for the State of New York. Professor Lyndon is the author of legislative and bar association reports and numerous law review articles.

HOLLY MAGUIGAN is a Professor of Clinical Law at New York University, where she teaches a criminal defense clinic and a comparative criminal justice clinic—both involving work with battered women in the criminal justice system. Her teaching, litigation, and scholarship focus on the obstacles to fair trials experienced by people accused of crime who are not part of the dominant culture. Professor Maguigan serves on the advisory boards of the National Clearinghouse for the Defense of Battered Women, the Society of American Law Teachers, and the William Moses Kunstler Fund for Racial Justice. She received her J.D. from the University of Pennsylvania, an M.A. from the University of California at Berkeley, and an A.B. from Swarthmore College.

ELIZABETH McKINLEY is currently a Senior Lecturer in the Department of Education Studies at the University of Waikato, Hamilton, Aotearoa New Zealand, where she contributes to courses on social issues in education, particularly in indigenous and women's education, curriculum, and research methods. Her doctoral research is on how race, gender, and colonialism have historically shaped, and continue to shape, the participation of Maori women in science as scientists.

JOHANNA NIEMI-KIESILÄINEN, LLM, Dr. of Law (University of Helsinki), lecturer in procedural law at the Faculty of Law, University of Helsinki, has written extensively on bankruptcy law and law of procedure. Currently she is leading a research project entitled "Violence in the Shadow of Equality—Hidden Gender in the Finnish Legal System."

L. AMEDE OBIORA is an Ibo woman who teaches law in the United States.

R. W. PERRY is a graduate of the Stanford Law School and holds a Ph.D. from the University of California, Berkeley. He teaches legal theory and cultural studies of law at the University of California, Irvine.

EDIBERTO ROMÁN, a graduate of the University of Wisconsin School of Law and of Lehman College, is Professor at Florida International University College of Law. His published work focuses on international law, postcolonial studies, and critical race theory.

SHARON ELIZABETH RUSH is the Irving Cypen Professor of Law at the University of Florida Levin College of Law. A graduate of Cornell Law School and Cornell University, she is a constitutional scholar who focuses on issues of racial healing and understanding. Her book *Loving across the Color Line* explains why racial goodwill is insufficient to eradicate racism.

BOAVENTURA DE SOUSA SANTOS is a Professor of Sociology and Law at the University of Coimbra and the University of Wisconsin-Madison. He has written numerous books in several languages and is widely published in political sociology, the sociology of law, and epistemology. He is involved in research projects in Portugal, Brazil, Colombia, India, South Africa, and Mozambique. Some of his recent books include *Toward a New Common Sense: Law, Science and Politics in the Paradigmatic Transition; Reinventar a Democracia; Globalizing Institutions: Case Studies in Regulation and Innovation.*

SASKIA SASSEN is a Professor of Sociology at the University of Chicago, visiting fellow at the American Bar Foundation, and Centennial Visiting Professor, London School of Economics. She has written numerous books on globalization and the world economy. Among her most recent are *Guests and Aliens* and *Globalization and Its Discontents*. Her books have been translated into ten languages.

KATHRYN SCANTLEBURY is an Associate Professor in the Department of Chemistry and Biochemistry at the University of Delaware, where she is the Secondary Science Education Coordinator for the College of Arts and Science. Her research focuses on gender and ethnic equity issues in science education, teacher education, and systemic reform in education.

CARRIE ANN Y. SHIROTA is a Staff Attorney at the Hawai'i Civil Rights Commission. She is a graduate of the William S. Richardson School of Law at the University of Hawai'i.

ERIC K. YAMAMOTO is a Professor of Law at the William S. Richardson School of Law, University of Hawai'i, whose activist and academic focus is on civil rights and racial justice. He was a member of the coram nobis legal team, successfully reopening *Korematsu v. U.S.* (Japanese American internment case): he represented Alice Aiwohi in her class action claim on behalf of Hawaiian Homelands Trust beneficiaries; served as procedure consultant to the legal team, successfully representing ten thousand political torture victims in the international human rights class action case suit against Ferdinand Marcos and family; and is senior counsel to the Native Hawaiian Advisory Council. He is the author of *Interracial Justice: Conflict and Reconciliation in Post-Civil Rights America.*

Index

Aba Women's War of 1929, 259
Abolition: of prostitution, 183, 184, 189, 198, 206–208; of slavery, 21, 23, 27, 28, 210. *See also* Antislavery; Prostitutes/prostitution; Slavery
Aborigines/aboriginal, 230, 236, 240, 302, 316. *See also* Australia; Indigenous peoples/populations; Native peoples
Abuse. *See* Child, abuse; Human rights, abuses/violations; Labor, abuses/violations
Acculturation, 89. *See also* Assimilation
Adoption (of children). *See* Child, adoption of
Advanced nation/society, 341, 342, 346, 347, 349. *See also* Developed nation/world
Africa/African, 3, 6, 10, 19–32, 34, 37, 38, 60, 89–93, 174, 192, 241, 255–259, 261, 264–267; women, 25, 79, 82, 257. *See also* Aba Women's War of 1929; African Civilization Society; Berlin West African Conference; Brussels Conference Final Act (1889–90); Congo; Niger Expedition; Scramble for Africa

African American, 31, 78–89, 91–95, 118, 120–124, 132, 188, 192, 230, 236, 237, 240, 273, 285, 338, 339, 343; church, 87–89, 95, 96; community, 79–89, 91–94, 119, 124; family, 80–83, 118, 131; lesbians, 78–88, 91–96; men, 6, 81–85, 88, 89; women, 78–85, 88–92, 192
African Civilization Society, 23
Ainu of Japan, 303, 313–316, 318, 319
Alaska, 236, 302. *See also* Yupiaq (in Alaska)
Allah, 63, 77. *See also* God
Al Qaeda. *See* Taliban (Al Qaeda)
America/American, 2, 10, 11, 15, 20, 29, 32, 42, 54, 78, 81, 82, 85, 94, 117–124, 127, 128, 130–132, 212, 214, 217, 226–228, 234, 235, 245, 255, 269–271, 273–275, 277, 280, 284, 287, 289, 291, 297, 300, 301, 303, 306, 307, 312, 315, 339, 340, 345, 350, 363; superiority, 118, 127. *See also* African American; Asian American; Convention on Human Rights, American; Cuban American; Declaration of Independence, American; Declaration on the Rights and Duties of Man, American; United States